bipolar bare

For you good mental health always!

Carlton.

bipolar bare

MY LIFE'S JOURNEY WITH MENTAL DISORDER—A MEMOIR

CARLTON DAVIS

Copyright © 2009 Carlton Davis
All rights reserved.

ISBN-10: 1-4392-2070-0
ISBN-13: 978-14392207-0-2

Library of Congress Control Number: 2008911249

Visit www.booksurge.com to order additional copies.

Art: Carlton Davis
Marilyn Tower: Carlton Davis, Marti Kyrk, and Jose Fonseca Architects
Author Photograph and Art Photography: Ed Glendenning
Cover and Book Design: Patricia Bacall

This book is dedicated to my wife, Virginia Tanzmann.
She has stuck with me through thick and thin,
good and bad, sane and insane.

THE WRITER WISHES TO THANK Michael Levin, founder of Celebrity Ghost, who worked with me for the past five years on this project, providing me with encouragement, sharp insight, and invaluable recommendations on how I could improve this work. He held the macro view. I could not have kept at it nor completed the project without his help. When I had lost direction, he kept me at the helm more than once.

I am also grateful to Pamela Guerrieri of Proofed to Perfection and her associates, who worked with me for the last four months on this project, providing a keen editorial eye. They provided the micro view. They made my words sing and soar in so many instances. When the struggle to complete this project seemed never-ending and I wanted to abandon ship, they helped me to complete the project.

And finally, to Patricia Bacall, cover and book designer, I want to give praise. She caught the vision and created a look for the book that is at once startling, engaging, and harmoniously designed.

FOREWORD

This book represents a high caliber commingling of imagination and reality. When I met Carlton Davis as his physician, he was embarking on his trek through the muddled waters of mental illness. The experience did not prepare me for this much beauty and strength in the self-revelation. That he has stayed the course has benefited us, his readers. It can only bring admiration into the heart of anyone who takes the time to read through these pages.

In truth, under Carlton's pen, a drawing can be said to be worth a thousand words. One becomes obsessed by the reverberating images. I can only compare some of the most powerful ones to the paintings of Lucian Freud or even Michelangelo, full of life and death.

As a practicing psychiatrist, I see his relating of his passage through the hell of mania, depression, and recovery as yet another source of understanding the experience on a very deep and intimate level. It is a special, unique, and high privilege to have accompanied him on his untiring journey. Through medical complications as well as periods of total obscurity, when his compass might have failed a less courageous man, Carlton kept on going back to his Herculean task. His strength lies in his ability to trust his intuition that his experience is universal in spite of its uniqueness.

I cannot forget the circumstances under which I met Carlton.

It was on a sunny Saturday morning. He had just been admitted to the locked unit on a seventy-two-hour hold a day or so before. I remember Carlton coming to our meeting on the patio surrounded by high grates and wire fencing, carrying an improvised briefcase out of an empty pizza box containing drawings of incredible strength. I have always thought that one reason for our bonding was my love of the visual arts in general and my appreciation of drawing. But I may be wrong in that.

There was a mixture of fear and trust in that first encounter. Carlton asked that I become his physician shortly thereafter. And so the journey began.

Any journey can be an eye-opener. Travel through time or geography and you will discover who you really are. Travel with a friend and you will find out more about your friend's character and your own than you ever would in years of friendship. Now, taking a journey through your own mental illness seems more reminiscent to me of a pilgrimage than of a trip to Europe, granted. It is one very long hike through history and foreign lands with only one sure thing: its destination. The destination was simple: staying alive.

Albert Camus said: "What gives value to travel is fear."

I believe that he was talking about the kind of far-flung exploration described by Carlton Davis in his new book. Fear is what will keep the reader entranced.

Carlton's travels (or more to the point, the travels of Carlton and Carlotta), so keenly described in *Bipolar Bare*, are reminiscent of a pilgrimage like a long dream to the Netherworld of the mind.

He has lived to tell the tale. And what a tale it is!

I feel privileged to have been there for the long haul and to have accompanied Carlton on his journey. Like him, I have experienced the fear at times but in a different way. My fear was that my technique would rob him of his enthusiasm and creative talent. And indeed at times it may have. Would he ever get it back? Would my knowledge and the science and art of psychiatry give him back to himself but without the essential part of his creativity?

This book proves otherwise. Like a chrysalis, this book seemed to grow internally, and to take on a life of its own. As I told Carlton, "It would not let you go." Many times Carlton thought of abandoning the project but the project would not abandon Carlton.

It seems that, in the end, the delivering of the book played a part in the therapeutic process. As if it had given its author an opportunity to take one last look around the inner landscape of this great insanity and finally allowed its author to say good-bye, taking a graceful exit. Or was it Carlotta who had to bid her leave?

This book may have been sparked in part by a conversation Carlton and I had in one of our early meetings. His view of his erratic behavior had been a traditional, dynamic one. I said to him something like: "This isn't about your mother, Carlton. You have a biological illness and it has a name. It is a bipolar illness." That was a shift in paradigm.

Carlton replied to me something like this: "That boggled my mind."

I was not the only one who walked along this road with Carlton. His wife Ginger—like Penelope who weaves her carpet during the day and takes it apart during the night, while she waits for her man to return from the high seas—never abandoned the hope of his returning home. To Ginger I would apply this German proverb: "Great things are done more through courage than through wisdom." It must have taken an enormous amount of courage and patience and love to stay the course without a clear picture of the end in sight.

What a strong and solid couple! I remember our first meeting: Ginger with her flowing burnished red hair, tall and physically impressive, and Carlton, immense and defiantly intense. There was a physical balance in their presence as a couple.

Carlton, this journey with you has been the occasion for many revelations about myself, and about my life's work. You have put down on paper at great expense of hardship, tenacity, and personal suffering a work that will enlighten not only the sufferer of bipolar condition but also the doctors who need to treat the disorder and the patient's kin who must live with them along the way of recovery.

> *"The great virtue in life is real courage that knows how to face facts and live beyond them."* – D.H. Lawrence

Bon Courage!
Nicole Poliquin, MD

CHAPTER 1

THE SHELL OF EMPTINESS

"Begin to search and dig in thine own field for this pearl of eternity that lies hidden in it. It cannot cost thee too much, nor canst thou buy it too dear, for it is all; and when thou has found it thou wilt know that all which thou hast sold or given away for it is a mere nothing as a bubble upon the water."

—William Law 1686–1762

I AM THE SHELL FROM WHICH EMPTINESS SPEAKS. I am the plague of negativity. I am clammed up in a prison of worthlessness. How can I find a way out? My quest began several years ago, and it all started in the back seat of a yellow cab…

The taxi drove me from the mental hospital to my home on the edge of the arroyo across the familiar sloped Pasadena landscape flanked by the San Gabriel Mountains. I was sober and perhaps stable. I thought about all the bumpy rides I had taken, where I was sober, but I didn't stay that way for long. The first ride from Las Encinas after my stay for drug abuse, the taxi took me down the long incline and quick upslope of Colorado Boulevard to Orange Grove Boulevard and the arroyo. I immediately went out and used. From The Betty Ford Center, I swooped home from Palm Springs and indulged at the first opportunity that arose. I found a tab of crack under the seat of my car and smoked it the day of my arrival. That was a quick relapse! I managed to stay sober for a week thereafter before I went to Henry Ohlhoff House in San Francisco, recommended to me by my Betty Ford counselor, to continue my treatment. After my infraction of their rules, a taxi took me up and down the hills of San Francisco from Ohlhoff House, a drug treatment halfway house for gay men, to the Abigail Hotel. I was smoking crack in a couple of weeks. I stayed hooked for more than a year until I decided, as the alcoholics say, to pull a geographical, returning to LA. After my long drive from San Francisco up and over the Grapevine to Los Angeles, I managed to stay sober for six months. I thought I had my jones beaten, but I relapsed and remained addicted for six years, fighting the desire every day to use and failing again and again.

Here I am again on another ride thinking about drugs …

Sitting next to me in the taxi, dressed only in a black bra, a black silk slip, and her bare feet, Carlotta smiles wickedly. Around her neck is a steel ring leather choker. Black leather cuffs adorn her wrists and a glass crack pipe is held between her thumb and three fingers. Gray smoke curls out of the end of the pipe.

"Ready to smoke again so soon?" she remarks. "I'm disappointed. I thought you could wait a few days this time."

Carlotta; sketch book; ink pen

"Damn you, Carlotta, you're reading my mind," I exclaim. "Get that pipe out of my sight!"

"You OK back there?" the cabbie asks, looking at me in the rear view mirror with a concerned look in his eyes. He sees that I am alone in the back seat of his taxi. He is probably worried about the nut case he has picked up from the hospital.

"I'm OK," I sigh. "I just remembered something. Sorry for the outburst."

Crack no longer gets me high, but I can't give it up completely: its allure still tantalizes me. Only my feeble attempt at suicide convinced me to get help for my obsession. Here I am again, crawling home after my fifth attempt—or is it my 1,550th?—to stay sober (that is if you count all the twelve step meetings I have attended). Worry sets in. How long will I stay sober this time? How long will I stay stable before anger, frustration, or depression turns my thoughts to go again to my dealer to get a hit of crack? I am free to do it if I want. I think about God. Can I give my life up to God? Will He/She/It keep me from doing it? It doesn't seem likely. The twelve steps do not work for me. Do I even believe in God when God seems so remote from my life? Can I say I have been given the gift of bipolar disorder from God, as the Reverend Saquety from All Saints Church suggested when he gave me communion in the hospital? It makes me want to laugh at the absurdity of the idea. Bipolar disorder is more like a curse.

In the brief period I have been in the hospital, only the medications the psychiatrist gives me stave off my addiction. I still have the thoughts about crack, but I don't have the craving. Even the appearance of Carlotta smoking doesn't make me want to use yet. I wonder how long this state will last. The cabbie drops me at my house. My truck is in the driveway; I could be on my way for a run in just a few minutes. I will pass on the opportunity.

In my empty dark house I sit in the big stuffed chair and think about one memorable ride I took back from Anaheim after a day at my job as a design manager at Disneyland when I was indulging myself in my addiction. That day, I lit up my glass pipe as I rolled along, took a drag, and placed the pipe in the cup holder between the seats of my Ford Explorer. I found myself in a most peculiar circumstance. I was in a gap on the crowded freeway. All lanes were crowded thirty yards behind me and thirty yards in front of me. I was alone on a little segment of freeway. Everyone was moving fast. All at once, the cars in the lanes in front of me screeched to a halt, their brake lights coming on in unison. I braked hard, too, but my Explorer fishtailed and spun 180 degrees. I looked and saw all five lanes behind bearing down hard upon me. I said to myself, "This is it. I am a dead man."

The car kept spinning. As I turned back, facing the cars in front of me, the Explorer went up on two wheels, spun a little further, and fell over on its side. The side view mirror smashed in the driver's side window and the broken glass cut my arm. I was calm, perhaps in shock or maybe just high, as I waited to be smashed by some car behind me. It didn't happen. I stood up in the smashed window opening, my only thought to hide the crack pipe. I found it wedged in the cup holder. I reached down, grabbed it, yanked it free, and jammed it in my pocket as a crowd of people surrounded my car. They looked at me through the windshield and asked me if I was all right. I said yes. They told me to get out of the vehicle. I tried to open the passenger side door above me but couldn't lift it—the door was too heavy. A bystander suggested I get out through the back hatch. I crawled toward the hatch while another bystander opened it.

I stepped out of the car slightly dazed and a little wobbly. Two men grabbed my arms to hold me up. One of the men said to me in a Spanish accent, "God must love you, man! You should be dead. You should go to church this Sunday and praise Jesus. God must love you, man!" The two men led me to the side of the road. The crowd righted my vehicle and pushed it over to the roadside next to where I was standing. All the drivers went back to their cars and moved on. I was left standing next to my Explorer wondering what had just transpired. All I could remember were the words, "God must love you, man."

My left arm was bloody, the left side of my vehicle was badly scraped, the driver's side window was shattered, and my side view mirror had disintegrated. I watched the cars speed by and waited for the police, but no police came. I laughed ruefully. The roadkill was out of the way and rush hour could resume.

I wondered if my car could be driven. I started it up and miraculously, it still ran. I decided to continue my drive home and pull over if a highway patrol officer came along. One pulled up behind me, passed me, and I followed him off the freeway. He didn't stop but drove on to a hamburger stand. I stopped, laughed again, turned around, and headed back toward the freeway. I rode home with my bloody arm hanging out the window, thinking about what the Hispanic man had said to me: "God must love you." The Reverend Saquety had said the same thing to me on Easter Sunday at the hospital. "God loves you no matter what you believe or what you have done." I went to church the Sunday following my accident and prayed for God to help me with my addiction. Nothing happened. I didn't change my behavior, and soon afterwards I forgot the statement. Ruminating in the big, striped easy chair, I wonder if this won't happen again. I will forget the cure of the hospital and return to my life on the run.

It is early evening. My wife, Ginger, hasn't returned home from work. I am sitting in the near dark ruminating about the past and worrying about the future. Carlotta emerges out of the shadows and stands before me. Fully dressed now, she wears her all-black dominatrix outfit: high heels, fishnet stockings, leather skirt and corset, and long-sleeved silk blouse. The corset covers the bodice of the blouse. Her graceful swan's neck is clamped in the leather collar with the steel rings and long dangling silver earrings reach almost to her shoulders. She parts her bright red lips in a wicked smile, revealing a mouthful of sparkling white teeth, and her fierce green eyes stare at me beneath a pile of orange red hair. She has a whip in her left hand.

"Are you ready for me to light the match to burn us to hell?" she asks, shaking the whip loose so the long leather lashes wiggle to the floor. "That's what you will do if you go again to visit Ike and get your hit of crack."

"Are you going to whip me?" I ask, cowering in my chair before the giant-like woman standing dominantly six foot six over me on her five-inch heels. "I deserve it, don't you think, for having these thoughts. As much as I know I should not do it, my mind says I am free and I could go there. And I want to go there! My life is ruined anyway."

Carlotta snaps the whip over my head. *"Wrong answer!"*

"Jesus! Carlotta, be careful with that thing! You could hurt me."

"I *will* hurt you unless you stop this pitiful thinking," she warns. "So, are you going to make another effort to set yourself free? Up to now, your efforts have been in vain. You have not accepted who you are. You have not used your strengths but have played to your weaknesses. You have one last chance to break out of your dark and empty shell. Are you up to the challenge?"

"I don't know," I answer wearily. "I am tired and old,"

"You need not be so fearful. I am here to help you."

"Who do you think you are?" I sneer.

Carlotta waves her hand dismissively. "I am whoever you want me to be. I will be strong if you ask and weak if you will it."

"I am naked in this shell. What tools do I have to break free?"

Carlotta paces the room, moving with a cat's grace, and traces figure eights in the air with her whip. "Nothing but your mind and your remembrances. Shall we begin our journey inside the dark shell, where there appears to be no exit? Perhaps we can find a way out. We can find the seam and push open the two halves. We can break through the walls. They are thin. You can do it, if you don't sink into despair. Remember what you were and where you came from. Follow the trail and find the tools to break open the shell. It is nothing, this enclosure. It is thin as an egg shell and only as large as you imagine it."

"Life tells me I am nothing, a zip, a zero, a colossal failure," I insist, cradling my face in my hands. "It was all determined before I was born. There is nothing I can do to change my karma."

"Karma!" Carlotta scoffs. "Don't hand me that hippie bullshit. Your karma is what you make it. Nothing is predetermined. Nothing is inevitable. Where do you want to begin to find our way into the clear light of freedom, to the fulfillment of all that can be?"

"Don't give me slogans! I don't know where to start."

"Start with your suicide attempt," Carlotta says patiently. "That was the culmination of your past and the beginning of the future."

"The future will be as horrible as the past," I counter morosely.

Carlotta's mouth twists in a viper's smile. "Could be, with that attitude—but you have nowhere else to go. You have reached the bottom of your shell of emptiness."

"One can always go deeper into the darkness."

"You must do something!" Carlotta snaps. "You can't wallow in self-pity anymore."

"Are there just the two of us who can follow this trail, which will lead nowhere? Why must you go with me? Can't you leave me alone?"

"No. Not until the time is right."

"Then light that match, Carlotta, and burn us to hell."

"No, I will light a match that shows a path out of the enormous void."

Carlotta strikes a match. In the dim light I stare at my judge. She is not so much beautiful as handsome. The orange-red hair, which is piled up on her head into a cone-like peak, is garish, promoting the illusion her head is on fire. Her skin is pale as alabaster. Her nose slopes softly down to her broad, red-painted lips, like I remember my mother's long nose and wide lips. Impossibly long lashes emphasize her green eyes. Her eyebrows are a sweeping curve, wide near her nose and narrow at the edges of her eyes. Her arms are long and slender, as are her hands, the long fingers ending in red, dagger-like nails. Her breasts are firm and erect. Curvaceous hips and shapely legs without end complete the decadent picture. With her face and body half hidden in the dark, she reminds me of a Georges de La Tour painting.

"What are you, Carlotta, a muse as well as a judge?" I ask at length.

"You will never know unless you try to find a way out."

"I think you should go away and leave me be."

Carlotta squints her green eyes. "Think something positive."

"Platitudes, you only give me platitudes!"

"Platitudes will suffice to begin this journey," she says dictatorially. "Carlotta is all you need for this journey to free yourself from this deep dark space where you are locked. Carlotta is your pearl. If you can set Carlotta free, you will find freedom from the prison of self you created."

The dominatrix fades into the shadows and I am alone again.

"Wait!" I call after her. "I thought you wanted to hear the story of my suicide attempt! Why are you leaving now?"

I hear a disembodied voice, supremely confident, somewhere in the gloom. "Carlton, you can start without me. I will be around when needed."

"Bitch!" I cry as Carlotta's laughter fades away in the distance.

"Artists should never call their muses names." Darkness closes in about me.

bipolar bare

Kill Him; sketch book; ink pen (drawn right-handed)

CHAPTER 2

LEAP FROM LIFE

Mr. Left chops Mr. Right to let all my pain fly out. Mr. Right draws the portrait to show Mr. Left he can. Mr. Down takes Mr. Up to the bridge to leap from life to let the depression out.

THE GREAT DEPRESSION ATTACK STRUCK EARLY IN 2003. It's mid-February, and I thought I might escape. I should have known better. The signs were there. I lost my wallet, ran out of gas on the freeway, ripped up my paycheck in a fit of anger, raged at my wife for minor irritations, and drew the drawing of Mr. Left chopping Mr. Right, and thus himself, to death.

Every year around this time, when the year is new, I have an attack. I'm never prepared for it. I am always surprised and devastated at the intensity. Two attacks happen each year: the first at the beginning of the year and the second in the fall. The latter is a reaction to the start of school, or so a psychologist once theorized.

The depressions creep up on me just when I believe they might not happen. My body becomes stiff and sore. My mind hurts. I hate everything, especially the government, the police, the rich, doctors, dentists, freeways, cars, food, the house I live in, my wife, my father, my mother, and me. *I want to die.* I must kill myself to end this misery. I can't go through this again. I can't put others through the hell I inflict.

Standing on the freeway overpass, I will throw my body over the railing into the racing traffic thirty feet below. Or, maybe I will stab myself in the heart with the ice pick I have hidden in my sleeve. *This time I must do it.* I stand on the sidewalk, hands gripping the railing with white-knuckle ferocity, trying to screw up the courage to make the leap. Suicidal thoughts have plagued my mind for months, but I haven't been so depressed that I was ready to do it.

bipolar bare

Now, I am. After a day of extreme irritation with the workmen fixing the heating system in the house disturbing my peace, and after yelling at my wife for no reason, I drag my aching carcass down our street to the freeway overpass two stoplights away. I mumble evil thoughts, determined to do it this time.

I wave my ice pick threateningly as an aggressive driver rushes me through an intersection. He smiles devilishly and speeds away. I don't even matter anymore. I have no future. After months of unemployment and now another job I can't stand, my sad career as an architect is fading into nothingness. Only yesterday, the boss put me on half time, citing cash flow problems, but I think my negative mood and unrestrained anger are to blame. I threw a set of keys across the drafting room and then ripped up my paycheck in reaction to comments that struck me wrong. Severe depression and desperate rage alternately afflict me. Each succeeding day is more miserable than the last.

I am in constant pain from the pinched nerves in my back that shoot waves of fiery sensation down my back. Fueled by immense anger, I limp to the overpass and push myself forward. Standing alone at the rail, a cop car passes me by. They do not stop. I fantasize what if they did. Two patrol officers, a male and a female, would approach me carefully. "Stay away from me," I yell. They keep approaching. I eye them maliciously, my hand gripped upon the hidden ice pick inside my jacket. I wait for them to get close. I whip out the ice pick and charge the female officer. She pulls her gun and shoots me.

My life force ebbing, I look at the officers standing over me. "Thank you," I say simply, a beatific smile etched on my face.

Suicide by cop would be an easier end, but it doesn't happen. I will have to do the act myself. I tighten my grip on the rail and start to sway in preparation to vault. All the justifications for my leap to death race through my brain.

"Don't do it, Carlton," says Carlotta, appearing next to me in a tight-fitting police officer's uniform.

"I must," I reply. "There is no hope. I am empty and lost. Why must you appear now? You only complicate the situation."

"You still have life left in you and there is the possibility of happiness."

"Oh, you are so wrong," I laugh. "I have wasted all my life and the future will only be more of the same."

"I guess I will have to arrest you for attempted suicide."

"You can't. Besides, look at all my failures—they are the indictment of an evil person. I deserve the death sentence."

"You are so wrong. There is much for you to do. Stand still, so I can put the cuffs on you."

"Stay where you are and listen to my thoughts, Carlotta," I command. "There is no hope."

The failed career (I can't help myself from pissing off employers) and the lousy marriage (I can't prevent the verbal outbursts against my wife) are good reasons to give myself the death sentence. There is the constant physical pain and the drug addiction. Crack cocaine has me in its iron grasp. For almost ten years, I have struggled with the addiction. I get sober then relapse badly when the depression attacks. I go on runs for weeks and months, chewing up money and trying to hide from detection. Alcoholic Anonymous' much-vaunted Twelve Step program doesn't work for me. After their meetings, I only want to use more. I hate the reliance on God. To me, God is the great torturer.

"You're doing wrong to yourself," says Carlotta, pulling her baton from her waist belt. "Do I have to beat some sense into you?"

"Leave me alone with my thoughts."

Carlotta stands stock-still, rapping the baton into her other hand with silent menace. "You know I can't do that," she demurs.

The same feelings I had then consume me now as I stand on the overpass. Life will never get any better. Life was a disaster in the past. Life is a disaster now. There is no improvement.

"Get it over with, you fool!" shrieks Mr. Down, the depressed brain state. "What you intend to do is inevitable."

"Don't listen to him, listen to *me*," Carlotta says softly, speaking in the reassuring tone of an officer confronted with a suicide in progress. "Think about others who will be affected by your actions."

bipolar bare

My body tenses. I lean over the railing, looking down at the highway below and visualizing my fall. In my vision, I am balanced on the railing like a swimmer poised on the edge of a diving board. Can I stand and balance? Probably not. My real fall will be ungainly, a stumbling lurch over the edge. No, imagine it this way: Think of it as a graceful vault and arch into space. Arms extended, I make a dive to death. The body falls rapidly in a straight line to the target far beneath. My dive is an Olympic effort, a smooth clean descent from the high tower. Does one die just in doing it, or it is the crash onto the pavement that kills? It's the crash, idiot. Thought continues until the moment of pulpish *smash*. What are the final thoughts, when you know death is imminent, and there is no undoing what is done?

carlton davis

Leap from Life; sketch book; ink pen

bipolar bare

Lots of vehicles are moving fast on the freeway. Their headlights are on—bright spots in the fading light after sunset. I watch them rush forward and disappear under the bridge. What if I hit the pavement in front of them or if I land on a car hood? The thought gives me pause. *This is not what I want.* I don't wish to cause others damage. What if they lose control, avoiding the falling body? What if it is a big rig that swerves to avoid me and crashes into another vehicle alongside? What if I fall on some unsuspecting driver's windshield and she panics, slams on the brakes, and the cars behind plow into her halted car?

Why do I care? If other people die, so what? My exit will be all the more dramatic. Maybe I will even make the nightly news. I can hear the handsome anchorman's sensationalistic teaser: "Suicide from freeway bridge causes major pileup. Details at eleven." I will finally get my Warholian fifteen minutes of fame!

I stare off into the dying light in the west, trying not to focus on the suffering my selfish act might cause others. I rock in horrible pain. If only I can rock myself to end the pain, to give myself the momentum to leap. *I can't do it.* I can't overcome the objection to hurting others. I'm locked at the edge. Stage fright makes me immobile. I can't even move my arms to let the ice pick slide into my hand. My hands are frozen to the guardrail. I stand and stare at the passing traffic, knowing the opportunity has passed.

"See," says Carlotta triumphantly, "when you think of the effect of your actions on other people, you cannot fling yourself off this bridge."

"It's your fault! I could have, if you hadn't arrived."

Carlotta smiles. "Let me walk you home. I will tell you stories of my exploits as protector of the peace."

"I don't want to hear it," I mutter.

Carlotta waves her baton in my face like a judgmental finger and is gone.

So, I won't jump off the bridge tonight. Defeated, deflated, and defused, I finally release my grip on the rail, turn, and walk slowly home. I go to bed without a word to my wife. The ice pick stays in my hand all night, poised against my chest. I toy with the notion of ramming it into my heart, but I can't.

Beside me in bed, Ginger, my wife, the long-suffering but strong-hearted redhead, who has remained with me in spite of my irrational actions, irritations to her, and aberrant infidelities, rises on one hand and places her other hand gently on my shoulder and asks me if I am OK.

"Yeah, I am," I splutter. "Leave me be!"

She rolls away from me and stays silent knowing well I will not react positively to her compassion. I stare at the ceiling, knowing I have reached the nadir of deepest depression. I will begin to crawl out of the abyss. Tomorrow I will be better, but I will never be free. I have documented the cycles since my thirties. The great depressions will come again. The next attack will be in September. Can—or do—I want to live until that time, when severe negativity will make me capable of suicide? I think about suicide all the time, but only twice a year—just after New Year's and come autumn time—am I ready to do it. I am convinced the terrible attacks are caused by the events of my childhood. The first depressive episode always coincides with the time when I was four, going on five.

I was kidnapped by my father and ended up in a foster home. I call it kidnapping, but it really wasn't. Dad took me from my mother's sister's house, where Mom had hidden me from the Davis family. I am obsessed with this history. I can't get over it. I think the war of divorce and custody they fought is the cause of my difficulty. I had to go to school as a seriously troubled child. The suspicion I felt was confirmed by a reading clinic report that I found later in adulthood, diagnosing me as an emotionally disturbed kid.

School was awful for me. I could not read properly. I reversed letters. Strange sequences of words came out of my mouth. I was slow at math. Some teachers thought me retarded. Other children picked on me. They called me "Stinky Chinky" and a dumb "Chink." I hated that name given to me because I had one droopy eyelid, which my family decided made me as a child look half-Chinese. I hated going to school. I was disruptive and spent a lot of time in detention. My parents and our society ruined me. The need for revenge follows me through all the years of my life. The greatest revenge would be to kill myself.

"I will watch you, Carlton," says Carlotta, "to make sure you are safe tonight."

"I don't need it."

"What are you saying?" my wife asks, rolling toward me and raising herself on her elbows. Once again trying to offer her compassion to me in my struggle against the darkness within, which she knows so well and is powerless to help me lessen its grip.

"Nothing," I answer. "I was talking to myself." Ginger lies down and rolls away from me.

Tears well up in my eyes as I watch the shadows on the ceiling from the moonlight passing through the boughs of the eucalyptus tree outside my window.

"Sleep well, Carlton," Carlotta is saying as Morpheus takes me in his arms. "Your life is about to get better."

CHAPTER 3

YOU NEED HELP

"You need help," Ginger says as I slump on the edge of the bed with my head in my hands. Ginger stands beside me in her nightgown, a warm loving look on her freckled face. She reaches out her pale left hand and places it on my shoulder giving it a gentle shake. "You're a suicidal mess, in terrible pain, and addicted to crack."

"Get out of my face," I growl shirking off her hand and staring down at the ice pick on the floor between my legs, which rolled off my stomach and the bed in the middle of the night.

Alarmed, Ginger steps back. "I can't live with you if you are going to keep on going this way," she cries, her head falling forward, her shoulder-length hair covering her face. "I talked with the doctor, and we think you need to go into the hospital. You're sick, Carl. I love you, but I can't stand to see what you are going through."

Rising to her full five foot five, Ginger moves her full body toward me again and tries to put her arms around me. I brush her away, get off the bed, rush out of the bedroom into the bathroom, and slam the door. I wait until my wife goes down the stairs before I come out of the room. The ice pick is gone.

I know she is right. I am a mess. Suicide remains on my mind. My back and my whole body hurt. Crack is my addiction that won't let go. The only choice is to go get help, but do I really want help? Would help dissolve my disillusion? Would it mend my sense of doom? No, it couldn't. I am too far gone.

I go into my closet with the small shelf and open the steel attaché case where I keep my pipes and supply of crack cocaine. There are four small pieces left, nestled between my junkie paraphernalia: butane lighters, glass pipes, razor blades, paper clips bent into semi-straight lines, scissors, a bag of mesh, and scores of stick and book matches. You don't need to use the rocks now, I chide myself. Get dressed and wait until she leaves for work. Hesitantly, I snap the attaché case closed, controlling the urge to get high immediately and savoring the small victory.

I put on my paint-splattered jeans, an ill-fitting T-shirt, and my ripped up sneakers. Dressing lousy matches my state of mind. Down on the first floor, Ginger is fussing in her closet, getting her clothes for work out for the day. She will shower next. She won't come back upstairs. I can do whatever I want. I sit on the edge of the bed, trying to think how I should proceed. Smoke or run away … probably both. Go to the bank, draw out my last couple of hundred bucks. Drive down to Ike's, buy a big wad of crack. Go off some place and smoke myself to death. That is one alternative. Maybe I can find another bridge to jump from. Maybe I can find someplace where I can crash my truck—a big tree or a concrete abutment. I can go the beach and swim out to sea and never come back. Or, should I try to live for the motives I won't acknowledge, because Ginger loves me? Because I love her? Because I care about my daughter? Because, because … because what? The reasons feel weak. Should I go to the hospital? Maybe there I can find some reasons to continue living.

Time to self-medicate. I need a hit of crack that will make things clearer. The mind will feel good. I go back to the closet and open the silver attaché case and slice off a small piece of the waxy white drug from one of the four rocks and pick up a broken pipe. The pipe was new a week ago. My thoughts go to my daily routine of crack purchases from Ike at his house on Hooper on the edge of South Central LA and the frequent stops I make to buy the paraphernalia for smoking. My daily crack buy is fifty bucks. The pipes cost a buck at the convenience store near Ike's and are called "roses" for the little plastic roses they have inside the glass tube.

There is a lot of ceremony in smoking crack. Once the piece of mesh is in place and far enough down that a piece of crack can rest on top and still be inside the pipe, you melt the crack into the mesh. I pick up the small piece—roughly a one-eighth inch square—cut off from the larger, medium-sized piece. I rest it on top of the mesh below the jagged point on the circumference of the glass pipe. With the butane lighter, I heat the outside of the pipe and watch the crack melt into the mesh. A small amount of the drug dribbles through the mesh and down the inside of the glass, turning a light brown.

I am ready to take the hit. The unfiltered end of the glass pipe is in my mouth and angled upward. The lighter is brought to the mesh end of the pipe, but the lighter won't light. I strike it several times and then toss it in frustration into the case. It lit before, why won't it now? I grab the second lighter. I carry two because of this problem. This lighter won't work either. The lever turns, the striking wheel sparks fly, but nothing happens. I stand in the closet in total annoyance. I can try to open the valve in the lighter using a paper clip straightened into a length of heavy wire, but if I do this, the lighter can explode into a six-inch flare. It's too hot for the crack, burns it up, and cracks the pipe further. This means I will have to use a stick match. Using a stick match means there will be an odor of sulfur left from the flame, which means I can be detected.

I don't like the risk, but I want a hit badly enough that I will have to take it. I light the match, put it to the end of the pipe, and take the hit. Luckily, Ginger does not come upstairs and smell the sulfur. I inhale deeply and hold the crack-saturated breath in my lungs for many seconds before I exhale what I believe is odorless smoke.

I get the rush of energy. It is wonderful for my head. My mind feels clear and focused. I can think and reason. I get the sense that I can do things and keep going, but the body screams in pain. I gag and cough. I grab my chest as it constricts in discomfort. A stabbing pain shoots down my leg from the pinched nerves in my back. The joints in my neck and in my arms hurt. I feel even more stiff and sore all over. With every toke on the pipe, the price I pay for the mildest increase in mental energy is becoming higher than I can take. Thus it is in these latter days of my use of crack cocaine. I refuse to do anything about my addiction. Sad to observe and chronicle, a junkie death isn't lurid, but dreary. I see my smoking as another method of suicide—a slow and deliberate decline as my body disintegrates.

"It's our body you are killing, and I can't prevent you doing the killing."

It is Carlotta, standing next to me in the small closet. She is dressed in a light terry cloth bathrobe and is snug against me in the tight space.

"All my protestation goes unheard," she goes on. "You talk about changing, but you choose dying. Why?"

"Go away! Leave me be!" I protest.

"I am just your conscience, poor Carlton. You know you need to stop this self-destructive behavior."

"It's hopeless!" I whine. "I can't maintain a positive viewpoint about anything more than a couple of days. Every time I say I will be strong and give up the use of crack, I fall into a pit of despair after a few days without the drug. I know it is killing me, but the negative desire to be high overtakes me. The drug does nothing anymore except relieve the mental pressure of black thoughts. High, I get mental relief at the price of a body that disintegrates a little more with each drag. There is no way out except in a coffin."

"This way cannot be," says Carlotta resolutely. "You must seek help. Go to your wife and have her find a hospital that will help you."

"I have been to three programs already and none of them helped."

Carlotta sighs exasperatedly. "That is because you still had not hit bottom. You are at your bottom now. To delay is to die and I don't want to die. Carlotta has many things she wants to be and many things she wants to give to you, including some much-needed humor. I am all the characters you need me to be. Now, I ask you to be the character I want you to be. *Please go get help!*"

I step out of the closet abruptly and close the door on Carlotta's entreaties. High, I stumble downstairs and sit down in the chair near the entrance to my wife's bathroom. When she emerges in her green pantsuit ready for work as an architectural manager, I say haltingly, "OK, I will go to the hospital, but these are my conditions."

"Wait, I have to go to work right now," says Ginger, eyeing me suspiciously. "I can call the doctor later and see when we can get you in. Can you make it through the day?"

"Yes, I will make it through the day," I assure her, but my words have a hollow ring.

I smoke crack the rest of the day and worry. Ginger calls in the afternoon and tells me they have arranged for me to go to Las Encinas.

"Don't you want to hear my conditions?" I say.

"We will talk about them tonight," she replies. "I'm sure they are something that can be worked out."

"They better be," I respond petulantly, "because I am not going unless they are."

That night, I tell my wife what my conditions are. I will not be put on a locked ward and treated like a total mental case, as I had been after my suicide attempt when I was much younger. Ginger says she has already discussed that with our doctor, and he agrees that I will be put into the open ward at the hospital when I am admitted.

The following morning, Ginger drives me to Aurora Las Encinas Hospital. I know this place well. I came here eight years ago for treatment of my drug addiction. It didn't work. The hospital is hidden behind ivy-covered brick walls that stretch down one long block in East Pasadena. Behind the walls are bungalows where the patients live. One larger facility sits near the front gate, a rambling two-story structure with walls of wood shingles. This is the administration office and main wing of the rehab facility.

I have my admittance interview in a small room with French doors that lead to the outside. Little chunks of stained glass are threaded through the lead-divided glass panel. The admitting nurse, an African-American woman, starts with her questions.

"Are you suicidal?" she says offhandedly.

"Not at the moment."

"Do you have a plan for committing suicide, should the urge overpower you?" she presses me.

"Nothing worked out at this point."

I wish I could have a hit of crack so I could deal with this situation. I concentrate on the stained glass panel in the door behind the nurse, knowing I have to be careful how I answer the questions. If I admit to a plan for suicide, the hospital will put me their locked ward.

"Do you know your French door is in poor condition?" I respond after a period of uncomfortable silence. "The lead is pulling away from the glass, and the panel is bowed and buckled." Criticism of the door distracts me from my nervousness.

"Please pay attention to me," says the nurse in a no-nonsense tone and fixes me in an icy stare. "Our conversation is not about the French doors. Do you have family in the area?"

bipolar bare

Childishly, I purse my lips and stare off into the lush lawn beyond the French doors. Ginger answers for me: "Only me in California."

I shouldn't have agreed to this. It didn't work before, so why would it work now? We fill out the admission papers, date of birth, mother's name—why do they always ask that?—emergency contact, allergies, and when did I last take any drugs. I won't answer that question. Ginger puts her hand on my wrist and keeps me from bolting.

"Who is your insurance provider?" the nurse asks.

"He is covered under my policy," Ginger replies and presents her card. I frown and feel resentful. I am always covered under her policies, since I never have insurance of my own, being unemployed much of the time.

"This is enough for now," the nurse says. "Please wait here, Mrs. Tanzmann. I am going to take Mr. Tanzmann down to the nurse's station."

"I am not Mr. Tanzmann! My name is Davis!" I say in a very loud voice. The nurse winces. Another insult to my status is added. I am always called "Mr. Tanzmann," my wife's first husband and the name she has kept. Immediately resentful, I am led down a long corridor to a room where I sulk and wait.

The room is institutional. Metal chairs with vinyl seats are arrayed around the four walls, flanking the double doors into the room. Worn gray carpet like a dismal sky stretches below the sickly yellow walls, adorned with framed prints of sunny vacation scenes. The curtains are drawn over a single, full-height window opposite the double doors. I sit on one of the chairs in front of this window, feeling belligerent and wanting a hit of crack.

"If only I had a hit," I mumble under my breath.

"That's not going to happen," replies Carlotta. She is sitting in a chair across the room from me, dressed in a sweater and jeans similar to mine.

"It's too impossible. This won't work. I will never get free of the addiction."

"You can if you put your mind to it." She stands up and looks at one of the vacation posters on the wall. "If you get clean, you can go to one of these beautiful places."

"Not bloody likely."

A nurse with glasses, light brunette hair, and an authoritarian air breezes into the room to interview me. She sits down in a chair across the room from me. She curls her legs up into the chair. I do not have a good feeling. I immediately associate her with Nurse Ratched, the dictatorial nurse in *One Flew Over the Cuckoo's Nest*. The name "Rat Shit" seems to fit her unfriendly face. I look away at the wall with the print of some Mediterranean scene with marble steps, ruined columns, gnarled green trees, beautiful blue sea, and colorful boats.

"Are you Mr. Davis?" she asks sharply.

"That I am," I reply sarcastically, keeping my eyes on the picture.

"Save the sarcasm for somebody else," she barks, "and look at me when I am talking to you."

I turn to look at her with a nasty look of defiance.

"You will pay attention to me when you are a patient on this ward," she says imperiously, giving me an equally nasty look.

I take a deep breath and reply, "So, around here I have to kowtow to you. Is that what you are saying?"

The nurse slams her notebook shut, stands up, and stomps to the door. "I will *not* have a person like you in my ward," she says acidly. "They will have to find other accommodations for you," she adds and exits in a huff.

"Good move, Carlton," says Carlotta, reappearing in the chair just vacated by the nurse.

"I don't care. I didn't like her and I don't like this place."

"I feel sorry for you. You are definitely off on the wrong foot."

"Bullshit!"

I stare at Carlotta in silence while she shakes her head slowly back and forth.

I am left alone for twenty minutes. The admitting nurse finally appears. "We have found another place for you, *Mr. Davis*," she says, emphasizing my proper name. "Will you please follow me?"

I get up and follow the nurse out of the building across an expansive lawn graced with tall palms and planting beds filled with exotic flowers. We make our way down a concrete path and across an asphalt road to a gate, which she unlocks with one of the keys on her tremendous keychain. Passing through the gate, she unlocks the door of a small one-story building. I am led into a small room where

bipolar bare

several patients are seated around two round tables. Doorways flank the room and there is a nurse's station at the far end. A blonde nurse greets me. The lady who escorted me to this place hands the nurse some paperwork and retreats from the building without saying a word. The nurse directs me to a room with a single bed. I notice the door contains a viewing panel of clear glass, and it dawns on me that I am being placed in a locked ward.

"Wait a minute!" I yell. "This is the locked unit of the hospital! You guys have put me in the locked unit of the psychiatric hospital. This is not what I agreed to. I am really pissed."

"Why don't you make yourself comfortable in here for now?" the nurse says, pointing to the bed in the room. "There will be a doctor coming along later that you can discuss this with."

Enraged, I lie down on the bed. I feel betrayed by my wife and my doctor. My jaws are clenched. My fists are banging on the bed while I stare at the ceiling of what seems to me a prison cell.

"You wouldn't be here now, if you hadn't been belligerent to the nurse," Carlotta observes.

"Where are you?" I ask from my prone position on the bed.

"I am behind you."

I sit up and see Carlotta standing by the steel-reinforced window. She is dressed in a crisp nurse's uniform—white dress, white stockings, white shoes—with a clipboard in her right hand and a pair of handcuffs in the other. She smiles through her bright red lips, revealing her brilliant white teeth.

"I look good as a nurse, don't you think?" she asks rhetorically.

"This not what I agreed to!" I rail. "And what are you going to do with the handcuffs?"

"I thought I might chain you down to the bed so you can't do something crazy."

"There is nothing you can cuff me to, so there!" I reply childishly. "Are you trying to make me even angrier?"

"No, I'm trying to help out."

"What with a little bondage and discipline? That would make my dilemma even more desperate."

"Forget the cuffs," Carlotta sighs. "I am sorry I brought them."

"Just tell me how I can get out of here."

"I can't. Too bad—you're stuck now. You will have to go with the flow."

Before I can reply, the door to my room opens and a nurse dressed in civilian clothes enters.

"Did I hear you talking to someone?" she asks.

"Just talking to myself."

"Hmm, very interesting. Well, I need for you to follow me. The doctor wants to interview you."

"Bitch," I mutter, turning my head to the window.

"What did you just say to me?" the nurse says challengingly, turning toward me.

"I wasn't talking to you."

"Your behavior bothers me, Mr. Davis," says the nurse. "Are you going to give us trouble?"

"Not much more than the trouble you are giving me."

The nurse leads me to an outside area behind the building beyond the nurse's station. A high fence encloses the grassy area. In the middle are three metal tables with integrated seats. I am directed to the middle table where a Chinese man is sitting. The nurse introduces the man as Doctor Chang. He is a youthful, chubby man with jowls, round glasses, a full head of dark hair, dressed in a white dress shirt open at the collar. He places a clipboard down on the table, bringing his hands together on top of it with a pen balanced between his fingers.

"I will be interviewing you," he says perfunctorily and asks me the usual preliminary questions: name, age, address, marital status, etc. I only half look at him and when I do, I don't hide my contempt. I am watching something else to keep myself from leaping across the table and strangling this Asian man. There is a man who circles the courtyard endlessly. He is silent and stares at the ground as he walks. He travels at the same steady pace. He wears a small-brimmed black leather cap, a tan shirt, tan pants, and black shoes polished to a glossy shine. He looks like a Middle Eastern man with his dark hair, dark eyebrows, and dark complexion. The seriousness of his visage never changes. I watch him pass behind the Chinese psychiatrist again and again.

bipolar bare

My hands are clasped together in front of me. I work the palms back and forth across each other below the knitted fingers. The thumbs move up and down before my eyes.

I blurt out: "I'm going to kill that goddamn wife of mine and my doctor too for doing this to me! This is not what I agreed to."

Dr. Chang tries to engage me in conversation. I silently resist his entreaties, continuing to rub the heels of my hands together harder and harder, all the while watching the man circle the enclosed area.

The doctor states he is putting me on a seventy-two-hour hold because of my threat to my wife and the doctor. His determination is that I am a threat to others and myself. I can endure the company of this bulldog-like Chinaman no longer. I stand up abruptly, causing the doctor to flinch. I walk away into the building—later, I learn this place is called the Mariah Unit—past the nurse's station to my room and shut the door. I plop down on the bed and stare at the ceiling.

"Now you *really* blew it," says Carlotta looking down at me. "Your threat to Ginger and the doctor has you in a real pickle."

"Oh, leave me alone."

"I can't do that," says Carlotta as she pulls out a pen and scribbles something on her clipboard.

"What are you writing?"

"Each incident that sets us back. The list is growing longer by the minute."

"What are you doing, keeping score?"

"That is part of my job. It helps me calculate whether or not you are getting better."

"I'd be all right, if I wasn't locked in this place."

I think about suicide, but committing suicide in the Mariah Unit is impossible. There is nothing to do it with and they will catch you before you can try. I think about the suicide that I planned earlier—to jump off the bridge onto the freeway. Oh, how I wish I had had the courage to do it! At least I wouldn't be stuck in this prison.

I am lying on a hard bed with a heavy wooden chest of drawers at its foot, looking at a pasty yellow ceiling with matching walls. The sturdy chest is constructed so that no madman, however strong lunacy might make him, can break it apart. The room is empty otherwise. I glance at the entry door with its clear pane in the middle, so a nurse or attendant can always spy into the room, and note the cleverly wire-reinforced glass that is impervious to a madman's fists.

My survey of the room complete, I turn to Carlotta and comment snidely, "Great décor. Sort of early cheap motel."

Carlotta nods her head silently and scribbles on her clipboard.

It reminds me of the room in Yale New Haven Hospital where I was incarcerated after my first suicide attempt—the same mustardy color, the same indestructible furniture, even the same slab-like bed. I am in hospital jail like I was at Yale. Thirty years and nothing has changed in my life. The ringing in my ears is a constant reminder of that first folly. My eyes fill with tears. I am trapped.

"Calm down," whispers Carlotta, leaning over and staring into my eyes. "Everything will get better." Her eyes are full of merriment. She disappears as I scowl at her.

I am listening to the tinnitus in my ears when the attendant comes to the door of my room and calls me to come for dinner with the other patients of the locked ward. I rise like a zombie and enter the common area outside my door. There are not that many other patients—two women and three men. We can all fit around one of the two round tables. A tall mobile service cart arrives, and an attendant is busy placing trays in front of the patients seated at the table.

I sit down between two vacant chairs. Across from me is a blonde. She immediately introduces herself as Fanny. The woman next to her appears quite depressed, but she still introduces herself as Rochelle. The three men at the table say nothing. One is the man in the black leather cap, who marches around the perimeter of the fenced yard. He never says anything to me the entire time I am locked up in the unit. The other is a much younger man, but also Middle Eastern-looking. He nods at me. The third man is much older. He appears to have no teeth and I suspect he might have Alzheimer's disease because he chops his toothless jaw and looks disoriented. He looks down at his plate in silence, concentrating on his food.

bipolar bare

Untitled; April 9, 2003; diary page; colored pencil

"You got 5150'd, didn't you?" says Fanny with a laugh. Her Southern drawl has a sparkling quality, like a pleasantly flowing brook. "I overheard the nurses talking after your interview with the doctor. You are a bad boy."

"What are you talking about?" I reply.

"It's a California law where the hospital can legally hold you for seventy-two hours to establish your mental competency and determine if you are a threat to yourself or others," Fanny explains. "Did you threaten to hurt somebody? If you did, the hospital and the police are obliged under the law to inform them that you have threatened them and can hold you in this locked unit for that length of time."

"Holy shit!" I exclaim. "I threatened to kill my wife and my doctor because they stuck me in this hellhole in violation of an agreement we had that I would go into the hospital only if I didn't get stuck in a locked ward."

"You blew it big time, buddy boy," Fanny chuckles.

I try to explain: "I was using a figure of speech when I said I would kill them. I would not kill them in reality. Now I'm legally stuck in a locked facility. I am behind bars and I am raging mad."

I jump up from the table, march to the grounds, and begin pacing like the fellow in the black cap.

I walk and walk and walk, around and around and around. The attendant comes to the door of the unit, asking if I want my supper. I tell him to stuff it up his ass. I wonder if I can scale the high fence and escape into the wooded area to the south. I decide I can't. I am completely trapped. I am trying to think if there is some positive aspect to this disaster. My part-time job is lost. At least I can rejoice in that. No more will I have to make the horrible trek to Whittier to be a lousy project architect for Dickard Architects. I can just stay here. Be a not-so-model inmate. Piss on the doctors and the staff. Write and read to my heart's content. Maybe being a prisoner against my will is a good thing.

It is my second day on the ward. The Middle-Eastern man has begun his daily circumnavigation of the fenced-in grounds. Seated at the big metal table, Fanny and I are having a pleasant conversation. I can't really understand why she is in this locked unit and ask her about her "civilian life."

"I live in a small house on the grounds of my Baptist church," says Fanny in her syrupy drawl. "I tend the gardens for the church. I like to garden. One day, one of the groundskeepers approached me and tried to rape me. I escaped, but I was scared out of my mind. I reported the incident to the pastor, expecting him to fire the groundskeeper, but he didn't do a dad-blamed thing. He said I was exaggerating."

"You are telling me a man of God, your pastor, didn't believe you?" I ask incredulously.

Fanny chuckles. "Honey, the pastor says to me, 'Fanny, you're too sexy in your Daisy Dukes and halter top that show off your big boobs. The groundskeeper just couldn't help himself.' Well, that horny old groundskeeper tries to do it again and I fight him off. I go to the pastor again but he still won't raise a finger. I'm hysterical by this time. That's why I came in here—for my own protection."

I look at her in disbelief. Fanny has the sunniest disposition. Her big broad smile is disarming. Whenever I am raging at the injustice of my situation, which is often, she has a hilariously sacrilegious answer that never fails to make me laugh: "Oh, get off the cross! We need the wood!"

bipolar bare

My seventy-two hour hold is almost up, and I hear from the nurses that Dr. Chang wants to put me on a fourteen-day hold. Rage wells up inside me again. From the other patients, I learn I can fight this determination through the Patients Rights Advocate. I call and make the request for a hearing on my competency and to protest the fourteen-day hold. Time to get down and kiss professional ass, if you want to get free.

When the hearing convenes, the hospital sends its spokesperson. An advocate represents me. An arbitrator comes to adjudicate between the parties. I get to speak on my behalf. We are sitting at the same table where I made the threat in the company of Dr. Chang and where I sit with my three friends: Fanny, Rochelle, and the senile old man with the choppy lips. The day is sunny and beautiful. The Middle-Eastern man is still circling the area.

I admit I threatened my wife and my doctor and try to explain that it was not a real threat, but merely rash words spoken in the heat of anger. I vow I would never really harm my wife or my doctor. "I said it because I had an understanding with them that I would go into the hospital only if I were placed in an unlocked ward," I explain in the calmest voice I can muster, being ever mindful that I must "play sane" in order to be free of this prison.

The hospital's spokesperson has very little to say. Likewise, the advocate appointed on my behalf is largely silent. The adjudicator admonishes me for issuing my statement in the first place.

I express my humblest apology and state that such a stupid error will never happen again. I am quite embarrassed that it happened in the first place. My contrite demeanor fools the judge. As a result, the hospital is not allowed to place me on a fourteen-day hold against my will.

I am free to go home as I wish! I win! I feel cocky. I have beaten the wily psychiatrist, Dr. Chang. Would that he were here so I could dance on his chest. Playing sane works again! But why does the victory seem so hollow?

I ask the nurse if I can admit myself to the regular hospital. She says she will check to see if they have room for me and advises me to pack up my belongings and get ready to leave. I do as I am told and sit on my bed in an awful, expectant silence.

The nurse returns and puts her head inside the door. "Good news, Carlton, they have a place for you," she says. "An attendant is coming to lead you to your room."

"See, didn't I tell you everything will get better?" says Carlotta. "I guess I won't have a need for my handcuffs."

Overcome with relief, I am silent.

CHAPTER 4

THE ATTIC OF CARLTON AND CARLOTTA

The Attic
She and He
Before gender identity
Played without Mommy
Had tea with Teddy
In grandma's attic
In the trunk of her youth
With sequined dresses, flowered hats
Peachy slips, creamy heels
Frilly limp bras, feather boas
Strings of beads
The dead fox stole
Out of sight, out of mind.

I AM FREE AND WALKING UP THE PATH toward the hospital. The attendant leading me to the main hospital is several feet in front. Smiling cautiously, he turns around to speak to me and make sure I haven't run away.

"We'll have you fixed up with a room in a few minutes," he promises.

"What do you think, Carlotta, should I just go home?" I mumble.

"You talking to me?" asks the attendant.

"N-no. No, I am just talking to myself."

Carlotta, still dressed in her nurse outfit, answers, "We've gone this far, let's give the hospital a chance."

I follow the attendant around the end of a building and along a trail that has a high metal fence separating the hospital from a swimming pool.

"Do I get to go swimming?" I ask him.

"No," he replies, "the pool is not part of the hospital."

The attendant passes a higher wall to his left where I can see people sitting at tables. Most of them are smoking cigarettes. Turning left, we enter the building between the smoking patio and another outdoor seating area. I am taken to the nurses' station and told to wait outside, while the attendant goes in. The nurses' station is the same place I came to on my first day at the hospital.

The attendant emerges. "You are going to be up on the second floor," he says and points to the staircase behind me.

We climb to the second floor and pass down a short corridor to another nurses' station.

"Wait here," he says, gesturing for me to sit down in one of three chairs along a wall next to the station.

"I think I should have gone home, Carlotta," I whisper, feeling nervous and apprehensive.

The attendant emerges from the station. "You're in Room 216," he says. "Follow me."

We travel down a short ramp and turn to the left. A long narrow corridor stretches out before us. Handrails line the corridor, interrupted only by doors to the rooms.

In Room 216 is a man asleep in the far bed next to the window. He is snoring and the room reeks of fecal matter and stale vomit.

"This is the room I am going to be placed in?" I ask, wrinkling my nose. "No way! This place smells like a barn." I step back into the corridor. "I'm getting the hell out of here if this is the best you can do."

The attendant asks me to wait in the corridor, while he goes back to the nurses' station to see what he can do.

"Carlotta, I can't stay here," I say to the empty corridor.

"Give them a chance to find a better room," she replies.

"I don't trust this situation. Remember what they did when I first arrived?

They are full of tricks."

"You need to stay here, Carlton. You need help."

The attendant returns and says a more suitable room has been found. We walk the corridor several paces and enter Room 209. The room is unoccupied and doesn't smell bad. The attendant points to the bed near the door and tells me this will be my bunk.

"Your roommate, a fellow named Smitty, has the other bunk," the attendant explains. "He's out right now, so make yourself comfortable. A nurse will come to interview you soon."

The room is pleasant. Opposite from the two bunks is a big closet, a bathroom, and a dresser with a TV on top. A large window nook with a desk and chair looks out to the east toward the swimming pool. I put my few belongings into the closet and lie down on the bunk. I am thinking about my whole life and the disaster it has become. The closet reminds me of the closet I remember from my earliest youth. It is very spacious. *Why is there such a big closet in a mental hospital?* I ask myself. *You could live in this closet.*

Teddy Bear

"What do you remember from being four years old, Carlotta?" I ask, lying down on the bed and staring at the ceiling. "That closet reminds me of the attic closet I played in when I was four years old. Of course, it doesn't have the dormer window." I breathe a big sigh, thinking more sad thoughts.

"Most people can't remember when they were very young," Carlotta replies. "A new place can spark the subconscious mind to reveal the hidden."

"I remember three things from this age," I say. "I remember my teddy bear, the tea parties with my sister, and the attic closet."

When I was between four and five years old, my companion was a teddy bear. He stood about seventeen inches tall standing upright and twelve inches high sitting down. He went everywhere with me and stayed with me until I gave him to my daughter when she was young.

Today, Teddy is worn from the years of holding and playing. The blue fabric is faded and slightly stained. Like the hair on an old bear, the tan fuzz on the body has become spotty, exposing the tight knitted fabric underneath. The fur is gone from the edges of the ears, as it is on the front of the paws and feet. The dark snout is nearly bare and the black stitched nose is losing some of its threads, but the stitched inverted V of the black mouth is still there. The bear looks serious, yet not unhappy. The black enamel button eyes are still in place and the arms and legs still rotate. For a teddy bear over fifty years old, he is still in good shape. He was well loved and he went with me on all my excursions into the wonderful world of my grandmother's attic.

At my grandmother's house—she is called Nonnie, although I never knew why—I played with my sister in the attic. I had no toys in Nonnie's house. We went to the small room where there was one small window above a window seat. A warm gentle light fell through an old gauze curtain ruffled at the top. Standing on the window seat and on my tiptoes, I could look out the window. It was directly above the front entrance. I could not see the door below because of a shallow-roofed portico, but I could see the concrete walkway that crossed the lawn to the three steps that descended to the sidewalk and Council Rock Avenue.

Up a narrow and steep staircase, the attic room inside a roof dormer was a secret and special place for my sister and me. The six-foot by six-foot space with

bipolar bare

the window seat along the front wall had, along the opposite side, a folding door closet. Two doors, one leading to the small hall at the top of the stairs and the other leading into the storage area under the eaves, occupied the other two walls of this room. Inside the closet, many old dresses and furs hung on the wooden rod spanning from wall to wall. Women's shoes were piled on the floor. Under the eaves, beyond the door amongst old furniture, lamps, and throw rugs, were two old wooden trunks strapped with metal strips. These unlocked treasure chests contained old silk slips, bras, belts, stockings, and hats. Sister and I would play dress up with the clothes in the closet and the trunks.

We put on bras, slipped on slips, cinched the silk with beaded belts, and placed our small feet into a set of old high heels. We wobbled around the room, the hall, and the attic in our getups, often tripping over the long train of the slips. The silk slips dragged on the floor far behind us, with our feet collapsing in the unsteady heels every few steps. We tried old hats on each other and wrapped each other's necks with boas. I had a favorite neck wrap. It was a mink stole that still had the mink's head on one end with black buttons for eyes and the tail on the other. The fur smelled of mothballs.

My sister had a tea set. After we were dressed we would sit on the window seat full of laughter and giggles, sipping imaginary tea. The teddy bear and dolls were our party guests. This is a fond memory never intruded upon, except for the sounds of yelling from beneath. The louder the yelling, the more we conversed with the teddy bear and the dolls, and the more "air tea" we gave each other and our guests.

From below, our mother's voice was the most shrill, but grandmother's was the loudest. We could hear her statement: "Quiet down, the children will hear." Mother would respond, "I don't give a damn. I won't be treated this way."

Whenever I visited my sister, dressing up and having tea was my favorite activity. The parties ended when my mother disappeared and I no longer went to my sister's house. As time went by, I forgot everything but the tea parties, the closet and my teddy bear. I even forgot my mother's name.

"There you have it!" crows Carlotta. "The beginnings of our story and the conditions it created later in your life."

"You think my problems began when I was four years old?"

"It is what you believe, is it not?

"What happened when I was four and five is the root cause of my difficulties—I am sure of it," I state with conviction.

"I can help you there," Carlotta says, brushing her long auburn hair from her eyes.

"Where is your nurse's uniform?" I ask.

Carlotta is sitting on the edge of my bed, wearing cut-off jeans and a halter top. Her legs are crossed. The upper leg dangles over the lower leg, letting her clog almost fall from her foot.

"I thought you might like it if I dressed like Fanny," she says. "Note that none of the nurses here are dressed like nurses in white uniforms. But never mind that. In my various manifestations, I remember all that you have forgotten. We together have an interesting tale to tell."

Carlotta and Carlton do have a tale to tell of childhood trauma, depression, being high, cross-dressing, sex addiction, suicide, and drugs. The stories we describe are part truth, part intuition, and some imagination.

As my feminine doppelgänger, Carlotta is both garrulous and articulate. I will let her explain our relationship:

"I, Carlotta, am not real. Carlotta is the voice Carlton hears in his head and what he imagines me to be. I appear in many forms. This is not schizophrenia, where the voice is audible and directs its charge, but a manifestation of thinking where the voice speaks the alternative viewpoints to every situation. Many people discourse with a voice in their head. Abraham Lincoln did.

"I am Carlton's other mind. Of course, I do not have a way to prove this conjecture, nor does he, but we both agree it is a plausible explanation. Carlotta is the left brain and right-handed. Carlton is the right brain and left-handed. I am more rational and much earthier than Carlton. He is more emotional and serious than I. Carlotta loves life and seeks freedom from the serious gloom of Carlton. I believe I can help him become a balanced person, but I, too, suffer the pain of Carlton. When we are both down, it is a serious situation. I go silent and Carlton withdraws into a dark corner of his mind, where he is unreachable and inconsolable. When this happens, we are at the greatest risk of suicide. Only time will break this prison of depression. Carlotta can only wait out this horrible circumstance. When Carlton reappears, he is usually charming, bright, and full of fun. We two make a joyous combination in this condition.

"Carlton is ambidextrous, but for everyday usage he prefers the left hand and thus the right hemisphere is dominant. I, Carlotta, struggle with him for control. I know that when the left hand grows tired, the right hand assumes command. Carlton does this when drawing or painting. For other activities, like eating and writing, Carlton only allows the right hand to take control occasionally. In childhood, the right hand/left hemisphere was dominant. Carlton's mother remembers him as right-handed, but we think he changed hands for this reason: He thought the right hand bad and the left hand good. Could this be the source of Carlton's later mental disorder? The psychiatrist and I think this unlikely, but maybe the switch is a contributing factor to his neurosis.

"I, Carlotta, am the protector and companion to Carlton. I am as real as the mind from which I spring. Carlton had another companion when he was a little boy, but the manifestation is me in a different form. My first incarnation was a teddy bear. Most children give some animation to their special toys and dolls. Carlton gave life to his teddy bear, which came with him on all his experiences. The bear remembers what Carlton first locked away in his subconscious.

"In his teenage years, the voice had no name, but he still talked to me, especially in moments of pain and frustration. He talked out loud to himself. He tried to do this secretly, because other people and even his family would think him weird. He was caught a few times and answered "No one" when questioned about whom he was talking to. I, Carlotta, had no name, personality, or physical description. He saw his conversation companions as old Indians, sea captains, or artists who gave advice when asked. Gradually, that internal voice became feminine and he called me Carol, Georgina, and Caroline—not to be confused with his sister, Carolee. He settled on the name of Carlotta, a name I approved, in his thirties. Carlton did not think highly of me, because he did not think highly of himself or women in general. Carlotta became a slut, a whore, and a dominating force, but like biblical wicked women, I knew the good in all people. I raised points Carlton would not consider himself.

carlton davis

"Before you say this man is obviously crazy to discourse with my character and imagine my dress, I must stress I do not tell Carlton what to do. I only provide commentary and humor when Carlton is too deadly serious. I do not direct him. In later years, when Carlton was stressed with his mental disorder, he decided he was split between two people, and he did attempt to become me. He played the role of hooker, but this is not what I am. I am a counselor, a jester, and a muse. My role is to provide another interpretation of events. I am the calm voice to Carlton when he is angry or full of excess energy, but there were times even I can't overcome the emotions that surge through Carlton's body. I must retreat and hope that we can survive another of his bouts of irrational anger. For Carlton is bipolar and could not control his blasts of energy and vacuums of lassitude until he found the right way to deal with his situation and mine. For thirty years or more, he did not know he was bipolar. Carlton knew something was wrong, but he attributed the wrongness to his early childhood.

"The psychologist said I was his state dependent personality. When he was high on drugs, I, Carlotta the slut, would appear. But this is wrong; I have always been with Carlton. Carlotta has been many things in Carton's life: muse, nurse, showgirl, cocktail waitress, and whore. I am half of a package that is nominally male, but whose aspirations and desires are at times female. The body of Carlton stays the same, but the mind splits. Drugs merely allowed me to assert myself. Carlton made me be a whore from his fertile imagination. High, we lost all inhibition and did crazy things. These were fun for a time, but we began to pay a heavy price for our dual self-indulgence.

"The body was injured and the mind was not as sharp. The drugs became self-medication rather than wild fun. The drugs kept us from finding a proper cure, which allows me to free myself from the slut's life and take up a role with ladylike demeanor. The drugs would not allow me to be like Ellen Dorland, the wise old woman at the arts colony, who influenced Carlton the first time he cleaned up his unstable life. In our tale, we will tell why we think this happened and assert that this dichotomy contributes to our creativity. Carlton, why don't you tell our story from the beginning?"

I take Carlotta's cue and begin thinking out loud.

bipolar bare

The dissatisfaction began as long ago as I can remember. In the early 1950s, when I was eight or nine, I always wanted to be a girl. Girls had it better. They got to wear pretty clothes. When I was young, they dressed me—Chinky—like my sister. With long hair and pink dresses, I am like the boys of the Victorian age. These clothes were just the hand-me-downs of an older sister until someone—was it my father?—blustered, "No more! He is a boy!" What he didn't know was that I liked it. Carol, my secret name for myself at the time, wanted only to dress up in his sister's, mother's, and grandmother's lace and satin.

When I am a teenager in the late 1950s and first become aware of sexual desire, I still want to be a girl. I slipped into the cabinet where my stepmother's belongings were kept to try on her girdles and bras. I did this when my parents are out for the evening and I am the babysitter for my young sisters. In the basement, beyond my father's work area, the washing machine, the extra refrigerator, and the freezer, is the family room, where I can enact my ritual pageant of modeling girdles and bras. This act begins after my sisters, then four or five, are in bed. With a girdle and a bra taken from my stepmother's dresser, I head for the basement family room. I have to be very careful to remember what the disposition of the garments was so that I can replace the underwear in their exact positions. No one ever confronts me, but still I suspect my stepmother knew. Her bras are a little bit stretched and her girdles perhaps a little bit looser.

I try to shoplift my own garments, but it is difficult. A male teenager is conspicuously out of place wandering amidst the female lingerie in a department store or a five-and-dime. I never am able to lift anything from the department store, but the local five-and-dime is different. Woolworth's could be easily raided, because I can pick a route through the store that leads me through the lingerie toward my favorite target of 45-rpm records. On a record stealing trip, I always go with a friend, but I make the lingerie raids alone, which increases the risk, but also the thrill. Several scouting trips are taken to locate my target.

Entering Woolworth's, I would head straight for the records and dawdle there, behaving very innocently and doing nothing suspicious. When all is clear and I know I am not being watched, I head for the lingerie and pinch a bra or a girdle. The snatch is quick and the item is easily concealed in my jacket. In seconds, I am out of the store and back home secreting my lingerie in the basement, where it would remain until my next babysitting assignment.

"Crook! Pervert! Addict!" storms Carlotta. "You do not portray yourself as a very sympathetic person."

"I was not, but I attribute my devious character to my childhood experiences. Later, I became a better person."

"You have no moral values."

"Don't you believe that change is possible?"

"Yes, but change for the mentally disordered takes a long time."

"Perhaps a lifetime. Look at you, Carlotta."

"Touché, comment received. Continue with our story."

My parents gone, my sisters in bed, I would retrieve the garments. The results were never satisfying. The bras were either too large or too small. I never could figure out what I should get. All I could do was snatch the most available item. I never understood the sizes, the Ds, the Cs, and so on, and there was no one I could ask. The same was true for the girdles. However, some of them I could get around me and they would squeeze me in a provocative way, even if I could hardly breathe.

The thrill of wearing the garments would culminate in masturbation. The thrill, however, involved lots of frustration. Putting on a bra is no easy task. Snapping or clipping the connections of a bra behind the back is beyond my ability to do. I became so tormented that the snapping would have me twisting in circles, desperately trying to hook the bra as my arms ached and my feet got tangled in the straps. I fell on the floor, winded, while in the late night movie I remember Errol Flynn swashbuckled his way across the Caribbean, saving English gentlewomen from the clutches of evil Spanish pirates.

The girdles required a lot of sucking, contraction, and pushing. Hooks almost hooked would come undone and the whole mechanism would release. After multiple attempts, I could manage closure, only to be immediately uncomfortable and calculating how many minutes I could endure the pressure. I could not understand how women endured the discomfort of wearing these insidious undergarments, and I abandoned them in favor of another idea: rope. I had more control of the cinching and no one could ever be suspicious.

"I can see the teenager rotating around in circles trying to snap a bra behind his back," Carlotta chuckles. "You hadn't learned then about snapping a bra in front and rotating it around your body."

"I was naive back then. The self-bondage worked better."

"The rope—that was a good one, Carlton. You would wrap yourself up in cord from chest to ankles and thrash around the basement. I was embarrassed."

"Well, at least I didn't have to steal women's undergarments," I say sheepishly.

"But it was so weird!" Carlotta says, shaking her head disdainfully. "And once you had completely tied yourself up, you couldn't even masturbate. You had to completely undo the knots in a hurry, just in case your parents came home before you freed yourself. How long did you practice this activity?"

"For years and years. Even when I was an adult."

"You didn't just start doing this activity when you were depressed," Carlotta muses. "You started when you were alone."

"I think so, but how do you know I wasn't depressed, Carlotta?"

"I think you were depressed. Try to remember."

"I can't!" I protest. "All I do know is that you, Carlotta, are a manifestation of the black depression. You appeared when I had my periodic downs. Downs that I tracked for years, convinced that there was something terribly wrong, and I just had to understand and plot their occurrence to avoid their effects. I thought if I knew when an attack was about to occur, I could somehow take measures to control it. I could prevent myself from becoming homosexual and living a secret life, but it never happened. The depression always caught me unawares, and I was unable to change. Maybe I didn't really want to change."

Carlotta smiles. "You liked living this double life. It had its exciting quality. By day, you were the straight-acting professional man and by night, you were the wild cross-dressing transvestite."

"Yes, but only in certain times, when the cycle of energy was low."

"Why is it that this cycle is always tied up with sex?" asks Carlotta, answering her own question. "I think it's because sex is the fundamental energy from whence we all emerge. It's messy, not particularly beautiful in its oozy essences, and is driven by urges humans can't really control. Thus, when the fire of perverted energy occurs, we go to our primitive sources, and in the embers we wallow in the results of the unresolved sexual issues of our lives."

"So philosophical."

"Then again, you and I could have just been horny."

"Spoken like a true slut!"

"You didn't have to make me *and* yourself into a whore," Carlotta argues. "I could have been something else: a muse, and a source of inspiration, a Simone de Beauvoir to your Jean-Paul Sartre. Say, I wonder if she gave him good head or if he was too involved with being intellectual? At any rate, I could be the left brain, speaking rational thoughts to the right, creative brain, and a means to make you whole. How would you describe me?"

I ponder the question momentarily. "Carlotta is obsessed with sex," I respond. "She likes to dress sexily—tight dresses, high heels, and aggressive jewelry. Carlotta sees herself as a slutty whore."

"I know that this is all you think Carlotta is, but think harder. Paint me in broad, vivid strokes."

Her challenge gives me pause and arouses my creative juices. "She patrols the streets," I say at length. "She takes tricks into sleazy hotel rooms. There, this wanton woman performs any sex act her client demands. She likes to suck big dicks, especially on black men, but she won't let them come into her mouth. The girl does have some discretion. Her favorite activity is to be anally fucked. She thinks she has a great ass, which acts as an attractive pussy. Her favorite customer is the man with a fat, long penis. It doesn't have to be really long—eight inches will do. The man must like to have her on her back, with her legs in the air, spread apart as far as possible. Or, tightly held together, pointing vertically, while the man makes deep, probing thrusts into her pussy. She also likes the man who is creative and moves her about until he finds the position where his penis will have the maximum penetration. Carlotta loves to get this kind of action everyday—maybe four or five times. This is Carlotta's sickness, and she won't let go of it."

"Very good," applauds Carlotta. "This is all the fantasy of Carlton for Carlotta. It is he who invents the sex his muse enjoys. Now, let Carlotta describe Carlton.

bipolar bare

"Carlton is weak. He is a little boy who never became a man. He always wanted his mommy, but he ended up with his weak daddy. Carlton Jr. never got over it. He hates himself, and he let this ruin his life. Carlton's problem is, he doesn't know what he is, unlike Carlotta, who knows she's a whore. Carlton would like to think of himself as an artist and an intellectual, but he doesn't have the self-confidence to make others believe it. He doesn't know that achieving this success is a matter of attitude, not based on accomplishment. Accomplishment happens when you have the proper attitude."

"You hurt me deeply."

"The truth always hurts, Carlton. Let me go on. Carlton can never make up his mind. He vacillates over options, then waits so long that certain possibilities become impossibilities. Carlton always shoots himself in the foot. He creates his own failure because he believes deep down he is too flawed to even become something.

"Carlton knows himself better than he knows Carlotta, but as usual, he fails to see the better side of himself and dwells in negativity. Too bad! For I, Carlotta, slut that you portray me as, see much within this weak, malignant soul that is admirable, despite the flaws. Carlton needs Carlotta to cut to the chase. The failed intellectual needs his whore."

"You wrong me, Carlotta."

"I never speak untruths. Carlotta gives Carlton his fire. Otherwise, he would always be a sad, depressed, unrealized person, but he never recognizes Carlotta's existence. He thinks Carlotta a manifestation of his addiction to crack, but she has always been with him. She is the forceful voice that gets him moving. Without her, Carlton would be dead. He would have killed himself. He tried once, but it was Carlotta who fought to stay alive as we lay on the bed, poisoned with aspirin. She is his life force."

"I am not an immature, unrealized person! How dare you call me that? I have assisted you in realizing your existence. You are more than a whore to me."

"Carlton, what a surprise!" Carlotta enthuses. "This is the first time you recognized my existence. Before, I was just a whore and everything you said about me was negative."

"Not always. I think you have some positive characteristics."

"Do you really believe it was I who fought to keep you alive when you took the overdose of aspirin at college?"

"You or God whispered in my ear not to give up."

"I have been whispering to you ever since not to give up, even in your moments of deepest darkest depression. You believe this, don't you?"

"I don't know. Something always does stay my hand from jumping off a bridge and running the knife through my heart."

"Does it matter what the something is? You never have the guts to go through with it, anyway."

"Carlotta, why don't you ever have anything nice to say about me?"

"Why should I? You never say anything nice about me, except for your earlier statement. You confuse me with the erotic female and determine me to be a whore. I have heard it said that boys who lose their mothers want to become the erotic female and thus you have turned me, Carlotta, your muse, into this great slut, to satisfy your hunger for the feminine. You invent stories out of your imagination, which is huge."

"Not every story I tell is out of my imagination."

"Then tell me the story from the beginning and we shall see."

"Once upon a time …"

"Don't be sarcastic, Carlton. Begin with the real beginning. What happened when you were four and five? You shall see how much good I have done for you."

A nurse, dressed in a sweater and dark slacks, appears at the door to Room 209.

"Did I hear voices in here?" she asks, looking around the room and seeing only me lying on the bed.

"You startled me," I say, sitting up quickly from my reverie.

"Whom are you talking to?" the nurse asks again.

"Oh, I was probably talking in my sleep. I do that some times."

The nurse looks at me suspiciously. "OK, but it didn't sound like that. Are you Carlton Davis?"

"Yes, but everyone calls me Carl."

"Fine, Carl, can we fill out this form I have brought for your admission to my ward?"

"Anything you want, nurse. What is your name?"

"Maria. Didn't I hear you talking to someone named Carlotta?"

"Don't be ridiculous!" I scoff. "There is no one here by that name."

CHAPTER 5

TEDDY BEAR'S NIGHTMARE

When I was eighteen years old in 1962, the Candy Bar Dream repeated often. I wrote it down to remember it. It was the first journal item I ever recorded. The dream made no sense to me, but it seemed to be full of portent.

The never-changing storyline went as follows:

A naked four-year-old boy stands in the white living room of an empty house. All the windows are covered with blinds. Beyond the living room, a white hallway leads from the front door to the staircase to the second floor. Beyond the stairs lies the kitchen. Light streams into the hallway from two panes of glass in the entry door. The light creates two trapezoids of brightness on the hallway floor. The boy walks carefully into the hallway, trying to make no sound. He stands on the two points of light. The hallway and the stairs in front of him are in shadow. He can hear loud voices on the second floor.

At the end of the hallway the kitchen, its door open, is bathed in diffuse light. The boy knows the kitchen is the place he must go. He creeps down the hallway past the stairs into the rectangular room with a counter along one side. The sink in the counter is below a window covered by curtains. A faucet is running water into the sink. The walls are white. The counter and cabinets are white. The curtain is white. The sink is white. The water is white. The young boy tries to turn off the running water, but he is not tall enough to reach the faucet at the back of the counter. The boy hears a woman scream. He hides behind the open kitchen door.

Peeking around the kitchen door, the young boy sees the woman coming down the stairs. He asks himself, "Is she the dark woman?" The woman is dressed entirely in red. Her hair is red. She wears a red dress, red high heels, and carries a red purse. At the bottom of the stairs, she stops and looks toward the kitchen. The woman strides to the front door, opens it and leaves, slamming the door behind her. The boy crosses the room to the counter.

bipolar bare

He slides past the window and sink and opens a drawer. There are candy bars in orange and red wrappers inside. He knows the candy bars are poison. He opens a wrapper. The chocolate is spotted with the white dots of age. He cracks a bar in half. The golden center has gone white. Inside the white center is a bright red spot. He believes the bright red represents the dark side, a feminine side. He takes a bite. There is a burst of bright white light. The boy disappears.

"In the burst of white light, you turned into the woman you always wanted to be," states Carlotta, sitting opposite me on the edge of the desk.

"I don't believe it."

"You know I was there for all of the events you have forgotten. I was your teddy bear, until you grew up and wanted a person to talk to, not a stuffed animal."

"You mean you are going to free my mind of all that is hidden?"

"Most of it," says Carlotta. "There are some things you are not ready to hear. The bear was your companion for many years. Teddy bear can tell you what you imagined and what is true.

"People think teddy bears are mute, but they are not," she continues, pacing the room with professorial authority. "Their voice is the voice of the child who speaks to them, who gives them feelings, and who listens to their thoughts. Teddy bears are sentient beings for as long as the dialogue takes place, until the child puts them on the shelf and takes the conversation silently inside. Carlton's nightmare was the bear's nightmare. You were called Chinky when the bear talked and he observed what happened. Chinky wants me to tell the tale because I know the whole story. I was there for all of it. I have forgotten nothing, whereas Chinky sealed most of it in his subconscious. What leaks out is too painful for him to tell. I shall begin with the crime."

Before my eyes, Carlotta transmogrifies from a comely nurse into the raggedy plaything I know and love so well.

"Am I what you remember?" asks the bear, sitting on the desk with its button eyes staring vacantly at me. The little upside-down V mouth moves jerkily, like a cartoon character's.

"Yes," I reply delightedly. "You are my teddy bear with light blue paws and the hair that thinned from so much playing."

The bear nods. "Good. Let us begin. We were with Daddy the night he disappeared. Carlton, Sr. took us with him, as he often did. We drive to the railroad siding, where the boat train arrives from Toronto. Dad knows how to gain access to the area because grandfather is in charge of the freight that enters the yard. Many boxcars are lined up along the siding. He pulls up next to a gray boxcar that has 'Baltimore' and 'Ohio' written in big letters on the side wall. Daddy parks his bronze Buick next to this boxcar. He gets out and we wait in the front seat while he goes to meet the man in the black uniform with the black-billed hat. The man in the black hat unlocks and opens the big sliding door and climbs into the gray freight car. The man passes small boxes to Daddy. Daddy walks back to the car, opens the trunk, and puts the boxes in.

"Daddy tells us we should be quiet when he does this, so we watch in silence. Daddy makes many trips back and forth from the freight car. He fills up the car's trunk and the back seat. On his last trip, the man follows Daddy to the car. Daddy places the last boxes in the back seat. The back seat is full of cigarette boxes. He stands outside the car, talking with the man with the cap. He takes his wallet from his back pocket and opens it. We can see Daddy giving the man money.

"Out of the darkness, bright lights shine. We hear loud words telling my father and the man to stand still and raise their arms. We slide off the seat into the space below the dashboard. We hear steps and the car's trunk open. A bright light appears at the car window.

"'Jesus, Frank, there is a kid in here!' a voice behind the bright light says.

"Another light shines in the window on the other side of the car. We try to make ourselves smaller in the seat well.

"'Get the kid out of there, and put him in your patrol car,' says another unfamiliar voice. 'I will take the two men in mine.'

"The car door opens. A man in a blue uniform reaches in toward us. We try to squirm away, pressing ourselves against the wall below the dashboard.

"'Come with me, kid,' the man says.

"He places one hand and one knee on the front seat and leans into the automobile with an arm extended, trying to grab us. The man's hat is knocked off. Chinky screams and clutches me close to him. The man grabs Chinky's arm—the one holding me— wrenching him up and pulling him from the seat well. I drop to the floorboard. Chinky is yelling and thrashing at the man with both arms, crying, 'I want my teddy, I want my teddy!'

"The man carries Chinky away. I am left alone in Daddy's car. The man comes back, picks his hat up, and grabs me roughly by my leg. I'm hanging upside down. He opens a black and white car door and tosses me into the back seat with Chinky. He slams the door and says, 'Here's your teddy bear, kid. Keep quiet.'

"Chinky takes me in one arm and begins sucking his thumb while crying and looking out the window for his father. The man goes back to the other man with a blue uniform and his black and white car. We can't see Daddy anywhere. They talk. He returns and starts up this car.

"'Where is my daddy?' Chinky cries.

"'Later kid, you can see him later,' the man says, driving away from the railroad yard.

"The man takes us to a place where there are a lot of other men in blue uniforms. We sit on a table against a wall with pictures of men and women pinned all over it. The men in blue uniforms walk back and forth in front of us. Chinky and I talk and watch all the activity. Chinky sucks his thumb intensely. One blue man comes and says you shouldn't be sucking your thumb.

"Another blue man brings us candy bars and a soda. There is a lot of activity at this place. Angry men and women come and go. We find out the blue men are called police officers. The angry men call them cops. They move in and out the front door and down the hall behind the wooden fence with men and women wearing iron brackets behind their backs. We are there a long time, observing the exciting goings-on. We even forget to cry, but we do get tired and fall asleep on our tabletop. Mother finally comes and takes us home to the white house.

"Four weeks later, she takes me to a photographer's studio. Mother tells us this will be a special moment before we go for a visit to mother's sister in New Haven. Neither of us knows that these days in the fall of 1948 will be the last we will ever spend with Mother. Mother, whose full name is Lynn Quinn Davis, suspects the worst. I overhear the conversations downstairs in the living room with the new man, Roger. Daddy is gone. A divorce is in progress, and the battle over Chinky is beginning. Panic and rage fill her voice. Roger can't calm her down. She says she will not be beaten, but the forces aligned against her are powerful. Roger counsels her to be cautious. She tells him *to hell with caution*. She will be bold and fearless.

"In the photographer's studio, I am placed on a stool next to the camera where I can watch the session. Lynn sheds her jacket and takes off Chinky's blue wool coat. You are dressed underneath in a blue and white sailor outfit. Your pants are blue shorts with a cloth belt attached. The weather is still warm enough that Mom thinks it's all right for you to have on shorts. Besides, this outfit is Mom's favorite for Chinky.

"You have on white socks and shoes with a strap and buckle that rides high on the socks. The white short-sleeved shirt has a wide blue collar with five narrow white strips across the collar just below your neck. A lanyard hangs around your neck under the collar. On the end is a whistle, hidden from view in the shirt pocket. How you love to blow that whistle! It makes our dog bark and makes Mom angry. I tell you not to do it so much, but you say its fun. Lynn instructs you to keep the whistle in the pocket during the photo shoot.

Chinky and Lynn

"'Chinky, look at the funny man behind the camera,' Mommy tells you, but you are looking at me, telling me it is really hard to sit still and not put your fingers in your mouth. I tell you to stare at the camera. Chinky tries to focus on the big square of the camera.

"'The boy looks like you, Ma'am—his hazel eyes and lips and wavy hair,' the photographer comments, starting another set of photographs.

"'Yes, he is my little Chinky,' Mom responds.

"'What's with the name? Kind of unusual, isn't it?' the photographer replies.

"'See, his left eye lid that is sort of slanted,' Mom answers. 'His grandparents think it looks Chinese, so they gave him that nickname. They love nicknames in that family and give each other silly names. I don't like it, but the name has stuck. The boy's name is actually Carlton.'

"'You ask me, the boy is in for a lot of trouble with a name like Chinky,' the photographer says.

"Chinky looks at mother and asks what the photographer means. Lynn tells the photographer to be careful what he says in front of the boy, because you are really smart for your age. Chinky looks at me and I tell you I don't know what the photographer means, either.

"'I didn't mean any disrespect Ma'am, but the nickname and the long hair could create difficulties with other kids,' says the photographer.

"'The nickname will go away soon and so will the long hair,' Mom says. 'Long hair until a boy goes to school is traditional with young gentleman.'

"'I'd get the boy's hair cut if I were you, Ma'am,' the photographer says as we are headed out the door.

"'Mind your own business, buster!' Mom retorts.

"She is silent all the way home to the white house where Daddy hasn't been for a month and the other man Roger now comes daily. When Mom is silent we know to watch out. When Mom is making noise, things are fun. She sings to us. She chases us around the house, and when she catches us she tickles us and we all laugh. Mommy is silent a lot since Daddy has gone.

"Before Dad's disappearance, our life was the same each day. Mom is home and sleeps all morning. Dad is never home. He is at the mustard factory or at school. At night, when Mom goes to sing at the nightclub, Daddy would stay home and study, except for the nights he takes us to Granddad's railroad yard to pick up the packages. After Dad first disappeared, Mom took us to the nightclub and we stayed in her dressing room. When she left to sing, Chinky colored in his coloring book, read books to me, and slept on the old blue couch with me, teddy bear, in his arms, but then we decided to explore and got into trouble. The manager didn't like us playing behind the stage and Mom got mad at us. Now we have to stay home.

"Before she leaves to sing, Mom puts us to bed, locks the door, and goes downstairs. Chinky refuses to stay in bed. You get up and take me to the door. In a darkened room, you start banging on the locked door, screaming that you want to go see your sister. Chinky bangs me, his friend, his teddy bear, against the door. You are very angry on this night.

"'Please let me go see my sister, I love my sister! Don't lock me in and leave me! Please, please, please! I will be good!' you yell.

"Light penetrates the room from under the door. The thin ribbon of light casts a dull hue on your pink pajamas with the blue sailboats. We can hear voices, loud voices. They are arguing.

"'What do you expect me to do? I can't help you out of this mess,' says the male voice.

"Is the voice Daddy's? No, it is the funnyman, the man who smells when he talks and staggers sometimes when he walks. We don't like this man. He is not the daddy, but he acts sometimes like he is the daddy. We hear a woman's voice, Mom's.

"'Shit, I've got to get that family off my back,' she says.

"'Mommy, Mommy, I want to go to see my sister!' Chinky yells as loud as he can, still banging me against the door with my leg. You drop me to the floor and punch the door with your right fist. It makes more noise.

"'I got to shut that kid up. I can't hear myself think. The bitch mother, she's taken most of the furniture. The house is nearly empty. What am I going to do with the kid?' Lynn cries out.

"Chinky is still yelling, 'I want to see my sister!'

bipolar bare

"'Shut up, Chinky!' Mom screams from below.

"Chinky crosses the room, goes to his toy box, and picks up an armful of blocks. He starts hurling the blocks at the door. *Bang! Bang! Bang! Bang!* The wooden blocks ricochet off the door panel.

"'Mommy, Mommy, I want to go see my sister!' you keep crying.

"'Roger, I got to go deal with the child,' says Mom. 'And make him shut up!'

"We hear hard steps on the stairs. Mommy and the man are coming up. We are afraid. We can tell by the sound that she is very angry. We have seen her throw things when she gets really angry. She stops at the door and begins fiddling with the latch. Chinky picks me up and we hide behind the door. Mom opens the door. There is a blast of light. Chinky is holding me to your face in your left hand and sucking on your right fingers.

"'Mommy. I want to go see my sister,' you say as she steps two paces into the room and sees us behind the door.

"'You can't go see your sister right now, Chinky,' she says. 'I can't take you.'

"Chinky is angry. You run into the middle of the room. 'No!' you cry, swinging your right hand at her. 'I want my sister!'

"'You can't go there now!' Mom screams.

"'Please, Mommy, I want to go see my sister, sister, sister, sister,' Chinky whimpers.

"Chinky runs toward the door. The man is standing in it. He frightens us. Chinky puts his right hand in his mouth, gripping me, teddy, more tightly in his left. Mommy turns and stands up. She has on a long, ruffled, red dress, red high-heeled shoes, and a red flower in her hair. She is ready to go sing. Chinky runs toward the man in the doorway. He stops Chinky and holds him.

"Chinky is screaming, 'Let go of me! Let go of me! I want to go see my sister!'

"'What do you want me to do, Lynn?' the man says. 'The kid is hysterical.'

"'Hold on to him for a moment,' Mom replies. 'Maybe I can calm him down.'

"'Let go of me! Let go of me! You aren't my daddy! I want my sister!' Chinky keeps yelling and tries to kick the man in the shins. Roger avoids the kicks and holds onto him more tightly. Mother is getting excited.

"'Quiet, Chinky, quiet! You'll wake up the whole neighborhood. Hold onto him, Roger!'

"'I'm trying, but he's a strong little fucker.'

"'Sister, sister, I want my sister!'

"Mom tries one more time. She bends down, looking you in the face. 'You can't go see your sister,' she says firmly. 'Not now! Not next week! Get used to the idea!' Chinky swings his right arm at Mommy, trying to push her away. You hit her in the face, but you don't mean to.

"'Goddamned kid!' she yells.

"Chinky put his right fingers back in his mouth. She stands up. She swings her open hand and slaps Chinky very hard across the face. Chinky bites down on his right hand and screams. Your fingers hurt. The man is frightened. He releases Chinky.

"Roger says: 'What the hell did you hit him for? *Jesus!*'

"'I wouldn't have had to, if you held on to him tighter.' barks Lynn.

"'Christ! It's not my job to discipline your children.'

"'If you are going to be with me, you better get more involved and less involved with your booze.'

"The two of them start to argue. We crawl away, get under the bed, curled up in a ball, and watch them argue where we can see them backlit by the light from the hallway. Chinky is sucking on all the fingers of his right hand to comfort them.

"Lynn is screaming at Roger. Suddenly, he grabs her by her shoulders and starts to shake her. Just as suddenly, he stops. Mommy looks at him and runs away. We hear her footsteps *clack, clack, clack* on the stairs. She goes down into the hallway and out the front door. The man looks down at us. He swears. We can smell his breath.

"'Stay where you are, kid,' he commands. He lumbers toward the guardrail, staggers, and catches it with his hip. We hear the crack of wood. He regains his composure. Erect again, he hobbles to the stairs and leaves the house.

"The house is quiet. Fluffy the dog is barking in the basement. Mommy is gone. The man is gone. Chinky's right hand hurts. You hit your mother with your right hand. Mommy always took your right hand out of your mouth. 'Don't suck your fingers,' she would always say. 'Be a big boy.' Now she hurt your right hand. Your tooth bit into the middle right finger when Mommy hit you and all four fingers went numb. Chinky says he doesn't want to use it any more. It is a bad hand now, you say. You claim it was your best hand before you hurt it, although you can use both hands. We lie under the bed, talking to each other. We fall asleep.

"We wake up. The house is quiet. Chinky's hand still hurts. We will go see your sister. She will fix your hand. She is the nurse, Chinky is the patient. Your pajamas are wet where you have peed on them. You decide to take them off and hide them under the bed. We creep down the upstairs hallway to Mommy's room. It is empty. We crawl to head of the stairs and listen. We creep down the stairs to find two old candy bars in the kitchen. The chocolate is old and spotted with white. Chinky eats one, but it doesn't taste good. You offer me the other, but I say 'no thank you.' We sneak by the empty living room. Mommy is not there. The funny smelling man is not there. We open the front door and go outside.

"We are naked. We start down the path toward the trees. Chinky tells me his fingers are throbbing, but you like the cold and the freedom of the night outside. The fall air is raising goose pimples on your naked skin. I tell you that you don't have fur like us teddy bears and you should get warm before we continue our journey to sister's house. We see the garbage cans at the end of the driveway across the lawn where we have played, pretending that they are igloos. We run giggling across the leaf-covered lawn to the driveway. We run down the driveway to the cans that are hidden by a car that is parked on the road by the big pine tree.

"Chinky places me on the ground next to a garbage can. You grab its top edge. You are careful not to make a sound while you turn the can on its side and take off the lid. There are several bags of trash and some of Roger's bottles in the bottom of the can. Chinky picks me up and we crawl in. The igloo can is very cold. Shivering, we curl up in the bottom of the can, pulling the bags around us to keep warm. Chinky offers me one of the bottles to drink from. I tell you I don't like the taste of that stuff. We are Indians on an adventure, we tell each other. When the sun comes up, we will make our way to sister's house and she will be our nurse.

"We are making our plan when a big fat man appears. He bends down, shines a flashlight into the garbage can, and says 'Whatcha doing in there, son? You're going to catch your death of cold. Come out!' He reaches his arm in. Men are always grabbing at us. We shake ours heads in refusal and push back. He gets down on his knees and reaches in with one arm, taking hold of my paw. He slips and curses. His body sprawls on the ground.

"He wriggles forward and with both arms, he grabs both my paws while Chinky holds me tight, resisting and yelling 'No!' The can is rattling. The bottles are crashing against the metal, making an awful clatter. The fat man wriggles back, dragging me out with Chinky holding on. He gets up to his knees.

"'The cops are sure to come after all this noise,' the man says, looking quickly up and down the street. 'This isn't what I'm paid to do, kid—rescue naked children with teddy bears from garbage cans. Now what I am I supposed to do with you?'

Adjusting his grip on Chinky's arm, he staggers to a standing position. The man, who smells like Roger, picks us up in his arms, walks around the pine tree down the street, and puts us in his car. He takes an overcoat from his back seat and wraps us in it.

"He drives off through the silent street of small suburban houses and evergreen trees. While we ride, he lights a cigarette and looks over at us. 'This ain't in my contract,' he keeps repeating. 'This ain't in my contract.'

"The man stops at a filling station and gets out of the car. He tells us not to leave the car. He walks to a pay phone and talks to someone. When he comes back, the man tells us he is going to take us to your grandmother's house.

"'I don't like this at all kid,' he complains, starting up the car and lighting up another cigarette. We listen as he keeps talking nervously to himself. 'It's getting complicated and that not good for me or the agency. But what am I supposed to do? I see a naked child waving a teddy bear in one hand, running from the front door of the house out onto lawn. The punk dances his way to the driveway, then runs down the drive. He disappears from view behind a large pine tree. I become concerned. I wait to see if anyone will come out of the house to find you. No one does. I decide to take a look. Am I supposed to just leave a naked kid outside in the cold all night? Shit the bed, there was no one around! No one came out of the house for you, for crying out loud. I am supposed to watch for the woman and the guy, not babysit a kid! Maybe Moe is wrong. Maybe I should just drop you at the police … let them deal with it. If I take you to the grandparents, it's sure to tip the mother off that she is being watched. Maybe what I am doing is illegal—it could jeopardize my license. I don't like it, I don't like it at all!'

"We listen to the fat man talk like this as he drives us over to Grandmother's house. Grandmother meets us at the door. She tells the man his agency will not be compromised. She tells him the police have been alerted. They will tell the mother that the boy was found in the street and the police brought the boy to his grandmother's house. The man tells Grandmother he isn't convinced the story will hold up, but he leaves. Sister is asleep. Grandmother puts us to bed in the guest room.

"See, doesn't that explain the dream?" says the teddy bear. "The naked boy, the woman in red, the candy bars, and the flash of light from the detective?"

"But what about the explosion of light and the disappearance?" I reply skeptically.

"Didn't you disappear? The detective took you to your grandmother's house."

"All right, what if all that is true? What does the dream mean?"

"Dreams don't have to mean anything. Maybe it is just a vision of your neurosis. After all, don't you like to be naked? Haven't you had experiences of the bright white light when you meditate?"

"Yes to both questions. But I am still not convinced you are making the right interpretation of this dream."

"I shall finish my story and we can revisit the dream's meaning."

The bear continues his tale: "You, me, and Carolee are playing in the attic when Mom arrives at Grandmother's house. Chinky hears a car door slam, climbs onto the window seat, stands on his tiptoes to look out the window, which is directly above the front entrance to Grandmother's house. Chinky can't see the door below because of the shallow portico, but he can see the concrete walkway that crosses the lawn to the three steps that descend to the sidewalk and Council Rock Avenue beyond.

"He sees his mother striding across the street from a taxicab toward the walkway to the front door. In the driver's seat, the cab driver looks down the empty street. In the back seat, Roger watches Lynn depart.

"'Mommy!' Chinky yells from the attic window. She hears him, looks up, waves and continues her purposeful stride toward the front door and disappears below the small porch roof.

"Nonnie calls out to Yoya, my grandfather, 'I will keep the child there, you deal with Lynn.'

"Yoya opens the door and places his arm was across the opening, holding onto the jamb and blocking Mom's entrance to the house. We can see Mommy beyond Yoya who is dressed in a light gray suit. She has on a flowered hat and wears an open brown overcoat that reveals a flower print dress.

"Chinky struggles to get out of Nonnie's grasp. He turns toward her, dropping me to the floor. He tries to peel her hand off his arm with his left hand. He can't do it.

"'Let me go!' he shrieks.

"Nonnie holds steady, paying no attention to his struggle. Her eyes are riveted on the two people standing at the end of the hall, about sixteen feet away.

"'You have no right to keep my son,' Lynn yells past Yoya to Nonnie at the end of the entry hall.

"'You are an unfit mother,' Nonnie yells back. 'The child was running around outside in the middle of the night with no clothes on.'

"'I don't believe you or what the police say,' says Lynn, shaking her fist at Nonnie. Her purse swings from the middle of her arm. 'You and that son of yours stole the furniture and the child from my house, didn't you?'

"Yoya remains calm and speaks to Lynn in a reasonable tone. 'I can't give the child back to you right now,' he says evenly. 'We will take the situation to court tomorrow or the next day. They will decide where the child goes.'

"Yoya closes the door in Lynn's face. Chinky kicks at Nonnie's thin leg and she drops his hand. He runs toward the closed door. 'Yoya, help me out here!' she demands of the silent and calm Yoya, standing at the closed door. Yoya blocks your hand as you reach for the doorknob.

"'I think you should let the child see his mother,' says Yoya equitably.

"'I will not permit that woman anything!' Nonnie shrieks.

"'Bitch!' comes Mom's voice through the closed door.

"'Mommy!' Chinky shouts and throws himself on the floor in front of the door, kicking at his grandfather legs.

"'This boy is impossible. He needs to see his mother,' says Yoya, pulling the flailing boy off the floor and taking him into the hall.

"'I swear, I will beat him myself if he breaks any of these heirlooms,' Nonnie threatens, pointing to the ceramic base of the clock on the hall table between the bronze dog and the bronze moose.

"Halfway down the hall, Yoya lets go of Chinky. You grab me and scramble up the stairs toward the attic.

"'I told you to hang onto the child, Yoya!' Nonnie wails. 'Why have you let him go?'

"Yoya looks passively at Nonnie, stating, 'I don't like any of this. The child belongs with his mother until the court decides otherwise.' He turns and walks through the archway at the base of the stairs toward his den.

"Carolee is in our attic castle, giving tea to her dolls. Chinky climbs onto the window seat, pushing her dolls aside. Carolee protests, 'Don't hurt my dolls.' You pay no attention and rise on your toes. We stare out the window. Lynn is standing in the street outside the cab, talking loudly to Roger in the taxi. She is gesturing with her arm toward the house, the purse still on her forearm, swinging with the rhythm of her shaking finger. Roger is alternately looking toward her and looking down to the floor of the cab. Chinky calls out to her, but she doesn't hear him. Roger gets out of the cab. He gestures for Lynn to get into the taxi. Standing for a few moments with her hands planted defiantly on her hips and shaking her head, Lynn at last gets into the taxi and it drives away. Chinky is crying. Carolee tries to console him. She offers him tea, but he just sulks.

"Three days later, Nonnie dresses Chinky in a new blue sailor outfit and a new blue overcoat. She brings us downstairs to the bench in the hall and tells us to sit. Mom comes to the front door and Nonnie opens it. The two women stare at one another. Nonnie calls to us, 'Come here, child.' We stand in front of my grandmother, facing your mother. 'The judge says I have to do this, Lynn,' Nonnie says, 'but know we will get the child out of your irresponsible hands.' Grandmother pushes you forward and Mommy takes your hand.

"'Go to hell,' Lynn replies, turning on her heels and leading us down the walk to the waiting taxicab, where Roger waits. Mother tells Roger that she is going to take the child away, where the Davises can't get him. Roger tells her that this is not a good idea.

"'I don't care what you think,' Lynn replies. 'You rich people think you can get away with anything.'

"Roger protests that he is not Lynn's enemy. He supports her, but he knows she is not helping her case by spiriting the child away. The Davis family is getting a divorce for Carl, Sr. based on her adultery with him. If she runs away with the child, the act will further stain her reputation.

"'I am not running away,' Lynn says, 'but I am not letting them have this child. They already took my daughter from me. They won't get my son.'

"'I'm just telling you to think before you act.'

"'I am thinking,' Lynn insists. 'That old woman is not going to beat me this time. You know what that woman said to us when I married her precious son—'Cocky' or 'Cock,' as they called him at school, the dashing young man riding around New Haven on the Indian motorcycle in the Yale sweater. He picked me up in a bar, you know, where I was singing underage. His mother said, 'What are you, a couple of dogs? Why don't you two just do it in the road?' I was very young then; little did I know he had no balls. His mother had cut his off.'

Roger says, "'OK, Lynn, calm down. The kid is here in the car.'

"'Better he should hear what a coward his old man is.'

"'You can't undo the past. Be smart about the future.'

Lynn laughs ruefully. "'You know, I was only sixteen when I married that bastard. Eighteen when I had my daughter. Carolynn was born the year after Pearl Harbor. His mother convinced us to give her up to her for adoption. It was the war, they said. We were too young. What if 'Carlie' got killed? Could I raise the child? It all seemed to make so much sense. So I went along. Nonnie said that after the war, if Cocky survived, they would give the baby back. Well, they didn't do it, did they? Now I think that the bitch just wanted to have a daughter since she had two sons, and this was the way she could get one. I was fooled. Well, I am not going to be fooled this time.'

"'Lynn, you have to be careful,' says Roger, trying to be the voice of reason. 'They are watching you. They have money and they have connections.'"

bipolar bare

The tale at an end, the teddy bear has transformed back into Carlotta.

"Is this all you have to tell me, Carlotta?" I say, drawing a heavy sigh. "It hardly adds anything to understanding the dream."

"I think you have to look at the larger context," says Carlotta. "The woman in red is yelling in your dream, and you are hiding. She leaves the scene, slamming the door, identifying her hot temper that she handed down to you. Each piece in the dream fits some aspect of the reality you experienced: the empty house, the naked romp outdoors, and the candy bars you ate. Parts are rearranged as they always are in a dream. I believe the dream is a metaphor for loss, disappearance, and your desire for the feminine. The woman in red disappears and you disappear. The self is lost. Didn't you say the blue at the center of the candy bar represented the dark side of life, and the feminine?"

"You speak a whole lot of horseshit."

"Don't you continue to have difficulty with women? You find them nefarious. You don't trust them."

"Yeah, what about you? I speak with you. I invented you and you toy with me, Medusa Carlotta, queen of the night."

"Now is that a nice way to speak to your own private nurse? I have to take care of you. Do you need a bed pan?"

"What made you think that?"

"It's just that I have noticed when you get excited, you need to relieve yourself. Isn't that what happened to you as a boy? Events get to be too much for you, and you wet the bed."

"I was asleep when that happened, not awake as I am now. A bedpan! You think the strangest thoughts, Carlotta. I think I like the teddy bear better. Shall I make you him again?"

"Too late—the bear is gone. You need a more mature muse and companion. Thus, it is I. Are you sure you don't want a bedpan?"

"The toilet room is only ten feet away. Why would I need a bedpan?"

"It is only a suggestion. A chance to relieve yourself might open up those pent-up memories that plague you every day."

"I'm going to bed. Back in your bottle, genie."
"Your wish is my command."

CHAPTER 6

THE BOGEYMEN

I RISE EARLY ON MY SECOND DAY in the main hospital to write about my experiences since I decided to admit myself to the mental hospital. My roommate, Smitty, is curled up in his bed with a blanket wrapped tightly around him. He looks like a gigantic burrito, legs and head hidden inside his wool tortilla. This is mostly how I see him during my stay at Las Encinas. When we aren't dining or participating in a mandatory group session, Smitty is always sleeping or watching TV from inside his blanket cocoon. He sleeps a lot during the day, a habit he blames on migraine headaches. He claims he contracted a strange syndrome in the war, which makes his sleep unbeneficial and so renders him unable to work. He seems perfectly normal to me, and I speculate he snoozes so much to keep the reality of our situation from penetrating too deeply into his subconscious. We are in the nuthouse, after all.

A tall African-American, Smitty is a Vietnam War veteran. He has nightmares, where he loudly relives the battles he endured in his days ferrying Navy Seals on the rivers of the Mekong Delta. When I ask him about his dreams, he reluctantly tells me they are flashbacks to the gory shoot-outs he was witness to. I want to hear more, but Smitty falls silent and retreats into his cocoon.

I think that if I tell him about the nightmares I had when I was young, he will open up to me. I tell him about the bogeymen from whom I hide under the sheets, clutching my teddy bear. Bogeymen crawled out from under my bed, came in through the door, emerged from pictures on the wall, and scratched at my window with long red fingernails. The apparitions came to steal me away. I scream until an adult comes to give me comfort and reassurance that there are not any evil beings outside the house, or in my room. They tell me I am merely hearing the branches of a tree scraping the window.

The Bogeymen; sketch book; ink, pen, and marker

The bogeymen dreams terrified me, and I wet the bed every night. For years, I buried myself under the covers with only a little bit of my face uncovered for breathing. I tell Smitty his sleeping position reminds me of how I used to hide myself under the blanket and sheet. I tell him that I haven't told anyone about the bogeymen before, hoping he might reciprocate and tell me his dreams. Smitty says his dreams are private, and we do not know each other well enough for him to reveal their content. He says my dreams are nothing compared to the horrific scenes he relives each night.

"You got no idea what it was like, man," says Smitty, rolling himself tighter into his tortilla blanket. Like a lot of black men, his deep voice has a militant edge to it. "I'm not going to tell you my dreams, sucker, and I'm not going to tell you why I'm in this hellhole. Now shut the fuck up and let me sleep!"

After Smitty turns his back to me, I begin writing in my journal:

"This is where you end up when you can't cope with the world as it is and when you either get too depressed, too wild to deal with others, or too addled by drugs. I have seen only one instance of so-called crazy behavior, when the attendants—assisted by the police—wheeled a screaming man strapped to a gurney across the lawn toward the locked ward. Otherwise, the people I have met here seem pretty normal—perhaps preternaturally normal is the best way to describe it. The drugs we are given must temper any strange behavior."

"Disordered behavior is hard to distinguish," says Carlotta.

"Carlotta, you are here again!" I exclaim.

"Who the fuck you talking to?" grumbles Smitty from his cocoon.

I lower my voice. "How delightful! I see you are dressed in your nurse's costume, but no bedpan."

"No, I have come with your chart." Carlotta waves her clipboard in front of me. "I believe we should continue our review of your early history."

"But you are not a psychiatrist."

"True, but I am the next best thing for you, for the time being. Didn't the nurse tell you that they do not have a doctor for you yet?"

"Yes, you are right. Nurse Maria told me that it might be four or five days before that happens."

"Precisely. I will function as your shrink in the meantime."

"Are you Freudian, Carlotta?"

"Not at all! I am Floridian," she quips. "We believe in sun and fun as we investigate your depressed and otherwise bent psyche. Our techniques are considered controversial, but all our patients remark that they had a good time when they're in our hands."

"Does this involve anything sexual?" I ask, continuing to speak *sotto voce*, so as not to disturb Smitty.

"I can't reveal our treatment methodology until we become more intimately involved with your issues."

"Knowing you, Carlotta, I would be surprised by nothing."

"Indeed! Shall we get started, then? I believe it is time we reviewed the experiences of your later childhood through college. You have already revealed your experiences with the bogeymen and I have recorded your description. However, we have not attributed any significance to the dream. What are your thoughts?"

"Well, the bogeymen are all the people grabbing at me: the detective pulling me out of the garbage can, and all the other people trying to restrain me—my mother, my mother's boyfriend, and my grandmother."

"Hmm, not bad for starters, but I think there is more to be revealed."

"You would know."

"We will move on to examine other important events in the formation of your personality."

"I'm ready. Shoot."

"I have in my possession a report from the Reading Laboratory at the University of Bridgeport, Connecticut, from 1951, when you were seven years old. I took it from your notebook. You didn't notice."

"You are acting like a Florida Mafioso!"

"Never mind the sarcasm. Let's get down to the report. They tested you to determine the causes for your retardation. The family went to the Connecticut shore for a vacation. You were sent off to this laboratory during the day."

I feel my face turning red. "I was never retarded."

"I know that, but the report says you were one year behind in all subjects in school at that time."

"Probably because of all that happened to me when I was four and five."

"I think that is probably right. Let me read you the report and give me your opinion:

'Carlton Davis seen on the afternoon of May 12. He has intelligence and superior ability, but is a severely upset child. Academically, he is approximately a year behind his peers. A certain amount of humor is evident. He faces and reveals his disappointments by fighting vigorously. He overreacts with aggressiveness.'"

"I have always been getting into fights."

"No comments until I finish, please. The report continues:

'The Rosenzweig picture frustration study (children's form) was given, as well as the figure drawing test. During these examinations, Carlton talked freely, giving his reactions to the tests and to the examiner. At times he struck the examiner or otherwise issued orders. Our impression is of a child who is accustomed to lashing out physically and speaking disrespectfully to adults. He was very active, climbing on the chairs, twisting his body, reaching with his arms, and kicking with his feet. At other times he was quiet and cooperative, reacting sweetly to the examiner and the test situation. This occurred when his mind was engaged, and when he felt that he was not alone in "giving."

Such as when he drew a picture while the examiner read a story about a whale. The Rozenzweig picture frustration study examines twenty-four situations. In all except one, Carlton reacts with excessive hostility toward the other person or persons involved.

'In other situations, his hostility and aggressiveness were exceptionally strong, with threats of gang action and physical violence. He shows neither respect for adults nor tenderness for smaller children. He uses temper tantrums frequently as a method for control of a situation. Carlton's story of the house suggests that he feels not only equal but also superior to many adults. Roughhousing and fighting form the family pattern, with the father returning to side with the wife. It is the father and wife who are punished, not the children. Again, Carlton's hostility toward adults is made evident.

'The figure drawing reveals the subject's typical reaction when other people are present. Carlton resisted this test by drawing parts of the people and offering them to the examiner to cut out and assemble, while he refused to do so himself. Carlton aggressively pointed to a red square on the classroom wall which he claimed contained directions for putting the people together. Superficially conforming to the test requirements by making people pieces, he cleverly avoids doing what is asked of him by insisting that the examiner assemble the parts.

This test shows a certain hostility toward adults as well as an unnaturalness for Carlton to think of people doing something together. While making these drawings, Carlton talked freely of the war in China, which he wanted stopped.'"

"I remember that test, but I remember it differently," I interject. "The examiner wanted me to draw a picture of my mother and father. I knew it was a trick and that they wanted something from me. So I drew only the hands and feet of my parents. I did it very slowly, until the examiner gave up on the test. I had outsmarted the old bat!"

"The conclusion about your character wasn't wrong, was it?" says Carlotta, ignoring my jubilation. "Did you at least have fun drawing the hands and feet?"

"Yes, I did. You know I love to draw."

"So, you had fun and time in the sun at the Connecticut beach. A true Floridian conclusion can be taken from that experience. Not all is negative or supercharged with meaning. I shall continue with my recollection of the report: 'These tests reveal an unhappy child seeking knowledge and satisfaction, which should be his in the natural course of things. Carlton needs discipline—not the punishment kind, but intelligent, constructive guidance that will develop self-control and permit the flowering of his many excellent qualities. A firm, intelligent, affectionate, and mature woman with a sense of humor is necessary in Carlton's life, if he is to develop into the fine man it is in him to be. Such a person will break down his hostilities (slowly, no doubt) by giving to him the security and affection, which he must have.' The report is signed Mary H. Grumbly.

"What do you think of that, Carlton?" asks Carlotta. "Didn't Dr. Wortz, the psychologist you went to for help with your depression, say you had attention deficit disorder and tell you to read a book on the subject?"

"Yes, he did," I concur, "and a lot of what is described in this report can be attributed to symptoms of ADD. The constant movement, excess energy, and temper tantrums are typical. The period of intense focus when your mind is engaged is a symptom. The distaste for authority is also common. What about the aggressiveness?"

"Carlotta has a theory how to diagnose the aggressive behavior, but now is not the time to discuss this."

"Why not? You are a psychiatric nurse, aren't you, even if you are one from Florida?"

"I am not from Florida the place, but Florida the mental perspective. We believe in appropriateness. We reveal our insights at the appropriate time for maximum therapeutic effect. For the time being, I shall say the aggressiveness is early evidence of later neurosis."

"Bullshit!"

"There you go, flaunting the aggressiveness and foul language that goes with your emotions. I have another example from your early teenage years, which is evidence of aggressive and inappropriate behavior. To wit: When you were a teenager, a huge and very special dump sat across from your family's small suburban house. Unlike most dumps, there are no rotting piles of garbage, no wrecked furniture, no bedsprings, and no mounds of moldy paper. Rather, this dump is a shimmering field of color, mostly white with flecks of red, yellow, green, purple, and blue. Broken and imperfect glass is deposited here from the big glass factory in Corning, New York, the town where you lived. Fragments of the clear glass from lamp bulbs, drinking cups, bowls, and assorted other things spread for acres from the street to the dike that protects the town from the Chemung River.

"Mixed into this field are the blue and red fragments of railroad direction lamps. Other green, yellow, and purple chunks, whose purpose is indeterminate, sparkle here and there across the wavy glass carpet. Buried like treasure in the rubble are the rejected waste globes from the manufacture of fine Steuben Ware goblets and plates. All the colors and shapes mound into low hills or are pushed flat into small plains.

"As young teenagers, you and your friends ran all over this fantastic world. You scrambled up and down the hills and hid in the narrow valleys. This mysterious world, silent except for your yells, the sounds of glass scraping against shoes, and the little avalanches of tumbling hunks sliding down the small hills, was the place you went to play every day.

"Your parents worried you would be hurt and warned you to stay away from this dangerous place, but to no avail. Your merry band of explorers went there to disappear amidst the reflective hills, to investigate any and all strange glitters on the white horizon. You discover odd shapes and weird colors. You find many riches buried in the glass: iron contraptions, Steuben globes, and magazines. Here, you discovered your first girlie magazine, all moldy and damp. You eagerly pried apart the pages of the magazine to see the photos of women's naked breasts and the lurid drawings of Red Chinese and Russian soldiers whipping scantily clad damsels in distress and our American soldiers descending on them with machine guns blazing.

"The wonderful land was destroyed when you were still a young teenager. Soil was piled over the glass and plowed into a level surface. A school sits atop this place now. A grade school building, surrounded by an immaculate green lawn, is the dump's tombstone. Your last memory of the dump starts with big trucks arriving to deposit loads of brown dirt on this bright place. The dirt and glass get mixed up and the hills become higher than ever. You charge up to the top and race down the sides. Hiding from your other pals, your friend Dewey and you shell them with dirt bombs. At one point, you pick up a piece of glass instead of dirt and hurl it. The engagement quickly becomes a pitched battle of chunks of glass. Fear and great excitement grip you all. *Someone could really get hurt!* You find the faux war exhilarating. Those dirty Commies on the other side of the hill are really going to get the shit kicked out of them, you think. And someone does: You hurl a chunk of glass and catch a friend above the eye, badly gashing his forehead. Your father physically disciplines you and forbids you ever to go on that site again. You did have a special ability to get your parents mad at you, I'll give you that."

I smile, recalling the Utopia that was the dump. "Carlotta, you and I certainly do have adventures and manage to get ourselves in all kinds of trouble."

"I did not approve of this violence. I told you not to start throwing glass, but you would not listen to me."

"I don't see this story as evidence of totally aggressive behavior. My friends were involved, too."

"But it was *you* who started the glass-throwing."

"I would attribute my behavior to ADD and a symptom of engaging in physically dangerous activity without considering the consequences. We have always liked danger."

bipolar bare

"Why do you persist in saying 'we'?" Carlotta protests. "It was always you who liked to cause trouble. There was the time you cut off all the heads of the neighbors' tulips when you were angry at their son."

"Young boys are supposed to be a little devilish."

"But not to the point of physically maiming others."

"Oh, forget all the aggressiveness rubbish!" I say with a dismissive gesture. "What I like here is the wonderful experience we were allowed. Perhaps the dump represents substantiation of a divine gift that came our way. How many others have a shimmering glass field across the street from their house?"

"According to you and what you experienced, the dump ultimately became a sad reality."

"They covered it up with a school, for Chrissakes. A bad fate, if you ask me."

"Carlton, there you go again, focusing on the negative."

"I am naturally disposed toward the negative because of my experiences. It is my turn now to recall for you the worst negative experience of my high school years."

"Keep it down," Carlotta admonishes me. "Your friend Smitty seems a mite agitated."

Indeed, Smitty is back in the Mekong Delta in his dreams, inhaling napalm and fighting off gooks. He twists and turns in his cocoon, moaning and muttering obscenities.

"At seventeen years old, my father forced me to spend my final year of high school at a prep school," I whisper. "He said going to Mount Hermon would help me get into a good college, since my grades weren't that good at the excellent high school I attended in Lexington, Massachusetts. I thought he just wanted to get rid of me. He had gone to a prep school himself and sent me out to interviews at Hotchkiss, Andover, Deerfield, and Mount Hermon. I didn't want to go, but I said I would if one of the schools were to accept me for just one year. Three schools said they would only take me if I redid my junior year. I thought I would escape, but Mount Hermon accepted me for a year. Resentful, I accepted to go to this school in western Massachusetts.

"My father pressured me to play football. 'It will make a man of you,' he said, 'and it's a good way to make new friends.' I went out for the team despite my dislike for the game. I wasn't good at it. Slow of foot, tall and skinny, and unsure of hand, I never liked tackling or slamming into others to block. I liked baseball. I liked being on a mound sixty feet away from a batter and firing a ball toward them. Playing football, I worried that some brute would step on my hand, ruining my fastball.

"The football coach sensed my unease and my rebellious nature. I was a third-string player who sat on the bench during real games and was the target for blockers in practice. I participated without enthusiasm, which annoyed Coach Percussion. He demanded eagerness and respect for him and for the game from all his players. I didn't cooperate. In practice, I got yelled at often for my lackadaisical attitude by this disciplined coach.

"I did have one ability. I was the only player who could shuttle the football between his legs to the punter with accuracy. The team's first-string center, a hulking 250-pound kid who liked slamming into others across the scrimmage line and who could do a halfway decent job of hiking the ball into the hands of the quarterback, was hopeless on the snap to a punter. In practice, I was called upon to do the shuttle so the kicker could improve his skill. In games, the first-string center would do the job, despite several spectacular failures when the ball sailed over the kicker's head or dribbled on the ground in front of him. The center could block. I was a disaster at protecting the kicker from the opposing line. During games, I could continue to goof off on the sidelines.

"The football field was down the hill from the main dormitories of the school, surrounded by a running track and flanked by classroom buildings and the chapel. It was considered by most to be the center of Mount Hermon. Once a week, the team would participate in a full contact practice game with the first-string team pitted against the second- and third-stringers. The practice is like a real game with all players in full uniform, helmet, and pads. My helmet has only one bent rod for a face guard, as the third-string doesn't get the better helmets with larger face guards. I don't think much about it, because as a third-stringer, I hardly ever play, even in these mock games.

"I am daydreaming on the bench, staring off at the hills in the distance brilliantly displaying their fall foliage, when the coach barks at me to pay attention and get my ass onto the playing field, because I am to center the football to the punter. I trot onto the field into the second-string huddle. I am to the snap the ball on three.

"The huddle breaks and I move into the center of the line over the ball facing the first-string players across the scrimmage line. The lineman facing me is much heavier than I, but about my height. Behind the lineman, two linebackers are positioned on either side. I know these guys to be gung-ho players, favorites of the coach. Both are shorter than I am but much more muscular. They eye me with loathing for my inattentive attitude. I try to look calm, but I am scared. I know these two guys are going to cream me.

"Our side crouches in unison. At least I don't screw that up. My two hands are on the ball, and I hope these guys won't deliberately spike my fingers. Through my legs, I can see the kicker about eight yards behind me. 'Hut one, hut two, hut three'—the quarterback calls the snap, and I shoot the ball back to him perfectly, the spiraling ball hitting his outstretched arms without adjustment. I rise, my knees still bent with my arms splayed, ready to block. The linebackers attack. An elbow from one of the charging linebackers hits me below the face guard, clobbering me. I fall backwards, thinking the puffy clouds above are beautiful before I go unconscious. I am carried off the field in a stretcher and don't regain consciousness until later in the locker room. My face is covered with blood. My lips are cut and my tongue bleeds. There is a vacant space where my front teeth used to be. I mumble incoherently. I sense the coach and team looking down on me with disdain. I hate them and myself for my weakness.

"An ambulance comes, taking me to the town of Greenfield's hospital emergency room. A doctor says I am not hurt too badly, except for the broken teeth. Dazed and disoriented, I am discharged from the hospital and taken to a local dentist by the school nurse. The dentist is an older, stocky man with a long mane of white hair framing large amber glasses. The face leans in toward me with a strong exam light behind him. 'We'll have you fixed up in no time,' he says reassuringly, 'and get you back to school.'

"My two front teeth are quickly capped and I am back in my dormitory while still groggy. I lie on the bed staring at the ceiling, wondering what has happened to me. I feel weird. My mouth doesn't seem right. The hard things behind my swollen lips don't feel like they are part of me. My tongue is numb and doesn't seem to fit correctly in the hole in the front of my face. My body is sore all over. My mind can't connect to this battered body. I wish I am somewhere else, but I realize I'm back in the prison of Mount Hermon. I'm stuck in a place I never wanted to be, a place where I have few friends and feel completely alien. I seem to end up in places like this throughout my life. Silently sobbing in the darkened room, I fall asleep.

"A day later, I go back to my classes and my job in the school laundry, where I am assigned to the shirt-pressing machine. I hate this job. The machine is set up to be operated by a right-handed person. Being left-handed, I have a difficult time keeping from being burned each time I place or remove a shirt from the metal mandrel, trying to avoid the enclosing piece that comes around to press the shirt. I get burned a lot and I swear, which causes me to be reprimanded by the supervisor. After the football incident, I am even more uncoordinated, burning myself on every shirt. I curse so much the supervisor sends me away. I tell him he can go to hell as I stomp from the laundry room. I do not return to the football team.

"Several days after the injury, my teeth start to hurt. I go to the infirmary. The nurse can find nothing wrong with me and accuses me of faking my pain to get out of work and football practice. The pain grows worse each day. On the third day, I go to the nurse again and am rebuffed a second time. I call her a bitch. She says she will report me. I tell her, 'Go ahead, I hate this damn school! Kick me out so I can go home!'

"By the evening, the pain is so intense I call my father in desperation. I tell him no one believes me when I say I am in awful pain. I tell him they say I was faking in order to get out of work and football. Dad doesn't believe me at first. I plead with him to come get me and take me to a doctor. Finally, he relents. He says he is too busy to come pick me up tonight, but if it is that unbearable, I should take a taxi to the station in Greenfield and get the next available bus to Boston. Call him, he says, when I am about to board the bus. He will pick me up at the Boston Terminal.

"The bus ride to Boston is a horrible experience. The bus takes forever, stopping at every small town on the way. The journey takes over five hours. The bus is not crowded, and I am alone in the rear, rocking back and forth, trying desperately to distract myself from the pain. Mid-journey, the throbbing becomes so intense, I slip down into the seat well and beat my head against the side of the bus. The sensation from beating my head against the metal wall below the window creates a painful diversion from the intense ache in my front teeth and face. I swear and curse. I yell out how much I hate my life, how much I hate the school, how much I hate football, how much I hate my father for sending to this horrible place. I scream I hate God for making me so miserable. He made me a misfit, a clumsy and stupid person whom no one understands, who can't make sense out of the world. From Greenfield to Boston, I rock, swear, and bang my head. The bus driver doesn't even notice the commotion going on in the back of the bus.

"I stagger off the bus, where my father is waiting. He rushes me to the Harvard Medical Center. An oral surgeon removes the caps from my front teeth. There is a terrible smell. They take an X-ray and discover that my teeth are also broken above the gum line. The teeth are infected and have to be removed completely. The surgeon knocks me out for the operation that removes my front two teeth. I wake up with a space in the front of my mouth. Dad takes me home, and the next day I go to a dentist who gives me a dental plate that has two front teeth attached. I am told that in several weeks I will have to return to have a permanent bridge installed. My father tells me that the infection in the broken teeth had almost reached my brain, and if it had I would be dead.

"I get to stay home for several days. My father tells me I will have to return to Mount Hermon. I beg him not to send me back. He says I must go. The tuition is paid and I am going to complete the year. He promises he would have a serious discussion with the school administration about how I was treated.

"On the ride back to Mount Hermon, I am sullen and silent. I am angry with my father who is making me go back, angry with the school, and angry at the world. I sit outside the headmaster's office while my father is inside. I can hear his raised voice but cannot distinguish what he was saying. The football coach is brought in. He looks at me severely as he enters the headmaster's office.

"I wait a long time outside the door before I am brought in. The headmaster says I will no longer have to work in the laundry. I am excused from the school's work requirement for the rest of the year. That is all the satisfaction I get. I go back to my dorm room, still upset. My father leaves. For the rest of the year, the teachers and staff avoid me. I become part of the clique of students who are not considered good Hermonites. I become friends with the pariahs who break the rules and thumb their noses at the ethos of the school. We sneak out of the dorm and go into the woods to smoke cigarettes and marijuana."

"That was your first experience with marijuana," says Carlotta.

"Yes. My new friend, Jim, had the substance, and smoking it made me feel good."

"This is your first step on the road to addiction."

"I don't think you're entirely correct. It was many years before I smoked weed again. In college, I drank alcohol."

"Who are the bogeymen in this tale of the dentist?"

"You ask a good question. My bogeymen were the school administrators, the football coach, the town dentist, and my father. They reached through my personal window and snatched me. They tried to convert me to their ideology, but I was different. I did not share their vision, and to me they were incompetent assholes. They reinforced for me all my attitudes of distrust for authority. They reinforced for me my negative perspective."

"Aren't you being unfair in your analysis? Your father did help you."

"Only after I begged for his help and he made me ride that bus for five hours in absolute pain."

"What else could he do? You should be thankful that you survived and not harbor hostility. You are never able to let go of the negative events—you hang onto them because they prove how the world has it in for you."

"Well, don't they?"

"No, they don't! The world is indifferent to your plight. It is up to you to find the good and the positive in all situations, especially this dental experience. You could take the Floridian approach of sun and fun. Look at the upshot: You got out of both football and the laundry drudgery. You were free to do as you wanted."

"Yeah! And I did get into Yale."

"See, there is a positive in the negative."

bipolar bare

"Going to Yale was no picnic and suicide was my game. There were bogeymen there, too."

Carlotta smiles. "You brought the bogeymen with you, Carlton."

CHAPTER 7

ASPIRIN IS MY POISON

WHAT IS IT LIKE TO ATTEMPT SUICIDE? How do you feel? What are your thoughts?

Such are my questions as I sit in my tiny garret dorm room at Saybrook College, one of the twelve residential colleges that comprise Yale College, with a bottle of aspirin at one elbow and a pint of Cutty Sark Scotch whiskey at the other. It is April 1, 1965, and I am in my junior year as I conduct a running dialogue with myself as to why I should or should not ingest both bottles in their entirety.

To say I was miserable only scratches the surface of the dread and hatred I had for my existence. I was flunking all my courses. I did not want to study because studying would make no difference. I was not smart enough to keep up with the pace of my brilliant peers. I was isolated because I was difficult to get along with. I was alternately angry or depressed.

I felt as if I were cornered, like some poor animal hunted down for no other reason than mankind saw me as a nuisance. The pit of my stomach ached, my skin crawled with invisible ants, and my head was crushed with the weight of unbearable failures. There was no relief. My thoughts were all negative. Nothing was right. My circumstances could not be changed. Only the release of death could free me from my prison of self.

I debated the pro and cons of killing myself. The reasons to die were easy to see; the reasons to live were murky and muddled. I worried how the ignominy of my suicide would adversely affect my estranged parents, my school, and my friends—if I really had any, that is. When I tried to think joyous thoughts, they fell flat. Spring was beautiful, but rain would soon come. Should I shuffle off this mortal coil, I would miss out on summer vacation. Should I choose life, I'd have to go back to Columbus, Ohio and get some crummy job to pay for two minutes at this high-priced joint. The future did hold some interest for me: I had my art, but everyone told me I could never make a living at it.

On my second day at the hospital, very late at night, Smitty has gone to sleep long ago and I am alone reading through my oldest journals at the scant entries before my suicide attempt at Yale, remembering with horror what its like to try to kill yourself, when I look up and there she is.

"See Carlton, I am always with you," says Carlotta with a stern look on her face, posing in her sexy nurse's uniform and sitting in the chair next to my desk in the hospital. "I tried to get you to think positive thoughts, but you didn't listen to me when you tried to get the two of us killed,"

"Oh, Carlotta, we were young then, and I didn't recognize your voice. I thought I was merely carrying on a conversation in my head with myself."

"But you are, dear boy. I am just your other mind, the foil to your negative thoughts. When you say you can't, I say you can. When you tell me life isn't worth living, I tell you it is. Tell me your lies, and I will tell you the truth."

"I want to be no more."

"Death will happen soon enough. Why can't we enjoy the time you are given?" says Carlotta, starting to file her fingernails.

"I could not, at Yale."

"You are good at telling tales. Tell me what happened next, after the debacle of Mount Hermon. I will shut up and listen." Carlotta blows on her vibrant red nails, looks up, and smiles broadly. "Be of good cheer, you still have a lot of life to live."

Smitty, still in the throes of his nightmares in the steaming jungles of 'Nam, gives vent to an anguished cry and shifts in his cloth tortilla. I slammed shut my journal and tossed it on the pile of composition books stacked ten high in two piles.

"I've got nothing I can read you here, but I don't need to. I know it so well I shall just spill my guts."

"A Davis boy is expected to go a good school, and that school is Yale. Going to Mount Hermon increased my chances of getting into Yale. Little did my family know or care how much I hated myself or the roots I had come from. By this time in my life, I had at least gotten my father and stepmother to stop calling me Chinky. I was Carl now, and I was on my way to Yale.

"I wanted to go to another university, but I did not get a scholarship, and I could not afford full tuition. I was headed for either my third choice school or the Marines, and I was favoring the latter. I was on the waiting list for Yale and got accepted. I think this was because of all the Yalies in my family history. Grandmother and grandfather were delighted. Yale was grandfather's university and my great-grandfather's too. My father went there before his downfall of marrying my mother. He never graduated. If I went there, I would be upholding the family tradition.

"My grandparents loosened their purse strings to help me matriculate. How could I resist? I decided to go, even though I did not want to go. I did not feel I belonged in this hallowed Ivy League university, having neither the brains nor the confidence to make it.

"I went and immediately felt overwhelmed. I could not keep up with all the brainiacs that breezed through the philosophy and calculus courses that I could barely understand. I couldn't keep up with all the brilliant young men who learned French with ease or who already spoke it. I failed French and had to go summer school, while my classmates went to Europe. I agonized over English papers, staying up all night without being able to write a word, paralyzed with fear.

"I drank a lot at Yale. Perpetually drunk and disorderly, I acted crazy and impressed my friends. At a party once, I dived out a third story window into a snow bank. The snow was piled up two stories high, so my dive was only ten feet or less, but it astonished my friends. In a fit of rage over a failed mid-term report, I slashed an emergency door with a fire ax. Daredevil Carl could always be counted on to do something amazing and daring that no one else would do. I had no fear of physical things. I only dreaded exposure of my intellectual defects. Drinking was good cover. Drinking lets you forget you are failing your courses. Getting drunk allows you relief from the worthless feelings you have about yourself."

"And you say you're not an alcoholic," Carlotta tsk-tsks.

"*Shhh!* I am not an alcoholic."

"The proof was in your actions," says Carlotta, bending down and fixing me in a chastening stare.

bipolar bare

Undaunted, I continue: "In the middle of my junior year, I sat on the couch in the suite I shared with Chuck and Ernie. Drunk and playing with Chuck's sharpened jackknife, trying to open it so I could slice an orange to squeeze it into a cup full of vodka, I managed to open the knife and cut the orange. Chuck and Ernie, also drunk, asked me to be careful since the knife was razor sharp. I told them to fuck off. I got distracted and proceeded to close the knife over the first joint of the index finger on my left hand. The knife snapped shut, amputating the top of my finger.

"'Jesus I just cut off the top of my finger!' I said bemusedly to my two roommates, holding the tip of my finger in the palm of my right hand and looking curiously at the severed digit. 'Quick, call an ambulance!'

"Ernie staggers to the phone lying on a chair covered over by several history texts and calmly dials the campus police. 'We got an emergency here,' he says nonchalantly, 'our stupid ass roommate just amputated his finger.'

"Chuck stumbles across the floor of our living room. 'Let me see the damage,' he says, peering drunkenly into my outstretched right palm cradling the severed fingertip with a segment of skin still attaching it to my left hand. 'Jesus, it looks like a cut through a mini piece of ham with the bone in the middle. Does it hurt?'

"'Of course it hurts, you macabre son of a bitch!' I rail at him. 'Looks like a piece of ham! What's with you? Is this like asking us to come see the big turd you crapped in the john? You asshole!'

"'Take it easy, man, take it easy,' says Chuck, wobbling like a stack of cards in a stiff breeze. 'I meant no offense.'

"The campus cops came and helped me off the couch. I kept the fingertip cradled in the right palm. Two cops kept me from falling down the narrow stone steps of the staircase that led up two our second floor suite and rushed me to the emergency room of Yale New Haven Hospital. I was too drunk to feel much pain. I stared dumbly at my hand and severed finger. At the hospital, they sewed the finger back on my left hand and told me I was lucky that I cut so smoothly through the joint. I was back at the university the next day with a big bandage around my index finger. I laughed about the incident, but my roommates seemed wary of me afterwards.

"They want me to move out. They say I am disruptive and weird: always angry, slamming doors, and yelling about this 'goddamn university.' We argue. I say, 'What about you guys? You drink every weekend. Chuck, you're the guy who spends most of his time in the john studying the size of his shit and reading pornography. Ernie, you're the guy who goes around wearing a Bullwinkle the moose plastic head on the top of his penis.'

"'Yeah,' Ernie says, 'but we're not depressed, moody, or wild, staying up all night like you all the time. We don't explode into anger at the slightest little thing, destroy stuff, and do things that nobody can fathom, like cutting your own frickin' finger off.'

"So, we didn't talk for a couple of weeks. My attention in class gets even worse. I spend even more time over at the fraternity house drinking and playing pool by myself. The tension became impossible to bear. When the master's office calls me in and tells me a single room has become available, I move there.

"The room is in the north entryway to Saybrook College. It is a garret on the fourth floor at the very top of the coiling stone stairway. I am up on this level all by myself in a tiny little room. I am isolated and completely cut off from the rest of my classmates. The place mirrors how I feel about myself. My whole situation seems hopeless. It is up in this garret that I decide that I did not want to live anymore. I have to find a way to do it.

"Suicide is difficult unless you have a gun. I visualize myself sitting at my desk in the garret with the gun in front of me. I am calm and deliberate. I try to convince myself that this is what I must do. I am failing my courses. I have no friends. I hate being at Yale. I get drunk to forget everything and gather up the courage to end this miserable life. I am sure that blowing my brains would be easy if I could hold the weapon steady. I would pick up an imaginary gun slowly and bring it to my temple and pull the trigger. One bullet and the pain, disappointment, and failure would over.

"I practice without a gun, just cocking my finger at my head and snapping off the shot, but I am not steady. My left hand shakes uncontrollably, as it always does when I become agitated. My right hand is no better. I will surely miss my head and probably shoot out a window. The campus police would come and I would be in big trouble. No, the gun was a good theory, but I didn't have one,

bipolar bare

didn't know where I could get one, and was sure I couldn't be steady and focused enough to do the deed. I had to find another way. The end to the self-hatred is one decision away.

"When you tell me this tale, do you realize how much it sounds like the person you are today?" asks Carlotta.

"I am aware. Isn't it sad that in all this time I haven't changed?"

"Yes, it's sad, but now you have an opportunity to change."

"So you say. I don't know if I believe it. Let me continue with my story. I bought a big bottle of aspirin one afternoon, thinking if I ingested all the tablets, death would be assured. They sat on the desk in front of me along with my bottle of liquor. I had a long debate with myself—not so much a debate, as a challenge to myself. 'Can you do it?' I asked myself. 'Sure I can,' was my answer, 'all I have to do is swallow.' I took another swig out of the pint bottle of Cutty Sark. I sat for hours telling myself I could do the deed and recounting the reasons why. Yet, I was unable to make the move."

"I tried to stop you Carlton," says Carlotta, "I told you that there was much to live for beyond the gates of this institution. You needed to think beyond Yale, but you would not listen. You were focused on the small world around you and mustering your strength to do this mad deed."

"Yes, that's true. I wondered: Did I have the courage to go ahead and kill myself? After all, there was no future for me. I was a failure here at Yale. I was sure I would be a failure at life. I hated who I was. I hated being Carlton Morris Davis, Jr."

"You always put yourself down. Did you ever think you had made it two and a half years at a tough Ivy League institution? You made it longer than your father. That is a big accomplishment."

I smile wryly at Carlotta's observation. "My father loved the place," I say, continuing my soliloquy, "although he never graduated, because he met my mother and was booted out. You couldn't be married in 1941 and still attend. I feared and hated the fact I might run into my own mother on the streets of New Haven—she came from here. What would I do if she appeared? There was part of me that wanted her to appear. But what would I say? She obviously didn't love me. She had abandoned me long ago. My own family wouldn't even tell me about who she was or what her name was. To my own family, I was just a vehicle to carry on the family name. They didn't really care about me. I was abandoned as a child, and now I was a forgotten cipher, sequestered from campus life in this forlorn loft.

"There is no reason for me to continue on. I might as well commit suicide. For hours on an early spring evening, I struggle with these thoughts and emotions, trying to work up the courage to open the bottle of aspirin and consume all 150 tablets. Past midnight, I finish drinking the small bottle of Scotch. I am drunk enough to do the deed. With a large glass of water, I gulp down full handful after handful of aspirin until the bottle was consumed. I go to lie back on my bed to await death, but instead I start to have this horrible ringing in my ears and pounding vibration in my chest. It grows louder and more insistent by the minute. I stand up and become very nauseated. I try to move, but I am paralyzed. I become very scared. This is not the death I envisioned—lying down and peacefully passing on. This is physical torture.

"I call my friend John, one of the few students I still felt I could call a friend. I tell him what I have done. He says he will call the campus police and hangs up. He arrives at my door with them a few minutes later. I am very dizzy and disoriented. The sound in my ears is deafening as I am rushed to the hospital.

"This time, they pump my stomach. Not a pleasant experience, with tubes being rammed down your throat like a Roto-Rooter to pump out your guts. I am completely woozy, gagging, and fearful. The master of the college comes, says some stupid words over my bed, and pats my knee. He is tipsy and smells of liquor. I don't pay attention to him. They wheel me into a room with another patient from the emergency room for the night. A green curtain surrounds my bed. I lie there all night with my ears ringing loudly and listen to the man next to me cough and rattle within his green cocoon. From the horrifying sounds he emits, I can tell he is dying. I decide I don't want to die and spend the night begging to live and for the ringing to pass away.

"Late in the night, the man next to me dies, exhaling his last drawn-out gasp. I peep through my green curtain when the nurses come and pull open the curtains around his bed. They place a tag on his toe and wheel him away. I fear it will be my fate to gasp and rattle to my death. I pray to God for succor, but I am alone with my nausea and labored breathing. This is not the easy death I planned. This is a horrible experience. I try to distract myself by tossing and turning in the bed. I can't do this for long. The nausea becomes too great, but I can't throw up. Toward morning the nausea subsides, but the ringing in my ears has never gone away. It's not as loud as it was, but I still hear it to this day.

"Once the critical danger has passed from the aspirin overdose, the doctors put me in the mental ward of the hospital. Tompkins One, they call it. I am wheeled through several sets of doors to one where the attendant has to use keys to enter. I am in the locked psychiatric ward. Beyond the entry double doors is a long linoleum-covered corridor that reflects the bright light of the fluorescent fixtures high above. The lights stretch past many doorways to another set of doors at the far end. The corridor is wide beyond the locked double doors. Several patients are wandering up and down the corridor like one-dimensional cutouts in a long tube.

"Just inside the doors to the right are the common rooms for eating, visiting, and group therapy. Next is the nurse's station where the medications are handed out three times a day. The male patients' rooms follow. Two patients share a room with a toilet space between two rooms. Beside each bed is a heavy wooden dresser bolted to the floor. One can store his clothes in the dresser, but nothing else. Shaving items are carefully monitored and kept at the nurse's station. A patient might try to commit suicide with his razor.

"Inside the entryway on the left, two doors lead to the treatment suites, where the ice bath and the electro-shock room are housed. Once, I saw the ice bath's room door open and there was an enormous tub filled to its edge with ice cubes. An attendant caught me staring and swiftly closed the door. I never saw the electro-shock room, but I imagine it to be like the electric chair on death row.

"Beyond the treatment rooms are more patient rooms. These are for women. One day soon after I arrived, I saw a middle-aged woman kicking and yelling as she was being dragged from her room down the corridor into the ice baths. The door was slammed shut behind her. Days later when I saw her again, she looked distant and worn out.

"Attendants guard us. They are big African-Americans with tattoos on their bodybuilder arms. They patrol the corridor to make sure no man gets rowdy or fraternizes too closely with a woman, or that no woman becomes hysterical or tries to seduce a man. If you get out of control, the two attendants are sent after you. This means a trip to the treatment suites, which all patients fear. All activity stops. Silently, we would watch as a patient, screaming and thrashing, is brought down the hall to the treatment suite and hauled inside. After a time, the patient reappears in a docile condition. One wants to avoid that fate at all costs. I am careful, and I never am sent to them.

"I was finished with Yale for the rest of the semester and for the next year. I had 'gone mental,' just like John, my roommate from sophomore year, who went crazy in Paris while traveling with his parents. He went running naked around the Eiffel Tower, I was told. Yalies go nuts a lot more than is reported. John ended up in the expensive treatment center nearby. I was in the public ward, but the place wasn't too bad, except for the ice bath and the electro-shock room.

"I have only one visitor during my stay, my father. He comes to one therapy session with me. The patients sit in a circle of chairs next to their family members. There is a lot of anger between the patients and their families. Most patients blame their situation on their mother or father. I aggressively ask my father why he won't tell me anything about my mother. He stands up, looks around the circle, and lets out an exasperated sigh. 'I don't have to answer to this stuff,' he says and walks out. He never comes back.

"I have a room I share with one other Yale student. We never talk. He is sullen and silent, while I am usually angry and sarcastic. I like spending my time in the enclosed porch at the far end of the wide hall of the psychiatric unit, where several patients hang out. Our ward is on the second floor and the porch sits over the hospital's loading dock. We watch the comings and goings of the service trucks from heavy metal lawn chairs lined up against a wall next to the double doors. Access to the porch is limited to evenings or times when we aren't in therapy. The patients sit behind and below a giant metal screen that rises off a concrete parapet wall about six feet from the porch's entry. The black screen rises up ten feet and then curves back to meet the wall of the building. We are completely caged in to prevent our escape into the outside world.

bipolar bare

"What strikes me as strange is that people declared nuts by our society and locked up for the mutual safety of themselves and society are the most interesting people I have ever met. I recall sitting on the porch in early May with Henri, a professor of French at Yale. Henri is a pudgy, worldly little man, full of amusing tales about what lies beyond the giant screen that separates 'us' from 'them.' He seems perfectly happy to sit in his chair and smoke his cigarettes and let the world pass him by. He does not seem angry or sad, but rather jovial and happy. I cannot figure why he is a resident of this particular funny farm with the rest of us misfits, nor would he speak of it. I don't have the heart to ask why he was in the psychiatric unit. He is so calm, I wonder if he was taken for a session of the ice baths or the electro-shock. Or maybe it is the drugs they hand out daily at the nurse's station. Was it Thorazine? I don't remember.

"We look out at the three-story brick wall across the street and the elm trees in new bloom. If we crane our necks we can see a couple of the aging two-story frame houses of east New Haven beyond the brick wall to our right. Out in the street, cop cars race by with their sirens wailing. Once, after a patrol car whizzes past, Henri mentions with disdain the Ashcan School of artists, who painted the rougher side of American life.

'Not much beauty in their images and our reality,' he sniffs. Henri prefers the work of romantic European artists like Cezanne, Picasso, and Manet.

"He talks of great literature, usually French. Henri is erudite and funny, with an accent like Pépe Le Pew, the amorous skunk from the Warner Brothers cartoons. 'Their words are beautiful,' he says, waving his cigarette at the black metal mesh in front of us. 'Not altogether unlike the delightful smells of spring and coming summer here before us,' He waxes rhapsodic over Voltaire, Balzac, Camus, and Baudelaire. 'Baudelaire's dark words are glorious,' he opines. 'He could make art out of our incarceration.' Henri chortles at his own joke. Most of the writers I did not know, except Baudelaire, whose *Fleurs du Mal* I studied and loved in my ill-fated French classes. 'You simply must go to France to learn the language,' Henri advises me.

"He talks on and on of beauty, creativity, and travel. 'You must see the beautiful villages of France,' he says. 'Go to see Arles, Avignon, the Dordogne, the countryside, and drink the wine.' Henri's talk fills me with wanderlust. I desperately want to get out of this prison and go to France.

"I have my sessions with the psychiatrist, who sits with me in a small office next to the nurse's station. He is in his leather chair and I am on a couch across from him. I find it curious I don't get to lie down. He wants me to sit up. He asks questions about my family. He asks about my mother.

"'What is her name?' he asks.

"'I don't know,' I reply.

"'Where does she live?'

"'I don't know.'

"'How do I feel about that?'

"'I don't know,' I say and I stare at the shrink with unalloyed anger.

"There is total silence between us. I hear yelling in the hallway and know someone is being dragged to the ice baths. He sits there smugly in control, twisting his pencil in his fingers.

"'Does the yelling bother you?' he asks.

"'I don't know,' I respond, unwilling to engage this quack in conversation.

"'I think that's all for today,' he says and stands up. I also rise and leave the office. There is no one in the hall.

"This psychiatrist disappears one day. I am given a new shrink. He flips through a manila folder.

"'You're not very communicative are you?' he asks.

"'Do I have to be?' I respond, 'And if I don't, do I get the ice baths?'

"'Depends on your behavior,' he replies. I am silent. I ask where my old doctor has gone and get a weird answer.

"'He left the hospital for medical reasons,' the new psychiatrist replies. The next day in the *Yale Daily News*, there is a story about my old psychiatrist, who was arrested after the police found in his apartment hundreds of stolen typewriters from various university departments. He apparently had a fetish for the machines and stole them at every opportunity. The article states that the university is not pressing criminal charges against the doctor but has placed him in a psychiatric institution for care and treatment.

"This article convinced me that sanity is a game you played. The keepers were no saner than I. Therefore, I would play the game to get out of the nut ward of Yale New Haven Hospital. All I had to do was agree to do all that they said they wanted me to do. I would answer all their questions in the nicest way I could, no matter what I felt like, no matter what I thought. I did my therapy. I went to my groups. It is all a hoax: You just play along, and if they like your acting they set you free. Lo and behold, they set me free!

"A year later, I go back to Yale and graduate. My old roommate John isn't so lucky. They let him out of the fancy psychiatric unit. He goes to New York, throws himself in front of a subway train, and dies a horrible death. I am a pallbearer at his funeral. His parents, wonderful but grief-stricken people, give me funds that rightly should have been John's to go to study in Europe. With this money, I study architecture in London and travel in France, having the most wonderful and free year of my life. I participate in anti-war demonstrations and even throw rocks at the American Embassy, never hitting it. The bobbies keep us too far away. With my history, I know I could never be president, but then, I never wanted to be. I want the creative life. The kind of life Van Gogh had. I sort of got it."

carlton davis

Self-portrait: 1973; 15¾ x 18 inches; conte crayon

"You let many years pass without seeking help," Carlotta interjects.

"There was the Adlerian psychiatrist I saw in Chicago. He did me no good."

"You never gave the man a chance. A few sessions and you bolted."

"You can't trust a psychiatrist. Playing sane is better."

"You didn't play it very well, and you still drank."

"Not fair! I didn't drink very much, but I never took aspirin again. It only increases the ringing in my ears."

"You weren't happy. You picked up a wife and drifted across the continent from Chicago to Wyoming and finally to California."

"I found I didn't like being an architect."

"Maybe architecture didn't like you, who were so reluctant to be a designer. You acted like design, the best aspect of the architecture business, was pure poison."

"I could not make it work for me, not in San Francisco and not even at UCLA, where I taught for two years. Architecture was pure poison to me."

"What about your wife and daughter? They were God's gift and you abandoned them in San Francisco."

"I did not! They refused to go to Los Angeles with me."

"Your ambition meant more to you than your marriage vows."

"That's not true! I wanted them to come, but they wouldn't."

"Why should she? You were depressed most of the time or angry at your circumstances. And the sweet deal of teaching did nothing to change your outlook."

"Teaching was pure poison! Do you know what academics are like? They stab each other in the back at every opportunity. I had to drop out and pursue a life as an artist."

"Your artist's life only increased your periods of depression and mania. Living like an artist was personal poison."

"Don't say that! I loved my life in the loft."

"You thought of suicide a lot. You were still obsessed with your mother. You were still moody and difficult, a person given to periods of despair followed by times of extreme energy and good behavior. You became a drug addict and a closet gay."

"I blame my childhood traumas for the mess my life became. Childhood was the poison."

"That was only a dream. I don't believe you, Carlton. You always said your brain was wired differently from the average person's."

"That's what made me an artist! All the great artists have thought about suicide or committed suicide."

"You are so wrong," says Carlotta, standing up and walking away as her short nurse's skirt swings right and left and her six-inch heels clatter on the floor. She disappears into the bathroom and closes the door.

"Some nurse," I mumble. "More like a slut! Reminds me of my mother."

"I heard that," Carlotta responds.

CHAPTER 8

DON'T OPEN PANDORA'S BOX

UP THE WHOLE NIGHT IN MY HOSPITAL ROOM, I am reading from my journals and thinking about my mother. The sun has not yet risen. Smitty is still asleep in his bed. I come across the confrontations with my father over the name of my mother. This was the beginning of my obsession to find her.

Carlotta opens the bathroom door. "You always emphasize the damage done to you," she says, stepping toward me.

She is wearing her sexy nurse's uniform. The short white skirt exposes most of her long white stockings, which end in her high white heels. Two buttons of her white blouse are open to expose her ample cleavage. A Red Cross nursing pin adorns her left breast. Auburn hair falls to her shoulders, framing her face. She has no nurse's cap.

"What about the damage you did to others?" she asks.

"Where's your nurse's cap?"

"I decided it looked too medical and detracted from my stunning looks. Do I remind you of your mother?"

"I wouldn't know."

"Oh, yes, you do. As the man who opened Pandora's box, you know what demon flew out and what it looked like. It looked like your mother."

"You don't look like her."

"We shall see." Carlotta hops up on the far edge of my desk next to the window and crosses her legs. "I see you ogling my legs. Will I be too distracting to you?"

"No, you won't."

"Very good. Then tell me your latest story."

"'Don't open Pandora's box!' my father says to me.

carlton davis

In the summer of 1971, I returned from my year in Europe. My father and I are standing in the foyer of his home in Columbus, Ohio, on either side of the grandfather clock, the heirloom Nonnie allowed my father to take from her house in Rochester. The tall wood clock with the long pendulum behind a glass panel stood in the entryway beyond grandmother's front door, along with a bronze dog and a large blue ceramic vase. This clock was one of the antiques Nonnie always feared I would break with my roughhousing.

"'Tell me about my mother,' I demand of him again, my voice growing more insistent, like the tick-tock, tick-tock of the clock between us. 'What is her name? Where does she live? How long were you married? Why did you divorce? And why is my sister my aunt?'

"My father is silent, but his face tightens as I ply him with questions. The clock chimes the hour.

"'Why won't you answer?' My voice becomes almost a yell.

"'Don't open Pandora's box,' my father says again. A look of anger and embarrassment spreads across his face. He turns and walks away from me into the living room.

"'Bastard,' I say to his back.

"'Don't you dare call me that name again!' he warns, stopping and turning to point a finger at me. 'You don't need to know this information. It will only cause more trouble if I tell you.'

"An hour or two later, I sat in the living room in my father's house, surrounded by the blare of television, the yelling of my father and stepmother in the kitchen, and the occasional bong from the heirloom grandfather clock. I fantasize kicking out its glass front.

"England was an escape from my family and the ties to them that I both detested and needed at the same time. They provided an identity even if I rejected that identity as elitist and shallow. All this I left behind a year ago. I left behind the history of the Davis family: a history I felt should be irrelevant to who I am, yet a history that perversely fascinated me. While in Europe, I had no desire to know more. I had no feeling it had any effect on me. Now that I was back, it was with me once again. I should have avoided the situation. Yet, I walked back into it, almost as if I really wanted the trouble it meant.

"My mother, the real one, was the secret force in my life. She seemed a ghost who could come out at any moment and cause ruin. I came home from Europe to learn from my stepmother she attempted to make contact with my sister and me twice in the past year, once through her daughter at Ashland University, once personally. My father plays down the story. He will tell me nothing when I ask him for details. I turn to Lois, my stepmother, for more details and she begins to cry.

"'Don't you tell him anything,' my father yells.

"'I will if I want to,' Lois screams back him. Lois heads for the kitchen to refill her glass of vodka and signals me to follow. A little tipsy, she exposes her worry that if I see my real mother, somehow she will expose her as a lousy mother. My natural mother, well preserved and happy, will show Lois to be a haggard, unhappy, mentally unbalanced alcoholic. She will show Lois to be an inferior mother.

"'What are you talking about?' I ask. 'You are a fine mother. Is there something here you are not telling me?'

"Lois becomes hysterical. I try to calm her down.

"'I can't tell you,' she demurs. 'It will only cause another fight and your father will accuse me that speaking out of turn because I am a drunk.'

"'You owe me the truth. Please tell me,' I beg.

Steadfastly refusing to talk at first, Lois finally relents.

"'Your mother wrote you a letter,' she sobs. 'I don't think it's right, what your father is doing, keeping the letter from you.'

"The machinations of the Davis family make me feel powerless, enraged, and obsessed. I wonder for how long my mother's inquiries have been kept from me. Nothing is being said. What is my grandmother's role? Why are my sister and I split up? Why was I made a ward of the court? Why did my mother never come to see me? *Why? Why? Why?* This story of my father and his first wife—my mother—has a mysterious quality, which torments my mind. I need to know the story. I go to my father and demand the letter from him.

"'Give me the letter my mother sent to me,' I demand. 'You have no right to keep it from me.'

"'I destroyed it,' he replies coldly.

"'You son of a bitch! How many other letters from her have you destroyed?'

"'Don't you dare call me names again,' Dad says, his voice rising.

"'I'll call you that and a lot of other things,' I yell back. 'Tell me, Dad, how many letters have you destroyed?'

"'None!'

"'I don't believe you destroyed it.'

"'Don't believe me! I don't have to tell you anything!'

"'You are a lying bastard, a wimp, a coward!'

"'You don't know what you're getting into! You don't know what I am saving you from!' He is bellowing now, a raving madman. 'I'm warning you: Don't open Pandora's box!'

"'Pandora's freaking box again!' I fire back, rolling my eyes. 'This is the third time you have said this to me. Open the damn thing! What is so horrible in it that you can't release it? I am an adult. You owe it to me. You know the whole story! Why are you giving me nothing but denials? Pandora found in that box of miseries the voice of hope. Give me some hope, Dad.'

"I block my father's way to the living room. I am bigger than he is now. He tries to push me out of the way. I push him back. He makes a fist and raises his arm, but I am quicker and stronger. I take a swing at him, hitting him in the chest and knocking him to the floor. He is dumbfounded and silent for several minutes with me standing over him.

"'Get out of my house!' he yells.

"'You've got it, you sorry excuse for a father,' I reply and stalk to the door, banging it behind me. I go for a drive then come home to gather up my things. I depart for my sister's house in Chicago. I intend never to go back.

"Carolee and I talk about my mother when I go see her. She is confronted with the same non-answers from the family. Things didn't fit together for her, either. She did not have a church wedding, motivated by the fact that our real mother might show up. It appears certain things are not done because of the specter of 'that woman.' Grandmother is the real power behind the scene. For an old woman, she still seems to be controlling many people's lives: my father's, stepmother Lois', Carolee's, and mine.

"I have an image in my mind of my grandmother's house in 1944, days before my birth. I see my mother pregnant, beautiful, bitchy, thoroughly sexy—the tramp!—in bed being served by my grandmother, the matronly Victorian aristocrat. The hatred is immense. The battle for the baby to come and the daughter is titanic. The aristocratic woman knows she will win out. My mother will be abandoned into adultery and crime. Or, is it something completely different? I have barely scratched the surface. Dare I dig deeper?

"In 1972 I live in Chicago, start my career as an architect, and begin dating. I try to forget about the sad saga of my mother and my father. My contact with the family is minimal, except for my sister, whom I see and talk to regularly. She calls me one day.

"'I received something in the mail which I think you should see,' says Carolee.

"'What is it?'

"'It's a copy of a magazine article. It came by itself in an envelope with no return address. Very mysterious, but enlightening. I think I have our mother's name now. She is called Lynn Ferguson.'

"I rush out to Glenview from my apartment in Old Town Chicago to look at the clipping Carolee received. It is an article from a magazine called *WE*, folded up in a business envelope. The postmark is Rochester, New York. Neither Carolee nor I can determine who sent the clipping, but she let me have a copy, and I still have it. Here, I'll read the clipping copy to you:

WE Magazine. October 10, 1949

ROCHESTER SOCIALITE INTRODUCES WIFE TO FRIEND WHO BREAKS UP HOME AND BRINGS ABOUT DIVORCE

John Ferguson faces suit for separation and support of a child born out of wedlock. Ferguson and his wife, Lynn Ferguson, lived as man and wife in Texas, where common law marriages are legal. A court hearing is scheduled to determine if common law marriages are recognized in New York. Mrs. Ferguson's suit against her husband will be heard before Judge Warner. If the marriage is determined to be invalid, there exists the possibility of charges against Ferguson for transporting a minor over state lines for amoral purposes in violation of the Mann Act.

The suit relates to Mrs. Ferguson's undisputed legal marriage to a young Rochester socialite, Mr. Davis, who introduced Ferguson to his wife. The former Mrs. Davis then promptly fell in love with the young Mr. Ferguson. The socialite, Mr. Davis, learned of his wife's unfaithfulness and friend's betrayal. He had grounds for divorce in New York, where adultery is recognized as a sufficient cause. The husband named Ferguson as a correspondent. The wife mentioned Ferguson's name, but without admitting she was intimate with him.

Ferguson objected to his name being mentioned at the trial. He said he loved her and when her husband obtained a divorce he would marry her. Thus, he added there would be no necessity of his name being brought up. The girl agreed.

She too admitted her love for him and agreed to marriage as soon as the decree became final. Consequently, with that promise ringing in her ears, the divorce was granted by default in August of 1948. The decree became final last November, but before that time Ferguson had moved in and was living with her.

She became pregnant. Ferguson's mother objected to him marrying a divorced woman and sent him away. When the child was born, the divorcee placed the baby in an institution and went to join Ferguson. They moved to Texas. In the eyes of Texas, they are legally married. Legal opinion seems to say they are married, since each state recognizes the law of another.

Returning to Rochester several months ago, Ferguson's ardor cooled, and he no longer wanted to marry his mistress, but overlooked Texas law. He denies responsibility for a second child born out of wedlock, while previously he had admitted it. Embarrassed and shocked Mrs. Ferguson retained a lawyer to bring Supreme Court action for separation and child support.

Ferguson denies he ever intended to marry the woman and denies his responsibility for the children. Judge Van Duser on September 12 made a motion denying alimony and attorney's fees, since it was not the proper time for such action, reserving the right to the trial judge to take such action as he saw fit.

Friends of Mrs. Ferguson's first husband are hoping he is not dragged into the case to reopen old wounds. There are two children by that marriage now in the custody of the paternal grandmother. The young socialite takes the position that as far as he is concerned, he is not interested one way or the other. To drag him into this new mess would only stamp his former wife and former friend as much worse in public opinion than he believes they are.

There is the possibility that the suit for separation will be settled out of court, but the threat of prosecution under the Mann Act, commonly known as the white slave law, still hangs over Ferguson's head.

"I tried to locate a Mrs. John Roger Ferguson in the Rochester, New York area. I met with no success. I had no means to track down the letter with the article inside. My guess is that the letter came from the one child of Ferguson and my mother, but there were too many Fergusons in the upstate New York area for me to call them all.

"My own life was becoming hectic. I fell in love with the woman who became my first wife, so I did not give a great deal of additional effort to the search for Lynn. The moths of sorrow simply attacked me on a regular basis. I sought help, but nothing seemed to arrest the periods of depression. These dark moods seemed to start when I began to obsess about my mother and when I wished to find resolution to my mother's story. My wife often caught me talking to myself when I was in one of my black moods.

"You weren't talking to yourself," says Carlotta. "You were talking to me. Pandora's box got open a little bit and you were smothered by moths of grief."

"Carlotta, the periods of depression grew more frequent. My wife said there was something wrong with me."

"She and I counseled you to get help."

"I did, but it didn't help."

"You had a prejudice against psychiatry because of your experience in college."

"I thought moving far away from the Davis family would be better."

"Oh, pshaw!" Carlotta harrumphs. "As moth-eaten an idea as any I have ever heard."

I ignore her one-liner and continue.

"I moved to San Francisco to put as much distance between me and my family as I could. It didn't work to resolve my many moods. Here is what I wrote in my journal in San Francisco:

November 1979. "I am living in San Francisco, my marriage is falling apart, and I have a child, who is a year and a half old. Est, a self-improvement system involving group awareness and training sessions, is popular. My wife did it and suggested I do it too, as it might help our failing marriage, so I went. I had a peculiar experience.

"The events of my est weekends are very vivid. The information told to us by the trainers has become hazy, but the experience hasn't. The est trainers did say many of us would find it difficult to remember exactly what happened in our training. I have not become that forgetful, but some has faded from active memory. However, the processes we did on the weekends after our mid-day break are not events I shall ever easily forget.

"In the cavernous space of the Marin Civic Center, the crowd is enormous on this first weekend of the training. Rows of chairs are lined up beneath an open ceiling crossed by large ducts. After several preliminary trainings, the est leader, Jerry, tells us to rearrange ourselves randomly all around the room in our chairs. An est trainer has us close our eyes and, following his command, we are to imagine ourselves afraid of the person to our right, to our left, in front of us, and behind us. A woeful din of wails and cries permeates the hall as we imagine ourselves afraid of more and more people. The trainer works us up to be afraid of not only everyone in the civic center, but in San Francisco and the entire world, as well.

"Suddenly, my stomach is seized by powerful contractions that grow worse and worse until I throw up into my hand, losing the hamburger I ate for lunch. I raise my hand for a sick bag, and I am given one.

"A few snickers are heard amidst the wails.

"'Some of you get it now,' says the trainer. 'Imagine now the whole world is afraid of you. San Francisco is afraid of you.'

"Laughter begins to spread throughout the room. By the time the trainer has worked his way back to the person to our right or our left, the room is filled with loud laughter and the process was ended. The weekend is over and we file out. Embarrassed and holding a sick bag in one hand, I slink out, smelling of puke. For the next week, I felt really good and positive.

"What happened to me on the first est weekend? Did the process get me in touch with some un-experienced parts of my past? I think the retching was the surfacing of the reaction I should have had when I attempted suicide in 1965. I never threw up then. But I prevented myself by a sick wish for death. I wonder if I could have had such an experience alone or with one or two others. Was the mass of people such that I became touched by some accumulated energy given off by the group? Could I have experienced not a transcendent event, but a form of mob hysteria? Did mob hysteria get me in touch with the un-experienced truth of my suicide attempt? If this is true, what a frightening power a large group can elicit. Is this a pernicious form of brain washing?

"On the second weekend in the Marin Civic Center the trainer, Jerry, talks about enlightenment, but it is different from the Buddhist ideas. To him, it is about casting off the weight of old experience. We have to 'lighten up,' he says. According to him, each new experience is a trigger to some old un-experienced experience in the memory records. New experiences are not experienced because the old experience is un-experienced. We have to get off it. From our mind's viewpoint, we have to experience our experiences as they happen; we have to lighten up. As we lighten up, we can return to our memory records and experience the successive layers of un-experienced reality. In this way, we lighten up and move towards enlightenment.

"What a mishmash of the beautiful Buddhist philosophy, I think. Est has massacred it and turned it into popular psychology. I am about to get up and leave the room, but then I think, OK, I have paid for this—I might as well complete the training.

"After a break, we trainees undergo a process in which we are to work on experiencing an item with which we are unhappy. We start by going through all the parts of our body and try to imagine ourselves at a beach playing. Tape-recorded sounds of the surf play in the background. I find myself at Cozumel, playing on the beach and swimming nude with my wife. The process leader brings us away from the beach and encourages us to imagine ourselves in a situation where our unhappiness can occur. I try imagining myself in the situation at work where I lost my temper over the Stockton, California Theater project, which I was designing for BFVS Architects. While I am trying to recreate this situation in my mind, I hear all around me the beginning of crying and wailing. I feel ill at ease. I don't want to throw up again. I am not successful in conjuring up anger. I try talking more loudly, calling my boss a bastard and other epithets. My conversation with myself becomes bolder as the sound around me grows in volume in the high space of the Marin Civic Center.

"I find my anger toward my boss converting into anger at my father. I am getting very mad at him and calling him all kinds of names. A rush of emotion sweeps over me. My rage is intensifying and changing into tears. I am becoming a little boy. I see myself in the back of a car with my head buried in the gray upholstery, yelling at my father in the front seat as the car pulls away.

"'I won't go, I won't go, I won't go!' I yell with tears running down my face. I join the mob in crying out loud. The din is deafening. My face contorts in agony, as I am powerless to change my fate in this resurrected memory. Eyes squeeze closed, lips pull tight against my teeth, arms press to my chest as I struggle to bury myself into the back seat and disappear. I am once again a five-year-old in a blue cap and blue winter coat. The whistle in my breast pocket of my sailor suit presses into the flesh of my arm, hurting badly, but I pay no attention, because I am being taken away and I don't want to go.

"The experience only went this far. The process leader begins to pull us back. We go to the beach again and come out of the process. I did not know what this experience was or when exactly it was. All I know is it was it had to do with my father and when I was a very small child. It felt very real. I was very shaken. I was disturbed to find that I could end up crying and making a fool of myself like all the others in the training who were carrying on in such an intense, emotional way. Later, many shared the revelation that nothing happened to them during this process. This bothered me even more. I did notice that after this experience of yelling and whimpering 'I won't go,' I felt relaxed and my body was without pain. Mentally, I felt very stunned. I wondered how much heavy emotional baggage I carried around with me every day."

"Good job, Carlton," Carlotta says. "You carry around a lot in your personal Pandora's box. My job is to get you to peek inside and let a few of the moths of pain fly out. Letting go of the pain is good."

"You are inconsistent, Carlotta," I reply. "First you tell me the moths are dead because they were so long buried in the box. Now you tell they are still alive and ready to escape."

"Time for me to change, as it was for you to change," says Carlotta. She slips off the desk and walks quickly into the bathroom.

"Where are you going?"

"I will be right back," says Carlotta, closing the bathroom door. Several minutes pass. Carlotta opens the door and strolls toward me.

"What's that you are wearing?"

"I'm in my scarlet toga. It's a present to you. You advanced your understanding of the past, but still you draw the wrong conclusion. Yet I am satisfied with the story, so I come to you as your muse."

"Togas are supposed to be white."

"Not all!" says Carlotta peevishly. "Dante Gabriel Rossetti painted his Pandora in red and she has a red box. His muse demanded it. Here, let me give you Pandora's red box." It is about the size of a large cigar box and has a clasp but no lock on the side.

"You are getting me off the subject," I protest. "I live with too much emotional baggage. Est, no matter how much I was offended by their philosophy, made me see that. I became determined after the est training that I had to find my mother."

"See, you are becoming willing to open the box without fear. How come you have put it off so long?"

"I was busy."

"Ha! You are scared, just like your father. You don't know if there is something hideous being hidden from you or if it is a dead issue. Pandora's box is empty, Carlton. Go find out if that is true."

"I didn't know if it's is true, but est spurred me forward to finally open the box. Listen to the rest I wrote:

"The est experience ends. All I get are uncomfortable memories evoked from childhood. What kind of dime store revelation is that? No other breakthrough occurred. I am deflated and troubled. Their philosophy is disturbing. The est revelation is that there is nothing to get. We must experience our experiences. There is no end to problems. That really leaves me unsatisfied.

"On Monday, I get up to go to work and am standing at the bus stop. The light is very strange. There are sharp shadows, cool pastel colors, and the birds are flying around, making strange sounds. I wonder if this is the way it is every morning, but I am unconscious to it. I think est has changed my life. I ride into downtown San Francisco, thinking I am a changed man, until a fellow tells me that I am seeing the aftermath of a solar eclipse. So much for instant enlightenment!

"I feel up for two weeks. Life seems good and I enjoy my job designing a ski resort's mid-mountain restaurant. A deep depression strikes thereafter. I am beginning to have a cycle of monthly up and downs. My wife is baffled by my behavior. Within a year, the marriage fails. I move to Los Angeles seeking work I like better, but it's a fruitless quest. I quit architecture and move into a loft to try to become an artist.

"The thoughts that surface about my mother, my father, and what happened to me as a child go with me and become an obsession. Pandora's box remains locked shut. I begin a long period of excessive marijuana smoking, which increases the depth of my depressions and the height of my good feelings. I think of myself as an artist to whom the range of emotions is a sign of my creative life. I am one with the great artists of the past."

I look up from my journal at Carlotta, who arches her eyebrows dubiously at my vainglorious reference to my artistry.

"Carlotta, it's time you went away," I sigh. "Take your red toga and get back in your genie bottle, your box, or the bathroom … wherever it is you come from. I don't want the staff to think I'm really nuts. Talking to myself might get me one of those electroconvulsive treatments. Smitty, wake up! It's time to go to breakfast!"

Carlotta retreats toward the bathroom. At the doorway, she stops and turns.

"Each step you took to find your mother moved you further from mental health," she says.

"I don't believe you."

"It's true. You became destabilized more and more," she says, opening the bathroom door and quietly closing it behind her.

Rousted from his slumber, Smitty sits up in bed and rubs his eyes with his fists.

"Man, I had the strangest damn dream!" he says, yawning and stretching. "I was trapped in the bottom of an enormous ammo box with mortar shells and cluster bombs and some psycho-babbling white guy with his sexy nurse."

CHAPTER 9

PRODIGAL SON IN THE WESTERN PARADISE

I OPEN THE DOOR TO MY ROOM. It is late in the evening of the day before Easter. Smitty is still down on the patio, smoking with the other patients. Carlotta is standing in front of the desk, leafing through my journal. She is still dressed in her red toga. Pandora's red box lies on the desk next to my writing books, unopened. The box reminds me of the box I used to keep my baseball cards in as a boy. That was a cigar box I painted red; it held the best of my collection: Mickey Mantle, Whitey Ford, Minnie Minoso, Nellie Fox; the greats of the New York Yankees and Chicago White Sox.

"I thought you were going to leave me alone," I say.

"I can't," she sighs. "I have appeared to give you hope. That is all I have left in my box. Here, open up the box. All the sorrows have escaped. I want you to have hope. It is so sad that you have none. My heart weeps for you. I have just read what you wrote in your journal. Why do you think of suicide all the time? There is much in life that is delightful and bright, even in the depths of darkness. Can I recount for you what you wrote?"

"Forget opening up the box and forget reading my journals. Will it be just another episode in a whole string of episodes? They lead nowhere. And I know the box is empty." Carlotta picks up the red box undoes the clasp and opens the box. It's empty. She shakes it upside down.

"Hope just fell out. Didn't you see it? Let's look at your journals; they have proof of hope. The writing demonstrates the ebb and flow of your sickness. How you improve sometimes and how you fall back. In this one, you totter on the edge, but you still have hope. Let me read to you this time."

"If you must."

bipolar bare

Carlotta begins to read from my journal:

New Year's Eve 1980: "I drive down to Venice, California to walk on the beach. A few people are wandering along the sand this late at night. I see two couples seated by a lifeguard shack. Their black shapes are silhouetted against the dark sky. They are huddling close together and laughing. Over the pockmarked crusty surface, I stumble toward the boulder breakwater I climbed Saturday. The tide is in. Near high tide I guess. The breakwater is completely offshore, a gray-black line of rock two hundred feet away from the beach.

"The ocean slowly rolls up into waves and arches into the surf along the open coast. The surf folds into curved lines of white flares when it collides with the beach. The ocean is a vast expanse of blue-black darkness laid out to the horizon beyond the many flows of mottled gray at the shore.

"A black shadow suddenly explodes against the breakwater seam with a muted booming sound, throwing a ragged tear of white into the sky. Two small waves appear inside of the breakwater. One arches right; one arches left. As the circumference of the waves grows larger, the waves collide with one another. Two curves of surf intersect and dissipate into one another. I stand and watch the phenomenon repeat again and again. I look at where I am standing and realize that the breakwater creates with its two small waves a small point of land on the big sweep of the beach. I am standing on that point. I am in a special place of land's end.

"My mind is full of thoughts, impressions, and urges. I contemplate walking straight out from my point into the intersection of waves to the deep water, where I will drown. This is a fitting end to a life so small and miserable. Quite a history—I work my way across America from New Haven to New York to Chicago, where I marry; to Laramie where I have a child, to San Francisco, where it all falls apart, to Los Angeles, where I drown. This could be the end of it all. I make it to a place where there is no more land to run across. I make it to the end of the decade, December 31, 1979.

"The romantic in me feels that a new decade is beginning and I should renew myself. The cynic in me says that Tuesday, January 1, 1980, will be no different from any other Tuesday of any year. My sense of reality says the cynical part of my nature is right. The sun will come up and go down. Breakfast, lunch, and dinner will follow in an orderly progression. I won't accomplish much, but I will do something. The romantic in me wishes that my life would be different. I want to have a new sense of commitment to life and the dawning of a feeling of satisfaction, but why bother? Why not just walk out into the waves to the end?

"1979 was a very difficult year. My marriage disintegrated. My career faltered. I didn't find my mother. I contemplated self-destruction and suicide. I still had not surmounted any of the problems which had plagued me for the past year or the past decade. The patterns of depression, self-absorption, and self-destruction were woven tightly into the fabric of my life. Irritation, tension, and negativity still welled up. A loving and positive viewpoint eluded me. Forgiveness of others, forgiveness of my own faults and failures, was impossible to imagine.

"My thoughts drifted from suicide, to my journey that brought me here, to all journeys across America. I thought about the line from *The Great Gatsby* about 'a continent commensurate with the ability to wonder.' Gatsby stands on the Atlantic coast, looking to the continent in front of him, pondering all that immenseness and wonder. I am standing on the Pacific, looking west, with all that immenseness and wonder behind me. I am looking into nothing and have in life experienced nothing but disappointment. California is the end of dreams.

"The wanderers, the lost, the pioneers traveled across America from the dirty industrial east through the cold flat plains and hot dry deserts to the end of the American dream. For some, California is the fulfillment of that dream, but for many it is the ruination of the dream and of all dreams. The beauty of the place masks a horrible reality. All grows rapidly and luxuriantly here but shakes and decays into nothing. California confronts us with the nothingness of our aspirations and our lives. That sad truth can either drive us mad or be the beginning of the 'Western Paradise' beyond our egos, if we can wake up to the divine.

"I want a revelation. This would be a good spot for it: edge of land, end of the '70s, and a Los Angeles beach with the great electronic Sodom behind me. I am thirty-five years old, with a marriage collapsed, and confused sexuality. My career dissolved and my self-esteem at its lowest ebb. It is perfect—roll the camera. I look up in the sky, wishing that I might see God. The clouds are a cottony mat. In the middle, I see a form. It looks like a head of a grouper, a big ugly fish. God is a fish? I stare at it some more. The grouper becomes a grotesque, like the gargoyles of a Gothic church. This is God? This is what you get. The sky will not open. A flash of light will not appear. A sound of trumpets will not blast. There will be no spectacular vision tonight. On my point of land, I realized the pain would never go away. This is the human condition in the Western Paradise. Enjoy the beauty while you can."

"Put the notebook away, Carlotta," I say wearily. "I have heard enough,"

Carlotta closes the book and turns toward me. "I wish you weren't so sad," she says sympathetically. "It's hard to be your muse when you are so mired in negativity. But don't you see the hope that's still there? You didn't give it up then. You need not do it now."

"I got better after that day. I didn't swim into the ocean never to come back. I went home to my loft and felt better the next day."

"That was good. I shall leave you now. Perhaps I should become your nurse again. I think you still need help." Her deep red toga dragging behind her, Carlotta strides to the bathroom and closes the door. "Think positive, Carlton," she says before she disappears.

Easter Sunday is a beautiful day at Las Encinas. My wife comes to visit me. I am feeling depressed. We have lunch together and sit in the grass courtyard behind the administration wing of the hospital. She knits; I draw and tell her about my reading of my journals.

"I have only worked my way through sixteen of the notebooks, but I am finding plenty of evidence to support my contention that my childhood is what makes me crazy," I say to Ginger while I draw the back of the administration building in my new sketchbook.

"I am not surprised," Ginger responds. "It is what you have believed all along."

"No psychiatrist has verified my self-diagnosis, since I don't have one."

"You still don't have a doctor? How can that be? You have been in the hospital for several days. I would think they would have a doctor for you by now."

"They don't, but I don't want to get into that right now, OK?"

"All right, I won't go there. Can you share with me some of your findings?"

Ginger puts her knitting in her lap and leans over, putting her hand on my shoulder. "You know I have stuck by you through thick and thin. It hasn't been easy, but I love you, and I want the best for you."

"I know you do, Ginger. Sometimes I wonder how you have put up with me. I have done some really horrible things. Please forgive me."

"I forgive you. Can you forgive yourself?"

"That I don't know. That I am still working on."

"Perhaps you can talk to Reverend Sacquety about it when he comes here later this afternoon to visit you."

"Maybe. Let me read you something I came across."

I open my notebook for 1979 and begin reading:

"April 1, 1979. This weekend after a photographic outing, I felt more depressed than I can remember for many years. The low feeling was precipitated when my camera went on the fritz while visiting the magnificent ruins of the Sutro Baths, the once-opulent public bathhouses on the San Francisco seashore, now nothing but curious concrete shapes at the edge of the surf and algae-covered pools at the base of a steep rock embankment. The failure of the camera's light meter was a small frustration, but added to all the other current vexations in my life, it triggered a massive depressive meltdown. At home, I lay in bed wishing never to get up again. My mind roams over thoughts of suicide and self-destruction. I could jump from the Bay Bridge, shoot up with heroin, stab myself, or be physically humiliated by some sadomasochistic gays. These are my images in my mind as I lie on the bed, feeling numbness spread over my body. I have felt like this before.

"It's this numbness that I am remarking upon. In what follows from the same journal I recall how I felt in 1965 before my first suicide attempt when I became immobilized. I wonder if this is some kind of biochemical malfunction?" Ginger shrugged and I return to the journal and read.

"In 1965, isolated in my room in Saybrook College, I lay in bed and felt the numbness come over me. I thought I was becoming paralyzed. This happened the day before I took the 150 aspirin tablets. At first I liked the feeling, but then I became frightened I would never move again After several hours, I managed to shake the feeling off. I felt the paralysis coming over me again after my failed photographic sortie. I have no real will to fight the feeling. In a sense, I long for the paralysis. Perhaps it will mean an end to my frustration. I thought about never getting out of bed again. I lie in bed on my back, arms at my side, feeling no desire to move and no ability to move. I concentrated and I was able to move. I knew I must do something to break this spell or I would descend deeper into this depression, which might lead to suicide. I forced myself to rise and dress and go for a jog. I ran for an hour. The fierceness of my ennui was broken. I felt somewhat better."

"What do you think of that?" I ask Ginger, turning to look at her.

"I am struck by the paralysis you speak of," she replies. "Does that happen to you often? I have never seen you in its grip."

"I often feel paralyzed when I fall into the deepest depressive state," I explain. "It is as if the body becomes locked in an inert position. The arms and the legs can't move. I can't raise my head. All the muscles are tense. The jaw is clenched. It takes a monumental mental effort to break the spell and move. At times, I have felt like I was falling into an abyss. It's a very enticing feeling—frightening, certainly, but at the same time, you want to fall into the abyss to see what would happen. Once it did happen—or, rather, I thought it did—and I felt like I was in the company of another being. I have told you before that sometimes I feel like two people. I wonder if this is some kind of epileptic fit or minor schizophrenic break. I shall have to ask the doctor about this condition."

"Is there more you want to share with me?" Ginger asks.

"Yes, there is. I wrote about my marriage and the dissolution of it. How exactly this fits into my symptoms, I am not sure. Perhaps it has to do with sexual adventures or boredom with things as they are. Maybe after you hear what I have written you can give me some insight."

"OK, I am willing to give it a shot."

"Let me say once again that I am not terribly proud of what I am going to reveal in this bit of writing. It speaks to the aftermath of the affair I had with Bonnie Wilson."

"Maybe this is what you need to forgive yourself for," Ginger says, touching my arm with her fingertips. I feel like crying. Letting out a deep breath I begin to read:

"July 20, 1979. Last night, I believe, is the end of my marriage to Christine. How quickly and unexpectedly it comes about! I come home after grocery shopping to find Christine enraged. She opens the telephone bill and finds a call to San Rafael listed on our charges. She surmises it is a call to Bonnie Wilson. Christine charges me, grabbing my throat as if to strangle me. She drops her hands and grabs my wrists, calling me all manner of names. I tell her to take her hands off me.

"Christine keeps up a steady stream of abuse at me while she searches for Bonnie Wilson's telephone number in the directory. She tells me to grow up. She tells me I am selfish and screwed up. She mocks my artwork and my pretensions.

"'Go to Bonnie,' she sneers. 'She understands you, your ideas, and your art. I am too middle-class to understand. Go to her, don't you understand? You don't want me. You want her. Here, you wimp, I'll call for you.'

"Christine tries to call. There is no answer.

"'How do you think it makes me feel, knowing you are lying to me? How do you think it makes me feel to find a wadded-up note you wrote on the floor, going into gory detail about how Bonnie had sucked you off in the car?'"

I explain to Ginger that this was a note I had transposed from my green booklet to my notebook. I had carelessly tossed the wadded-up paper at the trash basket, missing my target. The cats played with the incriminating document, knocking it around the house until Christine found it. Foolish me! I continue to read:

"'You told me the affair was over a month ago, but now I find this phone call,' Christine carps. 'What about all the other times? You said it was over. But Wednesday, you went over to Marin, and we all know a trip to Marin is a trip to see Bonnie.'

"'No, I did not see Bonnie yesterday," I reply.

The truth was, I confide to Ginger, while I hadn't seen Bonnie that Wednesday, I had wanted to. I tried to arrange a rendezvous, but she could not take the day off. I was relieved, actually, because I didn't have to worry about the guilt of meeting with her. I could continue to try and right things with Christine. I keep reading:

"'When was the last time you screwed her?' Christine demands.

"'I don't know.'

bipolar bare

"I try to explain to her that the note she found and the Father's Day weekend had indicated to me that the affair was becoming sick. I tried to explain that Bonnie didn't care about me—that she was using me for her own ends, that I was falling into an old trap, and that something wasn't right with me.

"Christine says something else about how sick I am, and how she is going to take Sarah, our two-year-old daughter, away from me. I become enraged. I grab Christine and push her into the bedroom. I throw her down on the bed. She stands up. I throw her down again and jump on top of her, pressing her arms down to the bed with my knees. I yell at her, push her face, and grab her throat.

"'How do you like having your throat grabbed?' I yell at her.

"Sarah, in her pajamas, holding in one hand by its long ears her favorite stuffed animal, a bunny rabbit, and with her other hand's thumb in her mouth, is standing at the edge of the bed, watching this awful scene, as her mother begs me to let her go. Mortified, I release her.

"Christine dresses and leaves the house. I give Sarah her bottle and rock her to sleep while I cry. What a mess, and what a thing for Sarah to experience. I am messing up Sarah's life, just like I am messing up my own. Christine is totally justified in her hatred for me. I have lied and covered up. Through blindness, selfishness, and self-destructiveness, I have created this mess. It is my fault for precipitating the events by becoming involved with Bonnie. I can't help but feel it would have happened anyway. Christine and I have been drifting apart for a long time. The blame perhaps lies with us both, but the blame for the break is all mine. Christine returns and I go out. After marching around the block three times, I return, and I fall asleep on the couch.

"The next day, we try to be civil to one another. I say I want our marriage to work, but I don't believe any marriage can work which has no sex involved. Christine leaps at me and starts pounding on my chest. She starts to cry and disappears into the bedroom. I put Sarah to bed and collect a blanket from our bed so I can again sleep on the couch. As I retreat from the room, Christine rises from the bed, shouting that since sex is what I want, why didn't we just have it and get it over with.

"'Forget it, you don't mean that,' I say and head down the hallway. Christine comes after me, cornering me by the kitchen door.

"'Pull it out,' she growls, reaching for the zipper on my pants. I brush away her hand and head for the living room. Christine follows. By the couch, she begins to undress me coldly.

"'Stop this Christine,' I implore.

"'This is what you want, isn't it?'

"'Not this way.'

"'I thought you liked it rough.'

"'Well, maybe I will make it real rough."

"I lunge at her. Christine grows fearful.

"'I don't like violence,' she whimpers.

"'What do you call what you are doing?'

"'It's not violent,' she says, her eyes big as saucers.

" I pull back from the urge to rape her. I feel impotent. I should have beaten her up and sodomized her, but I couldn't do it. Christine returns to her aggression. She strips off my pants and pushes me onto the couch and begins sucking on my cock roughly.

"'Are you going to bite it off?' I ask.

"'I could,' she says. 'You deserve it.'

"The whole mad scene has a mingled quality of repulsion and strong attraction. The sex is hateful, but I like it. Still, I am angry that I have not taken her as I pleased. I pull her up and enter her. She begins to fiercely work herself up and down on my erect penis. I come. She pulls off and moves away. We sit on the couch for a long time after this—me wrapped in the blanket, Christine in her gown. We talk about how awful it has gotten between us. I go to bed on the couch. Christine returns to the bedroom. In the morning, I see a patch of dried blood in front of the couch where were had intercourse.

"We have no sex again. We don't talk much. We argue in the park. Christine walks off. We decide we must separate. Christine remarks, 'Well, now you have got what you want. You are free.' "

I drop the papers in my lap, look off into the distance, and begin to cry.

"I had accepted a job at UCLA just before I wrote this and was commuting back and forth on weekends to San Francisco," I tell Ginger. "Christine and I were still trying to work things out on our marriage. The weekend I wrote about was the end. We separated after that."

Ginger kneels beside me and wraps her arms around me. "Carl," she says, "that is some pretty heavy stuff, and not very nice, but it was a long time ago. Think about what you didn't do. You didn't beat her up. You didn't sodomize her. You did hurt her in some terrible psychological ways, but not physical ways. When you had her down on the bed with your hands around her throat, you let go. You did not strangle her."

"But I wanted to."

"Maybe that was your illness speaking, or maybe that is the rage any human can get to when they are angry enough. Hadn't she just threatened to take your child away? Do you remember our friend who killed his wife when she threatened to take his children away from him? All of us are capable of extreme violence when we become enraged. Aren't all of us capable of becoming crazy at certain points in our lives?"

"Yes, I suppose so."

"Give yourself some credit. You didn't do it when you had a chance."

"You know what happens to me after I have an incident of extreme anger. I get really depressed and I want to kill myself. It happens every time. After I returned to Los Angeles I went for long walks on the beach to try to find some reasons to continue to live. I wrote another piece shortly after the incidents I just read to you. Would you like to hear it? It's called 'California, the End of Dreams'."

"Yes, I'd like that," Ginger says. She resumes her knitting while I read the piece. Just as I finish reading, the Reverend Charles Sacquety appears on the lawn in front of the administration building and waves to us. We invite him to join us. He walks over to the grassy spot where Ginger and I are camped. Ginger and I stand up to greet him. Charles asks if there is a place where he and I could go to talk and take communion. I look around the garden behind me and spot a concrete bench beyond a sidewalk, nestled in a group of low palms and flowering plants. I suggest we go there.

We sit side by side on the bench. Charles takes off his dark clerical jacket, drapes it over the back of the bench, and places his traveling communion leather packet on the bench between us. Charles is dressed in a white ribbed shirt with clerical collar, gray slacks, and high polished black shoes. With his full white hair and broad smile, he is the very picture of the beneficent cleric. I am casual in a red, short-sleeved shirt, blue jeans, and sneakers. With my twisted, receding, light brown-going-white locks and pained appearance, I am the unhappy parishioner.

"How are you on this beautiful Easter day?" Charles asks. "You don't look that happy."

"Eh, good, until I read to Ginger what a creep I was to my first wife," I reply.

"What did you do that was so bad?"

"I was unfaithful. I had an affair. I was selfish. I was uncaring. I was mean. I didn't help Christine when I should have. Some of it may have been my own problems with mental illness. But whatever it was, I did not treat her fairly, and I hurt her terribly. I feel a horrible sense of guilt about it that I have never been able to deal with."

"Maybe it is time you forgave yourself for this. How long ago was this?"

"Twenty-four years ago."

"That's a long time."

"God never forgets."

"You have a very strange view of God."

"God to my mind is the great torturer. It—whatever God is—tortures mankind from the day of birth to the day of death. The earth is the chamber of horrors."

"My goodness, where did you ever get such a viewpoint?"

"Experience."

"Can I give you a different perspective? Have you ever heard the parable of the prodigal son?"

"Yes, I sort of remember it. Tell it to me again."

"A man has two sons: the elder, who will inherit his fortune, and a younger, who will be given a share. The younger son says to his father, 'Give me my inheritance now.' His father gives it to him. The younger son goes out into the world and squanders his inheritance on gambling and loose women. He ends up impoverished. He works for others but is treated no better than a slave. The younger son decides to return to his father and ask for his forgiveness. When he returns, the father is overjoyed. He sacrifices the fatted calf for the son. The elder son is jealous. He says to the father, 'Why do you sacrifice the fatted calf for my brother, when I, who have stayed faithfully with you, get nothing?' The father says, 'I rejoice because he who was lost to me has returned'."

"So what am I, the prodigal son?"

"You could be, if you let yourself be. God loves us all. It is not a question of whether or not you deserve it. Start by forgiving yourself for the errors of the past. Some of those errors you made you may have had no control over. Others were your fault. Still you can forgive yourself. God forgives you."

"I find that hard to do."

"I see you in church on most Sundays. Why do you come?"

"I go because I support Ginger. Besides, I have always thought of myself as a spiritual person. Can I read you something I wrote a while ago when I first came to Los Angeles?"

I read Charles the piece titled "California, the End of Dreams." When I am finished, Charles claps appreciatively and comments, "Why, that was quite good! I didn't know you wrote so well."

"I write, I draw, and I am an architect," I say, basking in his praise. "As a matter of fact, I am embarrassed to say it, but I like to think of myself as the Leonardo da Vinci of our time. I know it's really silly to think this. I don't tell many people, because they laugh at me and think me mad. But then again, I am mad."

"You should never give up your dreams, Carl. God has given you many gifts. You need to appreciate them and enjoy them. Whether or not you will receive recognition for them is out of God's hands."

"You can't influence him a little to get me some recognition?"

"I'm afraid not," Charles chuckles. "I'm very interested in your writing about the Western Paradise. What are you speaking of here?"

"Oh, that," I say somewhat sheepishly. "I'm just mixing in a little Buddhist philosophy. Some sutras refer to the idea of a Western Paradise. I was thinking that California, stripped of the materialism that chokes the landscape, could be that paradise. It's not my idea. Many others have said it. California is a place where the life of the mind and the spirit can grow in a new way—where roots of Christianity, Buddhism, and Islam could forge a new kind of religion, incorporating all. A big fish where the madness of one swallows the normality of all."

"Will you take communion with me?" asks Charles.

"Certainly."

After we share the bread and wine, Charles departs. The sun is very hot. Ginger and I lie on the grass looking at the sky and talk about forgiveness. A squirrel tumbles from a nearby tree limb. The bewildered animal rights itself and stands statue-still, its feathery tail moving slightly from side to side. He looks toward us indignantly and slowly crawls away. We laugh at this ordinary circumstance of life. Ginger departs soon thereafter. She says she has to get prepared for work tomorrow. I go in to my room and sit at the desk.

Carlotta appears from the bathroom in her toga and asks me how I am. I tell her I am tired and I can't talk.

"Have you forgiven yourself?" she asks.

"I am working on the idea," I reply.

"To truly appreciate the gifts God has given you, your talents to draw, to write, to design, and your limitations of depression and of cycling up and down, you must forgive yourself. Forgiving will go a long way toward healing. Dance to the joy of life."

Carlotta dances in the middle of the room like Isadora Duncan. She twirls and lifts her toga. The long cloth creates an arch that falls to the floor. She sways, sweeps, and moves toward the bathroom. Before disappearing she says. "The wisdom of the mad lies in this direction."

I remain stone-still at the desk. *The Ten Commandments*, that perennial Easter favorite, is on TV, but I fall asleep, slumping over the desk before Charlton Heston parts the Red Sea.

CHAPTER 10

KALI MOTHER: LYNN JOAN QUINN DAVIS FERGUSON COLLIER

Kali Mother; 1981; 25 x 35 inches; pastel

ON THE PATIO BEHIND THE HOSPITAL DINING ROOM, three men and one woman are sitting around a metal table smoking cigarettes as Smitty and I approach. The white plastic ashtray in the middle of the table overflows with butts. Ryan has on a terry cloth robe over his pajamas. The words "Big Dog" below a Saint Bernard are printed all over the green robe. His slippered feet are propped up in another chair. Ray, Mauricio, and June are dressed in jeans and T-shirts.

"Can we join you?" I say, pulling up a chair from a neighboring table.

"Pleaaze do," responds Mauricio, a man with tan skin, thick glasses, and a strong Brazilian accent.

Smitty pulls up a chair, takes out his pack of cigarettes, shakes out two, hands me one, and drops the pack on the table.

"The Club Meds smoking lounge can come to order," says Ryan, leaning across the table and taking a cigarette from Smitty's pack. "We were running out of discussion stimulators."

"When did you decide to join?" asks Ray, turning to me with his lighter. He lights my Marlboro, then Ryan's, then Smitty's. I take a deep drag and exhale.

"Couldn't resist," I reply, coughing. "Everyone interesting around here smokes, and if I wanted to sit in on the scintillating conversations, I figured I might as well smoke. It's like a twelve step meeting where the best stuff goes on at the breaks. Everyone is crowded outside, puffing away."

"We're sending up smoke signals to Mauricio's friends, who are going to break us out of here," says June, stretching her arm across the table and picking up Smitty's pack. Ray, a man with long brown hair tied back in a ponytail, gives a big laugh.

"Hey, leave me a few," pleads Smitty. "That's the only pack I got."

"I'll get my connection to get you another pack tomorrow," Ray replies, lighting June's cigarette.

"What have Smitty and I been missing?" I interject.

"Mauricio is *saudaji*—that's melancholy in Portuguese," says Ray. "We are trying to cheer him up."

"Are you Portuguese, Mauricio?" I ask.

"Noh, I am Brazilian," replies Mauricio with a distinctive burr to his voice, "but in ah cossmick sense, I am ze male incarnasian of ze Hindu goddess Kaqui." Mauricio breaks out into a big smile.

"You don't sound too melancholy to me," says Smitty.

"Yeah, cut the crap, Mauricio," says June, ejecting a white jet of smoke from the corner of her mouth. She is a good-looking blonde in a tight T-shirt that shows off her firm breasts. "We've all heard about your days in the Indian ashram. Ryan is going to tell us about his days as a Hollywood stuntman when he rode his motorcycle all coked up. Nearly killed yourself numerous times in the desert, didn't you?"

"Those were wild times," Ryan laughs, "but now I have one of those stimulator things in my back from it. I have to go to have it charged up every now and then or I am in terrible pain. I can't work anymore. I tend my garden and walk my dogs. It's the simple life when I am not depressed."

"That doesn't sound very funny," says Smitty, ever the cynic. "What about you, Ray? I know you are a crackhead and you, June, I hear you are an addict."

An uneasy silence falls over the table, broken at last by Ray's voice.

"We don't know this guy Carlton very well yet to talk about our stories. Maybe he should be telling us a little about himself before we spill the beans about ourselves."

"What can you tell us, Carl?" asks June pleasantly.

"I am an addict too," I say, "but I don't know that I want to get into that right now. I don't know you guys, either. I am up early this morning because I am reading my journal about finding my mother. I didn't know who she was or where she was for thirty years. I hired detectives to find out for me."

"This is interesting," June enthuses. "Tell us more!"

"Well, I did a drawing of her as I called Mother Kali. It is a bust of a woman with no arms rising out of a plant. Her womb is exposed, showing a baby coiled in an umbilical cord. When Mauricio said that he is really Kali, I found that very interesting. Can I hear more?"

"Zat drawing zounds very mzthical—or should I say mzstical," says Mauricio, "but ze Hindu Kaqui has many arms and holds all kinds of tings in each one of dem."

"Let's not get into that mysticism stuff," Ray grumbles. "Tell us more about your Kali, Carl."

"The Kali drawing says a lot about me."

"Maybe," says Ryan, "but unfortunately, you don't have it here for us to see."

"All right, then," I say. "How about I tell you the story of the detectives and what happened to me when I moved to downtown LA and started making a loft space to live in? While I was painting the drywall on the walls of my studio, I decided to hire detectives to find my mother. I don't know why I decided then to do what I did. Maybe it was the effect of the paint fumes."

"Go on, tell us, it could be interesting," says June.

I rock back in my chair, pleased to have a captive audience. "Have you ever been in a detective agency?" I begin. "Well, it doesn't look anything like the places you see on television. The one I went to, The Sherman Agency, was a roomful of telephone books for the whole country where a couple of fat, sloppy-looking guys sat working the phones. I paid these creeps $300 for her name, address, and telephone number."

"It only costs three hundred bucks to hire a detective?" Ryan marvels. "I thought they cost a lot more."

"They tried to. The agency called me up a few days later and said they needed more money to complete the job. They demanded $450 more before giving me the information. I got angry. I told them to give me an account of the time they had already spent. They refused, so I check out this agency with the state finding out that they had numerous complaints against them for this kind of behavior. I decided to take them to small claims court."

Smitty whistles derisively. "You're busting their ass over four hundred and fifty bucks and taking them to court?" he snorts. "You're hard man."

"It's the principle of the thing," I reply coolly. "You want to hear my story or not?"

"Go on, Carl," says Ray, "we're all ears."

I recount my battle against The Sherman Agency in small claims court. The agency sends some tired little nervous guy named Wilson on their behalf. He looks like a pushover, but he is feisty and puts up a good fight. I argue that the agency will not provide me with an accounting of the work they've supposedly done and back my contention up with copies of the three other complaints against them. In the end, the judge decides the $450 will be split down the middle, with me having to pay half the cost for the information about my mother. I'm amenable to this, but only if Wilson will guarantee in writing the authenticity of his agency's findings. He agrees but insists on a cash payment.

"This is mildly entertaining," says Ray. "What happened next?"

"I went to the agency the following day and got her name and address. Her name is Lynn Joan Collier, or Lillian Quinn Collier, and she lived in Eggertsville, New York."

"Did you call her?" June asks breathlessly.

"Of course."

"And what did she say?" asks June.

"She was surprised, to put it mildly."

A nurse appears on the patio, telling us it is time for the first process group.

"I guess you will have to wait for the next installment of my tale," I say teasingly. "It gets better."

The group breaks up, stubbing out all its cigarettes. Ryan says he is going back to bed. The rest of us go to the process group and the other activities of the day. The following morning, I am up early, studying my notebooks and reviewing the rest of the story. My thoughts drift away from the difficult subject. I look out the window toward the patio to see if anyone is there from whom I could bum a cigarette. The patio is empty.

"Unpleasant to recall that time, isn't it?"

"Carlotta, you appear again!" I exclaim, startled.

Nearly nude save for a pendulous necklace of skulls and the severed hands and arms that hang from her waistband, she is coal black and has eight arms. She carries a sword in one hand and a severed head in another.

"God, Carlotta, you are quite a fright!" I comment. "Are these Hollywood props?"

"Hardly! They are as real as real can be."

"I know who you are supposed to be this time: Kali, the bloodthirsty goddess of the Hindus. Are you going to dance for me like Kali does over the body of Shiva?"

"I come to you as the true Kali, the Indian goddess of the feminine force and the primal force of all creation. I am here to help you get your metaphors straight."

Carlotta begins to dance, raising her left leg to her thigh and stomping down. The bells on her ankle tinkle. She does the same thing with her right leg and moves her four arms in rhythm with legs. She repeats the sinuous pattern again and again.

"Stop, please," I plead. "I don't understand."

Carlotta stops her dance. "Didn't you do a drawing around this time of your mother, which you titled *Kali Mother*?"

"Yes, but I wasn't trying to be literal, just symbolic of how I felt. My *Kali Mother* is a powerful feminine and destructive force like the Hindu Kali."

"If I recall, you had your mother emerging from a plant with no arms, like a Greek statue, and blonde hair on one side of her head and black hair on the other side. This is not how Kali is depicted. Kali has eight arms, a necklace of skulls, and a skirt of severed arms and hands around her waist."

"I know. It was just a drawing. Why are you getting all excited about?"

"You had your mother's womb open, showing a baby twisted up in its umbilical cord. Strangled, I would guess. Was the baby supposed to be you?"

"Maybe. I don't know. I was acting pretty crazy at that time."

"The understatement of the century," Carlotta jeers. "I know you weren't treating women very well. Kali comes to defend all women. See the sword and the severed head I have in two of my arms?"

"Are you going to behead me? If not, can I go have a cigarette?"

"No. You must stay. We must discuss this situation."

"What are you saying?"

"I think you should tell Kali what happened after you got your mother's name and whereabouts."

"No! If you are trying frightening me, it's not working. The sword and the severed head in your arms are plastic, I bet."

bipolar bare

"What if they aren't? The sword is steel and the head is Ray's. He didn't want to give it to me, but I insisted. See how I am holding up his head with his pony tail?"

"Now you are frightening me. Really, are you going to sever my head?"

"How could I frighten you? I am you. Only you can sever your head. If you did, you could put it back on straight, but I don't think you would. Men need our feminine force, the all-creating and all-consuming energy, to get anything right."

"That is bunk."

"You think so? Tell me the story of the night you got your mother's information. The gods demand it!"

Carlotta/Kali begins to dance again, waving her eight arms, undulating her hips, and alternately stamping one foot, then the other. "Get on with it, man!"

"All right, all right! Just stop your dance."

"As you wish. I will pose with one foot on my thigh and my arms in their traditional positions."

As Carlotta strikes the pose, I begin my tale:

"It is the first of December, 1980. I have received my mother's name, telephone number, and address from The Sherman Agency. I waited thirty years to have this information, and I was paralyzed. I spent the day and evening trying to get myself to make the call. What would I say to her? 'Hi, this is your son Carlton. Do you remember me?' That sounded stupid. I tried all kinds of introductions. None I liked. Would I get her on the phone or Mr. Collier? What would I do if he answered? 'Hello, may I speak to your wife? I am her long lost son.' How asinine that would sound!

"At the time, I am living in an enclosure made from a salvaged piece of the *Running Fence*, the ambitious—some would say insane—art project by the avant-garde genius Christo, involving miles of nylon fabric traversing Marin and Sonoma counties, while I work on building my loft. I call it my auric egg, a clean spot in the mess of construction all around me. The parachute cloth runs from ceiling to floor. The white shiny cloth covers the floor inside the enclosure on which sits my bed. The egg stands like a big white crystal in the middle of the loft, luminous, but not very soundproof.

"I sat next to the phone outside my Running Fence enclosure in my loft. The phone sits on a piece of Formica that's shaped like a green tongue sticking out of the wall and supported on a tree limb. I doodle and pace around the phone table, making figure eight loops. My head was full of all kinds of observations that made calling impossible. I smoke a joint. Stoned, I might be able to call.

"What would Lynn be like, I wonder? Would she be curt or friendly? Would she hang up on me? Why is she Lynn Joan Collier and Lillian Quinn Collier? Why Eggertsville, New York? What a funny name. At the UCLA Library earlier in the day, I look up the town in an atlas. A town of 55,000 people, Eggertsville is a suburb of Buffalo, that mercilessly cold city of rain, snow, and urban blight. Eggertsville didn't sound like a very exciting place, but at least I got a general idea where she was from the map.

"The phone mocks me. When should I make the call? I decide I can't do it tonight. It was already eight in LA; it will be eleven in Buffalo. I will do it tomorrow. Can I wait that long? If I do wait, will I chicken out? I'm afraid I will learn that there is nothing extraordinary about Lynn Joan Collier, or Lillian Joan Collier. She is a sixty-year-old woman and she and your father's tale is nothing special. The banality of it all is sad.

"I must face up to the ordinariness of it. She and he got divorced. They didn't love each other. She just drifted away from all connection to him, including a little boy. It's not a story of intrigue, but there is my father's comment, 'Don't open Pandora's box.' I needed to know what was in the box. There is the fact that I ended up with my father and not my mother. That is unusual for the time. In fact, I was not supposed to be with my father, but with my grandmother. I was her ward. No, rather I was a ward of the court. There is the fact that Grandmother legally adopted my sister. Could we really be my mother's children? Could we really be children sired by grandmother's favorite son, Carlie? No, it can't be. This is crazy thinking. A whole piece of my past is missing. One side is a blank; the other is full of an old and irrelevant heritage. I don't even know what my mother looks or sounds like. This is why I am doing what I am doing.

"Into this whirling maelstrom of thoughts came Gary, the artist who lives across the hall from me. He has slept in my loft the past few nights. The fumes of his freshly painted walls and floors forced him to find other sleeping arrangements. Last night, he was at Athena's, his art critic girlfriend's place. Tonight, he came back to my place, despite the fact that he tells me in a note that he will be spending the night with her. I ask him about it.

"'Athena won't show up,' he says. 'I may see her later, though, in a club. If she does show up here, could she spend the night here with me?'

"Gary notices me shifting my feet uncomfortably and looks sheepish.

"'As a matter of fact, I think I will go to her place if she shows up,' he says nervously. 'I could tell by your body language, you didn't like what I said.'

"I mumbled something about it being OK, but I didn't feel OK about it. I did not want to listen to Gary get it on with a woman while I was trying to sleep, my mind awash in thoughts of Eggertsville. I knew I could not deal with listening to the sounds of fucking tonight. I had listened to it all summer when Gary and other women banged away while I struggled alone with my guilt for leaving my wife.

"Athena doesn't show up. Gary and I go to bed. He lays his mattress a few feet beyond my curtain wall. I cannot sleep. My mind is racing with thoughts. Athena arrives after midnight. She and Gary begin to talk. I try not to be bothered, but I am. I am getting more agitated as they continue to talk. Eventually, her little murmurs of pleasure penetrate my egg as they start having sex. I get dressed, cursing under my breath. The moans outside my enclosure are growing louder and more frequent. My anger is boiling up. I hate this woman. I hate all women.

"I surge out of the curtained egg, slamming the door behind me, and go for a walk to cool off. When I come back, I hope they will be finished or at least be quiet in some deference to me. I smoke a joint on my loading dock. It is very cold outside. I do not stay out long. When I re-enter, she is talking louder than before. She is drunk. I make my way inside my curtain. I am thinking of *Beau Geste*, the classic 1939 movie where the Viking tradition of placing a dog at the feet of a fallen warrior is mimicked. The cruel sergeant of the foreign legion is the dog laid at feet of Beau Geste, portrayed by Gary Cooper, in the smoldering doom of Fort Zinderneuf. Gary, in the sack with Athena, is at my feet. They are my dogs.

"She is talking loudly, driving me to madness. I could easily kill her or both of them, set fire to the whole scene, and walk off. Instead, I say in a loud strong voice, "'Get that bimbo out of here! Please!'

"Surprised, Gary replies, 'We will be gone in two minutes.'

"I lie down inside my egg. Athena's incessant drivel tortures my ears. I want that woman out of my home. I can hear Gary stirring. In two minutes, they aren't gone. I go to the opening in my curtain and step outside.

"'I meant what I said,' I say meanly.

"Athena struggles upward, nude. I only see her back as she totters, trying to get her balance. Gary looks hard at me and says, 'I told you I was working on it.'

"I go back into my curtain and lie down, watching Gary's shadow play over the curtain as he gathers up his stuff. I tell Gary I am sorry, but I cannot deal with this situation tonight. I ask him if he is going to sleep in his fumes.

"'No, I am going to Athena's,' he says roughly. 'We can talk about this in the morning.'

"They leave. I get up to write. My life is falling apart. I am fractured."

"She and Gary were rude," says Carlotta, "but you weren't very nice, either."

"How could I be? I warned them once and they paid no attention."

"Mother Kali expects more of her consort, an enlightened being who understands the passing nature of human desire."

Carlotta starts to dance, stamping her feet and waving her eight arms. The bells on her feet and around her wrists tinkle. She spins on one leg. The arms swing over her head then drop to her side.

"Give me a break!" I whine. "How would you like it, if you were struggling with an important decision, and you had to listen to some babe getting fucked outside your curtain?"

"Such uncouth talk! You should have offered your services to help satisfy the earthly desires of the flesh."

"That would have gone over big. Gary would have smashed me in the nose."

"But you might have solved your problem without anger, and you never know— you could have gotten a little love, which might have relieved the tension."

"You are nuts. Gary never would have gone for a three-way."

"It would have been a better solution than the one you took. Take my sword of knowledge, sever your head, and put it back with a new understanding. You could have transcended the circle of creation and destruction with this act."

"I don't get it."

"I bet the woman might have liked two lovers. Her inhibitions were down. She was drunk, remember. Two lovers could have satisfied a fantasy. Why do I have eight arms? So I can take care of two men, of course."

"You are a mythical figure. Real people don't do such things."

"Get your head on straight. It could have happened. It does happen. In the complete cycle of creation and destruction, which is contained in me, many possibilities are real. I am only trying to get you to see another way that does not have to be full of anger."

"I could not bear another woman to deal with while I was dealing with the woman from whose womb I sprang. Women have ruined my life. I was born of a whore, and all women have made my life miserable."

"Too bad! Such incorrect thinking. This was not your finest hour. You were on a slippery slope and headed downward. It may have looked to you like you were resolving old issues, but you weren't. Finding your mother was a debacle from the very day you battled with the detectives. I felt so sad that I, the feminine Kali, the ultimate reality and the transcendence of all form, could not give you some insight. I might give you some pleasure to soothe your pain. But you were too full of craving for an answer to your need."

"What need was that?"

"The need to prove your mother was bad and by extension, all women were bad."

"I didn't believe that statement for one moment."

Carlotta laughs and dances toward the bathroom. She turns sideways to pass through the doorway. The sword smashes against the jamb. She turns her head to me and says before disappearing into the room, "At least you did call your birth mother. There was some good in doing that."

"Wrong. I called Lynn Joan Collier the next day. She said she was wondering when I would finally get in touch with her. Her manner was cool and guarded. We made arrangements to meet in Las Vegas over the New Year's holiday."

Carlotta puts her eight hands together in a gesture of supplication and bows. "Kali smiles at your good fortune."

Carlotta closes the bathroom door. "Damn modern conveniences!" I can hear her swear as she apparently stumbles over the bathtub.

"The experience was more weird than good," I shout at the closed door, "but I didn't hate her."

CHAPTER 11

PANDORA'S BOX IS OPEN

I AM SITTING ON A BENCH OUTSIDE the Las Encinas admissions office in the dawn's first light, reading from my journals, feeling sad, when Carlotta makes a typically flamboyant entrance. She is a study in madcap couture, with a riot of feathers protruding from her buttocks and the top of her head.

"How do you like my costume?" she implores with a Betty Boop-ish pout.

"Carlotta, you have an infuriating gift for showing up at the most inopportune times," I sigh. "What are you supposed to be this time, looking like a half-naked peacock?"

"Can't you tell?" asks Carlotta, a trifle hurt. "I am a Las Vegas show girl in honor of your trip to meet your mother. I think I have chosen a perfect costume. The Folies Bergère show at the Tropicana Hotel is my inspiration. A little old-fashioned, perhaps, compared to current tastes, which tend toward miles of cleavage and near-nudity. The sequined bikini, bra, and silver high heels fit me very nicely. The feathered headdress in pink is very traditional. The pink-feathered bustle does indeed make me look like an exotic bird. Shall I strut my stuff in front of you?"

Carlotta strides purposely up and down the brick pathway. She stops in front of me and shakes her body. The feathers swing and sway in all directions. She bends forward and blows me a kiss.

"You're a little hefty to be a show girl," I smirk. "Without a corset, you have no waistline. Josephine Baker, the Folies' most famous dancer, you're not."

"That is an unkind remark! You could at least see me as a curvaceous babe."

"I'm not feeling that way at the moment, I'm afraid."

"Too bad. I chose this manifestation to combat your deadly seriousness with a little humor."

"Oh, sit down and be quiet! I am reading the most crucial part of my story, the part where I meet my mother after so many years."

"I can't sit down in all these feathers," Carlottta frowns. "It will ruin my costume. I need to stand."

"Stand if you must, but don't do anything provocative. You will ruin my reading."

"What if I collapse? I am not used to these six-inch heels."

"Then pace if you must. No one will see you."

"Their loss. The other patients will be sorry they don't have such a beautiful alter ego."

"For Christ's sake, let me read!"

As Carlotta paces back and forth, making it all but impossible to concentrate, I read from my journal:

"After driving from Los Angeles, smoking dope the whole way, I arrive in Las Vegas after dusk and check into a sleazy, one-story motel, The Desert Paradise, across from the convention center. My mother has left a message that she and her husband are checked into the Frontier Hotel and I should call her. I do. We arrange that I shall come to their room, number 108, in several hours. Apprehensive, I take my time showering and have a nap afterwards. My intention is to wear a suit to this long-awaited meeting, but I forget to bring a tie. I am forced to change my plans and dress in my usual casual chic. Wearing my old beaten up leather jacket, tan chino pants, and a checkered Western shirt, I head off down Desert Inn Road to the Frontier Hotel.

"The Frontier is one of the big, tacky hotels in Las Vegas's early style. A huge sign like a flattened phallus marks its entry. Under the arch at the top is a big rotating letter F. Cascading down the shaft inside the long legs of the arch are red stars. Midway down, the word 'Frontier' passes through the elongated arch. At the bottom is a typical Las Vegas lozenge sign listing the headliners: Eddie Fisher, Robert Goulet, and Joan Rivers, whose names occupy the top half of the lozenge. The lower half displays the names of the performers on the second bill: The Treniers, Jimmy Rogers, and Jackie Leonard.

"The casino has a porte-cochere entry to its main gambling area, which

bipolar bare

extends down Las Vegas Boulevard behind a series of giant white luminescent panels. The hotel is a low, seven-story building of undistinguished fifties design, surrounded by an enormous parking lot. The Frontier is the least attractive of Las Vegas' big casino hotels. I wish my mother could have found a more interesting place—say, The Flamingo— for our meeting."

"Carlotta, this should interest you," I say, pausing in my reading. "The Frontier was imploded and has been replaced by a more thematic mega-resort."

"Do they still have showgirls?" asks Carlotta eagerly.

"Las Vegas will always have showgirls."

"Good, I shall get a job there."

"You're much too, er ... statuesque."

"Hee-hee. I like that."

I read on:

"I amble through the casino. The faces of the patrons playing the slots, roulette, blackjack, and other games of chance are bathed in a lurid orange-red luster from the tacky plastic décor and the velvet carpet. In the men's room, I try to converse with the black man polishing my boots, but he's a taciturn sort. The roar of televised football and the din of metal coins falling through the slots outside in the casino follows me inside the white-tiled refuge of a toilet. I am stalling. My mind is jammed with noise, external and internal.

"My bladder relieved, I pass back through the casino on my way to Room 108. Shouldering my way through the largely middle-aged, overweight crowd, I circumnavigate the banks of slot machines near the restrooms. Elaborately coiffed matrons in printed blouses and polyester pants account for most of the diehard slot machine players. I stop and watch. Like blue-haired robots, they pluck quarters from little plastic cups on top of the machines, feed them into the slot, pull the levers, and hypnotically watch the symbols spin. Occasionally, the monotonous kaching-kaching-kaching is followed by the happy jingle-jangle of quarters spilling into the tray, but the robot women just repeat the process, like they're programmed to do. I wonder if my mother will look like one of these blank-faced creatures.

"The gamblers at the blackjack tables and the crowds around the craps pits are predominantly older men. They wear jackets but no ties and tend toward red, blue, or green knit shirts and clownishly-colored pants associated with the golfing set. With a drink in one hand and fondling a stack of chips in the other, they try to affect an air of world-weary casualness, but the grim cast of their faces betrays their love-hate affair with Lady Luck. Arnold, my mother's third husband, turns out to be one of these men.

"I make my way to the first floor right-hand wing of the hotel. Determinedly, I stride down a long red-carpeted corridor lined with slots and VIP rooms: The Gourmet Room, The Branding Iron Restaurant, the small show room where the Treniers sing, and the party room where preparations are starting for the 'Gala New Year's Eve Celebration.' I climb up two small flights of steps, twisting and turning down a six-foot wide corridor with a brown wood wainscot and tan walls to Room 108. I halt, staring at the slightly ajar door.

"Taking a deep breath, I rap. From inside, I hear a female voice say something to the effect of, 'Come in.' Zombie-like, I comply. A scant six feet away, my mother stands before me in front of the bed. Mercy! She is a far cry from the dowdy slot machine automatons. She looks like my grandmother, but the eyes— they are different. I move forward to gaze into the eyes of my mother. They are dark and hazel. They are intense. There is a fire behind them. I step back to take her all in. She is a tall and elegant woman, aging gracefully and still beautiful, wearing a black sequin gown that flashes shimmers of light over her body. She has bleached blonde hair. Her thin face is dominated by an Indian nose, slightly bent at the bridge as can be seen prominently in all the early profile paintings of the Mohawk, Seneca, and Cayuga chiefs of the Iroquois Band. I have her nose, and her eyes. I look more like her than I look like my father. What a revelation! So this is whom I look like! I am speechless."

"See I told you the sequins were a good choice, but I should have chosen black."

Carlotta, stepping back to give me a better view of her sequined body, totters on the brick pavers and falls into the grass. Her headdress slips to the side and the impact crushes her feather bustle.

"Oh, pooh, I have ruined my costume!" she cries.

Exasperated, I make a motorboat sound through my lips. "Take off those ridiculous feathers and sit with me on this bench."

Carlotta struggles to her feet, removes the ruined bustle, and sits beside me. She crosses her outsized gams. One long, spiked heel dangles in front of me.

"Beg pardon," she apologizes breathlessly while rubbing her finger along the ridge of her nose "I am overcome by the drama of your meeting, that's all. Please continue with your story."

"We don't hug. We don't kiss. We just sit on the end of the bed. I can't remember much of what we say. I remember I apologize for not having a suit. I say I left my ties in LA. I am nervous. I almost cry. My mother simply stares at me in silence as if she were assessing me as her son. I feel embarrassed. This obsession to see my mother seems stupid and wrong-headed.

"'What shall I call you?' I ask.

"'Call me Lynn. My daughters do.'

"I am astonished: I have more sisters! I question myself quietly. Lynn breaks the awkward silence.

"'We will talk tomorrow. I have much to tell you, but now we must go down for cocktails. Arnold is waiting.'

"She excuses herself and goes into the bathroom to finish her makeup. I am left alone to survey the room. The bed is unmade and a tray table stands against the wall with two glasses and a bottle of Scotch. The closet is open. I can see Arnold and Lynn's clothes on hangers. The chest of drawers has several drawers open. Apparently, they made no effort to tidy up for my visit.

"Unprompted, out of nowhere Lynn says to me, "'No one ever gets the best of me, unless I want them to." She smiles broadly, reaching her hand out to me as she steps out of the bathroom switching off the light Lynn looks beautiful. I am silent and in awe wondering what she means "no one gets the best of her." Is this a warning to me?

"I rise from the bed. She takes my arm and we walk back down the corridor. Thirty-two years have passed since I last walked with my mother. My joy is undermined by displeasure at having to go meet Arnold. I want to stay and talk to this strange woman with the long legs and arms and the face that is my own.

I want to know everything immediately, but it is not to be. We head for the New Year's ballroom. Mother mingles with the VIP guests of the Frontier. They are all fat, old, and stink of money. My extroverted mother acts like one of the ladies who lunch, schmoozing expertly with couples from Buffalo, Boston, and Atlanta,. She gets all their names wrong and laughs it off. These strangers revolt me. They are posers and nouveau riche boors and their hangers-on. I feel strange to be in this plastic environment. The culture of Las Vegas is anathema to me. This is the culture of middle class American materialism gone horribly awry, and it is totally devoid of taste. And my mother seems to fit right in with them."

"There you go again, making snap judgments based on first impressions," says Carlotta. "You are setting yourself up to dislike your mother. You are letting your anger at her for abandoning you start to rise. Look at you, in your checkered shirt and leather jacket. You sure ain't no paragon of good taste."

"Well, I wanted to wear a suit."

"I'm sure that slip was Freudian," says Carlotta, pausing to adjust her shoes. "Damn, these high heels can really hurt your feet. I wonder how the showgirls can prance around in them. I think you are an elitist, Carlton."

"I am not!" I pout. "As usual, you have it all wrong. Let me continue. The best parts are coming up, and I want you to be quiet."

"I will, but first I must say you are slipping backwards in dealing with your obsession with your mother."

"I am not, I tell you," I huff, all too aware I must sound like a spoiled brat. "This is the beginning of resolution."

Carlotta gives me a wispy smile of encouragement as I read on:

"I meet Arnold. He is a short round man with drooping jowls like a bulldog. Next to his elegant wife, the aging princess, he looks like a grotesque toad that no kiss will ever transform. They make an odd pair and I catch myself staring at the two of them. Arnold takes us to the bar for a drink.'

"'This is all complimentary,' Lynn boasts. 'We always come to Vegas this way. The hotel pays for our drinks and food.'

" 'They get it all back, one way or another,' Arnold the toad grunts.

"He and I talk briefly. He wanders off back to his blackjack table. He is tipsy. Lynn admonishes him not to gamble too much after he has been drinking. 'Remember Monte Carlo,' she says.

"I go to get some hors d'oeuvres. Lynn retrieves Arnold and me. We stand at the bar. I have another gin and tonic. I am beginning to feel the effects of alcohol and pot. An abstracted state overcomes me. I hear the words being spoken, but I am disconnected, floating about in my own head, nearly insensate. Lynn tells me Debby, my sister, is coming tomorrow with her husband, Mike—I have another sister named Debby. I already have a half-sister named Debby in Columbus, Ohio. This whole situation is getting weirder by the minute. They are bringing Tykie, my other sister—I count them. Now I have five sisters: Carolee. Lory, I mustn't forget her, but I often do, two sisters named Debby, I wonder if they spell their name the same way, Tykie, what kind of a name is that. My head is beginning to spin. Mother tells me I have a brother. Incredible I have a brother too! Think of the birthday and Christmas card list! My brother is fathered by Roger Ferguson He is sickly and lives in Rochester. The child, named Bruce at birth, had a deformity: a growth on his neck. Rather matter-of-factly, Lynn says she gave the child up to a nurse named Lutz, who raised the boy. He is now called Peter Lutz. I wonder if it is he who sent Carolee the WE article. I am feeling woozy and retreat to the men's room where I splash water over my head.

"I wonder what kind of a woman my mother is. She gives up Carolee and me. She gives up another son because he has a deformity. After staring into the mirror above the sink for what seemed like an eternity, I return to my mother, who is alone at the bar chatting with a cocktail waitress. Arnold is nowhere to be seen. She turns and looks at me with a suspicious glance. Lynn must sense my discomfort at her statements. She asks me about my sister, Carlynn. I question the reference, because as long as I have known my sister, she has been Carolee.

"'The child was christened Carlynn,' she informs me. 'The name was a combination of Carl and Lynn, naturally.'

"'I always thought Carolee was just another Davis family name, like my own name, Carlton,' I reply. 'You know Carol and Lee.'

"'No, it wasn't. Lynn was in it. Carlynn, plain and simple. No 'O.'

"'Well, now she is called Carolee and you have been completely eliminated,' I reply with some satisfaction.

"'She has never been curious about me?'

"'No.'

"'I'm not surprised. I never raised her, you know. The minute she was born, your grandmother took over. I never had anything to do with her; didn't put a single diaper on her. With you, it was a different story.'

"Lynn tells me I was with her until I was six. I didn't try to correct her, but it was only until I was five.

"'It was too hard,' she says. 'I had to give you up. She was too powerful for me. I was singing everyday.'

"I can tell the drinks are loosening her tongue, but she presents a sanitized history brushed clean by the passage of time to suit her fancy.

"'I saw you last when you were six,' she goes on. 'I brought you back to your grandmother's house. She had detectives there. They pulled you from me.'

"'Why didn't I see you again?' I ask, wondering why we are having this conversation in the middle of a bar surrounded by all these strangers. It must be because it is neutral territory, where histrionics can be held in check.

"'It was too hard. There was Peter. I was singing seven days a week. My life was a living hell. Roger Ferguson was an alcoholic.'

"Finally, I screw up the nerve to blurt out, 'Why did you give me up?'

"'I thought you and your sister should be together,' she says.

"'My sister and I were never together. I lived with my father in Corning. My sister lived in Rochester with Nonnie.'

"'That's strange.'

"How could she think that strange? She knew that she had given Carolee up for adoption to my grandmother when she was born. We are silent. Lynn is searching the crowd for Arnold, who has wandered away toward the blackjack tables. I am looking at her, questioning myself for opening Pandora's box. I ask her about the divorce for adultery.

"'Oh, that,' she says. 'I agreed to that because I wanted a divorce and your father wouldn't give me one.'

bipolar bare

"I must have raised my eyebrows in disbelief, because Lynn gives me a devilish smile and turns again to look for Arnold. I order another gin and tonic from the bar. I don't understand her explanation, but I get no further clarification. Lynn tells me about the house on Dover Park.

"'Your grandmother set us up in it. You lived with your father and me. Your sister lived with your grandmother. We lived in this house until your father was arrested.'

"This startles me. 'My father was arrested? It is true then, what my suspicion has always been.'

"'Yes, for stealing cigarettes. Your grandmother never let me see him after that. She tried to get me to sign over the house to her. I wouldn't, and your grandmother told your father I wouldn't help him, which isn't true.'

"I question her about why she would need to sign the house over. 'Was it to pay for my father's legal problems?' I ask. She claims she doesn't know. 'But stealing cigarettes isn't a major crime.' I insist.

"'Your father was charged with grand larceny for stealing cigarettes on an epic scale.'

"'Why did he do it? He came from a moderately wealthy family.'

"'True, but perhaps your grandmother wasn't giving him enough money, and he wanted more to give to me.'

"Lynn tells me the full story of my father's criminal enterprise, how he was selling the cigarettes to the owner of the nightclub where Lynn worked, and how he was apprehended. This must be what is hidden in Pandora's box. I am mystified and shocked.

"I go to dinner with Lynn and Arnold in the Gourmet Room, which epitomizes the bourgeois trappings the American middle class dotes upon: candles on the table, plastic flowers in a vase, crystal water glasses, and plates emblazoned with large letter Fs. The service is slow. Arnold finally gets his clams casino and prime rib. The fare is cold, but Arnold just grumbles and won't confront the waiter. Lynn and I have rubbery lobster tails with lukewarm butter.

"When I go back to my hotel room, I can't sleep. I am happy and sad at the same time. At last, I see my mother, and I am glad to have the chance to look her in the eyes. I am amazed how much I looked like her. I am saddened that so much still remains a mystery to me. I know precious little more than I knew before, except for more on the larceny angle. Did my father have a big, illegal cigarette theft operation going? Then there are two new sisters and a brother. The cast of characters is complete, but the plot still makes no sense. The whys of this muddled history are still unanswered. I begin to feel that they will never be answered. The doubts remain. I try to put this thought out of my mind. I tell myself that I always expect too much. After all, this is only our first meeting! Tomorrow will be different."

I stop reading and turn to Carlotta.

"Do you think I should have left this all alone, Carlotta?" I ask.

Carlotta reaches down, undoes the ankle straps on her high heels, and shakes them off without answering.

"Well, do you think going to see my mother was crazy or not?"

"You were acting a bit crazy before you left for Vegas," she says at length. "You kicked Gary and Athena out of your loft. You were smoking more dope than ever before, and you were drinking tequila. Remember when you threw the empty bottle across the loft and the bottle lodged itself in the drywall? You ended up in bed for several days with the lights out. You stayed up many nights in a row without sleep working on your art. I think all this behavior was a little crazy. You want proof how crazy you were? Look at the drawing you did of yourself in 1981 with all the squiggly lines."

"I was having a hard time dealing with what I had done," I argue. "I had no one to talk to about my plan to see my mother in Las Vegas. The pressure felt enormous. No wonder I was acting so stupid."

"You could have handled the situation in a more mature manner."

"Yeah, right. I could have gone to Vegas dressed up as a showgirl."

"Maybe that would have been better than the stoned way you went."

"I don't know. I needed reinforcement to deal with the situation. As I read, you can see how the situation deteriorated. It wasn't my fault."

"It never is," snipes Carlotta.

Ignoring her, I resume:

"I rise early the following day and drive to the Frontier. Arnold and Lynn are still in their bathrobes. Their state of dishabille makes me uncomfortable. My mother's black bra is quite visible amid the loose folds of her navy blue robe with a white monogrammed 'Lynn' on the left breast. Without makeup, jewels, and evening wear, she looks decidedly more elderly.

"In fact, she reminds me of my grandmother, when I visited her as a child of ten or twelve perhaps, and she'd make me breakfast in her old-fashioned kitchen with the bulbous stove and the wood-framed refrigerator. Nonnie, with no makeup, dressed in a ratty green robe and red slippers, fried eggs and served me juice and cereal from a large tray covered with white china dishes. Her hair was white. Lynn's hair is white, too, or so it looks in the morning with the sun radiating from behind her smiling face.

"Arnold orders breakfast to be delivered to the room. Lynn disappears into the bathroom, and I am left with Arnold, who has his bulldog face buried in a newspaper. The room is even messier than yesterday, with clothes flung on all the furniture. I wish I had I met these two in more formal circumstances, instead of being invited behind the curtain to their private lives.

"Breakfast is delivered promptly. I sit down to hotel eggs and cold toast at a table meant for two. Arnold pulls up to the table in his brown robe with a red monogram. Arnold's robe is open down to his bulging stomach, revealing a reddish purple strip. Catching me looking, he parts the robe even further and says proudly, 'My hernia scar. This is what happens to you when the doctors gut you like a pig.' The hideous discolored seam runs down the middle of his chest from below the breastbone to where it disappears into the folds of the bathrobe above his groin. The scar looks like the lacing in an over-inflated football. Arnold lets out a deep chuckle that shakes the fat mass of his ruined stomach.

carlton davis

Self-portrait; 1981; 22 x 30 inches; colored pencil

"Still in her robe, Lynn reappears from the bathroom. She has put on makeup, which makes her appear years younger. Standing, Lynn nibbles on some toast and drinks some coffee. Our breakfast conversation is directed toward her. It consists mostly of Lynn fishing for compliments from Arnold on her beauty and her wild and crazy character. She ends each question with the word 'Right?' to which Arnold responds with a grunt. When Lynn demands a greater response, she says, 'Right, right?' and touches him across the table. Arnold looks down and with feigned malice says, 'Don't touch me. Watch out! Don't touch me.' He goes into the bathroom and reappears moments later, fully dressed. Lynn tells Arnold not to leave the room, but when she goes into the bathroom to dress, Arnold gives me a conspiratorial wink and slips away to his blackjack tables. I grow to like this man.

"Lynn emerges dressed in a white silk blouse, blue silk pants, and white flats. At the dresser, she puts on an agate necklace and several bracelets. She pulls out two oversized manila envelopes from the bureau drawer and sits down next to me on the bed.

"'These documents have been in Arnold's family for years,' Lynn says, handing the parcels to me. 'Arnold is French Canadian, you know.'

"'What are these?' I ask, opening the first envelope. Inside are twenty-nine pages, measuring eight by twelve inches, handwritten in ink in French. The first page, marked No. 31, is stamped with the seal of the Emperor of France: a circle surrounding a seated woman with her hand on a table, whereupon sits a bust whose chest plate represents the Roman eagle. Below the woman is written '75 Ces.' The pages are variously dated 1787 and 1788. The first page begins, 'Napoleon par la grace de Dieu et les Constitutions de Empires, Emperior des Francais, Roi de L'Italie…'

"'We are not sure, but we think they are something to do with the sale of property in France that was approved by Napoleon,' says Lynn. 'The seal is from Napoleon's court.'

'Are you giving them to me?' I ask.

"'Well, no,' says Lynn. 'We think they are valuable. You could have them appraised in LA and put them up for sale for us. We will give you a percentage of the proceeds. What do you think?'

"'OK,' I say slowly.

"I am thinking that the proposition is a little strange, but maybe this is their way of getting me involved with the family, so why not go along?

"Lynn picks up the second envelope, opens the clasp, and pulls out a stack of black and white photographs. She places a bunch of smaller photos behind her on the bed, keeping a group of eight by tens in her lap.

"'These are eight photos I had taken of you and me before we went away to my sister's place,' Lynn says, picking up the glossy photographs and handing them to me.

"I am astounded. 'I don't remember this at all,' I say. 'How old was I?'

"'You were four or five—I don't really remember. It was before the custody battle.'

"'These are professional pictures, aren't they? I can tell by the way a vignette has been added around the edges. This is the way photographers often do portraits.'

"'Yes. I took you to a photographer in downtown Rochester, near the nightclub.'

"'I have long hair,' I observe shyly. 'What's up with that?' My hair in the photograph falls almost to my shoulders. It has never been this long since my days back in the 1970s when I had really long hair like the hippies. Now that I don't have as much hair on top of my head I keep it shorter. It never falls over my ears like it does in this photograph with my mother.

"'Oh, your grandmother always insisted on that. It was I think a Victorian custom. Boys were supposed to have long hair up to a certain age. I don't remember how old you had to be when it could be cut short. It always seemed ridiculous to me.'

"'I like this one,' I say, pulling out a photo of me grinning ear to ear as my mother, also beaming, tickles me. My arms are rigid in a paroxysm of joy.

"'You loved to be tickled,' says Lynn softly.

"'All children love to be tickled. My daughter loves it. I still like it.'

"Much to my incredulity, Lynn asks me nothing about her granddaughter. An awkward silence settles over us. I continue to shuffle through the photos. The woman in these photographs is a handsome woman, possessed of an imposing rather than a soft or glamorous beauty. Her features are strong, with clear, penetrating eyes and a straight nose that suddenly takes an improbable bend. There is a prominent saddle below the nose. Her lips are not so much large as long, and the lower one curves in a gentle sway. A wry smile dimples her cheeks. A long Egyptian curve emphasizes her narrow eyebrows.

"'Do you think we look alike?' I ask tentatively.

"' Maybe in the eyes and the nose.'

"'Your hair used to be darker. I would guess auburn.'

"'Times change. Let's look at the other photographs.'

"Lynn holds out her hand for me to give her back the eight by tens.

"'Could I have one of these, Lynn?' I ask.

"'Go ahead, take one'

"'I take one, a photograph where both Lynn and I are intently looking toward the camera, and place it on the floor with the envelope of French documents.

"Lynn picks up a packet of small pictures behind her. There are six photographs of me in a sailor suit, taken around the house on Dover Park. In one, I pose with a black dog. In another, I'm riding a tricycle. A third shows me standing beside my mother, sucking my thumb. There are three wintertime pictures of me in the snow, bundled up in coat, boots, mittens, cap, and earmuffs, holding a shovel in my left hand. Lynn is surprised when I tell her I am left-handed.

"'That's curious, I don't remember you being left-handed,' she comments, scrutinizing the photo. 'No one in my family is left-handed. The only left-handed person I knew was Roger Ferguson. No, I'm mistaken. Come to think of it, Peter Lutz is also left-handed.'

"Oh, God, I wonder if I'm not even my father's child. Perhaps I'm Roger Ferguson's. Unnerved by this new possibility, I move on to the next small photograph.

"'That was Easter at your grandmother's house,' Lynn says.

"'I don't remember any of this,' I say.

Lynn laughs curtly. "'We had a hell of time getting you to stand still for the picture. This was right after the Easter egg hunt. Your grandfather wanted to take a picture of us all. He lined us up, but you kept seeing eggs or bunnies in the grass. Just when he was about to take the shot, you would break free and dart out to find the thing you fancied you saw. Of course, you never found anything. It drove your grandmother nuts."

"'Really?'

"'Oh, yes, and your grandmother kept screaming at me, 'Why can't you keep your son in control?' We got in a big argument. It took your grandfather to calm things down. Your grandfather was a good man.'

"'I learned he was carrying on a long-term affair with a woman in New York City, where he worked weekdays,' I reveal. 'He only returned to Rochester on weekends.'

"'Is that so? No wonder I liked him.'

I hand all the pictures back to my mother.

"'I have to go over to the convention bureau to do a little research for an article I am writing,' I say, but what I needed to do was get away for a while and mentally digest the images and information Lynn had just given me.

"As I depart with the eight by ten photo and the French documents in hand, Lynn reminds me Tykie and Debby along with her husband, Mike, are coming over that afternoon. We make a date to meet later for a shopping excursion.

"That afternoon, Lynn and I go for a walk to find a dress shirt and tie for me. A cowgirl hat perched on her head and her long blonde hair falling to her shoulders, she strolls down Las Vegas Boulevard, wearing sequined red shoes, tight red jeans, and a black sweater with pearl necklace, jeweled rings on her fingers. She protests, but not too much, as I backpedal, photographing her. I know the paparazzi treatment pleases her. I am struck by how much she resembles the young hookers parading the boulevard. Still, I am intrigued with this woman. She has spunk and style, where most women her age have descended into bland conformity. Age has not robbed her of a smidgen of her joie de vivre.

"Ungrateful lout! I feel guilty for thinking such thoughts. Still, do I wish my mommy would save my ass? Make everything all right? That's what they are for, isn't it? But no! Nobody is going to save my poor ass. Mom is tight with a buck. She's no intellectual, no fount of understanding. I don't get the feeling she really understands herself. The swagger and the style are an act, her nightclub act. They cover up the abyss of her failure, which she refuses to look into. She gave up two children. Now I find out it is three! She is a Mother Kali, metaphorically strangling her own offspring and dancing with the death's heads around her neck, oblivious to her acts of love denied.

"Or is all this my own projection transferred on to her? Yes, it is. We walk back to the Frontier with my bag of goodies—$124 worth—my mind bewildered and even more fascinated by this woman. I drive back to my motel and spend several more hours wandering the Las Vegas strip thinking all kinds of thoughts about my mother and our meeting.

"This is the real Lynn. She is more than I anticipated; less than I wished. I have to take a break from the contact. I drive around. Smoke a joint. Wash my car. Obsess about what I have seen that morning and early afternoon. I am becoming nervous.

"My mother is a wanton materialist. She is loud, bold, and cheap. She is unable to give me the understanding and sense of the past I want. She doesn't seem at all interested in who I am. She barely glances at the portfolio of my work I proffer for her approval. I feel like a nervous interviewee. Here you are, Madam: My curriculum vitae for the position of your son. My qualifications? I am creative, Madam, as my portfolio demonstrates. Why do I think I'm the best candidate for the job? Well, I have immense potential, and I can tell you with certainty that I would make a good son. All I need is a mother and I could really blossom. You see, I have been a failure so far. I am a big disappointment to myself. I keep thinking there is something missing. If I only I can get this or that, then I could make it. I have degrees. I have experience. I even get married, but nothing works. I am still the same old failure.

"Then I think—actually, I have always thought—what I need is a mother. I have two, but one is a step and the other my father doesn't think I should know. The step one doesn't feel right; the real one becomes my obsession. I find you. Now the whispered truth is, you won't provide what's missing, either. You don't have the key, the word, the thing I need. This is very disappointing.

"Yet I am glad, despite the fact that I am crushed, that I have found you. The void of dream and hope is now fulfilled. The filling isn't precisely what I wanted. Why can't you be a sagacious female writer, like Simone de Beauvoir, Virginia Woolf, or Eudora Welty, or at least some wise old woman? You don't understand me a bit, nor do I think you particularly desire to understand. The son, a caricature, will suffice for you. You are a real human being. I want a concept or a novel. My mother should not be flesh and blood but a desire and a chimera, impossible to achieve. There you are, just another human in the same messy boat. A victim too of the injustices that an indifferent world bestows. You breathe the breath of pain and I am struck numb.

"I wander away to recover from our contact, to try to understand if I love or hate you. Why should I love this woman, just because I emerged into this world through her body? On the one hand, you are the package I got delivered in, nothing more. On the other, I was with you off and on for almost five and a half years. You must have molded me. I can feel it, but the knowledge of what and how is still shrouded in the darkness of unconsciousness.

"What I feel is a bondage. I am constrained in some way. I am still in Mother Kali's womb, with the umbilical cord wrapped tightly around me like rope around a drum. Rebirth is my goal. The father is there, outside. He glowers and warns against transgressions. The father imposes guilt. Is it that I love her whom you blame for your misfortune? How can I not love her? She is my mother. How can I love her? She abandoned me. I must set myself free from this conscious dilemma. These thoughts race through my mind while I wander through the glare of Las Vegas."

"Las Vegas isn't interested in history," says Carlotta. "Las Vegas glorifies the ethos of easy come, easy go. It is as changeable as my costume. Your mother wasn't much for history either, Carlton."

"I know. I know. The history is probably too painful, but I needed some closure."

"You opened Pandora's Box. You couldn't close it then, and you can't close it now. It was a good thing you did find your mother, even if the results were not what you wanted or expected. You did advance our cause of hope for personal understanding."

"I had hope, but that got dashed in the dinner party on New Year's Eve."

"You know as well as I, good often comes with bad."

Carlotta rises from our bench with her heels dangling from one hand and walks away.

"Where are you going, Carlotta?"

"It's time for the next show. I have to change costumes. Maybe you should get dressed in top hat and tails for the next part of our story."

"I still have a suit with silk shirt and fancy tie."

"Then I shall await anxiously the next installment with you formally dressed. Perhaps I will tap dance for you."

"I will need a few gin and tonics to appreciate your dancing."

"Carlotta is a good dancer. You must be sober to appreciate it. Drinking and smoking will dull your senses to our search for truth."

"There are no drugs or alcohol around Las Encinas to get happy with."

"Oh, you would be surprised about that."

CHAPTER 12

DINNER IS "COMP," LIFE ISN'T

"Swedish meatballs!" Carlotta snorts. "I didn't know you liked Swedish meatballs. You wolfed down three helpings of them at dinner tonight along with all that heavy gravy."

"Christ, you startled me!" I exclaim. "Can't you give me a moment's peace without appearing out of nowhere? Keep it down or you'll wake up Smitty."

It is late at night and I am reading my journals at the desk in the alcove of my room in Las Encinas. I have gone through nine books already and I still have twelve to go.

"We are talking about Swedish meatballs!" Carlotta persists. "If you keep eating like you are, you will become one gigantic meatball and I will never fit into my costumes. Already, I am feeling a little squeezed."

"It's the medication, I tell you. This Depakote stuff makes you want to eat like a bear. I can't get filled up no matter how much I eat."

"Well, what are you going to do about it? I tell you, Carlotta is not going to become the Goodyear blimp. I have a svelte figure I intend to keep."

"We are stuck until they find me a doctor. It's either that or I don't take their medication."

"How long did they tell you we would have to wait?"

"Three or four days, the nurses said."

"It is only Monday now. In three or four days, I could look like Aretha Franklin, the soul sister diva! This is unacceptable—go talk to the nurse. I will need a derrick to stand me up."

"Those meatballs were good," I comment, smacking my lips. "I could use some more right now. Especially after the bad food I am reading about."

"You are back in Vegas, no doubt, reviewing the disaster of the mother and child reunion. Didn't I tell you not to eat anything while we were there?"

"The marijuana gave me the munchies."

"Oh, yes, I forgot about that, Carlton. Your affinity for pot will get us banished from the thin set, but it is not as bad as your Swedish meatball fetish. I swear, you become addicted to substances so fast, it makes my headdress spin."

"Not fair, Carlotta, you became addicted to other stuff, which turned you into a complete slut."

"No! No! No! I am not going to let you have that one. We are discussing Swedish meatballs."

"*You* are discussing meatballs. *I* am studying my Las Vegas adventure."

"Perhaps you should read to me. That way we can leave your meatball-blocked arteries alone and I can recall my fantastic appearances."

"OK, here we go."

"New Year's Eve, dressed in my European-cut pinstriped blue suit, pale blue Oscar de la Renta shirt, and blue floral tie, I return to the Frontier. Anxious about meeting my newfound sisters, I dawdle to watch the pudgy matrons chuck coins into the one-armed bandits. I stroll past The Gourmet Room, The Branding Iron, and the party room en route to Lynn's room. A television in the corridor is playing a bowl game. Arriving at last at Room 108, I knock and a woman who could be my sister Carolee opens the door. Surprised, I step back.

"You look just like my sister Carolee," I say. The woman says nothing and turns aside to let me in the room. Lynn is on the phone, dressed only in her flesh-colored bra and panties. She quickly covers up her breasts with her arm and waves gaily with the other. 'This is your sister Tykie,' she calls out before returning to her call. Lynn's voice grows loud and angry before she hangs up.

"'That call was your sister Debby,' she reports. 'She and Mike have arrived. They expect to be comped through Arnold's influence. I told them we can't do it, that the hotel is cracking down. Debby is angry. She's threatening to return to LA tomorrow if she and Mike and she aren't made complimentary guests like we are.'

"'I'm sure that's Mike's influence,' Tykie sneers.

"'Debby is angry about our choice of restaurant, too,' says Lynn. 'She wants The Gourmet Room and we have reservations for The Branding Iron next door. It's a good place for steak and Arnold likes his steak.'

"'That's a lousy place,' Tykie grumbles.

"'Too bad, reservations can't be changed this late,' says Lynn as she fumbles to find her robe amid the clothes piled on every chair while shielding her nakedness from my view.

"'Don't be so uptight, Mom,' Tykie teases her. 'After all, he's your son, isn't he?'

"Lynn shoots her a dirty look as she hastily dons a blue robe with 'Lynn' embroidered on the left breast. 'Oh, hush,' she says. 'Debby, Mike, and Arnold are down in the Casino, waiting for us. We need to get dressed.'

"'God, you look just like our mother!' Tykie gushes, searching my face. Your nose, your eyes. You are so talented, too. I looked at your book. You're not at all like Peter.'

"I laugh nervously and sit down on the edge of the bed. Lynn and Tykie start to clown. They do a vaudeville act, poking fun at each other, rough but tender. I am glad I smoked a joint in the parking lot before I came. It hides my nervousness and gives me the distance to observe their peculiar actions.

"'You have joined a crazy family,' says Lynn. 'Tykie is real crazy.'

"'No, Debby is more,' Tykie retorts.

"'Only in certain ways. Well, you will find out, Carlton.'

"They laugh and chatter away at each other, then ask me to leave so they can finish getting dressed.

"'You will find Mike and Arnold are at the blackjack tables, I bet,' Tykie tells me.

"I am relieved to leave the room. In spite of my stoned state, I find am very uncomfortable in this room with Lynn, who reminds me of my grandmother, and Tykie, who could be the clone of my sister Carolee. I haven't been confronted with something new, but a version of something old."

"What did you expect, Carlton, an re-enactment of upper class manners and neurosis?" asks Carlotta. "We are in Las Vegas, not the Hamptons or Martha's Vineyard."

"I see you have changed your costume again," I observe. "What are you bulging out of? The bust is booming and the hips are … how shall I put this? A bit cramped."

"You are most unkind! I am a cocktail waitress, dressed for New Year's Eve. Don't you remember me? I was trying to keep you sober. I couldn't bring you drinks fast enough to keep pace with your prodigious thirst. I remember your lascivious looks at my outfit."

"I don't remember that at all."

"What?" scoffs Carlotta, offended. "You don't remember my red-sequined top hat with the big red bow, my red bow tie over the starched white collar, or my long, red velvet sleeves?"

"Not a thing!"

"Surely you must remember my red-sequined bodice with the cleavage down to my waist, my fishnet stockings, and red heels."

"Nope. Nein. Nay."

"Well, there you go! You weren't very observant. See what alcohol and pot will do to you? You think it makes your senses more acute, but really it dulls them down."

"I wish I could forget the whole Las Vegas experience. Do you think I was crazy to go and meet Lynn?"

"I certainly think you were not well balanced in your head. Perhaps if you were, events might have gone better."

"At that time, I didn't think a little pot could hurt me. Everyone I knew smoked it. Marijuana is the artist's martini. It sharpens your awareness of space and colors."

"You didn't smoke a little. You smoked a lot."

"I guess I can't deny that."

"You smoked pot, and it colored everything around you. The colors may have been more vivid, but pot colored your perception of everthing else. It fed your neurosis."

"Was I sick then?"

"You were, but you didn't know it."

"Allow me get back to my reading."

"I could go serve some drinks to the patients. A Lithium Fizz, a Seroquel Manhattan, a Lamictal Tonic, or a Klonopin Daiquiri."

"Well, why don't you, then?" I bluster and continue reading:

"I wander away, wondering if I can find a man in tan blazer, a red Izod Lacoste 'alligator' shirt, and white shoes in the crowds of the casino. I eventually find him, playing with Mike, at the last table next to the casino door. Mike presents a contrast. He is Mr. Joe College, circa 1960, with a tweed jacket and an open white shirt. I see myself ten years ago. They are too busy to speak. I am distracting them from their playing. I head for the bar, where a waitress in a red-sequined top hat serves me a gin and tonic."

"See, you did remember," says Carlotta. "I even complimented you, big boy, on your suit and tie."

"I don't remember. Let me read."

"I don't gamble, nor would I waste my money in this manner if I had it. Debby, the other sister, finds me near the bar, watching the red-clad waitresses serve drinks. Debby looks amazingly like my other sister Debby. She bombards me with banal questions—'Did you meet Mother?' 'Are you happy you came?'—that are hard to hear given the volume of noise all around us, and even harder to answer given my state of confusion. She tells me she is just two months newly married. We are both uncomfortable. She stomps off to retrieve her husband. I drift away to purchase cigarettes, hoping the distraction of smoking will keep my anxiety at bay.

"When I return, Mike, Debby, and Arnold are standing at the red bar: red leather seats, red napkins, red fluorescent lighting, and red-dressed cocktail waitresses.

Mike asks me with utter nonchalance, 'What do you think about all this, Carlton, old boy?'

"I pretend not to notice how strange this is. The wayward son appears thirty-two years later. The meeting takes place in a Las Vegas casino. The son gets to meet the sisters for the first time. The sisters look just like his other sisters. One even has the same name as this other sister. What do I think, he asks? Oh, well, nothing unusual about it all. Perfectly normal, happens every day. I am silent, pondering my answers. I am about to make a witty and sarcastic observation when Lynn and Tykie arrive and deflect the uncomfortable conversation.

bipolar bare

"Lynn is wearing a silvery sequined dress with matching slippers. She has a diamond necklace on her thin neck and diamond bracelets on her skinny wrists. Her narrow face is made up with bright red lipstick and her eyebrows lined in the same long curve I saw in the vintage photograph. Her daughter is wearing the dress Lynn wore last evening. Arnold orders more drinks and drifts off. Lynn retrieves him. Arnold is impish, hanging his head like a schoolboy. He straightens up when Lynn pushs him back into the group. After this amusing scene, we follow Lynn to the Branding Iron for dinner. She has prevailed on the choice of restaurant.

"The service is really abysmal. Bickering breaks out between Lynn and the two daughters. It gets worse as we wait for our dinners. Civility breaks down between Tykie and Mike. Debby grows surly toward Lynn. We sit there an hour, waiting for our food. Other tables are served and guests leave, yet our dinner still hasn't arrived. I become dismayed at the tone of the conversation. It reminds me of home, where my father, stepmother, and Debby become discourteous with one another.

"'This wouldn't have happened if we had gone to the Gourmet Room,' Debby grouses to Lynn. 'You know this is a horrid restaurant.'

"Arnold gets up and complains to the manager, who comes to the table.

"'We are comp,' says Lynn airily. 'We shouldn't be treated so insouciantly.'

"The manager tries to explain his problems. It is New Year's Eve. Some help is off, some has quit. Mike jumps into the fray, getting hot with the manager. Tykie makes a disparaging comment to Debby about Mike's temper.

"'Mike is being nicer to the manager than you are to Mike,' Debby observes cattily.

"'Well, Mike is an asshole,' Tykie retorts succinctly.

"'Why don't you just be quiet, Tykie?' says Mike.

"'Don't try to tell me what to do,' Tykie snaps. 'You're always trying to boss me around.'

"I sit silently, bewildered by the animosity.

"The steaks finally arrive, cold and tough as an old shoe. The baked potatoes are tepid at best. The green beans are limp and tasteless.

"Tykie snipes, 'This food is terrible. It's like something Mike would serve.'

"'Why don't you shut the hell up?' Mike seethes.

"Debby rallies around her husband. 'Mike is always kind to you, Tykie, and all you do is give him lip. You stayed at our place for two weeks. Mike took care of you.'

"'I don't care!' Tykie roars. 'I am sick of him bossing me around, so butt out!'

"'You have no right to speak to Mike that way!' Debby replies, her eyes welling. 'I am sick of you.' She storms out of the restaurant, leaving everyone to contemplate their leathery steaks.

"'I have had it with you,' Mike informs Tykie menacingly. Tykie is on the verge of tears. Lynn tries to console her.

"'Leave me alone, Mom,' Tykie says.

"'Tykie gets very emotional,' Lynn confides to me.

"Tykie protests, 'I'm not the only one who is emotional.'

"Lynn looks at me apologetically and says, 'See what you have got yourself into? This is strange family.'

"Tykie vents her wrath on Lynn and Arnold. 'Are you two sure we are a family?' she says cruelly. 'Are you two even married?'

"'Watch out what you're saying, Tykie,' warns Arnold in a low, angry tone.

"'Every time I come home, you're in different bedrooms—separate bedrooms,' Tykie continues, grinning impishly. 'Curiouser and curiouser, cried Alice.'

"'Cool it, Tykie,' Mike interjects.

"Tykie turns to me and says, 'Don't you want to see what a strange family this is, brother dearest?'

"I say nothing, loath to give her encouragement.

"'Don't you two ever sleep together?' says Tykie, going for the throat.

"'OK, Tykie, that's enough,' says Arnold with quiet malovelence.

"'Sure we do, honey' Lynn insists, but her genial façade is crumbling.

"'When was the last time, fifteen years ago?' Tykie suggests.

"'Boy you really are an asshole,' Mike puts in.

"Tykie retorts: 'Not as much of an asshole as you, who has got to boss everyone around all the time.'

"I stand up at this point and announce, 'When civility reigns again, I will return.' I toss my napkin on the table and walk out."

"Not getting what you expected are you, Carlton?" says Carlotta. "You wanted to find an American family where everything was wonderful and everyone treated each other with respect."

"That's not what I wanted. I just wanted to find my mother and know more about her."

"What you got is reality, the big picture of your mother in her world, which isn't pretty. After all, Lynn never really bothered to find you. She was dealing with problems of her own."

"You know, I never saw those two sisters again after that visit to Las Vegas, nor Arnold either."

"You imposed that on yourself because you couldn't deal with them."

"We'll talk about that later," I say and continue reading:

"What have I got myself into? This family is just as dysfunctional as the Davises! The hatred and hurt are carbon copies of some of the Davis family's verbal rows. I have just exchanged one sick situation for another. Two hurt daughters of a second—or is it a third?—marriage rail against one another and their parents. I don't need this!

"When I return to the restaurant, a smiley waiter is clearing away the dishes. Arnold, Mike, and Tykie stand near the table. The waiter listens to their complaints about the horrible service. He keeps smiling while Arnold and Mike vent their anger at the indignities they have suffered. They are comp, after all, and deserve better. Arnold doesn't leave a tip. Mother has gone to spruce up. Mike leaves to find Debby. Tykie and I go for a stroll around the pool.

"'Lynn is living on diet pills you know—Dexedrine,' Tykie confides to me.

"'I never saw her eat a bite of steak, but no one ate much of anything, it was so lousy,' I reply, adding ironically, 'It was an amazing dinner, to say the least.'

"'I call her Ana Rex for anorexia,' Tykie says. 'Lynn has lost a lot of weight. She is twenty pounds lighter. She is the same size as me, her twenty-seven-year-old daughter. I am wearing her dress tonight.'

"'I hear losing a lot of weight too quickly is dangerous.'

"'She won't listen, she's too vain. Her chief asset is her good looks. Now that she's over sixty, her goal is to keep projecting an aura of glamour. She'd rather starve herself than see her figure go to flab.'

"'She is the most attractive woman I've seen in Las Vegas,' I gush. 'She knows it and flaunts it.'

"'In Las Vegas, she is a queen,' Tykie concurs. 'In Buffalo, she does the laundry, if she does anything."

"She didn't want to be a mother, and seeing you, a middle-aged man, probably didn't give her a good feeling about herself," Carlotta conjectures. "I am sure her emotions were equally mixed at the appearance of her first son."

"Carlotta, you speak with wisdom for once."

"You were too much under the influence of marijuana to be so wise at the time."

"I didn't think it influenced me that much."

"But it did. You thought it brought out the creative in you. All it did was slow you down and distort whatever state you were in. In this case, I think it increased the stress."

"Was I mentally ill, then?

"I can't attest to that yet. But you weren't sober. Too many joints! Too many gin and tonics!"

"Was it you who served me too many drinks, Miss Top Hat?"

"Only if your imagination can personalize the waitress."

"Then I *would* be crazy."

"A thought to ponder. Please return to your description of events."

"New Year's Eve is a complete bust. I go to the gala celebration for a short time and return to my hotel. I am tired. I want to go back to Los Angeles. On New Year's Day, Lynn, Arnold, Debby, and Tykie have breakfast with me in Lynn's hotel room. They seem to have forgotten the tempestuousness of last night. Lynn gives me her sister's name and telephone number and suggests I call her for further illumination.

"After saying my goodbyes, I drive back with a sense of relief. I have seen Lynn and learned a lot. I am not sure I want to see her again or learn more. I speculate that the sisters staged the fight and Tykie's baiting of Lynn and Arnold in an attempt to drive me away. If that is true, their ruse nearly succeeded, but I still have these French documents to deal with, and there is Lynn's sister. A week later, curiosity overcomes my reticence. I call Helene Carloni, Lynn's sister, for one more piece of the puzzle."

CHAPTER 13

QUESTIONS AND NO ANSWERS

SITTING BY MY WINDOW in Las Encinas one evening after medications and dinner, I am reading about events that took place twenty years ago. They remain vivid in my mind, with the journals only providing corroborating details. To be so obsessed is a sickness that I can't let go of. The answers to my questions never seem enough. I am left with an enormous void that demands exploration and filling.

Seeing my mother only increased that desire. Yes, I got to see who she was and what she looked like—satisfying in themselves—but the story of the little boy and what happened to him seems murkier than before. I opened Pandora's box and an enormous anger flew out, an anger that plagues me to this day. I am sure these events and the anger that arose from them are the root cause of my mental disorder. No hope came to me after meeting my mother. I have to dig deeper. The journals chronicle the search.

I decide to contact my sister Carolee to tell her what I have done. We haven't talked or communicated in four or more years, except for the obligatory Christmas card. It's pleasant to hear her voice, and we talk for quite some time. She says she is sad that she has a brother but grew up alone. I tell her I never understood why we weren't together. I tell her Lynn told me she had given me up thinking we two would be together. We never were. Carolee wants me to know that she understands and supports what I am doing.

"Did Lynn ask about me?" Carolee asks.

"No. Amazingly, she didn't seem too interested."

"She was never interested in me."

I try to ease Carolee's pain, reminding her that it was I, growing up, that spent the most time with Lynn. Carolee tells me that Lynn would leave her upstairs screaming in the attic apartment across the hall from the closet where we had our

bipolar bare

tea parties and go out. Grandmother told her Lynn was disappointed that Carolee was a girl.

"You have to remember," I say, "Lynn was less than eighteen years old at the time and Grandmother probably made her miserable, since she came from the wrong side of the tracks and snared her favorite son."

Carolee thinks she knows more than me of the whole sorry history, as comments would slip out over the dining table. I can picture that table, a thick articulated cherry slab that can seat ten with inlay around the perimeter in three bands of lighter wood, the middle band a two-inch wide checkerboard. The table stands on bulbous legs and fat clawed feet. It is always partly draped with a linen runner down the middle, and the runner covered with crystal goblets, decanters, small tureens, Tiffany candlesticks, and silver boxes for matches, salt, and pepper. Sideboards of the best American antique cabinetry full of the finest dinner linen, dishes, and cutlery flank the table on three sides. From above, the portraits of the ancestors look down upon the diners. Carolee is seated on one side. Grandmother sits on the end nearest the kitchen and the sideboard with the huge silver soup tureen on top. Grandfather is seated at the other end nearest the double doors to the living room with the parlor chair where he likes to sleep. Grandmother would pontificate. Grandfather would agree. Carolee would eat her food like a lady.

Carolee knows about the court cases—the divorce, the custody battle, and Roger Ferguson. She knows about the times Lynn came to the house to demand me back from the family and was rebuffed. She knows about the time Lynn came and the family had to give me up. On other points, however, she is as much in the dark as I am. She didn't know about our father's criminal career and how Grandmother got him off. I could not elaborate on his deal with Nonnie because it would be pure conjecture.

Carolee tells me how she found the log of the detectives who trailed Lynn and documented her affair with Roger Ferguson in an old desk she cleaned out at our grandmother's house after she died. The desk is part of her inheritance. She didn't have time to read the log, nor was she terribly interested. She gave the log to my father. I tell her I am going to call my father next to tell him I have met Lynn.

Carolee says she can visualize my father sputtering upon receiving my call. Daddy Carlie—Carolee has always called our father that to distinguish him from her grandfather, who was her adoptive father—will be dismayed and will call her. Once, not long ago, he called Carolee to say there are a lot of things in the past that required explanation, but he never followed up. She says Daddy Carlie and Nonnie are both very pigheaded and opinionated. They won't admit to anything unless pushed, and Carolee decided long ago not to do so. We laugh. Our conversation drifts away from this history. At the end, before we hang up, she says she doesn't want me to tell Lynn where she lives. I reassure her I won't.

I look up from my journal and see Carlotta standing before me, dressed in her nurse's uniform. Around her neck hangs a stethoscope and in one hand she holds a glass thermometer.

"So, you're back for a visit, eh, Carlotta?" I say. "I see you have abandoned your career as a showgirl and cocktail waitress. What are you now, an angel of mercy for the sick?"

"Maybe, or I could be an actress, playing the part of nurse," Carlotta replies. "You know how both of us love those old vaudeville skits with the doctor and nurse. Remember Groucho Marx striding about with his cigar, wiggling his eyebrows and calling 'Nurse! Nurse!'? A buxom nurse arrives and the comedy begins. I also remember when you went to the strip shows in Boston as a youth, and the nurse/doctor routines that served as segues between strippers. You have a thing for funny nurses. I am that nurse."

"No, I do not!" I argue petulantly. "Besides, I was only seventeen or eighteen when I went to the stripper shows. We had to sneak in, pretending we were legal age. The humor was atrocious. The strippers were funnier than the comedians."

"Nevertheless, I am here to lighten up your mood. You get so preoccupied with this long forgotten history, I have appeared to provide a different perspective."

"This history is not long forgotten. It is very important to me!"

"And no one else! Who cares if you had a difficult childhood? Only you. I bet every one else in this hospital had a similarly shitty upbringing, as it were."

"That's the point. If I can come to grips with this history, I can regain my mental health!"

"Now you are getting all worked up. Can I listen to your heart?"

Carlotta takes the stethoscope and puts the earpieces in her ears, then bends over and places the resonator on my chest.

"Make sure you peek at my cleavage—it's traditional," she says. "Don't you want to make some off-color remark?"

"No, I don't, you boob!"

"Darling, I have two boobs. Can't you count? Now you are getting overheated. How about I take your temperature? Rectal is best. Bend over and drop your pants," she commands, shaking the glass thermometer back and forth.

"Will you get out of here? Go back to where you came from!"

"Since I came from you, I shall return to you and you can read on. But remember, there is humor in even the most dreadful things."

"I'll remember that. I am going back to my reading now."

"My father answers the phone when I dial Columbus. I had hoped I would get my stepmother first and talk to her. A sympathetic soul, she would understand what I had done and thus ease the way before I revealed the visit to my father, but it was not to be.

"'I met my mother, Lynn, in Las Vegas, Dad,' I blurt out, 'I hired a detective agency to get her name and the telephone number. I contacted her and we met up in Las Vegas over New Year's Eve.'

"There is a long period of silence.

"'Why did you do that?' Dad castigates me. 'I could have given you her name and telephone number any time.'

"'What!' I yell. I want to jump through the phone line and grab my father around the neck and strangle him, but I am silent, breathing hard, trying not to call my father every curse word I know.

"'I said, all you had to do is ask me and I would give you her name and number,' Dad repeats.

"I am nearly beside myself with suppressed anger. 'For years, I asked you for exactly that and you refused me. When did you change your mind? Did you have this information when I came back from England and you told me not to open Pandora's box?'

"'I don't remember.'

"'You have a very convenient memory, Father. Now Pandora's box is open. I know about your criminal enterprise. You must have had a pretty good scam going to be indicted for a felony for stealing cigarettes.'

"'Yes, I did,' he says, laughing sardonically.

"'Well, what happened?'

"'Two days in the can. My life passed before me.'

"'Then Nonnie got you out. You struck a deal with her. She would get you out of the jam, but you had to leave Lynn. Isn't that right?"

"'Is that what she told you?' says Dad, irritation creeping into his voice.

"'Not in so many words.'

"'Did she tell you about her part in the enterprise? No, she wouldn't tell you that!' His voice is starting to rise

"'But you struck a deal with Nonnie, didn't you?'

"'Yeah. Sort of.'

" Where was I? Was I with you when you stole the cigarettes?'

"'No, you weren't!' Dad is yelling now.

"'Where was I then? Was I with Nonnie? Was I with Lynn?'

"'I don't remember.'

" Lynn says I was with you.'

"'Lynn's a liar.'

"'Then you tell me the truth!'

"Dad sighs heavily. 'I will send you the detective reports on Lynn's activities so you can decide for yourself what's really true,' he promises and hangs up."

Reading this passage puts me in a rage. I decide I must go for a walk to regain my equilibrium. I stride out of the hospital and march around the field of grass behind the administration wing. I want a cigarette but have none. Twenty years, and I am still angry with my father's response! He knows how to push my buttons. Why I am letting this get to me now? Unresolved issues, I think. My lingering animosity about my parents poisons my relationship with the world today. My mother is dead, but still I am angry with her. My father still lives, but I can't let go of the many ways he has caused me pain. The story makes me crazy.

bipolar bare

"You know, a nice ice bath would cool you off," Carlotta suggests. She is walking next to me, still holding her thermometer and shaking the glass tube like a wand. "Too bad you never had one when you were at Yale New Haven Hospital. It might have changed your life."

"Nothing would change my life. I have already lived it, and it is a miserable failure because of what happened to me so long ago."

"Other wounded beings have broken loose from their tragedies and risen above their circumstances."

"I can't seem to do it. I am held down by the past."

"You allow yourself to be held down."

"What do you mean by that? Your bedside manner leaves much to be desired."

"Figure it out for yourself. In the meantime, I suggest in lieu of an ice bath—they seem to have gone out of favor—why don't you take a cold shower? Then we can take your psychic temperature. You see, what I have is no ordinary thermometer. It measures your mental temperature."

Carlotta shows me the thermometer. Indeed, it is different. The bulb at the end is bigger than a typical glass thermometer, and the shaft is slightly larger and longer. Inscribed in very small letters on the side is a scale that goes from "calm" to "agitated" to "angry" and ends in "rage".

"Bunk!" I cry. "You're a charlatan, Carlotta. The thermometer is a toy."

"We shall see, Carlton. Your mood can be easily read with my device."

"All right, stick it my mouth, then, and let's see what it says."

"I am sorry, but this is not an oral thermometer. It must be inserted somewhere else."

"Right, right, we've been down this shtick before, if I'm not mistaken. Why do you plague me with these weird thoughts?"

"I speak only the thoughts that you do not allow to be spoken to anyone but me."

"All right, that's enough. Time for me to return to my reading. The part where I call Helene Carloni, Lynn's sister, is coming up."

"Too bad, I had a great routine for us with the mood thermometer."

"'Of course I remember you,' Helene says to me when I phone her on the second day after my return to Los Angeles. I tell her about meeting Lynn in Las Vegas after all these years, and Lynn saying how she will have something interesting to tell me about my childhood.

"'Do you remember what happened?' I ask.

"'Let me see. Your mother brought you here. Your uncle Vinnie, my husband, didn't think it was a good idea that Lynn should leave you with us. He said it was just going to make more trouble for her, but she wouldn't listen. My sister can be very stubborn. It was just before the court case. You always had a book. You could read even when you were so young. Macaroni, sausage, and sauce, that's what you liked to eat.'

"'What else?' I ask anxiously.

"'Let me collect my thoughts, it was so long ago. We were living on Spring Street near Howard Avenue and the Yale Yacht Club. You were four or five. Was it 1949 or 1950? It was 1949, I'm sure of it. It all happened on February 11, 1949, to be exact—my birthday. I remember the suckling pig we had for my party. Your father and the sheriff snatched you on that day. They came to our house after dark, making deep imprints in the snow. The street was full of police cars. They spoke through bullhorns, demanding entry. The police broke our door in. Your father marched in and took you. I was screaming at your father, 'You have no job!' Your father called Vinnie a wop and said we were unfit to care for you because of our dogs, the Great Danes. You liked the big dogs. You were screaming, 'I don't want to go. I won't go!' Your father had to pull you and your teddy bear off the rocking horse upstairs. You were yelling and kicking at your father while he carried you down the stairs. The cops held us back at gunpoint. That was a sad birthday. I always thought you were a brilliant kid.'

" Wow, that is quite a story, Helene,' I say.

"'That wasn't the end of it, either. The disturbance in the neighborhood was so big, we had to move. We never saw you again after that.'

"Do you and Vinnie have a deli and restaurant on Davenport Avenue called "Vinnie's?'

"Why, yes, we do. How do you know this?'

"'I just had a hunch. Actually, you did meet me again. I came into your restaurant once or twice and had a grinder, but you and I didn't know who each other were by then.'

"I didn't tell Helene that I was there on supervised walks from the psychiatric ward of Yale New Haven Hospital. Our group of patients on our way to release stopped at Vinnie's for lunch. I remember feeling there was something familiar about the woman who took our orders.

"'I still like macaroni, sausage, and sauce,' I tell Helene just before we say goodbye. I never talk to her again.

"In the weeks that follow, I take the French documents around LA to dealers who specialize in antique manuscripts. At each one, I hear the same story. These papers are commonly palmed off on unsuspecting tourists to France, especially those who visit the casinos in Monte Carlo. Agents will sell the documents to American gamblers, or exchange them for debt, misrepresenting them as priceless artifacts of the Napoleonic regime. Although the documents date from the time inscribed on the documents, the late eighteenth century, they are as common as dirt and worthless. Thousands and thousands of them were produced by the government at the time, covering all kinds of minor transactions. I feel like I have been had. These documents certainly didn't come through Arnold's family. They were gotten on a gambling junket to Monte Carlo.

"In March, Lynn and I have another meeting at a restaurant in Redondo Beach, where I accuse her of sending me on a wild goose chase with the French documents. She is unmoved and in turn confronts me with an accusation that the only reason that I came to find her was to get money from her and Arnold. She says Tykie and Debby believe this is why I contacted her. I am scalded by the allegation. It burns at my soul. Is there is some truth in it? Originally, I had never thought of contacting her for money, but when I find out Arnold is rich, I do fantasize that she will help me financially in my struggle to become an artist. She doesn't want to help. I leave the meeting angry, questioning why I ever made the effort to contact her in the first place.

"My anger swells to hatred as I mull over the conversation from the restaurant the next day. Lynn and I are to meet. I wait all day and stew, waiting for her call. Poisonous thoughts arise as I work on the construction of my loft. She finally calls me in the evening, precluding any meeting between us. She has spent the day in Beverly Hills, shopping with her daughter. I am enraged. I tell her I don't want to see her any more. She hangs up the phone with a terse 'fine.' Our reunion was without joy and leaves me crazed, full of fury, and depressed. I retreat into my loft, where I stay in bed and sleep for four days.

"Do you need a cold compress on your forehead?" Carlotta inquires. "I can see your brain smoldering."

I ignore her witticism. "That was the last time I ever talked to Lynn. My attempt to make contact with my mother turned out to be a complete disaster."

"Did you think your meeting was going to be like a movie of the week? Long lost son meets his mother and a happy ending to all his pain and sorrow ensues. What a crock!"

"Carlotta, I don't know what I expected, but that's certainly not how it turned out. The story was murkier than ever. What happened after my father got arrested? Where was I? Was I with my father when he was arrested? What happened to Lynn after my father took me from the Carlonis? I needed to know more. After I met Lynn, the scenario seemed to mushroom in scope and complexity, instead of growing smaller and becoming more manageable."

"You are denying the anger you felt. After all, she did abandon you. Only your father stuck by you."

"Stuck by me? What the hell do you mean? He denied me, too. He would not provide the information so I could learn the truth. He shipped me off whenever he could to get me out of the way."

"You are not seeing clearly. Your anger blinds you to the truth. It is part of your sickness. You must come to terms with all that happened to you. I am here to help you. You sure you don't need a cold compress?"

"Leave me alone."

"I did, way back then, and you went out and did crazy things. You isolated yourself in your loft, refused to talk to friends, and went out at night to bathhouses."

"I am better now."

"No, you aren't. You need the care of Carlotta, muse and nurse."

"Did you know I met with my stepmother a long time later to ask her why

I wasn't in any of her and my father's wedding pictures? Who am I kidding? You know everything, even when you pretend you don't."

"Carlotta does this so you can unscramble the images and events that have you walled up inside yourself. Somehow, some way before your days come to an end, we will get you beyond your obsession and your sickness. Now, tell me about what you learned from your stepmother."

"OK. This is what I wrote."

"Stepmother Lois shows me the photos of her wedding to my father in the summer of 1949. Flowers are in bloom all around. The pictures show Carolee, the flower girl, Grandmother and Grandfather, Lois and Carl, and Lois' parents. They are in the rock garden in Coudersport, Pennsylvania at Lois' parents' home.

"'Where was I?' I ask.

"'You were at the farm,' Lois replies.

"'The farm? What farm?' I respond quizzically.

"'The foster farm your grandmother sent you to when she couldn't handle you. She placed you there until we could collect you after the wedding.'

"'I was in a foster home?' I seethe through gritted teeth.

"'Yes. And right after the honeymoon, we came to the farm and picked you up and took you to Corning, New York.'

"'I don't remember this.'

"'It's best that you don't. You had nightmares every night for a year and wet the bed. I had to come in and hold you and read you stories. I tried to be a good mother to you, but often you would tell me how much you hated me. You wanted your real mother, you'd say. You really hurt me. Caring for you was very hard for me.'

"'I'm sorry, Mom. There are things I had to do. Things I had to know.'"

Overcome with emotion, I stop reading. A patronizing voice interrupts my reverie.

"Maybe Carlotta will have to tell you the whole story."

"Somebody needs to tell me something so this story will stop driving me crazy."

"You were drifting, unmoored, rudderless, and lost after you found your mother. This was not a good time for you. Your mental disorder became greater, your dependence on pot stronger, and your descent into deep periods of depression longer. I could not help you."

Holding my arm, nurse Carlotta guides me to my bed. She tells me I need to rest. She gives me a cold compress for my head. I thank her graciously but decline her offer to gauge my mood with her thermometer.

Later, at the process group meeting, I don't mention my journal readings or my conversations with Carlotta. All the patients and the staff would think me really crazy if I spoke of my muse.

CHAPTER 14

ATTACK OF THE BLACK BRAIN

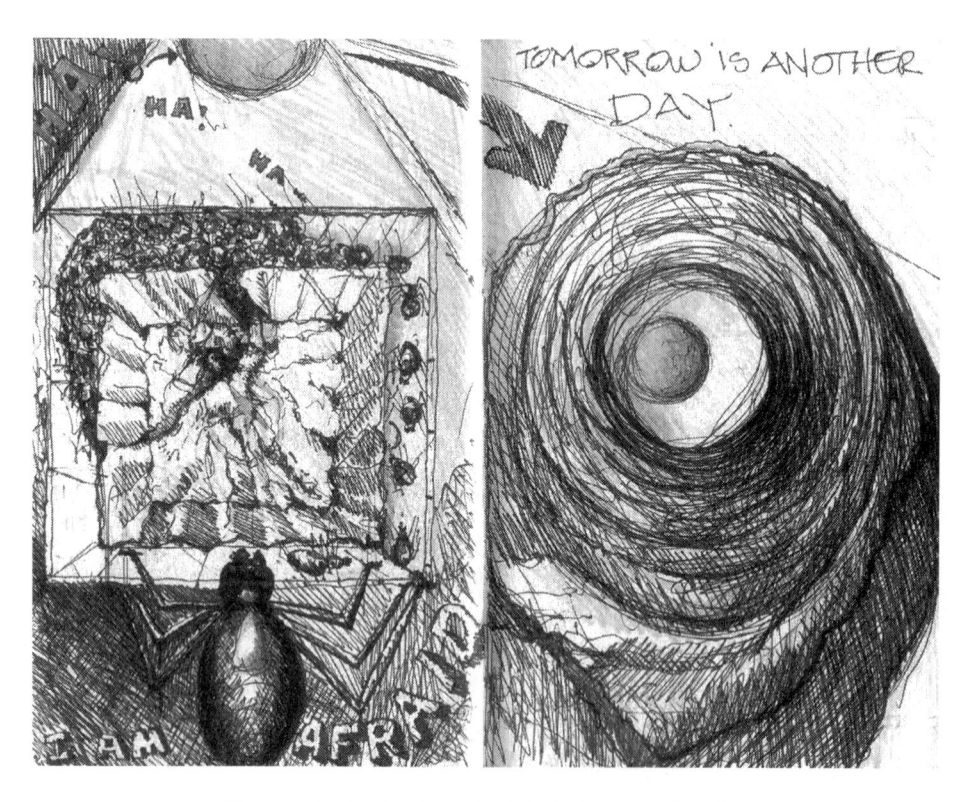

Tomorrow Is Another Day; sketch book; ink pen and marker

It is Tuesday, after lunch. After binging on spaghetti and meatballs, I am in my room alone, still unaccountably hungry. I have a sketchbook open to a page with the legend, "Tomorrow is another day." The sketch thereon tells the story of an attack of the black brain, where I retreat into my cocoon of the silken curtain in the midst of my half-constructed loft. I am in bed, beneath my quilt with the orange star in its middle, dreaming at midday. I am powerless to move as my prostrate body awaits the attack. Hundreds of black spiders skitter outside my curtain, seeking to get in. The largest mother spider, a poisonous black widow with a red hourglass on her shiny, bulbous back, has climbed over the top of the walls of the studio. She will drop down inside the curtain and strike any minute now, biting me and filling me with her poison of deep depression.

I laugh at my unavoidable fate. I mock the spiders, saying, "Kill me, see if I care." I am afraid of life, not death. When the black widow spider and her brood bite me and their work is done, I will be gone from life. Yet, the sun rises to the funnel of dark clouds. There is light at the end of the dark swirling tunnel, a tightening umbilical cord wrapped around the void. The sun shines, and tomorrow is another day. If I can survive until tomorrow, the black attack may pass.

Am I mad? I recall my depressions grew ever worse. The black brain attacks happened more and more frequently. I finished putting the silver insulation in my ceiling. Frustration and anger well up at the Sisyphean task of fixing up the loft. The whole loft seemed an exercise in futility. I didn't own it. The cost of fixing it up was draining all my financial resources. Even if I could afford to do it, the work could still come to naught, since we who live here were in violation of the building codes. The city's building inspectors could come here any day and kick us out on the street. With so much work to do just to make a livable space, I had no time to make art. I was an utter failure as a creative being, and as a human being, I was a total disaster. My career as an architect was gone; I quit to be an artist. My wife and child I had abandoned in San Francisco. All I had were the small sketchbooks that record my dreams, delusions, and ideas of what I might do if I had the time.

To be a creative being was my life's goal. The goal always seemed to elude me. Or I was never satisfied with what I got because others looking at me might say I got nothing but what I aspired to. I am a writer, artist, and architect. What I never got was satisfaction from any of it In that disappointment I found further reason for depression and wallowed in the pity of the self proclaimed failed.

"Are you wallowing?" says Carlotta appearing dressed like a goth artist. Her short hair is purple and spiked. She has on a black, knee-length dress with a neckline that plunges between her breasts. Her waist is cinched with a deep red scarf, and she is wearing sandals. Her legs are unshaven. Her make up is garish: purple and green eyeshadow, black-outlined lips painted neon lavender. Copper hoop earrings of increasingly larger size dangle almost to her shoulders. Her wrists are adorned with many circular, multicolored bracelets, and her fingernails and toenails are painted a deep purple. She has a ring in her nose and one in her eyebrows. A stud penetrates her tongue. She stands defiantly in front of me and spins around. A large red dot is marked between her exposed shoulder blades. I stare at her silently peeved at her remark. She changes the subject.

"How do you like my dress-up? It's a celebration of the days when you were on a quest to be an artist."

"The sandals don't work and the hairy legs are a turnoff."

"I wondered about that, but heels won't work, either."

"You should be wearing boots. Maybe cowgirl boots in black and white snakeskin."

"Snakeskin would clash with the purple."

"But snakeskin boots would be more ... malevolent."

Carlotta spins, revealing her bare back. "See the red mark on my back. I bet you think that is malevolent."

"Were you the big spider in my dream, come to end my misery?"

"A curious question," says Carlotta, turning around to face me. "The big spider in your dream could be me, queen of all the spiders!"

I shrink back from the bloodthirsty look on her face. "I know you are evil."

"No, I only jest. Muses don't come to destroy their charges. I was there and I am here to bring you back to life from the dead ends you pursue. I come for you to see the sun that lies at the end of your dark tunnel. The little spiders were then and remain today your enemies. They represent the thousand negative thoughts that plague your mind. My presence makes them frightened to enter your curtained shell."

"Did you like my description of the dream?"

"I did indeed, except for the negative parts and the tunnel being an umbilical cord. Why do you always go there?"

"I do it because it reminds me of my mother, who strangled my life. This is the dream that reveals the truth. The circumstances of my life have caused my difficulty."

"So you believe, but maybe the problem is different. Anything can happen in a dream. Your interpretation could be wrong."

"Speaking of interpretations, I think you could be a black widow spider. That red mark on your back might signify evil intentions."

"I have no evil intentions for you. I am your muse. I try to wring the sorrow from your mind."

"On the contrary, you are a fabrication of my *sick* mind."

"Touchy, touchy! You do get so upset at the luck I bring."

"Luck? You bring luck? You are part of my madness."

"I beg to differ. When you don't have me drugged, I can guide you to a better place, if you will only listen to me. You could even become normal and conventional all the time."

I harrumph at this. "I suppose next you're going to attack my unconventionality."

"I'll save that conversation for later."

"Why are you goth now?"

"I am a remembrance of all the female artists who came on to you, yet you treated them so badly."

"I couldn't deal with anything after the events in Las Vegas. I was stunned. I needed only to work on my loft and my art."

"There were lots of women who presented themselves to you dressed like this, but you rejected them all."

"Not *all* of them!"

"Yes, you did. You pushed *any* woman away. Remember Katherine, whose camera you lost when it was stolen from your loft?"

"I do, and I am not proud of what I did."

"She came to your loft to talk to you, and you literally threw her out the door, demanding she take the chair and small table she lent you."

"I was angry that I lost her camera and had no way to pay her back."

"How you treated that lovely woman was unforgivable."

"I was stoned."

"That was always your excuse for your rotten behavior."

"The state of being high protected me from feeling."

"Now you admit it! You were addicted to pot and made no attempt to get off it."

"How could I? Marijuana made life bearable."

"That is an illusion, and until you did something about it, you continued to have these attacks."

"Correction. I still have these attacks."

"But they aren't as intense."

Carlotta points toward the bedroom door and quickly disappears.

A nurse arrives. "Did I hear you talking to someone?"

"No. There is no one here but me."

The nurse looks at me suspiciously and brushes her hand around the green curtain to see if Smitty is lying on the bed.

"It is time for you to go to your music or art therapy," she says and departs.

After looking for Smitty to join me without success, I go to music therapy because I think the art therapy, where the participants make collages cut from magazine images to express their feelings, is silly. In music therapy, you spend an hour listening to everybody's favorite hits. We gather in the group therapy room on the first floor, next to the common room. Bob, the music therapist, brings his portable compact disc player and a box containing nearly every genre of music. Each person in the room gets to choose two recordings of their favorite artist or group. We listen to a lot of pop and country and western. I choose jazz and get to hear a little Duke Ellington and John Coltrane. I am thinking about my attacks of depression as Ellington plays "Diminuendo in Blue" and Coltrane essays "Some of My Favorite Things."

Paul Gonsalves of Duke Ellington's orchestra attacks his saxophone, working it into a great climax of repeated riffs. I see a similarity to my up cycles, which catapult me into a great crescendo before I collapse into the deepest, darkest depression. The saxophonist builds up to a melodic screech and quickly drops away. He has blown himself out. Similarly, I am blown out and depression sneaks up, making its commando raid on my brain, leaving me helpless.

I am a person of very wide mood swings. The fact that I am not constant is easily discernible. I go from very active and energetic to very lethargic and dull. This oscillation from up to down transpires in a continuing rhythm of varying intensity over six-week periods. I made a graph of my mood changes one fall. A cycle begins with a terrible "down" around the first week of September and lasts about a week, and then an "up" begins. In the up, I am energetic and ecstatic. This lasts about four weeks until the middle of October. At this point, a decline begins through the end of October. In the last week of October, I am in another down, irritable and angry, ending up buried in bed.

I have two terrible depressions each year, accompanied by intervening attacks of lesser intensity. The first attack happens in early September and continues through October. The second attack starts in late January or early February, ending in mid-February. My psychologist believed the first attack occurred because the time was the start of school. The second attack was a reaction to the divorce of my mother and father. His analysis never felt exactly right to me.

When did these cycles start? My guess is they began with my experiences as a child. While I didn't remember the incidents until recently, I remember my temper tantrums. Throughout my early youth, I had fits where I would throw myself on the floor and yell, scream, flail my arms, and kick my legs. At the dining table, I would throw food I didn't like across the table or on the floor. Often, I was sent to my room or spanked for my misbehavior. As a young boy, I attacked another child with a toy hammer because he was playing with my truck in the sandbox. As a teenager, I would stalk off in anger, giving the finger to adults. Alternately, I could sometimes be the best of boys, sweet and charming.

I would guess that it was during a down that I tried to commit suicide in college, and it was the countervailing up which served to release me from hospital confinement months later. The pattern of up and down is the significant characteristic of my life for at least the past thirty years. The dates of decline and ascent are never exactly the same. A period of down can go on for longer than anticipated, and a time of good feeling can last shorter or longer than predicted. There is no set pattern for these onsets, except for the two great downs of January/February and September/October. I can never be ready for when bad moods will strike or when they will end. I am always trapped unaware.

bipolar bare

Sitting in music therapy, listening to jazz, I am caught up in the rhythm and improvisation. The blues are like my cycle, which is never exactly the same but has nuances of aching and moments of tender sensitivity. I can be a perfect ball of fire, consuming myself in creative energy like the drive of jazz repetition, then slide away into a dead, burned-out hulk. My psychic jazz has moments of beautiful touches like Ellington and Coltrane. The rest of it is very painful and discordant.

Alternating between a sunny, positive nature and its dark, negative opposite, my warring dispositions make me a volatile "unperson" to both myself and others: *un*steady, *un*stable, *un*knowable. I can never predict how I will react. Friends tell me they don't know which Carlton will show up on any given day. Will I be sweet and charming or an irritable and angry person? By conventional standards, I am an unbalanced person. I am in perpetual motion between the points of high and low.

The moods of all people, I guess, ebb and flow within a shallower groove. I suspect this shift is traceable in all people. What is different is the degree of swing. I have a highly sloped psyche. While the ordinary human temperament might vary from an estimated ten degrees between high and low along a base line of equilibrium, for me the declination is more toward ninety degrees. From high, I slide down fast to low and climb the dark inclines slowly back to the bright of high. Up and down a roller coaster of life, wired for speed, burned up on danger, I cruise, charge, and sputter in a body capsule with faulty regulators. The tune I play is irritating to hear.

After music therapy, I return to my room and sit at the desk, flipping through my sketchbooks and journals. Smitty is asleep on his bed, the green hospital curtain half-drawn around his space. He is snoring and mumbling incoherent sounds.

Carlotta shows up again, emerging from the bathroom still dressed as a goth artist. She has hanks of fiber over her arm.

"You would never consider a fiber artist a real artist would you?" she asks.

"Fiber art is a craft, not serious art," I reply loftily.

"You have such limited views. What about the gigantic rope piece in the San Francisco subway? You know the one I mean. It's a long series of knots in strands of two-inch rope that hang down more than two stories at the end of a downtown San Francisco station. It's all black and looks like it's been discolored with train dust. I can't remember the artist.

"It's ugly and dirty. Name me some subway art that is any good."

"What about your work with the North Hollywood Station with James Doolin?"

"Too compromised. He quit when the politics got to be too much for him and I ended up with another artist, whose vision was not as good as Doolin's American Dream."

"You are so hard on yourself and everyone else. You become angry and frustrated. You cannot go along with the flow and accept the best a situation has to offer."

"Are you going to lecture me again, Carlotta?"

"I could, but what good would it do? You are not ready for the truth yet. I can only offer observations as you continue your misdirected search for mental health."

"My search is misdirected?"

"You will find out, when you are ready."

"Goddamn you, Carlotta!

"See, you can't control your feelings. First will be the energy and high spirits. Second will be the anger and frustration. Third will be the tiredness, isolation, and attacks of the black brain."

"You are right about that, Carlotta! I do know about being powerless, feeling frustrated, and getting angry. It is a bad thing for me because after I get these strong emotions, I get really sad."

"Are you going to read me something?"

"Yes, I'd like to. The first piece is from the fall when I was working on the loft, after my wife and I separated. I had just moved to downtown Los Angeles, and tried to become an artist."

Carlotta fondles her chime-like earrings, making a pleasing tintinnabulation. "Read on, then, I'm all ears."

"With each passing day, it grows more difficult to rise from my bed. I lie in my silk cocoon, unable to get up. I should have recognized the symptoms: the heaviness in the bottom of my stomach, the headaches, the inability to think clearly, and the tiredness. The body becomes paralyzed. Emotions throw me, like an exhausted swimmer caught in the surf. Again and again, I'm tossed onto the shore and dribble back into the waves, knowing a big wave will smash me down. I will be submerged and lost. I will drown in the horror of sorrow, never knowing that life tomorrow will become clearer and positive. I am losing hope. I am withdrawing. I go to bed praying I will die and never have to get up again. Despair overwhelms me.

"I can think only of death. I am acting as I did in college, when I withdrew into my room. I slept a lot, read a lot, and eventually took 150 aspirins. Fifteen years later, the situation is similar. I am isolated again. People steer clear of me. I reject Katherine, and she rejects me. I exile Brenda, another artist, from my life, and I am very much alone. The same emotions of self-created loneliness and the crushing sense of despair follow me everywhere. Acting strangely, I prowl the streets and the bathhouses late at night. I see myself as a diseased person. I can't get along with people, neither my friends nor my girlfriends. I argue and lose my temper at all of them. I am isolating my horrid self from these innocent people. I hate any nice people with whom I have contact. Hate is my favorite word. I hate everything, especially me.

"I am so melodramatic. If I rest and get up in a couple of days, I will be OK. Reason, intelligence, and experience tell me this, but emotion says no. A week, maybe two, maybe three, and I will be depressed again. I am the swimmer who can't resist one more chance to body surf, even as I know I am over the edge of tiredness. I will be caught in the emotional surf again. I will be wishing I could do anything to get away from the dark and tired feelings. These unhappy circumstances return again and again like the endless surf of the ocean. I am drawn to go there. There is no escape.

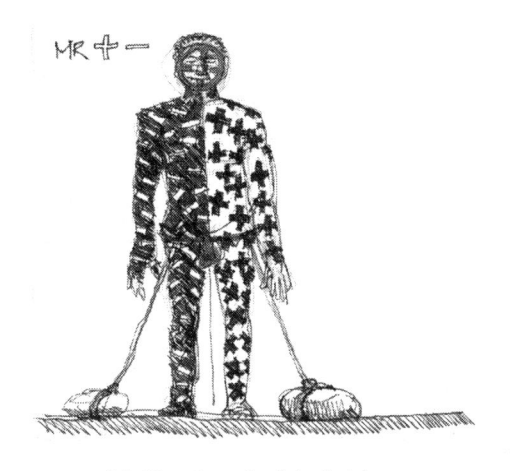

Mr. Plusminus; sketch book; ink pen

"Self-murder, I can do that. I almost did before. I shall make it a piece, a performance, an artist's death. The piece will be entitled *Mr. Plusminus Dances to the Sun*. I could even put out a program. That way, everybody would get a souvenir from my performance to take home. The book will outline the plan of action: 'Mr. Davis will develop the theme up to the point of his surprise culmination ...' The centerpiece of the program will be a signed color drawing of me as Mr. Plusminus.

"I shall paint myself half white and half black down the middle of my body. On the white half, there will be black plus symbols. On the black half there will be white minus symbols. I am naked save for a rope around my waist, from which two large stones are tied. My genitals will be painted red. A mysterious red box, whose unknown contents will surely tantalize the audience, lies on the ground next to a central pole upon which several long leather strands are tied. My dance will be reminiscent of the sun dances performed by the Plains Indians.

"According to custom, I will pierce my chest with wooden skewers, which are affixed to leather ropes and secured to the pole. Blood drips from my body as I lean with my full weight against the taut leather ropes, causing the wooden skewers to tug at my fragile chest muscles. The pain is excruciating as I circle the pole on the tether, dragging the heavy stones with me. All the while, I maintain a running monologue about my Indian heritage, my mother, and America's savage history. Increasing the speed and hanging with greater tension on the leather tether, I try, as the Sioux did in their gory rituals, to rip the skin and muscles from my naked, bloody chest. My frenzy reaches its culmination when the leather strands break. I collapse to the ground and crawl to the sinister red box. I open it to reveal a gun, which I put to my head and ceremoniously shoot myself.

"At the climax of the performance piece, the art community will be suitably stunned as splatters of blood decorate the floor and walls. The attendees scream in horror; several, overcome by horror and disbelief, faint in the aisles. The awful truth is that in death, I achieve my freedom and my fame. The dance of death is my life's greatest work."

"So gruesome!" says Carlotta, shuddering. "In the past, we muses danced around the maypole to music and singing. Painters painted us as a happy lot. But all you can talk about is suicide! I personally find it boring. Carlotta likes living more than you do. Maybe you should be on my side of the mind more often, dancing the maypole with garlands of flowers in your hair. You would look cute in a toga."

"And fruity," I argue. "I don't care to set myself up for more ridicule and trouble."

"Better trouble than death, my sweet Carlton."

"You heard my statements about isolation, the timing, the physical feelings, and not being able to get out of bed, didn't you? They are common to all my attacks of depression."

"OK, what has that to do with the tale of suicide?"

"Suicidal thoughts are the result of these feelings."

"Do they have to be? Maybe you could substitute sex for suicide?"

"Been there, done that," I reply wearily. "Sex is another kind of hell. *Your* kind! Be quiet and listen to what else I have written. You won't like it, because I talk about wanting to die again, but try to hear what else is there. It begins with the observation by Karen, my next door neighbor, of my depression cycles on the same day as today, a Tuesday, twenty-one years ago."

"See the lions leap and sense the fires burn. Fallen on my head from my loft ladder, skinned my skin, sliced and sprained my thumb. The damage wrecks me and the black depression consumes me. My body and mind have taken their wounds. I am trying to relax. Another black Monday has passed, and I remain depressed and suicidal. It strangles me in its blackness. I try to rise, depart, and seek life, but I can't break the isolation. Back I crawl to my bed and the dark safety and terror of the black. There is a flash of light. Where am I? Under the bed curled up with my bear?

"Karen opens my door and walks into my studio.

"'Exercise in fifteen minutes,' she calls out.

"'I would prefer not,' I say from the dark tomb of my bed, echoing the words of Melville's Bartleby, the sublimely disaffected scrivener from the short story of the same name.

"'Why so grim?' Karen responds.

"'I prefer not,' I mutter again from underneath my bed covers. 'The blob has descended.'

"'I have lived here long enough to see you have a thirty to forty day cycle of depression,' Karen says to me at ten feet away from the foot of my bed outside my curtain.

"'I prefer not!' I reiterate, louder this time.

"'You do have a cycle. You should think about it,' Karen says, striding out of my loft and closing the door behind her.

"I bury myself further into the covers and cry, mumbling over and over 'I prefer not to live, I prefer not to live …'

"Alone with my thoughts, I ponder the fate of poor Bartleby. The strange man's taciturn refusal to perform his scrivener duties lands him in prison, where, despite the efforts of his boss to see that he is well fed, he 'prefers not to' eat, and so dies.

"The lucky stiff.

"Ah Carlton! Ah humanity!"

bipolar bare

The Blob; sketch book; ink pen

"I won't see the truth of my impossible situation. Either I am very productive and engaged, or I am completely sluggish and depressed. Most of the time I am very productive, but every month or so I have a week, a weekend, or a day where I am feeling awful, physically immobilized, and mentally deranged. A Monday can be this. A dark cloud descends over me and, I erroneously believe, all the humans around me. Where do I lift this veil of blackness and peer beyond the shadow? It cannot be done. The veil is heavy, thick, and gooey, like molasses. There is no escaping its shroud. Yesterday, Monday, was another difficult day of this stiff slime.

"Tuesday, after the dark day of Monday, is a period of slow recovery. I am regaining my balance and beginning to take an interest in the world again. The feeling is one of tired relief. The death of doubt has receded, but only just. The memory of the paralysis of self-hate is very vivid. Wednesday comes and I am almost whole again. My energy has returned, but my head is still woolly. I can be irritable and short with people. I am angry all around the edges, but I am climbing and rising.

"On the Tuesday following a good Monday, there can be a reverse. An anticipation of bad things yet to come has me on edge. The senses turn to black hues. Perhaps it will be only a dip in a general up, but Tuesday can be the glide down from good things that can't last. Tuesday always waits to be over. Wednesday comes and I am fully down. The events of life speed by, and I have no time to reflect. I feel trapped in the inescapable forward rush of time. I have no control over anything, and the sense of powerlessness converts itself into depression. But first, the body must crash. My body feels stiff and sore. My back aches. My lungs are congested. My brain hurts. Behind my right eye, arrows of pain penetrate my skull. Both eyes are hypersensitive to light. I retreat from the light into the dark womb of my bed, burying myself in sleep and nightmares. The spiders will come, thousands of them, crawling over my body, biting me, and wrapping me in their web. I can't move. I can't speak. I can't eat. All I can do is wait in fear for the dread to end. Am I already eighty years old, like some crinkly bald Uncle Remus, waiting for the end? This Tuesday is a bad Tuesday.

"I am powerless. I non-exist. I am imprisoned by a matrix of circumstance inside the boundaries of time. Bound up in a joyless existence of perverted desire and failure, who would not wish for death? What is my existence but a meaningless set of functions? I eat, sleep, and defecate. I am an animal whose brain is given sensitivity to the horror and calamity of life, but no ability to change that reality. The pumping heart propels me forward into more loneliness and agony. The animal biology drives the flesh. The human consciousness is wounded. Thought follows the flesh, unable to direct or lead. Thought discerns the realities of survival and is turned sour. Allow me the courage to obliterate this vile consciousness.

"I am roused from my torpor by excitement in the street. A crowd has gathered to watch the antics of a young black man who is sniffing a can of glue at the end of the block, underneath the bridge. His mouth is a mess of foam as he dances and jives after each hit of glue. Presently, the police arrive. Four burly cops descend on the scrawny tatterdemalion, who capers about, dancing and howling, as they try to subdue him. Finally, after several minutes of putting up with the junkie's kicking, gouging, and spitting, one of the cops smacks him on the back of his knees with his nightstick. The junkie flutters to the ground like a high-flying kite that has lost its tail.

"That poor man could be me, I think, if I were to let myself go native. As if on cue, the junkie looks up at me as the cops are jamming him into the backseat of the patrol car and points his skeletal finger in my direction. I imagine him saying,

'Yes, I am one of your kind, mad like you!'

"Such self-indulgence! I have no right to think this way. My life is better than this fellow's. I am not a down and out bum, sniffing glue. I am not staggering down Fifth Street looking for a cheap bottle of Thunderbird and a comfortable pile of garbage to sleep off my alcoholic delirium. I could have a job if I wanted one. I am one of the haves, educated and employable. I still have a car. I should be full of joy for all the haves I have, but I am not. Give me liberty. Give me death."

"Oh, Carlton, I am so sad for you," says Carlotta, walking slowly to the bathroom. "You were headed in the wrong direction—clinging by your fingertips to a runaway rollercoaster going in and out of the darkest depressions and hurtling farther and farther away from mental health. I and others began to think there was no hope for you."

At the bathroom, she turns and sticks her studded tongue out at me, then steps inside.

"Give me liberty. Give me *life*," she says, gently closing the door.

CHAPTER 15

STONED NUDE STUMBLES DOWN THE STAIRCASE LOOKING FOR THE LIGHT

"Remember Giant Jane?" says Carlotta, sitting on the corner of my desk in black jeans, black blouse, and white snakeskin boots. She wears a long blonde wig with a black lace choker around her neck.

"Do I ever!" I enthuse. "At six feet five, she was unforgettable. You honor her memory to a T. I was just reading about her in my journal. What has it been, twenty years or more?"

"Verily. Read to me about her and the best conversation you ever had, until it got weird. You were stoned at the time. In those years, you lived stoned every day."

"I was drunk too, but that doesn't matter. It was a great dialogue. Like the great masters had in Paris in the 1880s and '90s: Van Gogh, Gauguin, Seurat, Cezanne, Balla, and Picasso. They were all drinking absinthe, the narcotic liqueur of the day. It didn't affect their work."

Carlotta snorts. "Ha! Van Gogh was a madman."

"If only I could be as good a madman as he," I sigh. Rummaging through my books, I find the correct volume. "I shall read to you and you will see I'm not always preoccupied with death."

"April, 1983. Giant Jane takes a drag on the joint, kicks her white cowgirl boots up on a diagonal chair, and rolls her head back. Her eyes scan the silver foil covering the loft ceiling; her long straight blonde hair cascades down the back of the plywood and tube steel chair. She exhales and leans sideways. Her extended right arm drapes across the square butcher-block table and dangles the joint in front of the elbows supporting my head. I move my right hand forward slowly and take the joint from her fingertips.

"'Don't bogart the joint this time,' she says, scooping up her glass of tequila in her long pale fingers with nails like blood-red talons.

"'I won't this time. I promise.'

"'This is really good stuff we're smoking, and you always forget you have the joint,' Jane carps. 'By the time you remember it's in your hand, the joint's a roach.'

"'OK, OK.' I take a hit and hold it, exhale luxuriously and pass the joint back to her. 'Are you happy now?'

"'Let's put it out for now and save some of this very fine sensemilla for later, after we have killed the worm,' Jane suggests, putting the joint in the crevice of the Caesar's Palace ashtray. 'Now, what were we talking about?'

"'Light! We were talking about light. The light in Vermeer's paintings. The cold clear light the Dutch seemed to catch in their best work.'

"'You were talking about Dutch painters,' Jane grumbles. 'I was just trying to get in the occasional word.'

"'You were rhapsodizing about Rembrandt before we got distracted by the joint,' I remind her.

"'That's right,' she says. 'The light in his paintings wasn't cold and clear. It is warm, almost hot. Take *The Slaughtered Ox*. You can almost feel the poor beast's snuffed-out life force. Remember, you showed me a picture of that painting once.'

"'Rembrandt is an exception,' I reply. 'He became too Italian. Give me some of that tequila so I can formulate a response to your challenge.'

"I reach for the bottle of Cuervo with the worm at the bottom and pour a shot in my glass.

"'Ha! I've shut you up for once,'" Jane gloats.

"I gulp down the shot. 'Whew! That tequila is good! Never! Never! Rembrandt is the master of shadow. He comes at light from its opposite, the world of darkness and shade. I bet he got depressed a lot. He does not even try to capture the elusive essence of the ineluctable.'

"'The what?'

"'The ineluctable.'

"Jane laughs. 'There you go again, throwing out one of those big fat words that nobody understands. I bet you don't even know what it means.'

"'I do, too! Ineluctable. It means you can't completely understand its fundamental ... er ... nature."

"'Bullshit! You are feeding me a whole lot of hooey."

"'No, I'm not,' I insist. 'I'm on a roll now. Light up that joint and let's have a couple of more hits.'

"Jane takes the half-smoked joint from the ashtray on the dining room table outside the kitchen construction by the stairs that go nowhere, takes a deep drag, and hands me the joint. I inhale deeply.

"Trying to understand ... (exhale) ... the nature of light visually wouldn't happen until much later ... (exhale) ... when artists like Van Gogh would paint the sky as little dashes of paint. Maybe it was Seurat who did it first with his pointillism, or it could have been one of the Impressionists like Cezanne, certainly not that sentimentalist Renoir. Wait, my head's a little foggy. No. It wasn't the Impressionists. It was the guys that were all making these little dabs of paint like light broken up into particles, just like the physicists were theorizing. The Futurists, that's who!'

"'You're too stoned,' Giant Jane understates.

"'Give me a break! I'm super high and on a roll. Along comes Balla and paints an electric light bulb the same way you see light coming off light bulbs as little particles of energy. This is true, because you can really see the light emanating from a bulb as little particles of light if you look at it carefully.'

"'I've never seen that painting and I don't think you can see light coming off a bulb as little particles,' says Jane skeptically.

"'No, it's true! Turn around in your chair look at the light coming off the fluorescent light bulbs in my studio. Can't you see the light energy coming from the bulbs?'

"'I need another shot of tequila.'

"'Come on, Jane. Turn your head and look at the fluorescent light.'

"'It's bullshit.'

"Come on Jane, you're an artist!' I cry. A maniacal note has crept into my voice. 'Can't you see it? Can't you see the light energy flowing from the fluorescent light bulbs onto the wood floor and bouncing back up? Can't you see the light energy reflecting off the silver foil ceiling?'

"'Man, you are totally stoned!'

"'I don't deny it, but the weed only increases my sensitivity to what is actually happening. The light rays are coming from the bulbs, filling the studio, and bouncing off every surface. You have seen the Futurist paintings by Umberto Boccioni, haven't you?

"'Umberto whosis?'

"'Boccioni, Italian futurist painter at the turn of the twentieth century. He painted these paintings that showed the modern city of the time as this riot of lines of force, color, and light. Very powerful. The best one was called The City Rises, I think. He was probably stoned on absinthe when he did them.'

"'I'm not into historical painting,' says Jane airily.

"'Not even Van Gogh?' I protest. 'How about his painting of the wheat fields where the sun is shown emanating all these rays of force as dashes of bright yellow color?'

"'I don't remember it,' says Jane, leaning back in her chair and laughing.

"'I remember showing you that painting. Well, if you don't like my art comparisons, how about if I compare this all to music? The lights are giving off rays of energy just like musical instruments are giving off waves of sound. If you were sensitive enough, you could see it.'

"'I can feel the waves, but I can't see them.'

"'If we were sensitive enough, we could see or feel all the forces traveling around us,' I insist. 'We could see the electricity traveling in the conduit in the walls. We could see all the energy waves traveling all around us: the microwaves, the radio waves, and the solar rays, to name just a few.'"

Jane guffaws. "'Next, you're going to tell me you have X-ray vision!'"

"'Perhaps I do,' I say with a Cheshire cat grin.

"'Wait a minute!' Jane exclaims. 'I may not see electricity in the wall, but I can see that it is raining in your kitchen.'

"'What?'

"'Turn around and look behind you,' says Jane, pointing. 'It's raining down through your silver foil over your stove and refrigerator.'

"'Goddamn that Zorba! He taking a shower again and has never bothered to waterproof his shower stall properly! I'm going to kill him!'

"I run into the back of my studio and begin rummaging in a pile of things against the far wall. Finding my baseball bat, I charge back across the studio, toss my dining chair aside, and run halfway up the stair that goes nowhere. I begin to swing my bat and bang on the floor of the studio above.

"'Zorba! This is the last warning! One more time you rain on me in my studio, and I am going to shoot you through the floor. DO YOU HEAR ME, ZORBA?'

"'Carlton, settle down.'

"'No, Jane, I have had it with this asshole. He did his own plumbing and he doesn't know crap. He has rained on me more times than I can count on two hands.'

"We can hear him creeping across the floor above.

"'DO YOU HEAR ME, ZORBA? I AM GOING TO SHOOT YOU THROUGH THE FLOOR!'

"'Carlton, the rain has stopped.'

"I stumble down the stairs, knocking over a small sculpture of a nude. It tumbles down six steps to the floor. My collection of postcards propped against the risers tumble with the sculpture.

"'*Goddamn it!*' I yell. '*I just stepped on* Duchamp's Nude Descending a Staircase*! My goddamn favorite!*'

"'Calm down, Carlton,' Jane cools. 'It's only a postcard, and it's only water.'

"'No it isn't! It is darkness invading my life! I'm in the light now and I intend to stay there. DO YOU HEAR ME, ZORBA? I AM GOING TO SHOOT YOU THROUGH THE FLOOR!'

"'I'm leaving, Carlton, if you don't give it up and calm down. Let's go out to the Zero-Zero.'

"'OK, OK, OK, as soon as I mop up this mess.'"

"I recall that evening with great fondness," I sigh, looking up from my journal. "This was a time when I was up and separated from my sorrow. How grand it was!

bipolar bare

How much fun! I was working again on my art and feeling completely energized. I had stayed up for several nights in a row working on my sculptures, bending wire mesh and soldering it together into a big pile of plus shapes and minus shapes. These pieces would soon become the parts of my best work yet, *The Ironic Column*, so called because it was a column of pluses and minuses suspended from the ceiling by a gigantic steel hook. I had finished a big, eight-foot-tall drawing of the piece, which was my mock-up, and all the parts were close to the point of assembly. Almost everything was good and positive, except for the rain and the rats in my studio."

"You were having a high time," Carlotta concurs. "You were in a manic up and everything appeared to be going in a terrific direction."

"True. I was having great conversations with my friends: Jose, Jane, Marti, Michael, Gary, Karen, and Ellen. Jane, my intellectual punk rocker and nighttime dominatrix, and I would visit the after hours clubs, talking about art and philosophy. Gary, my friend from across the hall in the loft building, and I would play Ping-Pong for the title of 'Master of the World.' I would talk for hours with Ellen, who had the loft behind me and played the sitar, about Asian or Indian spirituality. I was happy, living the Bohemian life I wanted, and I believed the negative times were behind me."

"Those were the fun times, or so you thought!"

"They were the best of times," I say with finality. "But why aren't you dressed completely in black? The white boots are too casual. I think you should ape Giant Jane in her dominatrix costume."

"Why are you steering me away from the real issue of your mental health, Carlton? And why is what I am wearing always so important to you? Can't I just be a feminine presence without being dressed to the nines?"

"Don't be coy with me, you insufferable fashionista! I know you love to get dressed up, put on your best sexy outfits and your most provocative make-up. You want me to ask, and you want to tell me."

"But not today. What I want to tell you is that I did not like us getting stoned all the time. It made my hands shake so badly that putting on my make-up was a very difficult chore."

"You never told me that, Carlotta."

"You never asked. You were too zonked to notice."

"We never talked about drugs. I thought you liked them, especially cocaine. Coke made you feel really sexy."

"We discussed drugs many times, Carlton, but you would forget most conversations after you were loaded."

"I remember many of my conversations with Jane."

"A most unusual occurrence. But I still ask: What about your mental health?"

"I was fine. I was happy. Must you spoil my good times?"

"I only question if they were *really* your good times. What about the Zero-Zero? Was that actually a good time?"

"I remember going to the Zero-Zero," I say wistfully.

"You and Giant Jane were quite the pair: queer cowboy and his gigantic queen go to the Zero-Zero, the after hours hole-in-the-wall club of rock junkies and Hollywood wannabes."

"Giant Jane wasn't a queen! She was a true transsexual and very, very smart. We had many wonderful conversations, if not much sex."

"When she was around, you never talked with me," Carlotta pouts.

"Jealous?"

"That emotion is beneath me! Let us say I was disappointed that you could be so easily distracted."

"She was an overwhelming presence."

"OK, I'll give you that. Recall for me the Zero-Zero. I was too inebriated or too high to remember anything. Zero-Zero was the after hours club somewhere in Hollywood. Right, right?"

"Omigod, Carlotta, don't start sounding like Lynn!" I say, my eyes bugging out in terror. "The Zero-Zero was in Hollywood on Cahuenga, I think. It didn't open until two or three in the morning, after all the bars closed. There wasn't even a sign outside the door. You just had to know where it was. Knock, pay three bucks, and someone would let you in, if they thought you were OK. They knew Jane because of her band, The Cage, and we could always get in."

"Sort of like a speakeasy, wasn't it?" asks Carlotta.

"Yeah, except I imagine more sleazy—a 'sleaze-easy,' as it were. The whole place was splashed with a coat of cheap white paint and otherwise practically bare. Everybody there was dressed in black, except for me in my blue jeans and blue-checkered cowboy shirt. I did wear my black leather jacket. The bar was a kitchen counter also completely painted white. You could buy a beer from the bartender for a buck. He would grab a can out of a plastic cooler behind the bar and hand it to you. Drinking wasn't a big thing. Drugs were."

"I remember *that*."

"The place was crowded and filled with cigarette and joint smoke. Everybody just stood around near the bar. Jane stood almost a foot above the crowd. I remember one time, we got into a conversation with a pompous guy who said he was a philosopher visiting from England. I can't recall what we talked about, just that a group of us were passing a joint around. Jane started to laugh."

"I remember her laugh," says Carlotta. "It had a deep, distinctive sound, like an out of tune honk that penetrated and rattled my brain."

"I drifted away when their conversation turned to punk music and stumbled down the three or four steps that led to a back room, where there were car seats arranged around big wood spools originally used for heavy cable. Musicians and their babes were jammed onto the car seats, cutting and spreading lines of cocaine on the tabletops. I watched while two guys and their girls did a couple of lines."

"I bet someone offered you a line …"

"As a matter of fact, they did. I was standing there, leaning against the wall, when one of the guys waves to me. I sort of know him through Jane. He was a musician named Carlo Cuitaro from one of the punk groups. He waved and pointed to the lines of coke on the table. I came over, picked up the straw, and did a line. It was good stuff. Quite a rush! That line was the beginning of my fascination with cocaine."

"I don't remember," says Carlotta. "I was stone-cold unconscious by that time from all the dope and tequila."

"Maybe so, but you loved cocaine. It always made you very horny."

Carlotta sticks her nose in the air haughtily. "I don't recall."

"Oh, yes, you do. You just don't want to get into what you would do when you had cocaine."

"I admit that delving into slutty proclivities when supercharged by that libidinous substance is distasteful to me right now. In retrospect, I think the Zero-Zero wasn't such a good place for the two of us, given the problems cocaine led to."

"It probably wasn't, but at the time I loved the outsider life it represented. I didn't think it had any impact on my mental health."

"It had a huge impact, Carlton, but let's leave that for later. Don't you have some more journal entries you wanted me to hear?"

"Maybe I do."

"Then let's hear it."

"Okay, but first, some backstory. This piece comes from a period when smoking marijuana was still fun. Jane was there. Cocaine—or rather, its more diabolical cousin, crack—hadn't started to replace my marijuana addiction. Curiously, I titled the entry 'I am the lamp maker in drug culture.' The reference goes unexplained."

"Darling Carlton, you precious boy," Carlotta coos, "I always think of you as lighting the way to a new understanding of life."

"Don't be sarcastic! This was a time in May 1986 when I was again high and going higher, but intimations of a down were appearing."

"I'll be quiet. Read on."

"Edith Piaf is singing on KCRW, the local national public radio station. 'Non, je ne regrette rien.' Translated into English, it means no, I regret nothing. How appropriate, I think. Jose is smoking a joint, inhaling some lines of cocaine, and intently drawing on our project. I lie on the floor, stoned—why do we call it stoned, I wonder?—looking at the silver ceiling behind the silky curtain, my piece of Christo's Running Fence. Jane is at the kitchen table reading a book and drinking tequila.

"I am depressed again, recalling all the ways I could off myself. Nothing has changed, but I know I'm not going to do it. Meditation, my newest activity, has dampened the desire. The vipassana scans have jackhammered the hard surface of my unhappiness enough that a big crack of joy leaks out. The plaintive wave of

bipolar bare

Madame Piaf's voice rolls over me and I cry for all that's lost. I am sentimental and bawling over the good things left behind when I turned Bohemian.

"After an hour and a half of lying on the floor and looking at the silver ceiling, studying the infinite reflections of light from the upturned fluorescent lamps darting across the crinkled surface, I rise, shower, and work with Jose on the Pershing Square Design Competition. Marti arrives and works with us on the design. Jane provides commentary and ideas. We create Marilyn, the tallest structure in Los Angeles. Jane suggested the name because the erector set-like structure reminded her of Marilyn Monroe in the movie *The Seven Year Itch*, in which her skirt gets blown up by the hot air from a subway grate. Our skirt, Jane says, is the bowl-like part of the tower above the four legs of the structure. Our Marilyn is a four-legged creature. On top of the skirt, soaring above a long shaft, is the world's largest and highest Ferris wheel. Marilyn is to be an Eiffel Tower for LA.

"It is late Friday night. We run out of dope. The lines of cocaine are all inhaled and the marijuana consumed. I can't even find a roach in the studio. Jose searches his car and comes up empty. Marti has nothing in his magic satchel. Nobody is home across the hall to mooch a joint from. We call New Mexico to get the new number of the dealer's house, because his old number is disconnected and we are desperate. A hundred fifty dollars would get us another quarter lid, but we will have to go to Venice for the score. Jose and I jump in my truck and head for the beach from downtown. We speed across First Street—no cops are out—and race down the freeway thirteen miles toward Speedway. I have no money, nor access to an automatic teller, since on Tuesday of last week, I lost my wallet—a sure sign that things are in decline. Jose has only eighty bucks.

carlton davis

Marilyn: A Tower for Pershing Square, Los Angeles; 1986

"We stop at a bank near the dealer and Jose tries his bank card to get more cash. It's a joint card with his soon to be ex-wife. It doesn't work. He can't remember the PIN number because he fought with her. We drive from one instant teller to another near Venice Boulevard as Jose tries different number combinations. None work. His Spanish accent gets thicker and thicker as he grumbles and curses his esposa for scolding him over his enormous drug use. She made him forget his number. He shall never forgive her for that.

"Jose and I are desperate for our high. We give up on getting the additional $70 more and go to the dealer. Jose—short, stocky but quick, an ex-professional soccer player—scrambles out of the truck and scampers up the sidewalk to the small dark house. He pushes the bell and waits, moving impatiently like a midfielder expecting the ball. A man appears at the door and Jose disappears inside. He convinces him to give us the quarter lid for the cash we have, with the promise we will bring the hundred more by Monday.

"We have no rolling papers. Jose directs me to liquor store a few blocks away and we are fixed up. In the truck, I roll two joints. I do it because I roll better joints. We light up our joints and head for the freeway. I feel immediate relief. Our journey back to downtown is happy. We dump on our ex-wives. How they screwed up our lives and forced us into rely on dope to get through the day to remain sane. We discuss crazy ideas for Marilyn, our design project for the competition.

"'What if we put a waterfall between her four legs?' Jose suggests.

"'No! No! No! Too obvious,' I laugh. 'Everyone will get that Marilyn is peeing on LA!' (Which, come to think of it, is not a bad idea.)

"We work on Marilyn into the wee hours of Saturday morning. Perched on red steel high heels, Marilyn gets ever taller: sixty, seventy, eighty stories high. Inclined elevators take visitors thirty stories up from four, erector set-like legs. A giant three-story bowl of steel and glass full of concessions constitutes her hips and waist. From there, clear glass elevators rise up to her head, affording visitors an amazing vista as they ascend fifty-seven stories through a network of woven steel to the restaurant deck and the observation deck above.

"On the observation deck, the ultimate ride awaits: the world's highest Ferris wheel, and maybe the biggest, at twenty stories, larger even than London's Eye.

We imagine the Ferris wheel as Marilyn's head and a rider as spinning around her head in brilliant circumference of moving lightings that can be seen for miles, perhaps even one hundred miles by approaching aircraft. In a glass cabin at the crown of her head, a rider would be at a point one hundred and seven stories high with a magnificent view out over the Los Angeles basin with the ocean's flat rim bordering the west and south, the San Gabriel Mountains jagged rim forming the North, and all of the megalopolis spreading endlessly beneath and to the east. As the wheel turns the riders would be rotated out into space with nothing supporting them below or above. They would feel as if in a space capsule hovering above the city until pulled back into the safety of Marilyn's boney steel structure. The Marilyn traveler would get the best of two greatest exhibition thrills ever created: the Eiffel Tower observation platform and the Columbian World's Fair Ferris wheel. But now, a century later, the two exhibitions would be combined and surpassed, beyond the belief that a shaft could be this tall in earthquake country and carry the forces of an enormous mechanical wheel to the earth. This would be the greatest view and the best thrill ride in the world. We think people would pay money to do this. We hoot and laugh. The tower is so LA. We are truly high. I have forgotten my negative thoughts. I am sped up, charged with energy, and my mind is on fire. Passion has arrived. I am ready to ride."

"Ah, Marilyn," I sigh. "It was Jane who came up with the metaphor."

"No, she didn't," Carlotta hisses. "It was I who whispered the idea in your ear. Marilyn had other, less subtle nuances that did leap from Jane's febrile imagination. What about Marilyn's little offspring, the alligators that would drop down a slide between her legs into the big pond?"

I laugh, recalling Jane's madcap suggestion. "I'd almost forgotten. The slide was below Marilyn's hips, quite wide and ten times the height of a normal slide. From the underside of her hips, alligators would drop and slide down into the big pool that flowed out below her legs into the rest of Pershing Square. It was a brilliant recreation of the alligator slide, one of Los Angeles' first attractions at the turn of the twentieth century. A sly homage, to my mind, to Los Angeles' darker side."

"Only you would choose to go there," Carlotta says.

"We toned the idea down, you know. I wanted Marilyn to drop alligator eggs every four hours onto a special pad, where they would bust open and little alligators would wiggle out and slide down the slide."

"Eww! Disgusting!" says Carlotta, pulling a grotesque face.

"After Marti and Jose stopped laughing, we figured the alligators would never survive the drop, even if we provided a soft landing. They would end up alligator mush. I reluctantly agreed to abandon the idea, but I thought it had great symbolic potential: the great mechanical Marilyn, a Hollywood dinosaur, drops her eggs on LA as an indictment of its cultural pretensions."

"It's probably why you didn't win."

"We never *expected* to win."

"You *never* expect to win! That was your problem."

"We did get mentioned in the newspaper article about the competition. I believe the reporter said something to the effect of 'there was even an entry that mimicked the Eiffel Tower.' He did not get the originality and subtleties of Marilyn. Oh, well, that is my fate. A genius is never really recognized in his own time."

"I am still upset about the alligators, and I need a rest in the ladies room to recover my equilibrium."

"Why don't you do that?"

Only moments later, Carlotta emerges from the bathroom in a new costume: leather skirt, corset, spiked choker and wrist bands, fishnet stockings, and five-inch heels. She wears bright red lipstick and brandishes a riding crop.

"Wow, look at you!" I say admiringly. "Now you're dressed as you should be to play the part of Giant Jane."

"Be quiet, little boy," replies Carlotta, beating the crop rhythmically against her meaty thigh like a Nazi torturer. "I've come to teach you manners and administer some overdue discipline. Sit up straight at your desk!"

I obey mechanically, sniggering in spite of myself.

"You think this is funny, little boy?"

"I think it is hilarious."

Thwack! The crop comes down hard on my desk. "Do you admit you are powerless over drugs and your life became unmanageable?"

"Oh, no! You're not going to start in on me with that twelve step stuff."

Carlotta glowers at me. "I said, 'Do you admit you are powerless over drugs and your life became unmanageable'?"

"I will not say it, because I don't believe it. I could manage marijuana. I could even stop it, which I did several times."

"You are a pothead and you have no control over your addiction. I ask you again. 'Do you admit you are powerless over drugs and your life has become unmanageable'?"

"No, I don't," I reply, crossing my arms defiantly.

"Get up from your chair!"

"I will not."

Thwack goes the crop. "Yes. You. Will," says Carlotta, enunciating each word with coldhearted menace.

"Hey, wait a minute," I blubber. "This isn't real. Go away."

I bolt upright from my chair and stumble. The chair falls backwards.

"For the last time: Do you admit you are powerless over drugs and your life has become unmanageable?"

"I, I'm not going to say any such—"

Thwack! The crop sings through the air, stinging my arm.

"Fuck! What are you doing to me?"

"Get down on your hands and knees. This is what we do to little men who won't follow their mistress' orders. Down *now*!"

"All right! All right! I will do it. Just don't hit me again."

"That's a good boy."

I assume the position. Carlotta puts one of her spiked heels in the middle of my back.

"Crawl, little man," she commands, straddling my back. "You are going to give Carlotta a ride."

"I am not!"

Thwack! The crop smites my buttock.

"Ouch! That hurts."

"Do you admit you are powerless over drugs and your life has become unmanageable?"

"Never!"

Thwack!

"Carlotta thinks Carlton likes to be treated like this. Crawl, you little bucket of slime, crawl toward the bathroom." I obey. "Now, I will ask you one more time: 'Do you admit you are power—"

"What's going on in there?" barks Nurse Maria, flinging open my door. "I heard yelling. Mr. Davis, what are you doing down on the floor?"

"Ah … I dropped my pen," I mutter. Standing up quickly, I realize I am only wearing my underwear and blush fiercely.

"There is something fishy going on in here," says Maria. She conducts a perfunctory search and, satisfied that only the slumbering Smitty and I are present, strides to door. "Leave this door open in the future," she orders me and disappears down the hall.

"Carlotta, you almost got me in a lot of trouble!" I complain, although she isn't there.

From somewhere in the void, her laughter peals. "The stoned nude has stumbled down the staircase and found the light," she whispers. "Shall I show you?"

CHAPTER 16

SEEDLESS IN THE GLORY HOLE

CLUB MEDS CONVENES ON THE PATIO outside the common room beyond the dining room early Wednesday morning before breakfast. Ryan, June, Greg, Mauricio, Ray, and I are in attendance. We are talking marijuana.

"I was into purple green outs," says Ryan.

"I get it," says Greg, bobbing his head.

"Whaz's dat?" asks Mauricio.

"Purple buds and green weed! Smoked as much as possible," replies Ryan with a laugh, rocking back in his green plastic chair. "I used to ride with a motorcycle team that had purple jerseys with green lettering. We called ourselves Team Seedless. We rode and did movie stunts stoned. That's until I crashed and hurt my back. Now I have a stimulator in my back to stop the pain. I have to go to the doctor regularly to get the device adjusted. Now I walk my dog, tend my garden, and try not to be depressed. All too often, it doesn't work."

"Pot makes me dreamy," Ray puts in. "My smoking buddies used to tell me, 'Don't bogart the joint!' when we were smoking, because I'd forget I had it in my fingers. Why did we say bogart? I forget."

"It came from Humphrey Bogart, the tough guy actor, who always had a cigarette hanging from his lips. His nicotine habit killed him," says Greg, shaking a cigarette from his pack and lighting up.

"My friends always said bogart, too," I concur. "I spent six or more years stoned on the best dope from Northern California, Thailand, and Hawaii. I'd get the packets of dope that mainly had the bud of the marijuana plant with very little leaf. The buds were still semi-damp and a beautiful reddish, purple-brown color. I'd crumble up the buds in my fingers and roll a joint. My fingers would get sticky from the resin. My routine was an espresso and a joint first thing in the morning for all those years. I thought I was cool, living the artist's life beyond the boundaries of normal people."

"Ganja was everywhere. Nobody I knew didn't smoke it," says Ray.

"Not everyone was into pot. I never smoked it. My drug of choice was crack," adds June.

"Crackheads are a whole different story. Let's save that for another meeting of Club Meds," says Ray. "I am sure many of us have tales to tell about our misadventures with that drug." Everyone smiles and let out little snorts of laughter.

I tell the group, "Dr. Wortz, the psychologist, to whom I went for help with my depression, said to me that marijuana augments the state that you were already in. If you are happy, you are happier. If you are sad, you are more sad."

"Is dat zo? I never heard dat before," says Mauricio. "I would zust get high and trip out on da colors, forms, and da look of peoples. It made me real quiet, and never more melancholic zan I already was."

"I couldn't get away from it," I reply. "Marijuana was everywhere in the loft building where I lived. I paid a heavy price for my use. Everyone knew I was a pothead. I lost my teaching position at the university over it. Some of the students complained I taught loaded. I did, but I didn't care. Stoned, I thought my words were brilliant. What a joke! The joke was on me."

The three of us in the group without a smoke lit up cigarettes and inhaled deeply in remembrance of our times as druggies. The group grew quiet, and when the cigarettes were short like roaches, we put them out in the overflowing ashtray and split up, heading for breakfast.

I wished I could smoke a joint. It would mellow my thoughts. The words of the guys on the patio are troubling to me. My attacks of the black brain were caused by childhood traumas, not my abuse of pot. When would I get a psychiatrist, I wondered? Three days have passed and the hospital still hasn't provided me with a doctor. I could discuss with this person the medication that is making me eat like a horse and never be satisfied. I could discuss with the doctor my use of marijuana, which I am sure was tangential to my problems with depression.

"You are wrong about the drugs in the '80s, but first you must confront your drug abuse, which grew worse as marijuana failed to provide the relief you desired."

"Carlotta, you're always turning up, like a bad penny!" I exclaim. "Come to challenge my beliefs again? What's with the funky toga? I thought black was your favorite color?"

"I am making an exception this time. The reddish-brown toga and the green of the laurel leaves symbolize your marijuana use. The colors of the toga harmonize with my auburn hair. The greens of the laurel leaves are my victory crown. Unfortunately, the leaves come down too far on my head and tickle my ears. Shall I dance for you to make you smile?"

"As long as you don't make like Isadora Duncan, prancing around the forest in her flowing togas. Can you do a hip-hop routine? Bust a coupla moves?"

"Never! It would be unseemly for a muse to … shake her booty."

"But not a hooker or a whore."

"Don't go there, Carlton! There are things we both have to seek redemption for, and it was while we were loaded on drugs."

"Marijuana wasn't that way," I counter. "Marijuana was good. Ideas flowed like the swirling, circular currents of the sea. Thoughts would travel to interesting places, then come back to where they began."

"That is a lie. Marijuana was a vortex, a cone into which you sank. The analogy is more like wastewater in a toilet, spinning down the plumbing of the mind. You already admitted the big price you paid for smoking dope. What about the gay sex you got into?"

"I don't want to go *there*."

"Another time then."

After my morning process group, I lie on my bed and wax nostalgic about the copious amounts of dope I used to buy. I had a secure source of pot. One of Trader Josh's representatives delivered it to the loft in a business suit with an attaché case full of pre-packaged dope. He handed me a price sheet for the "Tea Club," which listed and described nine kinds of marijuana. The cheapest, "Compañero," cost less than $100 a quarter lid and was described as "a traditional south-of-the-border solution for work that is too hard, days that are too long, and tempers that are too short." The best stuff was "Big Kahuna," described as "a baby seal skin coat decorated with bald eagle feathers" and costing $1,100 a lid. I could afford a quarter of this every once in a while at $275. Big Kahuna was all bud of an intense, reddish purple-brown hue. No twigs needed to be removed from this marijuana, and it was seedless too. The dope really put you out there where the colors, the forms, and the thoughts were the most intense. You thought your mind was full of brilliant ideas, but for the most part, you were almost comatose. Playing in my loft, I would drift off into a most pleasant place of inactivity. Anxiety is forgotten. Emotional feelings are buried in the buzz.

"Green Mountain"—"a triumph of agro-engineering"—and "Dragon Lady"—"a pungent brown green tea with an exotic spin"—were, at $135 and a $150 a quarter lid, respectively, my favorite buys. These were mid-range dopes that were mainly bud with a few seeds, requiring careful separation of the drug from the tiny pits. Dragon Lady and Green Mountain kept me pleasantly stoned and still able to function. I could carry on a conversation without drifting into an out-of-body experience. I could talk about art, architecture, play Ping-Pong, and drive a car.

My trip down hallucinogen lane is interrupted by a knock on my door and I sit up in bed. A tiny woman dressed in a black suit, showing a hint of a red blouse at the neck, enters my room. She introduces herself as Dr. Poliquin and says she will be my psychiatrist. After a few pleasantries and a promise that she will adjust my medication to address my appetite issues, she heads for the door, calling over her shoulder that the nurse will fetch me for a full-fledged session on Friday.

"What time on Friday?" I sing out belligerently, but the brusque headshrinker is already clip-clopping down the hall.

After lunch, despite my misgivings, I decide to attend the art therapy session. I make a collage of images cut from magazines of women of various sizes, surrounded by an rough oval of leaves and grass. I name my paper and paste creation "Seedless in the Glory Hole." My creation is an homage to the feminine, marijuana, and sex. I think my creation isn't too bad, but I still throw the picture out at the end of the session. Therapy doesn't make art, I say to myself. I go back to my room feeling depressed and still absorbed in remembrance of marijuana and the problems I had with women and sex when I was a pothead. I sit at the desk and begin thumbing through my journals.

"You didn't have a problem with women, you had a problem with homosexuality," says Carlotta, standing next to the desk still wearing her sylvan toga and green laurel.

"I was only queer when I was depressed."

"Carlton, you were depressed all the time, and especially depressed when you went to San Francisco to see your daughter and confronted your ex-wife. And what did you do? You smoked as much marijuana as you could, then went out to find the gay bathhouses."

"I can't deny what you say, but I still liked women."

"No you didn't. You were mean to women. You liked the weird sex with men. It appealed to your stoned mind. Open your journal and read the pages where your thumb has fallen."

With great reluctance, I oblige:

"I did not want to go out at night to find women. I'd rather go to San Francisco's South of Market neighborhood, the unfashionable zone below Market Street where the homeless lived in the alleyways and few Victorian houses had been restored because they were mixed in with cheap commercial warehouses, flop houses, and auto shops. There I could delve into the world of homosexuality represented by the leather bars and the sex clubs sprinkled liberally in the dinge. My friend suggests we go to a singles bar, but I realize his offer has little attraction for me, since the likelihood of success is so minimal. Women make me angry. I turn him down, smoke a joint, and go to South of Market.

"A gay newspaper acquired on Polk Street advertises the various clubs in South of Market. I pick the South of Market Club. On a dark street the club, a single story commercial building, is identified by one door painted black with a white circle around which the name South of Market Club is written. Inside the door is a short black hallway leading to an open counter cut in a wall where you can purchase entry, a membership in effect. The club is through a turnstile and around a wall into another large and high black-walled room with very low illumination.

"White painted cubicles with red doors and eight inch holes in the end and side walls fill the center of the black room, leaving only a narrow aisle around the perimeter. Men wander around the path from cubicle to cubicle to the constant

bipolar bare

blare of disco music. The cubicle doors have two white painted numbers: the number of the door and the number of the door opposite on the other side of a central partition. The door numbers look like fractions: 6/12, 5/11, and 4/10. It takes a few minutes to understand the code. The first number is the number of the door to the little room in front of you. The number below the slash is the number of the little room on the opposite side of the corridor. Sure enough if you walk around the corridor those doors are numbered 10/4, 11/5, and 12/6. As I wander the circumference with other men, this place reminds me of Russian constructivism: the odd numbering, the black, the white, the red, and the holes in the walls. Men stroll along the line of doors pulling on the handles until an unlatched door opens, and they disappear inside.

"Inside, three walls of the cubicle are pierced by oval holes at the height of the genitals. Glory holes, I learn they are called. You squat and look through the hole to see if anyone is available in the holes surrounding you. Sometimes, looking at you through the hole, there is another face, sometimes more than one. Either party drops his trousers and presents his penis through the hole to be sucked by the person on the other side. The only sight one has of the partner is a bulge of the balls protruding from the hole and the erect penis pointing outward. One's penis is sucked while amyl is inhaled.

"Upstairs are movies, more booths, and a place where men suck each other in the open and crowds gather to watch. The music throbs and creates an eerie silent world where no one talks. From a white railing, you can watch the activities in the cubicles below. Two men in one large booth work on each other and on anything that presents itself through the walls. One man has his buttocks pushed up against the wall while a man on the other side is screwing him. Men lean against the black walls and others circle the booths furtively. Two men exchange nods. A blond biker goes into ten. The bearded man in business attire opens the next door, number eleven, and slips in, latching the plywood door. The suit drops his drawers and wiggles his ass to the hole in the wall. The biker's cock and balls dangle through the hole in the wall. Suit squeezes the balls and the cock goes erect. Biker leans against the hole, pressing his body hard against the wall. His hands grab two small drawer pulls positioned at the top of the wall. Suit drops to his knees and begins to suck upon the proffered penis. Each man inhales from the top of a small brown bottle of amyl. Biker presses harder against the wall. Suit tries to engulf more of the penis. Biker's head and upper back arch in orgasm. Suit pulls away, fumbles with his pants, and, removing a handkerchief, wipes his chin, stands, pulls up his pants, cinches his belt, and opens the door. Biker is already gone.

"From above, I imagine animated Egyptian hieroglyphics, cartouches full of cocks, balls, buttocks, and bald heads. I watch many men suck each other. I get sucked and suck other men. I lose my glasses and my wallet, which causes me considerable inconvenience but does not deter my return many times to the club. The sexual promiscuity of men is much more weird and enticing than the pain of female companionship. I like this gay activity, but I am repulsed. Is this the culmination of a free market, where anything can be purchased for a price? Should we call it Cockitalism?"

"You became a prime participant in the economy of Cockitalism, going to that club every time you came to San Francisco," comments Carlotta.

"I can't deny it. I did a drawing where one man's penis protrudes through the glory holes to ejaculate five cubicles away. The semen explodes to fill San Francisco Bay. A giant eyeball watches, while connected to an electrical socket on a boat floating on the sea of semen."

"This drawing is one of your strange concoctions. What does it mean?"

"An artist doesn't have to explain his meaning. You take from it whatever you want."

"And this you did at the height of the AIDS epidemic."

"I wanted to get AIDS so I could end my miserable life. Call it suicide by fucking."

"But try as you did, you didn't get AIDS."

"I know it was insane, and I regretted each incident after my depression passed, but I could not help myself when I was angry and down, which I often was."

"You didn't think clearly about the consequences of your actions, even when you saw wasted men ravaged by the scourge of AIDS."

"I didn't want to, I wanted more strange sex and I found it. Here is another piece about my activities."

bipolar bare

East in San Francisco; 1981; 14 x 24 inches; colored pencil

"I go to the Folsom Street Club down the street from the first club, pay my dues, and go in. The place is totally black. The club is full and most of the men are dressed in leather. Some have on only leather chaps that reveal their genitals and asses. Many have leather straps crisscrossing their bare chests and backs. A few wear military caps. These tough guy posers are patrolling the corridors and inhabit many of the white cubicles. I investigate the series of white rooms inside the black shell. Unlike the cubicles at the South of Market Club the little rooms here have two doors for entry. One on each corridor, making the room a long narrow slot divided in the middle by a raised platform. This makes possible three way action in each booth.

"I am a wandering, aimless outsider. Upstairs are more rooms. One has a leather swing. No one is in it. Down another set of stairs are more cubicles. These have large holes in the wall. They look like they are for the presentation of the buttocks—more glory holes. The men in the rooms are up on the ledge with their legs in the air and their buttocks presented to the door. I watch for a while. I see men enter the cubicles and fuck the men inside.

"I enter a cubicle, undress, get on the ledge, put my legs up, and wait. Many men passing by my door look in the peephole of the outside door, but nothing happens. I am getting discouraged and thinking of leaving when a man enters. He drops his pants. A large and long penis pops out. He lathers up his penis with the Crisco available in a paper container next to the ledge and enters me. He fucks me for a long time. I breathe amyl and love the sensation. He asks, 'You want it slow?' 'Yes,' I say. He has me roll over and works in and out of me very hard and very slow. The pleasure is mixed with pain. He rams his penis in as deep as he can, grunts, comes, and pulls out slowly. He puts a handkerchief over his penis. 'Your ass is made for fucking,' he says and departs. I can hardly walk but contemplate staying longer. I am not up to it. I dress and leave depressed.

"I didn't even know what the man looked like. He was wearing dark sunglasses, a military cap, a leather jacket, and jeans with chaps. I am sick and repulsed when I reach my car. I feel guilty. I hate myself. I want to die, but I also want to return and do this again. I like this dark anti-world. The black and white spaces speak of a divided universe, which I believe is my home. The aggressors are in black; the victims are in white. In this gay world, I reverse the stance I take in my daylight life. In this dark world, I become the receiver, the passive one. I don't want to be the masculine one. I want them to come to me and give it to me. I become the dark feminine: the witch, the bitch, and the killer woman."

"I don't know that you do me justice," says Carlotta. "The feminine in you does not have to be dark and full of revenge. I believe that you have cast me in the role of whore out of your own insecurities. You are educated enough to know that man, in the largest sense, is a union of the masculine and the feminine, the yin and the yang. Your own version is born from mental disorder, which is our goal for you to mend, appreciate, and use for a greater good."

"Oh, please Carlotta, I am you, and you are a two-bit whore. You fucked anything that moved."

"Carlton, you prude, I don't think you should be ashamed of a little good sex. I personally like a good lay every one in a while."

"Once in a while! Every chance you got, you would get laid."

"I was a tad horny. After all, you did keep me shut away like some genie in a bottle for far too long."

"You make me blush. That was pure pornography. Many men have homosexual experiences—women, too, for that matter. What we don't usually see or hear described is the full detail of those experiences, what people liked or why they liked it. I struggled with my proclivities for years and I find they came only at certain times. When they came, they ruined any desire I had to be with a woman at other times."

"Maybe you are bi-sexual."

"You could be right, Carlotta. Clear your ears for the next batch of this sexual saturnalia."

"Am I a homosexual? I refuse to confront the truth. While married, I did not yearn for homosexual interludes. Prior to marriage, I attempted several liaisons without much success or satisfaction. I accepted homosexuality as a human reality and did not regard it as morally wrong, but as a lifestyle, it was not one for me.

"When my marriage dissolved and my dissatisfaction with female relationships was at its zenith, I ventured out and tried homosexuality. I regarded my excursions as purely experimental. While it wasn't my normal predilection, I found I enjoyed the act and indulged in it more and more. Should I perhaps call myself bi-sexual?

"I dated women. Social evenings were spent with females culminating in sex. The insertion of the penis is done with a curled lip of disgust. Female intercourse gave me little pleasure. Sex was work, a puffing and grunting toward release and revulsion. Lying over a female body, penis gone limp I wish for something else. Anger knots in my body. I wish to be gone, out of sight of the abhorrent form prostrate in the bed. Is it the knowledge that this intimacy is *not* intimate? The closeness of the contact failed to bridge the gap of loneliness. My center is never reached and I am never seen, never revealed. The squirt of sex creates a screen that forever distances. The sea of semen fills the bay inside the Golden Gate Bridge.

"I stand alone behind the screen in my dark cloud whose only physical manifestation is the dribbled sexual juice, mine and countless, anonymous others. I am gone from myself because I live a lie. I make love to women but do not desire them. I desire to be screwed and suck like a woman. The logic of mind and action are inverted.

"But there are days when this does not happen. There are days when I truly enjoy the company of women and enjoy sexual intercourse with them. If I have a choice, I always choose female companionship over male. They are more interesting, more sensitive, and more caring. Then the change comes. I know not what I am, a traumatized heterosexual or a natural homosexual. Ambivalence is my prevailing state of mind."

"Very interesting," says Carlotta. "When you were depressed, which happened every month, or when a bad event occurred, you went to the bathhouses to search out gay sex with a view toward killing yourself by contracting AIDS."

"Carlotta, I am heterosexual when I am not depressed," I reply. "Yet, AIDS was a constant worry. I did not want to give it to someone else. That is why I eventually stopped dating women."

"You knew you were in trouble. Your emotions ran wild. You were up one day, working feverishly on your loft and your sculptures, and down the next. Your emotions ran the gamut from manic energy and humor to extreme frustration, irritation, and anger, and finally to utter melancholy, where you would hide in your bed, dreaming that spiders were descending on you from every direction."

"Meeting my mother made me sick. I was just a little bit off balance. It went away after a year or two."

"No, it did not. You are in denial. You are lying again. You were running wild, staying up all night to work for days in a row, or going out to bathhouses late in the evenings and rejecting all the women who presented themselves to you. Your cycle of depression to high energy became faster and faster."

"I was running from and toward you, Carlotta. The feminine in me was driving me crazy. Why couldn't you be a male presence?"

"As if! I am female. Muses always are."

"You are odd, a terrible visitation on my life."

"Odd? I will grant you that, but the oddity starts with your psyche. I am your lucky charm. You refuse to recognize the gift I bring you."

"Gift? You are a product of my depressed imagination."

"Are you depressed now? Full of medication, you shouldn't be."

"No, I am not depressed now."

"And here I am, still with you, a rich and essential part of your very nature."

"Maybe I am depressed."

"Carlotta thinks you like your depression. It's a good excuse for your failure."

"That was an unfair comment. I can't control the coming or going of depression. I must wait it out."

"I think Carlton loves his dreams and his drawings. You never let go of the dreams or do anything with your drawings, except hide them in a drawer. You see in them great significance. Maybe they are just will-o'-the-wisps, nothing more than the result of your pot smoking. Perhaps your mind was trying to cleanse itself of the poison you ingested."

"That could be true," I admit. "I remember my dreams better than reality. They are certainly more interesting. I can't control them and I can't stop thinking about them. They present so many possibilities. They spread my focus over a hundred possibilities. I say I would like to focus like other people can, but I can't. It eludes me. I am lost in a sea of recurring darkness. Isolated in my bed, I can watch these illusions like a movie, without going out in the world and facing real failure. Even if the dreams are nightmares and I scream, the unreal world is better than the real."

"This path got you nowhere, Carlton. You needed to stop smoking marijuana."

"I didn't want to. Marijuana made me feel good."

"Feel good? What about the debilitating depressions, where you went to bed for days on end? Did you think marijuana didn't contribute to your painful isolation?"

"I don't know."

"I *do* know. I was so drugged up, I had to bury myself within you. Marijuana masked all your other emotions and only left you angry, which is still your base emotion."

"I laughed sometimes. I was often light and entertaining. My friends called me the Cosmic Humoroid."

"You created this situation for yourself, Carlton. You wanted a life that was different and you got it."

"I didn't expect it to be so difficult."

"The difficulty was predictable. When you consciously decided to become an outlaw, you should have expected what you got."

"We looked at ourselves as cultural outlaws and reveled in that fact. Being depressed about it was not something I expected. Carlotta, let me continue my reading please. The next passage may answer your challenges."

"Five years on marijuana. I know I am an addict. Yet, I thought the causes and sources of my present condition, my failures as an architect and artist, was a consequence of meeting my mother, not a result of my drug use. In the art world, drugs of various kinds are readily available. I became a devotee of what on the surface may appear to be the least detrimental of these drugs. Pot was certainly the most pervasive stimulant available. I liked smoking it from the times I had it in the '60s until today. In art school and graduate school, there was almost always some of this exotic smoking material available.

"Like most of my contemporaries, I tried puffing the weed and found it more enjoyable and less debilitating than alcohol. I drank alcohol to excess as an undergraduate. I can remember very drunken evenings of wild behavior, jumping from the dormitory window into snow banks followed often by sessions of puking over the toilet, wishing for a blackout to end the spinning. I can recall the Scotch I drank before attempting suicide. Marijuana worked differently. I was not belligerent but sat in conversation or alone, delighting in the variations of my circular thoughts. Spaced out was preferable to pissed off.

"The smoking I indulged in was minimal, a joint at a party and the odd few during the week. My memories of the occurrences are always pleasant. At parties, friends passed around a joint happily, laughing and engaged in intense debates on contemporary issues. Friends sat in a gazebo on a summer evening smoking, talking about ideas, observing the shadows of the trees, hearing the sounds of distant trucks rolling past our little island of dreams. Our activity was a conscious defiance of bourgeois norms. After all, we were barely twenty—it was the '60s, an era of questioning old ideas—and we were artists whose role was to tromp on the established mores of society to foment a new and better vision. A joint loosened that vision for my generation, as perhaps alcohol loosened the visions of previous generations.

"This first period of drugs lasted not very long: a summer, a fall, and several times a year in the late 1960s. For most of the 1970s I smoked no dope. I never took mushrooms, LSD, or cocaine. I was afraid of these more potent drugs. My experience of attempted suicide in the mid-60s warned me off any substances where I thought I would lose total control over reality. While I was fascinated by the prospect of taking a trip, I was fearful of the consequences to someone like me who was given to immense anger and self-hatred. The propaganda books in circulation at the time about the horrors of LSD made me even more timid to take the plunge.

"Drugs were never a big part of my life until I came to California. In San Francisco, I began to smoke dope regularly and took magic mushrooms. Getting high mitigated the boredom of employment. At lunch, my friends and I would toke after eating. We would go to the park with bag lunches, eat, smoke, and complain about our lot as exploited architects. Others similarly imprisoned in white-collar work were seen huddled in small clusters, commiserating as the sweet smell of pot wafted from their camps. When I moved to Southern California and joined the artists' community, my habit became an essence in my life.

"Once on the drugs, I couldn't release myself. I was too unconscious for too much of my life. I was full of hope for my new life and full of anxiety for the choice I made. Thus, I found myself in that place where I neither knew what I was doing or who I was. I knew I had no control. I knew I was operating in two selves. The first I imagined was an infantile self, screaming but unheard, unseen, and unalterable. The second was a mature, rational self who could deal with the disappointments of adulthood. You see, I was a person who became stuck in duality.

"Drugs fed an infantile, homosexual self. Weed woke it up and it emerged again and again, each time hungrier and more irritated than before. I could not stop feeding that self. I was fascinated by what I perceived to be the energy there. The state of high sucks me into its whirlpool, where feelings are anesthetized and intellect is given freedom to run and run, motoring on oblivious to the feelings that confuse my mature self. Dr. Wortz said I take dope as an anesthetic. Anesthetic to what, I wondered at the time. Now I think it is an anesthetic to the sensations and feelings in my body. You don't have them when you get high. You want everything condensed into mind awareness. You are wide awake in one half of your mind by anesthetizing the other half.

"How many personality parts are there? Fourteen, at least—probably many more. There is the infant and the mature man. There is Carlton and Carlotta. I am alternately the man playing woman, then the woman trapped within the man. There is the negative I see altogether too much. There is the positive I did not see enough. There is the irrational and the rational I. There is the self-destructive and a constructive I. The shift between heterosexuality and homosexuality is the most apparent manifestation. When I take drugs, I can't control the appearance of the alternate me. They come as they wish to come. They rise and fall at will. Each of these characters comes to life without my awareness. I find myself in a persona seemingly after it has already acted and asserted its nature. I am a sequential being for whom there is no solid center of self, but rather a shifting structure of mood condensing into the alternate selves."

"Carlton, what if you were weedless in the glory hole?" inquires Carlotta, sitting on top of the desk and looking down on me like a giant Greek goddess in her toga.

"I don't understand your meaning."

"I mean, what if you went to the sex clubs sober and participated in the gay sex without benefit of the drugs."

"I couldn't do that. Whenever I was sober, I had no desire to go."

"Could you not be a gay man?"

"No, I could not. I had to be the woman dressed in male clothing. I was you, Carlotta, my female alter ego."

"But I did not require you to be stoned. I am accessible to you sober, too."

"What should I be as a sober Carlotta? A lesbian?"

"I did not say that. I am your muse, who can speak to you of the positive and the beautiful."

"No, no. You are the whore of my addiction. The more I released you, the more crazed I became, and that happened when I switched from marijuana to crack."

bipolar bare

"I admit a predilection for that substance. It loosened my inhibitions and made me forget my role."

"Women are nothing but trouble!" I declare. "I recall what one said to me recently: 'You have so many separate lives and none of them are integrated into one another.' Another truth, and she didn't even know the extent … she didn't know I was a queer. She didn't know I don't like women for sex, yet I loved women otherwise. They are all unsatisfactory in some way. Sex with them was a hardship. No, sex with them was a horror. I was always torn apart, wanting to be in a relationship. I was always damned because a decent relationship was impossible because the feminine me is a whore. I was always saved the possibility of a relationship because the she in me satisfies my need for her. I can be she. Being both solved the difficulty of life, and for this self, there was no need for another. But wait—it didn't work, we were never companions to each other. We were solitary separateness, sequentially fulfilling fantasies but never creating any relativity. Each sound from self is spoken to an empty opposite. Sad days for the one who knows loneliness."

"Can't our relationship be different now?" Carlotta implores. "We are sober and getting treatment for our mental illness."

"But we are still separate, when we should be one," I state firmly. "There are many things remaining to talk about. Now, get your toga-wearing ass off my desk. You are intimidating me."

"As you wish," says Carlotta, smiling. "But remember weedless in the glory hole."

With a swish of her toga, she is gone.

CHAPTER 17

QUESTIONS RELATED TO MIND

It is Wednesday morning and the process group room has filled up quickly. There are twenty people in the room. All the chairs in the circle are filled and several people have to sit behind them. How many people show up each day is an unknown. Some days there are few, as the patients go back to bed after breakfast or never get up at all. Other times, it is standing room only. Today is one of those days when so many people appear little can get accomplished.

Several patients are reluctant to talk in front of a large group. Other patients love having a big audience and talk forever. I look around the room. Julie has come. She's a crack addict whose boyfriend abuses her. The state took away her children, and she is having trouble getting them back. There are two new faces next to her. Annie, who is depressed, sits next to Peggy, an alcoholic. Peggy likes to read and always has a book with her. Dostoevsky's *The Idiot* lies in her lap. Todd, an alcoholic, sits next to her. Next is another person whose name I can never remember, but she's a lawyer, a lesbian, and depressed. I probably can't remember her name because I don't like her. She whines and gets upset when she feels she doesn't get enough time to talk.

Then there's Kelly, a young woman who's very depressed and suicidal. Inez, the former model, is tucked into a corner as if she is trying to hide from the group. Rafael, the gay postman, sits up very straight in his chair and smiles at me. I wonder if he senses my past. Mary sits next to Alma, a heroin addict. Mary has one of her big flowered hats in her lap covering her arms. She is a cutter, a person who likes to slash her arms with a knife. In the group yesterday, she said she wanted to pour boiling water on her arms.

Rick sits next to me. He is a former police officer who took some bullets in his spine in the line of duty. He now walks with difficulty on a cane and is severely depressed. Steve is in a wheelchair near the door. He is paraplegic from a trucking accident. He is severely depressed and suicidal. Wendy is bipolar. Her husband abandoned her. She lives alone near a freeway, doing her yoga and unhappily tending her plants. Even Smitty has turned out, as have Ryan, Ray, June, and Mauricio. They sit in chairs behind the circle. Jeanine, the group leader, takes her usual chair between Wendy and Julie at the corner of the room.

"How is everyone doing this morning?" Jeanine asks. The group mutters some incoherent response. "We'll go around the room now. You will introduce yourselves, say how you are doing, and if you want some time from the group. We'll start with you, Julie."

Julie says she's fine. She doesn't want to talk because the group's too big. The two new people introduce themselves. Tony says it's his first day and he just wants to see what happens. Bill feels the same way. Peggy complains that nothing can be accomplished when so many people are in one room. She has lots that she wants to talks about but will not do it in front of so many people.

Rachel—that's the bitch's name!—the lesbian lawyer, makes a long-winded introduction of herself. She says she is lonely and wants to discuss how she can deal with that loneliness. Kelly can barely be heard as she speaks.

"Are you all right?" Jeanine asks. Kelly bursts into tears. "We are going to come back to you first after all the introductions are done."

Several more people introduce themselves, but I have mentally drifted away. Jeannine turns to me and asks me why I look so grim.

"I'm a little angry at my situation," I say.

"You have problem with anger, don't you?" Jeannine replies. "I have the report from the Mariah Unit."

"Yes," I respond. "I need to talk about that and my feeling that I'm split like two people."

The introductions move on around the group, but I am not paying much attention. I am looking at Kelly, crying in her chair, and Rafael, who is always bitching about his unfaithful lover, leering at me as if he can read my mind. I want to flee the room to avoid talking about my past, my sexual escapades, and my split personality. There is an anger that wants to challenge anyone who might think ill of me. There is the feeling that if I want to rid myself of guilt and to understand what I did, I must bring it all to the light of day. But it is so hard. It is not pretty. It makes me seethe with fury.

"Kelly, tell us what's going on," Jeanine says, turning her attention to the downcast Kelly once all the introductions are done. Kelly looks up. Her eyes are red. Her cheeks are streaked with tears.

"I don't know if I can," she says.

"Try. We're here to support you," Jeanine says. "Aren't we?" She looks around the room. Everyone says, "Yes."

"I tried to hurt myself with scissors when I went home last week," says Kelly.

"What happened? Tell us more," Jeanine prompts her.

"I thought he was my friend. He was so kind to me while I was here," Kelly says. "I saw and talked with him every day in the hospital. Last week, after I left I had a conversation with him on the phone that was really weird. I should say something in the group about it, but I can't. On Saturday, I had a two-hour conversation with him on the telephone. He threatened me. He said he would come and hurt me when he got out of the hospital. I was really scared. That's when I tried to hurt myself and ended up back in the hospital. Now I am afraid. He is here."

"Do I know who this patient is?" I ask.

"I won't say his name," Kelly says.

"You don't have to," I reply. "I know who it is. He is a genuine wacko. I will mess him up good. I will break the bastard's knees. He deserves it. He does this to all the women he meets at the hospital."

"Carlton, you will *not* go after this guy!" Jeanine rebukes me. "You will not take your anger out on him! Do you hear me? The staff will be talking to him about what he is doing. You are to stay out of this."

Her words bring me back from the edge of my desire to be an avenger—the hunter without fear. I hesitate for a minute, thinking of the chance to beat him up. I imagine myself in the patient's food line in the cafeteria in front of the ever-smiling David, turning to him with my empty one-by-two brown plastic food tray, kicking his legs out from under him, while I smash his head with the flat of the food tray. I lean down over his confused prostrate form and say calmly, "Don't ever threaten any ladies again."

"OK, you're right Jeanine, I won't go after him," I promise, "but Kelly, you know I am your friend. I support you." I sink back into a silent sulk as the group moves on to other topics.

Staring across the room at Kelly, I am daydreaming about anger. The times I have scared the hell out of people and made them back down. Once a man approached me with a tape-wrapped pipe. I backed him down unarmed, because he knew I was going to tear him apart just by the way I looked at him. I used to be able to walk through skid row or a tough neighborhood without fear, because I showed no fear. Lowlifes backed away when they knew I would take them on and go to my death in a fight. It was all in how you looked and how you walked. The attitude was another way of flirting with suicide.

I thought the only way ahead in the world was to beat your way forward. You fought with the maximum amount of anger to overcome the obstacles thrown at you. I used to believe I could fight my way to the top.

"Carlton, talk to us about your anger," Jeanine suggests.

"What?" I come back to the group from my private thoughts. "Because life sucks. Life has no rewards. I need my anger to survive. Without it I would be nothing. I am a fucking queer when depressed and on drugs. I don't like it. I have a split personality, one male and one female. Got any other goddamned questions?"

"That's a lot of stuff to be carrying around," says Jeanine. "Anybody else have some feedback for Carlton?"

"Why do you call yourself queer? You don't like gay people?" asks Rafael.

"Oh, man, I don't want to have to deal with this right now," I respond.

"How come you are so angry all the time? Do you like pushing other people away?" says Wendy.

"I can't deal with this," I say. I get up and stalk out of the room. I go to my room, climb into bed, and stare at the ceiling.

Late Wednesday night, the sky is clear. I am at my desk, gazing intently at the full moon reflected in the apartment complex pool beyond the hospital's fence. My hands are knitted under my nose. My anger over the process group has reached a crescendo. I think of Carlotta and voilà, she appears.

"You're a tad upset tonight," she says, taking her customary place atop my desk. "Things didn't go well at the office?"

"We're back to the old sarcastic Carlotta."

"Just trying a little levity. Tell me about what has you in a tizzy."

"Today's process group, mainly."

"Want to talk about it?"

"No."

"Oh, come now! The nighttime is the right time to get down to the nitty-gritty. And you've got to admit I've dressed the part."

Indeed, Carlotta is as Stygian as midnight from head to toe. "Back in black, I see," I comment wearily. "Black dress. Black hose. Black hair. Black *everything*. Your attire fits my mood."

"In your negative state, we are often more focused because there are no other distractions save the black state of mind. Try sitting back and relaxing. Tell big Carlotta, the black widow, what has you down."

"Carlotta, I am so tired of being angry. Being angry leads to being depressed. Being depressed leads to being suicidal. Being suicidal leads to being split. Being split leads to being queer. Being queer leads to wild behavior, then to disgust, to guilt, and finally to really deep black depression where I go to bed for days. I feel like going to bed now, never to get up again."

"Not good! I won't let you go to bed. We have to discuss the issue of your anger and being split. Describe the sequence, please."

"After hiding in bed, the whole anger cycle starts again in some fashion, including the use of drugs—especially marijuana years ago and crack cocaine today. You appear when I reach the nadir."

"Are you sure you have the sequence right? You used to smoke pot even when you were up and not angry. You thought it gave you inspiration to be creative and see things differently. Your muse appeared whenever you wanted."

"You are the other side of self."

"Other side of self? How can you be so sure that is true?"

I sigh and stretch, feeling my backbone pop. "I am not sure of anything. I can see the cycle of suicide and depression in my notebooks. I can follow the

bipolar bare

symptoms of physical change, the stiffness in the body, the headaches and irritability. It's hard to talk about, but it's not embarrassing. What follows is something else. Written in my notebooks is the other side of self I have kept secret. In the process group today, I tried to admit that I had a homosexual side. I could not do it because I feel I don't *have* a homosexual side. I have a *feminine* side. There is a distinction. I have *you*, and I am not sure I even understand that. All I know is, this side emerges when the anger becomes too great and finds its expression in the destruction of the masculine Carlton."

"You did not admit to having me as a part of your personality, if I remember correctly, until only a decade ago. How long ago is the writing you are studying?"

"Long ago, before I gave you a name. Shall I read?"

"Of course. Nothing can come between us."

"The dark and angry feminine force comes to divide me in two. Today, I am the feminine queen. I desire to suck and be fucked. The anus seeks to be the vagina. I want sex to be weird. Pleasure comes in the exploration of peculiarity and fantasy. I dreamed I am lying on a sling, bound up. Legs are strapped down and spread apart. Arms are trussed out. The head is bent back. A collar around the neck pulls the head back. The face can see the approaching erect penis, upside down. He walks forward, his stiff cock projecting out from the leather pants. He inserts it in my mouth and I begin to suck. Another man approaches unseen between the outstretched legs. His hands are greasing my body, squeezing hard the breasts, and oiling the genitals and buttocks. The penises stand erect—his and mine. He grabs them together, rubbing them rhythmically. The sling begins to move. He inserts his swelling member into me. The movement becomes frenetic. More men gather around. Some are squeezing my breasts. The breasts swell and become feminine; milk begins to flow, pouring out over my body. Another stranger begins to suck my penis. Everyone and everything is throbbing. Leather pants comes into my mouth. There is a flood of white fluid, pouring out onto the floor, creating a shallow pond of whiteness in the gloom. The second stranger comes, swelling my innards with hot juice that flows out of my anus, making the pond a lake. I come and more white juice flows, filling the room to the height of the sling with fluid. The men withdraw, slogging away through the white lake to disappear. I am left alone, slowly vibrating, dripping white ooze from my orifices, and slowly changing from human to an amoebic mass, while laughter splits the surrounding darkness. I scream and sink into the white soup."

"Gadzooks, how vivid!" says Carlotta. "Were you hungry?"

"What are you implying?"

"I had a momentary flash that the white soup was clam chowder, and your dream was a metaphor for hunger, not sex."

"Please be serious."

"All right. Personally, I found sinking into the white soup a metaphor for the return to the primordial. I didn't find it pornographic at all. There was nothing titillating in the story in the slightest. It was sad, rather, and a reflection, I think, of our depressed state of mind at the time. Why can't you find a way to call on your feminine energy at times other than when you are down in the dumps? It's very discouraging to me."

"I don't know, Carlotta. I guess it's a problem I have of integrating the two parts of a split being. At the time of these writings, I was only dimly aware that I was split. Should I attribute my sexual dysfunction to the peculiarity of my systems, left-handed, dyslexic with minimal brain dysfunction, and my upbringing? I'm weird—what can you do? I am the artistic type. Given to rages on occasion and homosexual exploits here and there. The rest of the time I behave properly."

Carlotta smiles. "Keep talking, Carlton. We're making progress. Spill your guts: I'll catch them."

"OK, you asked for it," I reply. "When I was younger, I always had two women to be my companions, each kept separate from knowledge of the other. My attempts to find one suitable female partner were unproductive. The ones I craved, I was unsuccessful attracting and far too successful with the ones who craved *me*. That was always the case with my lovers. I could never commit. I went for an older woman, who taught me the ways of love, and left my young, sexy lover with the dancer's legs and the lithe body.

"I thought about gay sex and tried several times to become experienced.

bipolar bare

I never succeeded. Dark bars and strange old men did not speak to a freedom of choice I so strongly advocated. There is nothing wrong that I can see with homosexuality, I told my girlfriends. I said that often to my future wife after we first met and found we liked to spend time together. We fell in love. The sex between us was fantastic and we had fun together at first. I was a delightful person who became full of rage without warning. I was the sunny person who became depressed and darkly suicidal. I was the person who split into two, a vengeful queen one day and a doubtful king the next.

"I am bi-sexual. They have the best of both worlds, someone said. Somehow, I don't think so, because I am not happy. I am sad. I think life's a sewer. I think myself a loser. I think I have no future. I am alive, plagued by doubt in the sunny Southern California climate. No one can be negative here. Everyone has to be positive. The good vibrations will it. It is only oneself who bars the way to joy, and I believe it. I am trapped in the prison of self. What should I do? What should I be? There is nothing to anchor oneself except the confining walls of life. If only I could laugh about it. Laugh so hard the walls of consciousness would fall in and I could get out. Maybe I can find God to help me out of my confusion."

"Carlton, what I don't get about you is the tremendous contradictions," says Carlotta, furrowing her brow. "On one hand, you see your mother as an evil whore and on the other, you loved and liked her. You are angry with women, yet you prefer them to men. You like the power and strength of men, yet you see them as weak and unreliable. You say you are not a homosexual, yet you act like one. It is as if each and every aspect of yourself is contradicted by another aspect. You cross and re-cross yourself in an ever-increasing weave of complex currents, like unsheathed wires in an electrical network that sometimes works brilliantly and other times short circuits without explanation."

"Carlotta, this is why I see myself as fundamentally split. Not that I am schizophrenic, but it is as if two beings split into multiples of two live within the body that I carry around with me. If I am not mad, then I am close to that edge. This fact became clear to me when I did a drawing, which I showed to my therapist, Dr. Wortz. The drawing, loosely based on Andrea Mantegna's three iconic paintings of St. Sebastian, is half man and half woman. Dr. Wortz had me be parts of the drawing while we talked. My writings record making the drawing and those sessions I worked with it."

"Will reading that entry provide some insight into your dilemma?" says Carlotta, leaning forward and staring straight into my eyes.

"I think it's central," I respond, turning my head aside nervously.

"OK, as long as it moves our story forward in the quest for mental health."

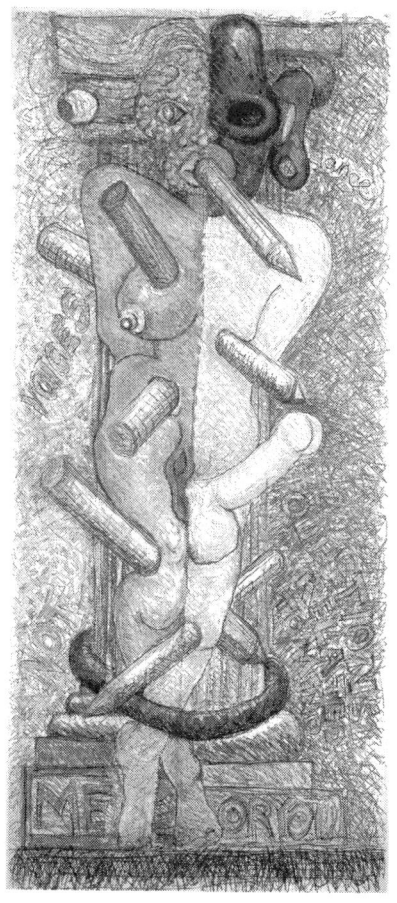

Questions Related to Mind, Me or You; 1984; 2 feet, 4 inches x 8 feet; oil stick

"I drew a huge drawing titled *Questions Related to Mind, Me or You*. The drawing, more than eight feet high, is of a large monster—half man and half woman. Each side is partially distorted. As is typical in anatomy, the right brain hemisphere controls the left side and the left hemisphere controls the right side.

bipolar bare

Thus opposite her blue body, the woman's head, represented as a dark blue mask, hides the brain that controls the right side. The hole in the mask for the eye recalls the iris-less sculptures of antiquity. The ear is an empty hole in the mask. The woman is both blind and deaf. The woman's body has one breast and two holes at her pelvis. One is her vagina, the other her anus.

"The male's body is flesh-colored and has an erect penis. The male's head is opposite his body and looks like a brain. The eye to the brain is floating in space. The male can hear and see, but the seeing is strangely disconnected from the body and thus not integrated with the person. A stake penetrates the mouth. For both the male and female communication is blocked. Other stakes penetrate both the male and the female body, which is standing against a Greek column, held by one loop of rope at the ankles. The base of the column is inscribed 'Me or You.' The body's arms are held behind it and the body's legs are crossed. Mantegna's *St. Sebastian* series, but in particular his painting in the Louvre, is the inspiration for this enormous cartoon. From the Renaissance onward, the theme of St. Sebastian pierced with arrows was a testament to spirituality. The idea motivated the commission of numerous paintings. Homosexuals, too, found common cause in St. Sebastian's martyrdom.

"I started to draw on this enormous paper with the thought that I would draw without thinking—just let the drawing happen. I would enjoy the process without conscious intervention. Very Zen of me. I leap up, saying, 'OK it is time to draw, don't ponder, and just do." I go to the paper and draw a hallucinatory image of an androgynous St. Sebastian pierced with long wooden stakes sharpened to a point at the ends. In this drawing, I see the bogeyman of childhood who crawl in your window and yells into your ear, 'Anybody there?' and he bleeds into your mind's eye. You pee in your bed and wake up alone.

"The artist wanders into his mind, looking for monsters and calling for relief from his unhappiness. The mind confronts two tendencies: one is female, the other male. The artist finds two states: the conscious observer and the unconsciousness actor. Whose voice is talking in the drawing: the voice of consciousness, or the voice of unconsciousness? Is it just I—inconsistent, judging, and weighing every decision? That judge says, sees, and does two different things. Each tears apart the other by its conflicting view. They must be tied up and knitted together by stakes.

"The pierced soul's anger acts, full of adrenaline, and one brain seizes control. I can't distinguish which one it is. I am talking now of a binary nature. Today, am I in the brain's right or the left hemisphere? Who is my voice? I thought I heard a Carlton calling to me outside myself. Yesterday, a Carlotta called to me. Do I hear voices? Have I gone schizophrenic? The voice I hear talking to me is one in all the jumble of the conflicting twos. Which 'I' am I? Is it: the I who hates women, the I who hates men, the I who loves both, who is verbal or who draws? Is it: the I who is heterosexual, the I who is homosexual, the I who hates me, or the I who loves me? I am flooded with a host of identities. From where they come and where they go, I cannot tell. One is in the right brain controlling the left-handed me. One is in the left brain controlling the right-handed me. The right-brained I is generally dominant, but there are the days when everything is possessed by the left brain. I switch easily from left hand to right hand.

"In the minority, the lefties, the right-brain people, are given to aesthetic interest, pictures, and space. However, the right-handed people with their left-brain ability are dominant in culture, more conventional in their thinking and writing. There is an ambidextrous I with traces of both brains. Can I not write with either hand? When drawing, if I become tired or bored, or if a spot is better suited to the different hand, I switch seamlessly from one hand to the other. Perhaps I am an unnatural lefty. That would be peculiar. My mother remembers me as right-handed. Could the childhood trauma of striking my mother with my right hand have caused me to become a southpaw? Did I change hands to forget an injury? Was I changed at the home for court-remanded boys, or because the monsters come in the middle of the night and take bad boys away to hurt them? Or was I sexually molested? Good reason for a boy to split into two to preserve his mind. At five, hand preference is not completely set and can change for no reason—so say the psychiatrists. Is all this conjecture merely a mix between two brains?

"'Your personality is split, severely split,' Dr. Wortz says to me. 'But you are not insane,' he adds for reassurance.

bipolar bare

"I am in good humor and smile at his remark. In our four o'clock Monday session, we speak and work upon my separate personalities. I feel rational, level-headed. I can think. I arrange to see him again when the cyclical blackness strikes, when I see another me, irrational and angry.

"For my next session with Dr. Wortz, I take with me *Question Related to Mind, Me or You*, which I finished on the previous Sunday. I sense the drawing has become a visual device for personal insight. The drawing is a means to give voice to the unconscious. However my analyst is required to decipher the code. We move the furniture out of the way in his office and roll the eight-foot long drawing out on the floor. Dr. Wortz asks me to be parts of the drawing.

"'First, be the blue woman,' Dr. Wortz directs me.

"'I am the blue woman because I am unreal, a vision of death,' I say. 'The stake is driven through my heart and I'm furious. My cold body has a large, firm breast and two red-rimmed genitals. One hole is the fissure of fecundity and other the anti-hole of pleasure and perversion. They turn up to receive divine inspiration. They may connect; they may not. Between their ambiguities surges the erect penis of the male's unbridled biology.'

"Very good. Now be the pink male,' says the doctor.

"'I am the fleshy living male. Males are pink. Women are blue. No male would be blue. Males are horny and ready for action. The cock is erect like the member of a hanged man. Saint Sebastian in ecstasy salutes with his penis. The female voice says the male likes pink, he's a fairy. He should dress in red.'

"'What is this female voice you refer to?' asks Dr. Wortz.

"'It isn't exactly a voice. I don't hear people talking to me when they are not. I don't hallucinate. The voice is the dialogue that runs through my mind. It's like the soundless dialogue that I carry on when driving. You know, there is the self who is driving, watching the road, the cars, sensing the accelerator, ready to apply the brake if necessary. Then there is the other self, mulling over details about the past before the drive or the future lying at the end of the trip. That is the voice I hear in my mind. Sometimes there are two voices, point and counterpoint. If I stop and try to hear, I hear nothing. The gods do not speak. Occasionally, I am startled by sourceless sounds, which call out of the everywhere of noise and the nowhere of silence. I swore I heard someone call 'Carlton' a few days ago, but I could discern no physical source for the sound. Must have imagined it, I surmise. Or was it the voice of the other hemisphere, reaching out to be heard?'

"'Most intriguing,' Dr. Wortz comments. 'Now, be the blue mask.'

"'I am the blue mask. The blue brain, small but powerful is hidden in the dark emptiness behind the façade of the mask. From within that vast space, blue brain controls the blue body and wars on the male, who is useless and weak. The mask has no eye and no ear. It is not needed. Blue brain, sees, hears, and speaks through cables and wires like the blue hairs above the male brain that lace themselves into the male brain to its ear and to its eye floating in space. It laughs a cold laugh and orders hard tasks. Get up and suck my breast. Get it up and find my pleasure. Fight your fear! Don't be weak! Go to your death like a man! I, Shiva, scream from my eyeless void. I am angry in the place where I am blue and penetrated by you.

"'Excellent. Now, be the right brain.'

"'I am the mind which sees with the eye. I am aware of the confusion the blue brain creates. Amongst my fellow brains, I am unusual. The right brain speaks for most. This makes the person left-handed and a member of another significant and oft-misunderstood minority. My responsibility as right brain is to control this undisciplined left brain. You see, the left brain is diseased and damaged. It has been so since youth. It is now my heavy responsibility to do most of the work for this pitiful human. Quite a good right brain I am. However, my strengths are the special and visual, and in our modern world, this skill is less honored than those of the left hemisphere. Thus, I have trouble with the left hemisphere functions. Language is one of these difficulties. I have had to incorporate some of these skills within my structure, and I am less organized to do this. Quite often, I have to allow the left to do work. This is always a risky situation. The chemicals over there are not right. They go off erratically.

"'Left brain protests. Don't you see it is you who are the peculiar one? Since your youth, you set up some strange, unnatural functions, and the right hemisphere has assumed supremacy over me and refuses to allow me my due. I am hidden behind the mask because right wills it that way. Right's voice is more powerful than the left because it hallucinates through the eye. Devil, I shout.

Right sees, but does not see what is real. This is the struggle I endure. I had to have him plunge the stake through his own mouth to shut him up.'

"'Be the eye floating in space,' directs Dr. Wortz.

"'I am the eye detached from the body. I see all. I see this terrible division. I wish that it weren't so. I wish that I could be reinserted in either the left or right brain. If I were, I could see existence clearly. I shall try to pat the eye into the right body. I see the past. There is a woman taking a pencil out of the left hand and putting it in the right.

"'Use your right hand, Carlton,' she says, turning the page of the paper so the lines are parallel to the edge of the desk.

"'I like to use my left when I write,' I respond as I put the pencil back in my left hand, turning the page of paper so the lines are perpendicular to the edge of the desk.

"'Use your right hand, Carlton, and turn the paper around. You are not writing Chinese,' she says, her tone annoyed. She takes the pencil from my left hand, places it in my right, and turns the paper around.

"'I can see the letters better in my left, with the paper up and down,' I insist, switching hands and rotating the paper.

"'In your right hand, child!' she demands, grabbing the pencil from my left hand, forcing it between the fingers of my right, and spinning the paper. She takes my left hand and places it behind my back. 'Now, use your right hand, child!' She leans over me and looks fiercely at me with her old creased face beneath a mat of ratty gray hair.

"'No!' I scream and put my right hand with the pencil in it behind my back. Secretly, I move the pencil to my left hand.

"'Do as I say! You are to use your right hand,' she barks and pulls my hands out from behind my back. I resist. I am disobedient. I will not release the pencil from my left. She can't pry it from my fingers.

"'You brat, do as I say,' she commands.

"I move away from the desk and stand defiant. All the other children in the class are staring at me. This is my pencil. I was drawing pictures. I was having fun. I will not let Mrs. Morgan have it. The teachers are always mean to me. Mrs. Morgan moves toward and grabs for me. I swing the pencil, trying to stab her, but miss. She is really angry now. She swats me on the head. I start to cry, scream, and throw a tantrum. I thrash about on the floor, kicking my legs and swinging my arms wildly, and stabbing myself with the pencil. Other teachers are called into the room to calm me down. My parents are called. The principal tells them, 'Your child is severely disturbed. We will not have him disrupting our classes.'

"'Maybe the stakes are pencils,' Dr. Wortz suggests.

"'Yeah, I think you are right, Dr. Wortz. I think the drawing is partly an allegory about going to school when you have learning problems and a split personality. I always get depressed in the fall after Labor Day and in the winter after Christmas when children return to school from the holidays.'"

"What do you think of that, Carlotta? Carlotta! You're not talking to me now. You are angry with me."

Carlotta gazes mutely at me, looking as black and inscrutable as Poe's raven. I grow uncomfortable at her silence.

"You don't like the two-brain idea? Talk to me! Cat got your tongue?"

"I can see this drawing explains a lot and does further our understanding of your situation," she says at length, "but I, the *feminine* I, am angered that you have put a stake through my heart. Your anger always manifests itself against women."

"Jesus H. Christ, Carlotta, it's just a drawing."

"Ah, but it says everything. I can't talk to you for a while until I have regained my composure. You have wounded your muse deeply."

"OK, we will talk later after you've had a good sulk. In he meantime, think about the two brain concept."

"Silly boy," says Carlotta, rising from my desk and disappearing into the bathroom without looking back, "you have only one brain."

CHAPTER 18

MEDITATION REHABILITATION

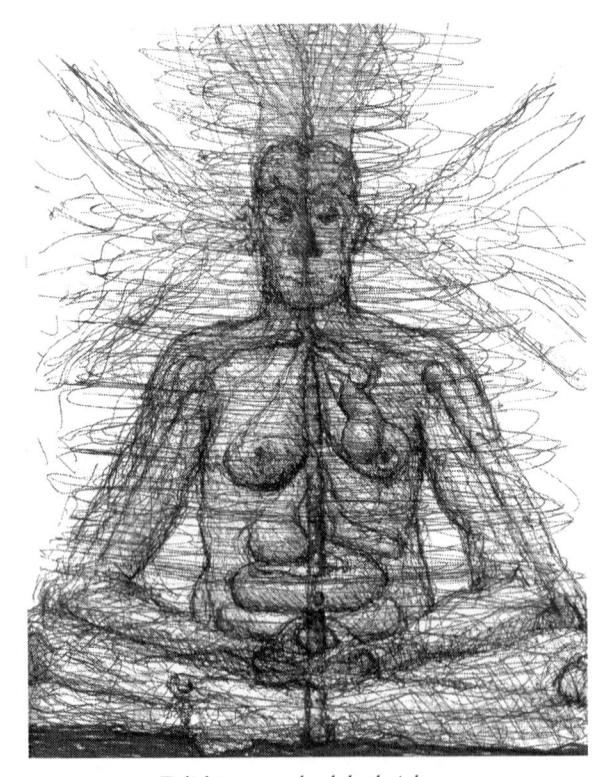

Enlightenment; sketch book; ink pen

THE NEXT DAY, EMBOLDENED BY THE REVELATIONS from my latest tête-à-tête with Carlotta, I go to the process group and apologize for splitting in a huff. I admit I still have unresolved issues with myself about anger, but I feel I am getting better. I tentatively broach the subject of my homosexual escapades and the group is most supportive, to my eternal relief and gratitude.

Early Thursday morning, Smitty has again flashed back to 'Nam in his dreams. His strangled cries let me know another firefight is underway on the Mekong Delta, with Smitty and his crew giving as good as they get in a gunboat to gunboat duel with the commies. The hospital is still except for Smitty's nightmare. The sun is hours away from rising. Moonlight is reflected in the apartment house swimming pool beyond the fence, defining the hospital from the sane world. I can't sleep. I am at the desk reading from a notebook and thinking about the past. *I* live in the past. *Smitty* lives in the past. Is that our problem?

The journal tells the story of my struggle to become clean from drugs the first time. Meditation was suggested as a way for me to free myself from my addiction to pot. For many months after beginning to meditate, I still smoked and participated in the underground artist's life.

Carlotta emerges from the bathroom wearing the black robe of a Zen Buddhist monk She walks up to the desk and bows slightly from her waist with her hands clasped in front of her chest.

"I return to you, Carlton, but I am still angry with you because you put a stake through my heart," she says by way of greeting.

"Tough titty," I mutter. "You are a bad girl."

"I will ignore that," says Carlotta with supreme dignity. "In my current guise, I have an overwhelming desire to recite a haiku of my own composition."

I sigh and shake my head. "Go ahead, if you must."

Carlotta bows again and recites the poem in a most mellifluous voice:

"Coming down the mountain path

There is a beautiful city in the plain

Full of rats."

"And what, pray tell, is the meaning of that rot?" I ask.

"I won't tell you. You must figure it out for yourself. That's the way of a Zen poem."

"Is this your way of joking about my experiences?"

"Not at all. I am only adding dimension."

"I am not Zen and can't relate to your haiku," I reply dismissively. "Now, listen up, while I read something intelligent and not so damned obscure."

"Carlotta *hopes* it's something intelligent, but it's probably obscure, as well.

bipolar bare

Besides, where is all this leading? Why are you telling me one episode after another? Where is the theme? What is the big picture?"

"You mean I have to explain it to you?" I say hotly. "You, who says she is the other half of me, should be the one person who does understand. Didn't you just say in one of our previous conversations that we were painting a portrait of my mental state?"

"Did I say that or did you?" says Carlotta, feigning ignorance. "I get confused sometimes."

"Never mind who said what," I reply indignantly. "The important thing to remember is that I am explaining the root causes of my mental disease, and now I am about to explain how I cured myself. It should be no more obscure than your poem!"

"Read on, grasshopper," says Carlotta with a grin. "Can I tell you if you are on course or not?"

"I couldn't stop you if I wanted to," I sigh and begin reading.

"One evening, several weeks before I moved out and sublet my loft, I was meditating, sitting on my cushion in my usual position in the center of the four wood columns. All lights were extinguished except the bright spotlight illuminating the column behind the loading dock door in the area of my loft I call the Art Dock. In this place, I positioned the fiberglass prop of a composite column, the Roman elaboration of the Corinthian order. Over the top of this shaft, I draped a segment of Christo's *Running Fence*. The fabric swags down to the floor on both sides of the column and peaks to the ceiling above in a rough triangle.

"In the dimness of the loft, the back-lighted shaft and curtain create a silvery illumination. The column's volutes and acanthus ornamentation are richly shadowed. The curtain becomes a veil of light shaped by the folds of the hanging suspension. Near the top of the column the spotlight reveals an intense yellow pyramid of light. This is the fourth day I have observed the set in meditation, studying its every nuance stoned.

"On the fifth evening, I added another idea. Positioning a square mirror on the floor in front of my meditation cushion, I am able to observe the pyramid of light reflected in the mirror. Sitting in the meditation position, eyes downward, I can watch the triangle in the square. I am fully concentrated for many minutes. My observation of eye movement and changing light values is fascinating. Surely this is the goal of meditation. My attention is fully engaged in the phenomenon of the set and its partial reflection in the mirror, when I hear a rustling in my kitchen.

"The rats have returned! For several days, I wonder how these animals have gotten into my space. I hear suspicious sounds but never the culprits themselves. I investigate their rattling and scratching near my kitchen but never find any evidence of intrusion. I return to my seat. This time there is a thud as if something has dropped from the ceiling. I turn my head to look. I see a rodent emerge from the shadows and scoot into the darkness behind the dining table. I wait. The animal appears and runs toward my bed. Alarmed, I break off my sitting and go to chase the intruder away from my sleeping spot. I grab a pillow from the floor. A spot of brown fur darts away. I can't find where the rat has gone. I decide to return to my meditation, watch, and wait. My high is wearing off.

"I sit down on the cushion and put a mallet between my knees. If he comes close, I reason, I can wallop him. I do not wait long. The animal emerges, this time on my left. It is small. I think it could be a mouse. He moves cautiously around the perimeter of my space. I see it every few minutes somewhere on the periphery of my vision. My legs have gone numb from the sitting position, but I do not move. I do not question the purity of my motives. I want to kill the sucker. The animal grows bold and moves out into the open floor. It halts by the mirror. I can easily see its full shape: large ears, long snout, a long low body, and a long ringed tail. It is a rat.

"It darts again to the right and scurries into the kitchen. I wait. It reappears and runs straight at my tucked knees. I fumble for the mallet, swing, and miss. I jump up and the rat disappears into a pile of clutter on my left. I stagger around on numb legs, lighting all my lights, mumbling 'So much for enlightenment.' I cannot find my visitor. The meditation on light is finished.

"That night, I position a mousetrap smeared with peanut butter under the sink counter. In the morning I find it tripped but no rat in its clutch. Six feet away is the carcass of a large dead rat. Neck broken by the trap, it had extracted itself, only to die before reaching the safety zone behind the fire door. I put the body in a plastic bag, freeze it, and reset the trap. The following night, meditating again on my lighted column, I catch another, smaller rat. This vermin dies a nasty, bloody death: head nearly severed from its body, eyes burst from their sockets. I place it, too, in a plastic bag in the freezer. I thought about woman and rats."

"Well! Not much enlightenment in that tale!" Carlotta declares. "Do you think what you were doing was meditation in any form? Do you equate all the feminine gender with rats? Do you think that showed much recovery from your dependence on marijuana? I must protest! That tale told nothing about recovery. It merely showed how you used meditation to further your own sick agenda."

"I told you this story documents my very early experience with meditation," I reply. "I wasn't very serious. Notice how I did not have much concentration or focus. If I had been truly awake and aware, I could have walloped that rat with the mallet when it approached my cushion. As it was, I missed completely! I was high with excitement, my mind was racing with thoughts about rats and their character."

"You were high! That much we know; and your marksmanship has always been poor. You could never hit anything with accuracy. Remember when you threw a baseball? You were lucky to get it anywhere near home plate. But let us leave that aside. Isn't the Buddhist philosophy to be kind to all living things? Why are you trying to murder rats while meditating? It goes against the basic tenets of monkdom."

"Because they are *rats*, for Christ's sake! Rats are supposed to be killed. Man does not let rats run around freely in his abode."

"What did you do with the rats you froze?" asks Carlotta. "That's beyond macabre, if you ask me. Did you make art out of them? I wouldn't put it past you, doing something weird like that."

"I wish I could remember, but I can't," I answer truthfully. "Maybe I was going to try my hand at taxidermy and make a *tableau vivant* out of them."

"Weird, as I said. You are like some little boy who likes to come home with some really strange dead thing to show Mommy and Sis just to gross them out. When will you grow up?"

"You have done some weird stuff, too. I just can't think of anything at the moment. How about I tell you another story?"

"All right. I still can't see where you are going with this. Maybe if I sit in meditation and listen."

Carlotta pulls up a chair and sits with her hands loosely held over her knees.

"Now, get on with your story and make it quick before my legs go to sleep," she bids me. "And it had better not be about rats."

"It's not—it's about radishes," I assure her. "I went to a fellow artist's costume party, which took place after I moved away into the meditation center. At the party I met up with Leslie, an old friend, long ago former lover, and sculptor, who works in the movie industry building sets.

"Slowly, languorously, Leslie puffs on her cigarette and speaks. 'No longer,' she says, 'will I think of coming to a Halloween party as a nudist. Now, in my middle age, I come as a radish, my favorite food.'

"Her body is covered in a big red dress tied at her waist and puffed up with stuffed clothes to create a bulbous shape. The toes of her white stockings are unraveled into dirty strands like the roots of a radish. She notices me staring at the plastic leaves that festoon her back and shoulders.

"'I tried to get the leaves to stand up like on a fresh radish, but I burned my thumb trying to get the whole apparatus glued up in a rigid standing position,' Leslie explains. 'So now the leaves dangle and I am a wilted radish.'

"I laugh. Hers is a great costume and so aptly chosen. And this is a great party at Peter's loft, an enormous work space filled with metal parts. Small bolts, angles, and rods are stuffed in bins and large pieces of sheet steel from old aircraft lie about the floor among the welding equipment. The littlest living area is to one side of workshop along the big steel windows. A couch, a kitchen table with three chairs and a TV on it, a refrigerator, and a small counter with stove and sink separate the living-dining area from Peter's bed. I wonder how he can get all his metal out of this place, for we are celebrating the end of the artists' tenancy in the Third and San Pedro Building, an old shoe factory. A large crowd of imaginatively costumed downtown artists is gathered amidst the mounds of metal. Joints are being passed from hand to hand. Groups of people are packed in the john, sniffing lines of coke. I do not partake of the drugs.

bipolar bare

"The building is slated for demolition in a month. The party is the celebration for a dying community destroyed by its own success and superseded by the art groupies and the speculators. The Los Angeles Building Department has marked other illegally occupied buildings to comply with code or vacate. The building I live in is on the list.

"Leslie, the wilted radish, ties her dirty white roots around her ankles. She and I climb three stories up winding concrete stairs that seems almost medieval in its steep and narrow enclosure to the roof. On the door one flight up from Peter's loft is a flyer offering lofts from $900 to $1,200 a month. The lofts the artists occupy in the building cost less than half that. Someone has written on it in big letters 'Such a deal!' On the roof, Leslie offers me a joint. I decline. We look out at the lights of downtown LA to the west and the darkness of the warehouse district to the east. I remember five years ago when the artists started occupying the grimy warehouses. I talk about all the artists hidden in the buildings between the river and us. Leslie tells me about the female artists who were arrested by the cops, thinking they were prostitutes because they could not believe women would be on any of those streets after dark.

"Here is where it all began for me. I saw it as an adventure to join the artists' community that pioneered living in the seedy, worn-out industrial landscape of Los Angeles next to the railroad tracks and the concrete culvert of the Los Angeles River. We lived in our illegal residences of abandoned warehouses and used illegal drugs— marijuana, cocaine, and speed—which increased the feeling of living in the land of the rebellion. The ambition we all had was to make LA the new Paris. One artist said, 'We are living in Los Angeles in an era reminiscent of the flowering of Impressionism a hundred years ago, in the 1860s. We are poised to become an artists' community of great significance, rising out of the squalor on the streets below.' A noble aspiration, but it didn't happen. The future was in shadows around the Texaco station several streets away, where crack dealers sold their wares. The radish wilted.

"I gave up on the downtown LA artist community. It was killing me. The drugs, the building inspection raids, the earthquake reinforcement work on old brick structures like the one I lived in, and my own battles with depression forced me out. I go home to the Community Meditation Center. I go home to my little room in the old house on an edge between the emerging Korean community and the drug infested Central American neighborhood just west of downtown. I go home to meditate and be sober.

"Will the move to the meditation center break me of the habits before it is too late? Dr. Wortz once said, 'There are two ways to give up an addiction. One is to move away from the circumstances in which you carried on a certain behavior. The second and best way is to focus on your addiction and root it out. There are several ways to do this. Meditation is one, and I recommend it highly.' I am trying both ways simultaneously."

Carlotta slowly raises her head and looks into my eyes.

"You certainly did smoke a lot of pot," she says. "It didn't help our communication. You were often too stoned to talk and would simply sit in your chair, staring at a wall."

"I know you are right, but I was using pot to help me with the symptoms of my neurosis. That is how I now see it."

"But ultimately it did not help. It only delayed the downs and made them worse. Isn't that right?"

"Yes, but who knew that then? I thought smoking pot was wonderful. I thought it gave me such creative ideas."

"Bunk! It made you stupid. It cut you off from everyone and from me. You silenced me with that damn weed. I was too stoned to know where or what I was. I don't know if I can forgive you for that."

"The story I just read documents the first time the meditation was taking hold. I found the will to refuse drugs, and I was able to act normally."

"That is true, but what is the purpose of all your stories? What is their theme? Are they just amusing stories or do they have some higher purpose?"

"Yes, they do. The stories document my progression into and out of complete neurosis. At the time of the rat tale, I was at my low ebb. Although I didn't know it at the time, when I met the radish I was beginning to recover. And with this final tale I will read to you, I am on my way to recovery."

"Carry on, but I am still skeptical."

bipolar bare

"Very well. This last story was written after I moved into the meditation center."

"Onward, Master Navel-gazer."

"I have no control. I am unable to stop myself from my compulsive smoking and doping. I tell myself I shouldn't smoke. The more I lecture myself, however, the more I want to smoke, and the more I do it. This is a vicious cycle. I can't seem to find a way out of it. And it is not just the vicious cycle of smoking. I can now see the compulsions operating in other spheres of my activity. There is eating, for instance. For most of the week until Wednesday night, I am eating healthy. Sam, who has lived at the meditation center for a long time and occasionally teaches grade school as a substitute teacher, is cooking macrobiotic food and I am enjoying each meal. How wonderful to arrive home and find wholesome food on the table. Wednesday night, though, I come home, peer into the refrigerator, see the veggie leftovers from last night, and say to myself, 'No way! I can't eat vegetables again. I need meat.' I bolt from the house, head over to the burrito stand by the Boys Market, and wolf down an al pastor burrito. I try to focus on the eating. I try to bring all my awareness to the act of eating: the placement of food in my mouth, the chewing, the swallowing, the sense of it descending my throat, and the pleasant feeling of fullness attained with each morsel consumed. I try to slow it all down. Chew slow. Swallow slow. Bite the next piece slow. I cannot do it. All I want to do is consume food as quickly as possible. I am still ravenous. I walk down the street to another food stand, The Double Eagle, and I eat another burrito. I try to bring my awareness to the act, and again I cannot.

"I am deep in the throes of the eating binge. The conscious me is completely anesthetized. I am controlled by the robot me, driven by some unfelt desire, gulping down the food. I want to feel full, but even a second burrito won't produce that sensation. This is not hunger from the need for nourishment: This is hunger from some unconscious craving I cannot identify and cannot satisfy… a craving I have to follow dumbly like an ox pulled by a yoke. My yoke pulls me to a donut stand, where I consume two heavy, doughy pastries and milk. My stomach is increasingly uncomfortable, but the hunger still will not leave. I walk back toward the house, passing the first burrito stand. I almost go in, but conscious restraint wins out. To eat another thing is absurd. I see how helpless I am against my unconscious cravings. I feel depressed. The old feelings of hopelessness and anger at my weakness fill my mind.

"On Thursday, I continue my binging. I eat breakfast at Denny's, scarfing down eggs, pancakes, and syrup, then more food mid-morning, and later a humongous lunch. What is driving me? Is it the tiredness from a long week of work? All week, I have fought my craving for gay sex. On Tuesday night, I did not go the bathhouse, as has recently been my habit. I felt so proud of myself! I thought I had finally overcome this perverse craving. It is not so.

"The thought of finding a big hard dick to rape me continues, becoming intolerable by Thursday afternoon. I go to the bathhouse and wait. The black man I rejected last week with the sore on his cock comes back. The man, full of disease and death—I think he will cure me of my abnormal desires—comes into my room, and I let him fuck me. The craving overcomes all my aversions: the fear of AIDS and the fear of death. In fact, it seems to me that the craving itself is a desire for death. I can dimly perceive extensive interconnections in this act I cannot stop myself from doing. I know the act to be self-destructive. I want it to be self-destructive.

"The interconnections weave into all my compulsive behaviors: eating, smoking, and sex. The Gordian knot is huge. I can see no way to unravel it, cut it open, and set myself free. The impossibility oppresses my mind and makes me desire more actions that will ensure my death. I want to control the destructive behaviors. I know I can't. I find it hard to believe that the answer lies in no control. The meditation leader says you have to give up the idea that you can control it with your will. You have to experience it with equanimity. You must allow it to be there.

"Who says these cravings are wrong? Only you beat yourself with your failures. Let yourself fail. Feel where the failure lies. After all, it is only a feeling and that feeling is only a sensation located in some particular part of your body. Become aware of your body. I protest. How can I become aware when I can't even bring any mindfulness to any part of my body when I am full of these cravings? The meditation leader says, 'Just keep trying and don't blame yourself, don't fill yourself with guilt.' I say I will try. Acceptance of things as they are is difficult for me.

bipolar bare

"Do I accept myself? No! Have I ever accepted myself? No! Have I hated myself and rejected myself? Yes, for years, for my whole lifetime! To wish to be as I am, to live in equanimity with myself, is a task I find hard to allow, but I shall try. I shall say, 'From now on, I am OK. I accept all that I am. I feel it.'"

"And it worked, didn't it, Carlton?" asks Carlotta. "After your stay in the meditation center, you stopped smoking dope, you stopped going to bathhouses, and you stopped trying to kill yourself."

"Yes, it did," I reply, rather pleased with myself. "The transformation was slow, but after a year and many months, I did stop smoking dope and my depression lifted. I moved back to my loft and had a few good years after my meditation experience. I was calmer and clearer. I was stable enough to get married again. But you and I stopped talking."

"That wasn't my fault. You were too involved with your new woman. Not that I objected. She is a very fine lady and takes good care of you."

"But it didn't last! Why not?"

"Because the beautiful city was still full of rats. You had not rid yourself of them. You had only swept away a few."

"I thought I was free."

"You know why you weren't free."

I ponder this with a shudder. "Yes, I drifted away from the meditation and got all involved in business. The stress of that sent me right back into my disease. I took the wilted radish image with me. I'm going back to bed now. Talking with you has made me depressed and sleepy."

Carlotta stands up. She turns and walks toward the bathroom door. As she places her hand on the knob, she turns and says, "I ask you again—what is the theme? Your stories are interesting, but where do they go?"

"They follow my path from addiction and mental disorder to recovery, to relapse, to addiction, and disorder again … and, I hope, to recovery once more. It is the route to the beautiful city through the habitat of the rats."

"Your route is as strange as yourself, grasshopper," says Carlotta, bowing courteously. "You are a riddle, wrapped in a mystery, inside an enigma. That's why I like you. Peeling you apart makes life worth living."

carlton davis

Self-portrait ; 1984; 29½ x 21 inches; colored pencil

CHAPTER 19

IT'S NOT THE CAUSE OF YOUR DILEMMA

THURSDAY MORNING, I AWAKEN IN A SWEAT from a vivid dream. There is a modern house with a large wall of glass next to the sea. I walk into the glass-faced room when someone yells, "Watch out!" I turn and look out the glass wall toward the sea. The sea is flat and the sky cloudless. As I stare, an enormous swell of water rises up, cresting into a gigantic whitecapped wave. The colossal arc of water crashes against the house in slow motion. The glass wall caves in. The water submerges me in great depth. I am swept away. The landscape returns to calm sea and empty sky. The house is gone. I am gone. This is oblivion.

The sequence repeats itself over and over again. Someone yells, "Watch out!" The wave comes. I see it and I think coolly, *I could move out of the way, go behind a solid wall, move into another room, or get into a boat, but I know nothing will do any good. Oblivion is impossible to avoid.* The flat sea and blank sky will return. There is no fear, only curiosity and seconds of musing.

I'm sitting in the process group, hearing June talk about her cocaine addiction, but not listening to her meaning. I am replaying my dream and pondering the image of the sea. The sea is I. From the calm waters a swell of anger rises up. The anger becomes so great that the swell turns into a gigantic wave of anger. The wave crests and destroys all that lies in the direction of its surge, including me. I can't save myself. I am aware that the tidal wave is coming. I accept it coming. I even *want* its coming. Positive action is impossible. I am stuck in place, unable to prevent oblivion. Is oblivion what I seek?

Carlotta sits in an empty chair opposite me in the circle of chairs. She is in a bikini, wearing flippers, a snorkel, and a dorky scuba mask. The sight of her wide, winsome smile magnified to goofy proportions behind the glass visor makes me laugh out loud.

"Do you find what June is saying humorous Carlton?" asks Jeanine.

"Oh, no, please forgive me June, I had a funny thought," I apologize as June gives me a dark look.

"I suggest you pay attention to the group," says Jeanine.

Nurse Maria opens the door and points to me. She flexes her index finger for me to come out of the room. Thank goodness, I can get out of the group without more embarrassment! Carlotta wiggles her flippers goodbye. I frown, excuse myself, and follow Maria down the narrow, twisty corridor toward the nurse's station. She stops at the head of the stairs to the first floor and waves to the small room to the right of the stairs. The room is the size of a telephone booth. Inside, a black-haired woman wearing a gray skirt and white blouse is sitting in a chair. She is the same woman, Dr. Poliquin, who visited me several days ago. She is studying a folder in her lap.

"Your new psychiatrist wants to interview you," says Nurse Maria. "Please take a seat in the interview room."

I enter and sit down in a chair opposite the doctor. The chair barely fits in the room. The doctor slides the door to the room closed.

"I'm Dr. Poliquin," she says. "I will be your doctor."

"We've already met. Guess you're too busy to remember," I reply sarcastically.

"How are you today, Mr. Davis?" says the doctor, unfazed. "May I call you Carlton?"

"I prefer Carl. Carlton makes me sound like a banker, which I am definitely not."

"Carl, you have been here about a week. Is that right?"

"Yes. Eight days, to be precise. Three of which I spent in the prison ward." This last statement is delivered rather tersely.

"You are referring to the Mariah Unit?" Dr. Poliquin responds, her voice calm and level. A pleasant smile emerges on her face. She is not going to take my bait.

I reply affirmatively. I am feeling claustrophobic in this little room. Our chairs are about a foot apart and the walls are less than an arm's length distant in any direction. I wonder if they use this room on purpose to make the patients ill at ease.

"You came in after planning suicide," the doctor continues.

"Yes."

"It says here you threatened to kill your wife and your doctor."

"Yeah, but I didn't mean it. I was angry at them because they duped me and I ended up in a locked ward after I had an agreement with them that I would go into the hospital only if I was put in a regular ward."

"Do you often lose your temper, Carl?"

"Sometimes. What that got to do with anything?"

"Patterns of behavior. How have you been getting on since you have been in the hospital?"

"Fine! Fine! Food's great. People are great. You should call this place Club Meds. Advertise it big time. It's better than most vacation spots. I find myself relaxed and more together than I have felt in years. I've been rereading my notebooks to get a sense of the issues that have driven my life. As a matter of fact, I think I have figured out what has caused me to be so screwed up over the years. My self-diagnosis is, I think, brilliant."

"Is that so?"

"You want to hear it?"

"Please. I'd love to."

"I had a horrible childhood. At least I did from ages four to five and, as I understand childhood development, these are the formative years, when everything you experience is embedded in your brain and forms the basis of your makeup as an adult."

"Some people believe that theory."

"You see, my original assumption is that my mother and father made the mess that I became. Their divorce and their battle for custody of me, which involved my vindictive, prejudiced, and arrogant grandmother, is the root cause of all my problems."

"Go on."

"They emotionally abandoned me. They physically abandoned me. At first, my father disappeared, and then he reappeared to snatch me from my mother's sister, the only woman who actually showed me complete, unconditional, maternal love.

My mother disappeared nightly and then finally disappeared altogether. Her nightly disappearances to her job—she was a nightclub singer—meant nightly imprisonment for me. I was locked in my room. This is one reason I think I can't stand small rooms and especially small rooms with closed doors. Do you think you could open the door just a crack? I am getting really anxious sitting here in this closet."

"Certainly," says Dr. Poliquin, sliding the door open about six inches. I immediately feel a tremendous sense of relief.

"My mother was a temperamental woman," I go on. "She struck me on occasion. I was once right-handed, but because I once struck back at her with my right hand, I became a leftie."

"That sounds a bit far-fetched."

"Well, maybe. Actually, I'm ambidextrous, but my left hand remains dominant."

The doctor raises one skeptical eyebrow and scrawls something on her pad. I continue.

"Anyway, back to my diagnosis. I resent—no, resent isn't the proper word—I *detest* the upper classes, their snootiness, their materialism, and their sense of superiority. I get this from my hatred of my grandmother, who made my life miserable. From thinking about her, I was able to put together the whole picture in the past week here at Las Encinas. My grandmother, who ended up with custody of me, or should I say she had me as her guest after the court made me its ward, decided she didn't like me as a guest. The old bag was afraid I would damage her heirlooms, so she put me in a foster home."

"An interesting tale you're spinning so far."

"Wait, it gets even better. I had forgotten that I had even been in a foster home until a few years ago, when I asked my stepmother where I was when she and my father got married. She told me I was at the farm. The farm, I asked her, what farm? She told me I was at the foster farm. You mean, I was in foster care, I asked her. She told me yes. I had completely forgotten all this crap and buried it in my subconscious. This is not the end of it, however. What happened at the foster farm is the real kicker. And this is what I completely blocked in my subconscious until recently, when I was in San Francisco at a halfway residence for my drug addiction."

Dr. Poliquin's face remains inscrutable. She nods for me to go on.

"I was beaten up continually at the foster farm and I was sexually abused. The experience is what I have been unable to accept. Unconsciously, I relive it every day. This is something my mother and father know nothing about, but they are responsible. They know nothing of what happened because of the war between them. This fact made me the angry, bitter, distrustful, and depressed human being that I became. Knowing my story, I think I can overcome it."

"That is quite a story, Carl. It certainly may explain some of your neurotic behavior, but I think there are other factors to be considered."

"Like what?"

"The medical transcripts we received from other doctors who treated you indicate a history of repeated periods of depression. You have also been hospitalized for drug abuse here at Las Encinas and at The Betty Ford Center."

"So I'm a drug addict. Who wouldn't be, carrying around that kind of subconscious wound and the hate growing out it?"

"I think there is something else going on here. I think you are bipolar one."

"What the hell is that?"

"Bipolar disorder is the modern terminology for what used to be termed manic-depression. This is a mental disorder we now believe is probably genetically and certainly biochemically based."

"How come no one told me this earlier?"

"Because diagnosing bipolar disorder and treating it is relatively new. It is only in the past ten years that we have had an effective array of drugs with which to treat the illness, and in the past twenty years, there was only one drug at all to deal with the disorder. That drug is lithium. In the far past, unless the patient's symptoms were acute and unambiguous, no one could diagnose the disorder, and if diagnosed, there was no treatment. Even now, unless one is in a wildly manic state or in extreme depression, the condition can go unnoticed."

"Look, I have been going to psychiatrists and therapists for thirty years trying to find out what is wrong with me. Now you tell me I'm bipolar one. Is there a bipolar two?"

"Yes, there is, but bipolar one is the more pronounced form of the illness."

"Why should I believe this? Isn't this just the latest fad mental illness so the drug companies can find another sucker whom they can pump full of incredibly expensive pills? We're probably going to hear that every Hollywood actor who's weird, or in trouble with drugs, or his agent, has it. Right?"

I smile my know-it-all, sarcastic smile and stare intently at the doctor.

"There are quite a few creative people who are diagnosed with the disorder," Dr. Poliquin replies, looking back at me with gentle eyes and a warm smile. "Why don't you look for yourself? You told me you were looking at your notebooks. Look through them and see if you have written about any incidents that might fit the characteristics of the disorder."

"And what might they be?" I ask, raising my eyebrows.

"Let's start with mania. How about looking for times of expansive mood or what might be called high energy? Do you have periods of inflated self-esteem? Grandiosity, it's called. Do you have periods of greatly increased career-oriented activities, maybe combined with nights of no sleep and a relentless parade of ideas? How about excessive sexual adventures? Does your behavior involve anything like that?"

"I used to have many sexual adventures."

"Are you often impatient? Are there times of extreme distraction or lack of focus? Can you be extremely irritable?"

"Yes to all of the above. But doesn't everybody have these types of experiences?"

"It's a matter of degree, not experience," Dr. Poliquin clarifies. "Then look at depression. How often are you depressed? Are you suicidal when depressed? Do you retreat from the world? Do you go to bed for days?"

"Depression I know about. I am frequently down. I often hate life and wish I was dead."

"Do you have decreased interest in friends and activities? Are you sluggish and tired? Do you have vividly evil or apocalyptic dreams?"

"I have wild and colorful dreams. I had one this morning."

"Tell me about it." says Dr. Poliquin asks. She nods with interest as I recount the dream and comments, "Sounds apocalyptic to me."

"One dream doesn't make me bipolar, does it?"

"No, but a repeated pattern of them might be an indicator. The diagnosis is not based on dreams alone. Let's discuss your current medications. How they working? Are you experiencing any side effects?"

"They seem OK, but I am having difficulty sleeping."

"I will add a sleeping tablet to your medications." Dr. Poliquin stands ups and opens the sliding door. "Look into your experiences and we will talk again tomorrow or over the weekend."

She steps out of the room and strides down the hall toward the nurse's station. I am left alone in the tiny room, pondering her debunking of my dearly beloved diagnosis.

In between therapy sessions, I study my journals the remainder of Thursday. I only go through the first twelve, as most of them I have already reviewed for the story of my mother. Identifying what I think are pertinent issues, I write out notes to discuss with Dr. Poliquin at our next meeting. I am crestfallen when she drops by Friday morning and dismisses my research. She inquires briefly about my heightened appetite and promises another adjustment in my meds, drops a cryptic reference to attention deficit disorder, and is gone.

Later that evening, I go down to the smoking patio with my handwritten notes rolled up in my right hand. I sit down at the metal table by myself and light a cigarette. I have relapsed to smoking cigarettes and recruited Paul, a fellow patient who has a connection to a local pharmacy, to buy me a pack. When Ray and Mauricio arrive, I try to interest them in my findings and am again rebuffed. Angry that no one wants to hear my observations, I return to my room in a funk. Even Smitty, curled up in a white blanket like a huge, snoring burrito, is unavailable.

Sitting at the desk, I read the dream of the tidal wave aloud softly. The tidal wave dream is definitely apocalyptic. How else could it be interpreted? It could be a symptom of bipolar disorder. I have had other tidal wave dreams. In one, I am in bed with a woman. Our bodies are intertwined. A wall of water splinters the cabin wall, engulfing our bodies. I have had many other dreams that were either erotic or mysterious. I remain unconvinced that the evidence presented so far proves unequivocally that I have this mental disorder.

Looking out the window at the palm fronds, the pool, and the stars, I hear the familiar voice. Carlotta is standing next to me in her red bikini, wearing a silky red beach coat with white flowers on it and carrying flippers and a mask.

"Which way to the ocean, landlubber?" she cracks.

"Carlotta! You've come back again. I never thought I'd say this, but I'm almost glad to see you. The past couple of days I've been miserably lonely."

"I'll bet. But I hasten to inform you, I was not the woman in bed with you during your dream. Muses don't become lovers of their charges."

"I don't believe that. Incest is not something I think is out of bounds for the slutty Carlotta. A weird twosome should appeal to a sex addict like you. After reading my journals, I've come to think of you mainly an expression of my drug intoxication."

"Once again, you misinterpret my role. I will forgive you for the insults, though I don't know how much more of your ingratitude I can take without retaliating in kind. You need me more than ever, especially with your clinician and your fellow inmates turning a deaf ear on your findings. Tell Carlotta, siren of the sea, all about it."

"Give me a break! I don't need your wild slutty ass to cause me confusion."

"Can't do it, baby. I am here no matter what you want, so stop with the nasty attitude."

"Look, go away! If I reveal I talk to you, the psychiatrists will think I'm not only bipolar but schizophrenic as well."

"But we know you are not. Didn't Dr. Wortz say you were split, but not insane?"

"Insanity is a choice—that is what one psychiatrist said to me. I choose not to be insane. Therefore, I am not going to talk with you anymore. Go away!"

"You might as well enjoy my presence. I have done a lot for you. I can do more, like helping you interpret your research. See me for what I am: a gift from God."

"Stop being hilarious! You are no gift, but a grim reminder of the gutter I tried to immerse myself in."

"I kept you from suicide."

"Are you suggesting that was you talking to me on the bridge? I don't believe it."

"I'm not saying. You could have been hearing a voice from God."

"God never talks to me. If there is one, which I doubt, He, She or It has made me miserable."

"Small thinking. The light is great. You need to dig deeper to see the truth that lies behind the shadow."

"Now you are getting all poetic on me. Do you have another haiku? Or are you all tricks?"

"Don't be so close-minded. You are so conservative beneath that rebel veneer you project. Haven't I always been the more adventurous one and, conversely, the more rational one?"

"*And* the one who gets me into a whole lot of trouble."

"That was then. You know how drugs get me wild and sexy. It was you who took drugs, not I."

"I took drugs under your influence."

"Now that is a big joke! Can't you put aside your crazy thinking? Today we are both sober. Carlotta is a reformed girl. She is ladylike. Why, you could even take me to a stuffy cocktail party and I would behave."

"I doubt that. You would say or do something outrageous, as you always have. Like showing up in a red bikini or in a Zen monk's robes."

"Well, I can't completely go against my nature. Some things have to be said or done. You have always secretly liked it."

"But I need to be serious now. I must have my act together. There can be no talking with you if I want to finally become whole, stay sober, and cure myself of mental illness."

"Cure! What cure? You know as well as I do that there is no cure for what you have. You are not sick, like having the flu or typhoid. There is no magic pill that will kill the illness. The illness is not ill. It is a fundamental aspect of yourself, like me, your other self. You need to learn how to enjoy us both and not let it destroy you."

"Are you getting philosophical on me?"

"As the writer Jorge Luis Borges says, for every thesis, there should be an antithesis. I am your antithesis. Between the two of us, maybe we can reveal the reality behind the thesis and the antithesis."

I laugh incredulously. "Are we going to solve the problem of mental illness for society? That's rich: The nuts reveal the real truth. You have got to be kidding!"

"You have to think big, but we can discuss this at greater length later. Right at this moment, I believe you need to accept my presence, which up to now you haven't. After all, I am a different girl today. Too old, like you, to go out and get into all the interesting adventures that we once did. I like to sit, smell the flowers, take a swim, and meditate on the major issues of life. Think of me like that old lady you met at the Dorland Mountain Arts Colony, the one who sat on her porch on the edge of the oak grove listening to the sounds of nature, composing music in her head, and reading all the great works of literature."

"You mean Ellen Dorland," I reply. "She was quite a gal, well into her nineties when I met her and still sharp. She invited me to join her on her porch and read my writing to her. She would raise her hand and move it rhythmically to the flow of my words. That was unnerving."

"I know. I was there. I remember her speaking of the great artists of the early twentieth century: Picasso, Kandinsky, Matisse, Nolde, and the Mexican painter Sequieros, whom she met and had several works by, including a lithograph from which I made a copy drawing."

"I don't recall her saying that, but she did know Arnold Schoenberg well. She was a concert pianist and traveled all over Europe in her youth. Einstein, too, was a guest at her retreat on the mountain. I heard she and he played the piano together in her cabin."

"Think of me that way: a wise old broad with knowledge of the arts who's here to broaden your horizons."

"She did give me many insights," I muse. "You know, she liked my writing and was amazed that I was an artist and architect, too. She said I had so many talents, it was going to be difficult for me to sort them out."

"The operative word is 'we': Carlton and Carlotta."

"All right! Have it your way. She said WE need to listen to the music in our words, and suggested WE look into Schoenberg. We did, but his atonal work lost us. I did start to listen to the sound of what I wrote."

"Neither of us is very musical. We didn't get that gift."

"That's the truth for sure."

"So, are we in agreement? Carlotta will listen to your words and you will heed my feedback."

"OK, I'll give it a try."

"Excellent!" Carlotta exults. "What have you got for me to ponder?"

"There's a line in Maxim Gorky's play *Enemies* that struck an emotional chord with me: 'A man who knows where he is going pursues with calm deliberation.' Out of school and living in Chicago, I was inspired by Gorky's statement to pen these thoughts."

"I am not pursuing with deliberation. I do not know where I am going, and I am not chasing calmly. My anger gets me out of control. I have so many things I wish to do, but I get so wrapped up and so keyed up, I can't do them. My goal is to find a way to self-control.

"Dealing with my bad temper is the first goal. What is the reward of anger? People distance themselves from me. Petty annoyances build up until I explode at the wrong time. Instead of speaking to an issue when it first arises, I put it off until it eats at me so much that I snap. Confusion is created and situations are left unresolved. Why? Am I afraid to speak my mind openly and calmly when I should? Do I secretly believe so little in myself and my own ideas that I can't express them save with the authority of anger? This must be, because when I'm put on the spot without anger involved, my body trembles, my hands shake, and I feel very vulnerable. Anger covers and defends me from anyone seeing how small and afraid I am. I remember that, as a child, I would quiver when confronted with a threatening situation. I could not control it. I could not mask it, even as I felt able, ready, and desirous of meeting or initiating aggression. I cannot free myself of the shakes except through rage.

"My aggression is self-preservation. Anger protects me. It distances those who threaten me and confuses those who might see me as I really am. How can I solve this problem? I must find ways to think more highly of myself. I must realize that I have as much to offer as the next man. Not that I should obscure my own faults, but rather I should have a positive view of myself. I don't. The strength to attain this has to come from within my own soul.

"I want success and happiness, but I am afraid that I will fail. If I never attempt my dreams, I can't fail, but I can never succeed, either. Success will always be a dream, frustrated today and tomorrow, keeping me forever unhappy. I will be forever bitter, forever condemned to the hell I deserve. I am angry at being afraid. My fear is cloaked in laziness. Why do anything when everything will end in disaster? This is my downswing. My upswing is trying to do everything: to paint, to draw, to write, and to design. Thus, I spread myself so thin I can never achieve anything. I am safe this way. I create the illusion that I am trying hard.

"Hyperactivity is punishment for periods of laziness, and laziness is punishment for the lack of success in the periods of energy. I punish myself because I am unsuccessful, unintelligent, and no good. Throughout college, I thought myself dumb. I worried over how stupid I was in comparison to my classmates. My worst fears were realized: I flunked out. Proof achieved that I am a bum.

"I came back and did well, then scoffed at the degree that was gotten easily in gut subjects like art. I said that the courses had gotten so bad anybody could get a degree. Yet under all that hubris, I was proud. I did it. Arrogance covered how small I felt. Instead of feeling dumb, I called everyone else dumb. I caught myself on the way to work the other morning, thinking how brainless everybody was, and how this was a big change over what I used to think. I realized the old insecurity had transformed from the super-negative 'boy, am I dumb' to the super-arrogant 'I can't be as dim as I feel when everyone else is so dimwitted.' To be up, you have to place all others down. A victory over such people is thus hollow, because it isn't a victory over someone worthwhile. The vicious cycle rotates between the arrogant direction and the inferiority direction.

"I expect people to operate rationally, and when they don't, I become angry. Many times, my own behavior is totally irrational. I opine that chaos and irrationality are the essence of life. Why? Could it be that I crave irrational acts in others? I can delight in getting angry and self-righteous. By seeing them as dumber than me, I am able to place myself above someone else by intimidation, or, at the very least, I make them keep their distance. Like the wizard in *The Wizard of Oz*, the humbug masquerading behind his imposing façade, I can bellow and fume at interlopers. Behind my façade of fire and volume is a little me. Outsiders are controlled from hurting me or from seeing my small self. I fear. I tremble and I conceal. Time to come out from behind that façade and stand tall to take my defeats and successes with grace and calm deliberation.

"I am often bored, especially at work, where being in a subservient position makes me angry. Doing work that I think is beneath me makes me irritated. 'A baboon could do this,' I think. Being cooped up inside on beautiful days makes me annoyed. At work on Sunday—I hate working on weekends—nothing would go right. Becoming nervous and infuriated, I began to throw things around the office and curse at no one there. I am bored with myself for putting up with it and unable to free myself from the situation.

"I am morose. The pressure builds. My muscles compress. Anger stiffens the shoulders and tightens the neck. Teeth clench. Hatred fills me more than love. I see the dancers by the window backdropped by the summer time Chicago skyline, the beautiful and the witty chatting next to the boss' office, and the privileged gathered around the punch bowl at the architect's annual Founder's Day Party. Alternately, I long to be with them or to cut them to ribbons. I am locked into myself, in a prison I cannot escape. The ravenous rot of my soul seeps out. To Sue, a pretty blonde, I can only expose my hate of America. Or is it of her or of me? My lips draw back and reveal the set teeth. My eyes stare straight at her. I want her.

"I want each one of the luscious women: the little one, young and so beautiful, with sleek legs, soft brown hair and eyes, and smooth, tanned skin in the white chemise that comes only half way down her thighs; Pepe in hot pants, with a blouse tied around her midriff and over her loose breasts; Joy, in the red velvet dress, a full bodied and rich woman; and Sue, a curvy blonde with a pretty face. I have nothing to say to them. My feeble attempts at conversation ring hollow, glib, pointless. I am locked away unable to engage. Other men engage them in conversation and get their attention. They leave the party in the company of these other men and I am envious. They seem half-alive and I am half-dead. I am jealous of the little air and space outside themselves they have. I feel I have none. My life races in slow motion. It relentlessly churns toward death, gaining velocity inside my self. Life moves too slowly. It waits too long in each second—so long, in fact, I know how much I hate each time and place. I am constantly drowning in my own life. I am choking on my own perceptions. I want out, but stay in fascination, watching and waiting for death.

"Around and around I go. I want to get off this circle. I know I can't continue as I have, yet that is all I seem to do. The past several days were agony. I am utterly alone, and I can't stand it. I want to end everything, yet I don't. I want to live, be happy, and give happiness. I can't seem to find a way. Jan, a woman I knew from graduate school at Yale told me that Sherry, a fellow graduate student who lived in the same house we did, had jumped from her window in Boston. Sherry hurt herself badly in the fall, but didn't die. I have wanted to write to Sherry and offer my help and friendship, but I can't help feeling that it will do no good. Is there anything I can say to her to make life seem worthwhile when for me, it hardly seems worthwhile, either? I think of her lying in an alley, nearly dead. What can I offer to such a person? Aren't people going to do what they are going to do? All one can do is stand by and watch.

"These depressing thoughts are swirling around in my head. My own anxiety is increasing. Although I feel calmer now for writing, I wonder if these are not signs that I am becoming unglued. Before my last suicide attempt, I became increasingly isolated, anxious, and depressed. My behavior became weird. I can't let this happen again. Is it a conscious choice to go insane? My old psychiatrist thought so. If this is so, I must make pro-life and pro-sanity decisions. I want to live."

"The classic symptoms of bipolar disorder are revealed in that piece," says Carlotta. "The cycling through enthusiastic and morbid moods seems to Carlotta to be a perfect indicator that we have the disease. What remains now is to follow its history closely. Does it get worse or better? What else can we learn about our fate? What advantages and disadvantages does it have? Is there a silver lining to this mysterious gift God has given us?"

"Gift?" I scoff. "You would say that, Carlotta. I find the whole thing depressing. This is an abyss that encircles my being. Yet I did get better for a time ... for years, in fact."

"My God, you had a positive thought! Should I alert the media?"

"No, you should get thee to a nunnery, you licentious old bimbo."

"That sounds a bit drastic, but I think I will take a dip," Carlotta says, shrugging. "Cowabunga, dude!"

Carlotta disappears into the bathroom. Minutes later, I see her at the swimming pool beyond the hospital's fence. I watch as she takes off her robe and dons her flippers and facemask. Giving me a jaunty thumb's up, she mounts the diving board, bounces once, and executes a picture-perfect cannonball into the shimmering blue water.

CHAPTER 20

THE CLEANED-UP ACT FALLS FLAT

FRIDAY'S LUNCH IS FINISHED. The pork chops are gone—four wolfed down in record time. The patients have gone to the smoking porch or to their rooms. I climb the broad stair and walk down the corridor toward my room. At the nurse's station, I inquire angrily when will I see the psychiatrist again. The nurse tells me it will be soon, but she can't say when. I swear and head for my room to take a nap. I pull the curtain around my bed, lie down, and sulk. Is Dr. Poliquin correct that I am bipolar? I need to discuss my findings with her.

Anxiety builds. Judgments, feelings, and resentments race through my head but can't find an exit. The brain is clogged with a hundred thoughts. The motor is revved without the gears engaged. Energy piles up at the consciousness door with no way to get out. I struggle to be free, but the blockage grows larger. I spin, but I can't move. The body becomes paralyzed. I am drowning in a gasoline of my own volatile emotions. She holds a lighted match and won't let me go. Will I explode and disappear?

Behind my curtained hospital cocoon, I am stretched out on the bed like a corpse. I begin to experience an old terror and the weird delight of my spinning mind and bound body sinking into a black void. I want to go into this black abyss, but I am terrified. In the past, while I watched the mind race and body become stone, I have alternately fought against this feeling or tried to hold myself steady against the fear as I sink. A racing mind is one of the symptoms of a bipolar person.

But what about the body turning to stone and sinking? Is this a symptom? I always become afraid and struggle to make my body respond and break off this descent. Each time it is as if I have to battle with a downward burial force. I must make my body move to prevent myself from becoming forever inert, a cadaver in the dirt.

This time, when I sense the fears begin and the sinking starts, it is accompanied by an awareness of someone else in bed with me. I become aware of a reality more real than anything I have experienced before. I want to go to this real place with this invisible person, but I am petrified. The warm tongue of this being is slowly penetrating deep into my mouth, gagging me. Her name comes to me out of the blue. Who, I think, is Jean Delanuit? She is French. Jean of the night. Is she my French lover out of the long lost past? But her name was Janice? What am I doing in bed with a woman I have never heard of before? My body strains against the bonds and with a convulsive move, I snap back to normal. I am not falling anymore into some dark place, but the body is still immobile concrete. I look around. Carlotta is in bed with me. Why is she here? Why am I here? I must go home.

"Because you need the help," Carlotta says. She is lying in her nurse's uniform next to me in the narrow bed.

"Are you Jean Delanuit? Were you holding me down? Did you have me in bonds?"

"That wasn't me, baby. Muses don't put their tongues down their charge's throats in an erotic way, nor put them in restraints. That was some other dominatrix fantasy. Jean Delanuit is some other lady you liked to play with. Maybe giant Jane Delanuit."

"She didn't share that part of her life with me."

"Maybe you wished she did."

"But she didn't. Besides, what are you doing here in bed with me?"

"I'm here to protect you and present to you warning signs."

"What warning signs? Am I going completely mad? Am I going to explode? I feel like I will. The drugs must not be working. Nine and a half days I have been in the hospital. The psychiatrist has seen me twice. I need to see her again. I need my medicines changed. I must discuss the bipolar diagnosis with her."

"You need more patience."

"Leave me alone! I'm not getting help. And you are taking up most the bed, while I am practically falling out. And why must you always take the other side? Can't you side with me for once?

"Because your side is silly, dear Carlton. I must crowd out your stupid ideas. Maybe you will fall on the floor and wake up to your best interest: me! Don't I always see things better than you? A muse would not be worth anything, if she didn't push you in the right direction. Here, I am going to push you a little." Carlotta nudges me toward the edge of the bed.

"Stop! I am about to fall on the floor."

"That's the idea. I am trying to make you aware, accepting, and ready for change. Falling on the floor will wake you up."

Carlotta nudges me again. I grab instinctively grab for the mattress before tumbling out of bed. I stand up quickly, no longer paralyzed.

"Are you all right in there?" asks Nurse Maria, sticking her head inside the curtained enclosure. "I heard a big thud."

"I'm OK. I must have rolled out of bed during my nap."

"It's not time for you to be sleeping. You should be out and going to the music or art therapy."

"Art therapy, what a joke."

"Joke or no joke, get out of bed and do something." Nurse Maria pulls her head out of the curtain and leaves.

"See what you have done to me?"

"Did I wake you up? Don't you see you need to be here? No leaving the hospital!"

"What help am I getting? Not much, if you ask me. Two visits from the shrink and all the drugs you can take at the nurse's station. Can't you see the drugs they are giving me aren't working? I am still hungry, depressed, and now I am very irritated, another sign of bipolar disorder."

"You haven't given the drugs long enough to work."

"How long does it take?" I whine. "Street drugs work better. At least I felt good after the first hit. I could at least find my dealer. He is always around as opposed to these doctors, who never appear and never talk to you."

"You know, you are not a sympathetic case. You are impatient, irritable, and a drug addict. Your escapades—or should I say *our* escapades with sex and drugs—are not behaviors that ordinary people find attractive or are willing to forgive. You violate all the rules of normal society, and we haven't even talked about the most outrageous parts. Your escapades with sex are another symptom of bipolar behavior. You owe it to yourself, your wife, and me to stick it out."

"Society be damned! I don't want to be a sympathetic patient. After all, I'm not trying out for a part on *ER*. All I seek is relief from the agonies of my life."

"You are *not* going to get relief by leaving the hospital and going to get street drugs."

"I am not convinced. I should be getting more attention."

"The psychiatrists are probably dealing with the more severe cases. What about Mary, the woman who likes to cut her arms, and Renée, the French woman whose lover beat her to a pulp and stole her millions? They are suicidal. They are bipolar, too, and in far worse shape than you."

"Are you saying I am bipolar?"

"The description fits. I want you to admit it."

"What I want is to get back in bed and take a nap."

"You don't need a nap. Come, let's go play nursey. It will make you feel better. Why don't we go from room to room collecting urine samples with a bed pan?"

"Ridiculous!"

"It's a wonderful idea. We could say we are doing a comparative study of urine color. The darker the color, the more bipolar the patient is."

"Now you're just making fun of me. I need to talk to the psychiatrist."

"But I am serious! A little absurdity can go a long way. Such are the curative powers of laughter."

"Where would I get a nurse's uniform like yours?"

"Mine is a special one made for medical muses. Note the white dress, the white stockings, the white shoes, and the white cap with the very wide wings. Perhaps I can fly! Besides, the nurses here don't wear uniforms, so you would have to imagine yourself in one. You can do that, can't you? You do it all the time."

"They don't wear the nurse's costume because they want to obscure the fact that this place is a funny farm."

"Boy, are you ever in a sulk. Get into bed, and I shall get out." Carlotta rises and stands beside the bed with the big thermometer in her hand. "It's time to take your psychic temperature again. Roll over."

"Please leave me to my funk. I want to think about meditation and if I should abandon this hospital."

"Promise you won't leave."

"All right, I promise, but I need time to think about the years I was sober after becoming a meditator."

"Tell me your memories," says Carlotta, pulling up a chair. "I will tell you if it is true."

"The transformation began in 1987 when I rented out my loft and moved into a small garret on the third floor of the Community Meditation Center. I began serious meditation two times a day. The first meditation was early in the morning before I went to work. The second meditation was in the evening after I returned home. On the weekend, I indulged in meditation marathons. I ate healthy and well because the center provided meals. I lived like this for more than six months, after which I moved to a storefront artist's live/work space at the beach. These were good years, 1987 to 1993. I was sober. I don't remember any major downs from the time. I can't document this, however, because I stopped writing."

"Your memory is faulty," Carlotta interrupts. "Don't you remember the pain and anger you experienced while you meditated? At the first retreat in January of 1987— January historically marking the advent of your depressions—the pain in your arm and shoulder crazed you. You could not sleep. You begged for relief at the meditation leader's door in the middle of the night. He and his lover volunteered to take you to the hospital, where you waited in agony for assistance. Since you weren't outwardly hurt or bleeding, they left you to suffer in a room. You became so angry you barged out of the hospital and took a cab back to the center. The pain kept up for days. You were ready to abandon meditation forever. So don't tell me how wonderful your meditation experience was! Only when you got acupuncture and a cortisone shot did the pain go away. Wasn't this when the acupuncturist spoke of the wind blowing over your soul, stirring up the anger?"

"That was the guy," I confirm. "He and two assistants looked at my tongue and made that observation. He was weird, but the acupuncture worked. My meditation got better. The pain in my shoulder subsided in subsequent meditations, and I became more skilled in bringing my attention to the pain and dissolving it."

"Your memory is still defective. What about the ten-day retreat you took at the end of the year in Northern California with the master Goenka?"

"It's hazy, but I remember the red scarf I wrapped around my neck for protection from the cold. And we ate a lot of prunes, which gave everyone gas."

"Remember, they asked you if you had any addictions or if you had any mental problems. You lied and said you didn't so you could stay."

"Yeah, and I had a wonderful experience."

"Once again, your selective memory chooses to forget the trouble you had. What about the first meditation at four a.m., where you had to keep your attention on your breath? 'Anapana,' they called it. Attention was brought to the nostrils, where you had to feel the breath coming in and going out. You started to shake violently. Your whole body was convulsing and shaking back and forth. You thought what you were doing was insanity. You thought of only one thing: getting out of the meditation hall, driving away, and smoking a joint."

"I don't remember any thing like that."

"Of course you don't! On the second day of this retreat, you passed through anger into a profound sadness. You felt you had ruined your life and wrecked your marriage by your selfish behavior. And you were still shaking. You asked Goenka what you could do about the shaking and he gave you a startling answer. 'Stop it,' he said simply. You tried and you could do it—to a degree. The gross shaking you could end, but the fine vibration up your spine you could not control. The vibration sent shivers up your spine into your head. You asked Goenka again about these sensations. He told you these were good vibrations and you should stick with them, allow them to happen, and you did. This was the joy coming out, he said. And your reward was the image of the tiger leaping through your equanimity. The tiger devoured humans and your anger. You experienced not joy, but the carnivore and the blood that seeped through your soul."

"I was getting the hang of meditation and at the end of the ten day retreat," I reply, nodding. "I felt really good. I drove back to Los Angeles and was not affected by my yearly down in January and February. As a matter of fact, I had a really good year. There are no journals from this time. Maybe that is a good consequence. Nor do I exactly recall the sequence of events—they all flow together. I do remember

I moved to the beach and had to move out under peculiar circumstances. I came home one day to find the studio's toilet atop a pile of dirt because the landlord was doing improvements on the space. He planned to put a new commode, but forgot I was living in the place. I could not move back to my studio because the artist with whom I had traded my place was using it to make an enormous sculpture out of huge logs. My studio was much more like a lumberyard than a place to live, so I had to find other housing. I did this without my usual irritation and anger. I felt I had found freedom from my guilt and depression. I was acting moralistically—*sila*, the meditation teacher called it."

"You did give up your immoral behavior, but it was short-lived."

I nod. "The years 1988 and 1989 were good ones. I moved into my future wife's house in Pasadena as a paying guest and I meditated every day. That was the start of our relationship. We weren't lovers, but we got along with each other very well. Somewhere in this time, I went north to the Montalvo Artist Colony to work on my writing. I was completely sober. I was healthy and writing and exercising every day. I ran or bicycled down the mountain and across the landscape around Saratoga, California. My life was in good order. I didn't have any major depression. Life seemed good, and I didn't have a major depression after I left the artist colony, nor in the coming years."

"You had depression attacks, but you have forgotten," Carlotta corrects me. "They were not as severe, but you had them. They were delayed. Depression came to you in October and November instead of September. January's down was postponed until February. You can't deny it. You were often grumpy. You lost things. You lost your keys one time and your wallet another—that is characteristic of your down—and you went out to a bathhouse for the first time in two years."

"I don't have any of those recollections. How do you know?"

"I looked at your daily diaries. You weren't writing, but you did record your moods in diaries for each year. Too bad you lost the one for 1988. It would have told us a lot. Continue on with your remembrances."

"I left the colony and returned to my loft in Los Angeles. I was still meditating at least once every day. I got married. I went on another ten-day retreat with Goenka in the redwood country north of San Francisco. After I left this place,

I remember how well I felt. The whole world seemed changed to me. I felt as if I was cleansed of all the negativity that plagued my life. I had achieved what the meditation leader called P.I.E.— peace, impermanence, and equilibrium. The good feeling did not last very long. After a few weeks of being back in Los Angeles, the stress of living got to me. I wasn't on the road to enlightenment any more, but I wasn't smoking pot, plagued by depression, erratic behavior, or visiting the bathhouses, either."

"I remember that time bittersweetly," I tell Carlotta. "I was free and working hard with my wife in our office. We designed all kinds of projects, including the Los Angeles Mission and the Metro Red Line subway station in North Hollywood."

"Yes, you did, but you also drifted away from meditation."

"That was the beginning of my downfall. I vowed to keep up my meditation practice because I felt it was the foundation of my newfound equilibrium. Regrettably, I didn't follow through. Over a period of five years, I slowly stopped meditating altogether. First, I ditched the twice-daily habit. Then, the once-daily habit gradually lost its new car smell, until I stopped altogether. My twice-yearly major depressions started to return, attended by my irritation with people. I was stable before this happened."

"No, you weren't. Your recollection is warped by what you want to believe."

"OK, so maybe I got a little down here and there, but life was good. I thought I had left my problems behind me."

"The delusion of stability is what you had."

"I admit to you that in the end, I came unglued."

"Indubitably. You abandoned your marijuana smoking for something more sensational. Marijuana no longer gave you the kick it used to—your body had adjusted to the drug. You needed something else to get you high. However, the price you paid was amazing. You really split in two when you discovered crack."

"I admit that, too. Crack gave me more energy and energy is what I wanted. There still was me, but you emerged as a dominant force."

"We were definitely a twosome residing in one body," Carlotta agrees. "I loved being free, but you were choking on the fumes of your own creation."

"How did I exit these noxious fumes? There must have been an egress and a trail beyond."

"There was, but you just needed to practice some patience. You were not as bad as you think you were."

"Perhaps," I sigh. "But I lost interest in all my personal work. I couldn't seem to find the time to break out from where I was. I liked where I was. I was a shadow of my former self. Formerly, I had many different aspirations. Now I had none save the one to become a woman. How could I escape when I didn't want to escape?"

"There was no escape. You had to live as you were."

"But I was deceived! I was not myself! I was not who I thought I was. These sad confusions raced through my mind in an endless circulation to the same place. I ran like a flywheel, spinning faster and faster. Engagement would strip all the gears, ending in disaster. The machine went out of control, burned out, and became inert. I was a walking corpse, a retarded adult ready for the grave, ready to fall into the black abyss."

"Ah, but I wouldn't let you," Carlotta gloats. "I held you back, even when you teetered on the edge of the abyss by using heavier drugs."

"Most often, I just wished for an end," I confess. "I found my life an immense failure and existence too painful to find any joy in the simple passage of the day. I didn't love life. I didn't care about anyone, least of all myself. I spent the next few years trying to destroy myself. I saw the previous twenty years, ever since the 150 aspirin incident, as destructive."

"Since you don't love life, life does not love you. All is gloom because you see it that way."

"I can't argue with you. I love my negativity. To be otherwise would not be right. It would not be *me*. Myself is not self, but the anti-self. I dwell in my own feces, gorging on that waste like an addict. Addiction to pain is my *raison d'être*. Addiction to dope is my reality. Can you attribute this grim slide into hateful negativity or to substance abuse? Crack augments any state you are in, and prolonged use can alter personality. In my case, I became so addicted that nothing could dissuade me from use. My need for crack was so intense I would start my day with numerous hits and end the day with several more. I did not sleep. I waited, patient as a spider, anticipating your flamboyant appearance."

"Carlotta loved her freedom but hated what it did to Carlton."

"I loved being Carlotta. I could not release myself from you. I found myself in that place where I didn't know who I was. I knew I had no control, no matter how much I wished to break the addiction. Once on the drug, I couldn't come back. I was too unconscious for too much of the day, for too much of my life. There was no hope."

"It was sad and pathetic."

"Drugs fed you, Carlotta. With each hit, you emerged more demanding than before and more sexually charged. I was fascinated because there was so much energy there. The state of high sucked me into its vortex, where feelings and intellect were anesthetized. Oblivious to the feelings of others, I had a wild time."

"The doctors said you took dope as an anesthetic. Anesthetic to what, I wondered? Now I think it was an anesthetic to the sensations in your body and the feelings that you thought. You don't have them when you get high. You had your sensations and feelings condensed into your subconscious. You are wide awake in one half of your mind by anesthetizing the other half—the Carlton half."

"I am a divided being for whom there is no solid center, but rather a shifting structure of moods condensing into the two selves," I reply.

"You were alternately the man, then the woman trapped within the man," Carlotta retorts. "If Carlton thinks Carlotta is a whore, then what would you call a female who hunts for sex as much as you do?"

"I would call her Carlton, the male trapped in the female. Who determines who is what?"

"No one—the drugs determine that. Crack created the endless circulation between male and female. High, the male thinks like the female, and hung over, the female thinks like the male."

"No, I, Carlton, made the determination. I refused to admit what was my predilection when high. The male me lived with a woman and didn't like the intimacy. Sex was a horror. No, sex was dreadful. I was always torn apart. I was damned because a decent relationship was impossible, because you, Carlotta, intervened and you wanted only sex. Thus, I was a pervert denied the possibility of a decent relationship because Carlotta satisfied Carlton's need to be with a woman. The difficulty of a relationship is resolved by being both. Thus, for the masculine self, there was no need for another. But wait! It doesn't work! We were never companions to each other. We were solitary, separate beings sequentially fulfilling fantasies and never creating any bond."

"Carlotta never left you alone. I was there to be a companion."

"If it weren't for drugs, I would not have released you. My inhibitions would have kept you buried."

"No. I am you and no matter what you did, I would have appeared."

"If I had not lapsed into crack use, I could have kept you under control."

"I would have made my appearance no matter what you did. You always wanted to be a woman. I was the woman you desired me to be: a muse, an intellectual, a sensitive person, an interpreter of reality, and a whore."

I sigh world wearily. "I am a severe case! If the powers that be are right, and I was an undiagnosed bipolar for years—no, decades—I need help. But they are just letting me languish. It's not fair."

"Who says life is fair, bub? Life is unfair and it has always been that way."

"My life should be different. I have given up everything, including my freedom."

"You seem a little better than you were before, when you were racing all over town trying to get high, cross-dressing, and seeking out the clubs for sex."

"No, I am not. My mind races and my body is uncoordinated. I stumble when I walk. I can't focus on anything. The mess I am in remains the same."

"Give it time and everything will be better. I promise."

"I don't care what you promise. I want to talk to the shrink. The bipolar diagnosis has me in a quandary."

"I thought you inferred from your journals that Dr. Poliquin's diagnosis was true?"

"Yeah, but true to what degree? The fact is that meditation ended my entrapment within the confines of this disease. If Dr. Poliquin isn't going to see me, why shouldn't I leave the hospital and return to the daily habit of meditation? I should go on retreats and free myself of the corruption in my character. I should become the red Buddha again, stripped down to my essentials: brain, heart, liver, and intestines. The meditative energy would cleanse my being."

"I should give you a mental enema that would clean out your thought rubble," Carlotta threatens. "Please remember you are only half-right. You remained vulnerable to your twice-yearly downs and still had other times of depression. It is like what you are doing now: hiding yourself inside the drawn curtain."

"It's not the same. I will get up after I have a little rest."

"You are not hearing me. You were *not* fine. You had your yearly major downs, recall them or not. You could be a real bastard."

"I don't believe you. I know I was fine because I went back to work and I got married. I never thought I could get married again, given my fits of temper and irrational behavior. My memory tells me I was free of manic depression. Jeanine, my process group leader, says it can go into remission."

"All well and good, but you have no proof of your sojourn in Normalville."

"I would if I hadn't lost my diary of that time."

"Carlotta finds it interesting that you lost the records of the time period when this sobriety allegedly occurred. One might say the lapse is Freudian."

"Whatever. I'm going to try to see if I can dip into my memories without the crutch of a journal."

"Go ahead, see if you can convince me," Carlotta urges. "I will protest again when I think you are dreaming an untruth."

"All right. My stay at Montalvo was delightful. Ginger, my future wife, came to visit me. The wonderful time we had together sealed our relationship. I felt as if the anger and irrational behavior had left me. I could again attempt to have a relationship with another person."

"What about the time you went looking for a bathhouse to have some gay fun?"

"Nothing ever happened. I wasn't depressed enough."

"But you thought the thoughts."

"Yes, I thought the thoughts, but I was without stress. It is stress that makes me go wild. If I kept meditating, I could handle the negative thoughts and negative actions."

"Are you saying gay sex is bad?"

"No! I think gays and gay sex are all right. Except for me, it signifies that I am under a lot of stress and going gay is a way I handle it."

"An unlikely argument if I ever heard one. Can't you even admit you are bi-sexual?"

"But I'm not, when I'm on an even keel. It's when I get overwhelmed that sexual aberration overtakes me."

"I don't believe you. You are lying."

"I am not. Let me continue with the story that will explain my actions."

"I doubt that, but proceed."

"When I left the artist colony, I went to live in my loft again. The temptations to use and to go to the bathhouses were the same before I disappeared, but I was able to resist them. I meditated every day at least once. I dated Ginger, and we decided to get married. At the time, I felt stable enough that returning to the architecture profession was an alternative I could accept. I needed the money and was willing to put up with the peculiarities of a design office. I had a new perspective: architecture was only a job for me that kept me off the streets and away from drugs. My life's desire remained the pursuit of art and writing. I took a job that required me to work only four days a week. The remaining three days, I could make art and write. I kept the stress at a minimum."

"I seem to remember times when you smoked a joint or two."

"I may have, but I wasn't making a habit of it."

"So you say. I believe old habits die hard."

"Meditating in my loft and at the center, I felt I had my life under control. I was happy."

"But the thoughts and desires remained."

"No, they didn't."

"Oh, yes, they did. You didn't get rid of your sex toys and ensembles."

"I did, I tell you. I gave up my negative behaviors for years."

"If you insist. What went wrong, then, to make you fall off the wagon?"

"Stress! Stress was the problem. When we got married, Ginger and I started to work together in her office. The architecture office was always under her name, The Tanzmann Associates, but the reality was we ran the office together. She marketed our services and managed the finances. I ran the production of the work and led the design. The loft was only blocks away from our office. We could walk to work. Our circumstances were good and loving. Everything seemed to be going in a positive direction. Our office grew. We had art shows in our office. Our reputation was growing. We were getting new clients. I remained sober for four years in this arrangement. I remained satisfied, but circumstances began to change. The work we were doing became more and more stressful and the hours grew longer and longer."

"You lie. It wasn't four years. It was two at the most."

"Let me continue! After several years, the careful structure of my life started to come unglued. I drifted away from my meditation. We became so busy that I was working long hours and would come home to the loft too tired to meditate or to partake in the energy of group meditation at the center. The loss of this stabilizing activity was gradual and did not happen overnight. I would complain to my wife that I was losing contact with the painstakingly constructed plan that kept me stable. She did not understand that stress brought out all defects in my psyche. Soon, I was back to smoking marijuana.

"At this time, I had to give up my loft, which was traumatic for me. I lived in that loft for ten years, but my lease was up and the rent had become unaffordable. We moved into Ginger's house in Pasadena. It became our primary residence. I moved into a smaller workspace behind our architecture office. I kept increasing my pot consumption. In less than four years, I was back to smoking marijuana all the time. I smoked during the day in my studio, and I would go down into the park after getting home, roll a joint, and get totally loaded. I soon found this activity failed to elevate my mood or alleviate my anxiety, as it once did. I no longer got high or full of ideas. I was slowly going mad.

"I have never handled stress well and the stress of my work environment was attacking the meditation pillars of my established stability. I started again to experience the roller coaster mood changes: up one day and down the next. My depressive episodes in January and September came back with renewed severity, as bad or worse as they had been before I began meditation."

Carlotta puts in, "Your sobriety was less than three years. I was there, Carlton. I should know."

"It doesn't matter. What happened was, I made an easy transition from marijuana to crack cocaine. One day, driving in downtown LA, I went by the service station near our office and purchased my first pieces of rock cocaine from a filthy man who slipped out of the throng of homeless people behind the station and approached my vehicle. After convincing him I wasn't a cop, I bought twenty dollars worth of a waxy white material wrapped in plastic that the man spit from his mouth. I returned to my studio and lit up. The rush was incredible! I felt energized, supremely confident, and very sexy. I could work on my art and do architecture with great enthusiasm. I had found my new drug. As the effect wore off, I needed more to keep myself going. I start to use more and more. When I came down, I was confused. I tried to write or make art, but the desire had disappeared into a need to smoke crack. In my journals, I found one or two entries where I explored what was happening to me.

"I started to cruise the area around the seedy hotels off Fifth Street where there were more dealers. I would cruise by one place in particular daily. If my man wasn't there, I found other dealers who were. They started calling me Papa because I was such an old addict."

"You are an intelligent man. Did you not know what the consequences would be from your dalliance with this deadly drug?"

"I didn't care. All I wanted was relief from the stress of my work and my melancholia."

"Didn't people know you were a druggie?"

"If they knew, no one ever said a word to me."

"Carlton may have gone mad, but Carlotta found a drug that really turned her on. All Carlton's hidden desires to become a woman were released from inhibition."

"I'll say! We had a wild time together when I released you from my mind and so much trouble came our way. I left the architecture business with the excuse that I wanted to work on my art and writing. I did no such thing. I spent my money on crack and I dressed up like a woman in my studio. And as the night came, I went out to the transgender bars to hunt for sex. I was a big bear of a man searching for excitement, which I found very rarely."

"Carlton had disappeared into the big rock candy mountain of crack cocaine," says Carlotta. "Your headlong descent into mental illness was heartbreaking, and there was nothing I could do except travel with you."

Carlotta gets up from her chair and walks out the door of the hospital suite without looking back. Mentally exhausted, I stumble to art therapy and make a collage of fifty women around a can of shaving cream.

CHAPTER 21

TWELVE STEPS TO NOWHERE

INSIDE MY CURTAINED COCOON, I DREAM. My tiger and I are camping in the national park along the rushing stream near the rocky round stone edge. Our tent is hidden in a small clearing amidst the bushes between the rippling water and a wide grassy meadow before the aspen trees signal the ascent to the high mountains. We are camouflaged and safe.

My tiger is a real tiger, more Hades than Hobbes. She is a hunter and wild. My wildcat lies by the campfire, stretched out, lounging and lazy. Her head is on her forepaws. Two attendants, a man and a woman, dressed in white-white shirts, white pants, white wide-brimmed hats, and white shoes march into my clearing and walk toward my campfire. They have ropes with nooses dangling from one arm. They see the tiger and abruptly stop. They tremble. My beast stirs and raises her head. She starts to growl and bare her large incisors. I turn to the tiger and say, "Quiet, girl." The big orange, black, and white-striped cat stops growling. I scratch her head. The attendants approach timidly. "It's OK," I say, "she is just guarding me." I put my hand on her jaw. The tiger opens her mouth. I put my hand in her mouth and stroke both her large incisors.

The attendants come up to my campfire and sit down. The tiger stands up and walks around the campfire, sniffing and nudging the interlopers before she returns to my side and lies down. The attendants are still. The comfortable tiger rolls over, and I scratch her stomach. The mammoth cat purrs and drops her paws over her underside. She wiggles her back on the ground. "She's a good cat," I say. The attendants look at each other.

The woman says, "You are not allowed to have such an animal in the park. We have come to take it away."

bipolar bare

I shrug my shoulders. "You're going to take her away? Not with those ropes, you're not."

The man states, "A wild animal like that is dangerous. It's against all the regulations!"

"Not dangerous for me." I respond.

"Well, the park doesn't like it," says the woman. "You shouldn't have such a beast. It's too scary."

"You can leave, if you wish."

The man and the woman stand up. The tiger rolls over and looks at them indifferently. "Cool it, girl," I command.

The tiger rises on her haunches and sits like an Egyptian cat, staring at them. The attendants uncoil their ropes and lasso the tiger. I laugh. Before the attendants can tighten them, the tiger raises one paw and sweeps both ropes off its head, holds them between her teeth, and shakes her head violently until the attendants drop the ropes. The big cat gives off a fierce roar and stretches back her front legs like it might leap. The two attendants stumble backward, turn, and run for their lives out of our campsite. I hear them yell when they are some distance away, "We are getting the warden to deal with you and your tiger!"

The tiger sees a herd of deer. She is gone in a flash, loping away in the same direction as the retreating attendants. The attendants are petrified. The tiger races past them and into a valley beyond. The deer scatter in terror. The tiger picks a big buck and tracks it across the valley meadow. She overtakes it and throws it to the ground, her jaws clamped around its neck. The deer is dead in an instant. The cat drags the deer back to our camp.

I yell to the attendants. "What can I do? My tiger is really a wild beast!"

The attendants run away in fear. My tiger and I have venison for dinner. I say to her, "Tomorrow, I think we must move higher up the mountains to a safer place."

"Who's your tiger, baby?" asks Carlotta, stepping out of the bathroom dressed in a silky white blouse and tiger-striped pedal pushers and heels. Her hair is bright orange.

"Yes, you are my tiger, Carlotta, and a handful of tiger you are," I reply, "but you should protect me more like the tiger in my dream."

"I do protect you," Carlotta brushing her hand through her orange locks and pushing them away from her eyebrows.

"What about the time I went into Las Encinas the first time to end my addiction to crack cocaine? Where were you then?"

"What proof do you have that I wasn't there?" retorts Carlotta, cocking her hips and giving me a big, wicked smile. She noisily chews a piece of gum—Juicy Fruit—with her sensuous lips parted.

"My journals tell the tale."

"Read to me then, bwana."

Carlotta saunters to the window places her hand flat on the glass, cocks her head to one side, and crosses her legs, which kicks her hip up sexily. I open my notebook, look out past Carlotta's provocative stance, over the swimming pool, the apartments beyond the hospital's fence, the palm trees in the distance, and sigh.

"This is the beginning of my serious attempts to be clean and sober," I say.

"Were you meditating?"

"I can't answer that question. I think I had given up the practice. Serious depression had seized me."

"You weren't fun to be with, that's for sure," says Carlotta, blowing a giant bubble that pops against her nose. "This girl just wanted to have fun."

"Las Encinas Hospital December 22, 1994: The African-American nurse who leads me to my room in the brown, one-story ramshackle cottage they call the Briar Unit, located in the middle of the grounds of Las Encinas Hospital, is old. Her dark skin contrasts with her short and nappy, nearly white hair. She is dressed in civilian clothes: green sweater, blue jeans, and sneakers. My bed is a metal-framed unit with a heavy mattress, covered in a dull green army blanket, situated along a wall in a narrow room with two other beds. Mine is closest to the door. I toss my suitcase on the bed; it bounces once on the mattress. Not very comfortable, I think.

"'Follow me to the common area,' the nurse says. 'We need to do your paperwork.'

"To get to the common area, you exit under a wide eave right next to the enclosing concrete block wall and walk past two more patient doors into the Briar Unit's main hall. On the left is the nurse's station, on the right is the wall where a big list of the twelve steps of recovery is posted, and in front is the big room with chairs and couches scattered in front of a grand stone fireplace. Two women are lying on couches reading books. Two men are gathered around a TV set in a corner next to the fireplace, watching a football game. One young man with headphones sits by himself, oblivious to his surroundings.

"'Wait here,' the nurse commands. I am standing in the hallway between the nurse's station and the wall with the twelve step poster. The nurse disappears into the nurse's station. I am left to contemplate the poster, which is designed to look like an ancient parchment scroll. This is my first encounter with the twelve steps of recovery— twelve steps that will be hammered at me for the next six days of my self-incarceration in the Las Encinas drug rehabilitation program. The twelve steps will be the road map for my drug rehabilitation program for the next three years.

"Step 1 on the poster reads: 'We admitted we were powerless over alcohol— that our lives had become unmanageable.' Alcohol? I don't have a problem with alcohol. I have a problem with drugs. My stepmother has a problem with alcohol. I am certainly not like my stepmother. My life has not become unmanageable. Do I believe this?

"Step 2. 'Came to believe that a Power greater than ourselves could restore us to sanity.' Am I going to come to believe that there is some God or something like that? Ha! There is no God. If there were one, how could such an omnipotent being create a world as screwed up as this one? Am I going to do this? NO WAY!

"Step 3. '"Made a decision to turn our will and our lives over to the care of God as we …"

"'This is a twelve step program here at Las Encinas in the Briar Unit.'

"Startled, I turn to see a red-haired woman behind me. She has a narrow, freckled face with curved bangs reaching over her lush eyebrows. The bangs part in the middle, creating a point in her forehead. The rest of her hair falls to her shoulders in numerous rope strands, like the coiling arms of an octopus. Her eyes are green. A long nose turns up suddenly at the end, and her lips are a narrow band covered in a coppery lipstick. The mouth is smiling slightly, lifting the peak of her lips to reveal two gapped white teeth. She reaches out a hand with brass-colored fingernails for me to shake. Her many metal bracelets rattle.

"'I am Alex, one of the counselors here,' she says. 'You will get to know me in our group sessions. Can I help you with anything right now?'

"'I don't know. I don't know if I agree with this twelve step stuff,' I respond.

"'That's typical. Why don't you give it a chance for a few days and then see how you feel? We can talk then.'

"Alex walks away. I had many future interactions with this woman and none of them were pleasant."

"That Alex, she was quite something," says Carlotta. "Loved her flaming red hair and the red high heels she always wore. The rest of the her wardrobe varied between red and green dresses with matching nylons that I found a little tiresome and unimaginative, but then again, she *was* unimaginative. However, I bet all the boys wanted her, or wanted her to be their higher power ... except you."

"Carlotta, you nasty woman, there you go again, making snap judgments."

"The snap judgments were yours, Carlton, dear one. It didn't take you long before you hated the lady. Am I not correct when I say you could not stand her?"

"Yes! I secretly called her Medusa and the Alcohol Nazi."

"The very first day at the very first group you attended, did she not tell you that you were an alcoholic, in spite of the fact you did not drink, but used drugs? The statement infuriated you, did it not?"

"Yes, it did! I thought I would get some understanding from her being as she was an ex-heroin addict."

"Alex got in your face and told you there was no difference between an alcoholic, a drunk, a drug addict, or a junkie. She said any intoxicant—beer, gin, whiskey, marijuana, cocaine, heroin, or any other mind-altering substance—was a chemical with the same effect. They all clouded your perception of reality. You became enraged and stormed out of the meeting."

"I did, I did, I did! My stepmother is a drunk. I can't stand drunks. I am not a drunk. I have a problem with drugs. Not with alcohol. She really pissed me off."

"Truth hurts, doesn't it, Carlton?"

"Listen, you hardheaded spawn of a whore, I AM NOT A DRUNK!"

"Excuse me! So, the little boy had a temper tantrum and retreated to his room and pulled the covers over his head and sulked for the rest of the day."

bipolar bare

"Yes, that's right. So, shut up and be quiet. My ear hurts."

"If memory serves, your ear hurt you a lot during your brief sojourn in the Briar Patch."

"Good term for the place! You are not going to side with THEM, are you?"

"I am neutral. Carlton was the one who got all tangled up in the briars. What more did you write about the experience?"

"After the paperwork, I am interviewed by the African-American nurse with the white, close-cropped hair. She asks the same question they asked at the admissions desk: your date of birth, your Social Security number, your drugs of choice, your using habits, etc, etc. Why? For the remainder of my first day at the drug unit, December 22, 1994, I sleep—except for that first twelve step meeting. The staff leaves me alone while I detox. My ear begins to hurt. Am I having an earache like the ones I used to have as a very young child? Can this be a phenomenon of detoxification from crack cocaine? I think not. I go to the nurse's station to ask for something to kill the pain. She ignores me. I struggle through the night without sleep. I get cranky and agitated.

"I sleep all the next day, but as the night grows near, the pain in my ear starts again. I go to the nurse's station and beg for something to relieve the pain. They refuse my request. I explode in anger. 'This isn't detox' I yell, 'this is real! This is something unrelated!' The night nurse looks at me blandly and states that unless I quiet down and go back to bed, I will be escorted to a locked unit for patients who can't control themselves. I retreat to my bed. I feel as if I have a hot poker inserted into my brain. All I can think about is dying. I pound my head against the wall throughout the night to stop the misery. I swear at God, who has to be a sadistic bastard to allow me to remain in such a state of pain. I am convinced Las Encinas is denying me treatment for my ear, confusing detox with a medical emergency. They are idiots, I am sure.

"Crazy with pain and angry beyond measure on the early morning of Christmas Eve, I walk out of the hospital and stumble my way six blocks to a telephone booth at a convenience store at the corner of Colorado and San Gabriel boulevards in Pasadena, where I call a taxi to take me to Huntington Hospital. In the emergency room, the doctor confirms that I have an infection in my right ear and prescribes an antibiotic. I call my wife and ask her to return me to Las Encinas. She reluctantly complies after first reprimanding me for leaving the hospital. We argue over the phone and in the car on the way back to Las Encinas.

"December 25, 1994: My return to the Briar Unit causes a commotion. When I appear, the patients are all in a group meeting in the common room. They stand, turn at my arrival, and comment amongst themselves. Several point fingers at me. I feel like an escaped con returning to the penitentiary after his aborted attempted at freedom. The three duty nurses come out of their station and stare at me in silence until the head nurse orders Ginger and me to follow her. She escorts us out of the unit and across the lawn to the main administration building and leaves us at the door of the Briar Unit supervisor. We wait uncomfortably outside for several minutes before the door opens and we are waved inside. A tall thin man signals us to sit in two chairs in front of his desk.

"'I am Dr. Harvast,' he drones, flipping open a manila folder. With his right hand, he touches his forehead and sweeps his red hair back. He studies the contents with his chin cradled in his small pale hand. He looks up at me. I can see he has clenched his teeth because the muscles in his cheeks become prominent.

"'Why did you leave the hospital, Mr. Davis?' Dr. Harvast asks in an aggrieved tone.

"'The hospital refused to treat my infected ear,' I respond.

"He proceeds to accuse me of being insane for running away and calls my wife a co-conspirator for abetting my conduct. He threatens me with forced institutionalization, unless I relent in my uncooperative behavior. I shout back at him that I went to Huntington Hospital to get treatment only after my repeated requests for help at Las Encinas were ignored. I state that I had to abandon Las Encinas because the nurses treated a legitimate medical emergency as withdrawal from chemical toxins.

"'I have prescriptions and documentation to prove my assertion,' I say. 'If you incarcerate me as insane, I will sue this hospital's ass.'

"The doctor leans back in his chair, looks up at the ceiling, and expels a breath through pursed lips. He reiterates his analysis of my insanity and again threatens me, but the force is gone from his first threat. We hiss at each other. I tell the supervisor I don't much like him or his hospital.

"'What you plan to do now, Mr. Davis?' the doctor asks.

"'I came back to the hospital, didn't I?'

"'If you do something like this again, I will expel you from the hospital and make sure you never come back.'

"'I hope I will never have to come back,' I say, looking directly into the doctor's eyes.

"The doctor lifts the telephone receiver. A nurse arrives momentarily and I am escorted back to the unit. I didn't leave, they didn't institutionalize me, and the situation got better."

"Two things strike me from this altercation."

"What's that, Carlotta?"

"Maybe you should have been institutionalized. Maybe then they would have recognized your bipolar disorder and we would have saved ourselves ten more years of grief."

"You think that's possible?"

"Why not? Is this not very same hospital that ten years later finally deals with your mental disorder and puts an end to your drug problems?"

"Yes. And your second observation?"

"Doesn't this event remind you of anything, dear Carlton?"

"What do you mean, Carlotta?"

"Oh, just a little story from the past, where a young man gets to bang his head against the wall in pain. Daddy saves his ass. And back he goes to the school, where he doesn't have to pay any attention to the institution because they injured you. They ignore you. You get to ignore them. Am I not right? The ear hears perfectly well right now."

"Are you implying I was faking it? Untrue!"

"Oh, no, I know you were not faking it. It was my ear, the *right* ear that was in pain, if you recall. I was the mind you could not hear or listen with, the mind of reason that became infected. The infection allowed you to operate only out of your left ear, only out of pure emotion."

"That is bunk!"

"You think so? Let me examine the facts. You could establish a position that everything they said about recovery from your drug addiction did not apply to you, since once again they—the powers that be, the higher power if you will—were as corrupt as you believed them to be. You proved you were right, didn't you, Carlton? Why did you go back? Did you want to rub those bastards' noses in it? Prove one more time that doctors, lawyers, administrators—any persons who would control your life—are evil and don't operate in your best interest? That they only operate in their own best interest?"

"Stop trying to confuse me. I was the injured party."

"You are always the injured party."

"Damn, I hate you sometimes, Carlotta. Why won't you defend me like my tiger?"

"To hate me is only to hate yourself. Listen up; I think I'm onto something here. Those right ear infections that you had often as a child, while real, I believe were metaphorical manifestations to prevent hearing what I, your other self, was telling you."

"You are too smart by half, and I wish you would shut up."

"Time for you to listen to me, rather than I should listen to your emotionally charged, intellectualized fairy tales."

"That is a low blow."

"It is meant to be."

"Forget you not that ever since the incident of the 150 aspirin, both my ears have buzzed," I counter. "My hearing has never been too good since. At least the pain in my ear went away and I could hear the miraculous stories of recovery in the last three days of my stay at the Briar Unit before I had to leave."

"Stop play acting! So you left the program meant to help you with your drug problem after only a week? You proved the program was bogus. Right? Right!"

"Yes, damn it, and don't you bring my mother into this again, you witch!"

"Oh, so sensitive, Carlton."

"On December 28, 1994, my counselor, Alex, informs me that my insurance will cover only detoxification and not the rehabilitation portion of the Las Encinas program. This means either I am discharged, possibly the next day, or

I have to pay for the entire program myself. The full cost could run as high as $10,000, which will be beyond my means."

"Stop kidding yourself! It is more than you wanted to invest in this particular program, and you should have been willing to do anything to preserve your health, but you weren't."

"But I did look at all the different options. I could continue in the program but not live in the hospital—several addicts came for the days but left at night. I could return for the evening program of groups, family therapy, and meetings. Alex suggested this. Or, I could continue with the rehab program. This was Dr. Wortz's suggestion. Initially, I did not want to do any of the alternatives. I wanted to get out and get on with my life. Dr. Wortz said that thirty days was not too much to invest in my sanity and health. I had to agree with him, but that, of course, was before I reckoned it could cost me $10,000 of my precious personal savings."

"Your precious personal savings, what a joke!" sneers Carlotta, smacking her Juicy Fruit contemptuously. "So you opted for number two, and it wasn't long before you relapsed, was it?"

"I was committed to working the twelve step program whether or not I remained at Las Encinas."

"Baloney! Did you not hate Alex the Red, who kept calling you an alcoholic?"

"I changed my mind."

"No, you did not. You called her the Drug Nazi. You are lying to me. I can tell because of the way you have your fingers in your mouth and are biting on your nails."

"Damn you."

"What about your depression? What did you write back then? Read for me from the notebook you are hiding behind your back."

"I won't."

"Yes, you will."

"I refuse."

"You can't refuse the opportunity to expose you ability, assisted by me, of course, with your kind of peculiar, right-minded left-handed prose … or is that pose?"

"Carlotta, someday … someday I will put a stake through your cold heart."

"Not today. Not until you have grown up. Then you won't want to. "

"December 29, 1994: In the hospital, there is a stronger support system and less temptation to revert to my favorite drugs (marijuana and crack). Yet even after I complete a full program, I still have to face leaving and continuing a program on the outside. The temptation will still be there and depression still lurks. It is the depression that most concerns me. As Ginger has said, and I concur, I am long-term depressed. I have been depressed all my life. The marijuana, as Dr. Pinsky, the director of Las Encinas, points out, is a major contributor to my depression. Marijuana, the hallucinogen, is my long-term drug of choice. It is my meat and potatoes, so to speak.

"My depression, frequent and often severe, has been exacerbated by my continued use of this drug. I am committed to stop my smoking. The question, of course, remains: if I become depressed by other means (a likely occurrence), will I return to pot and the descent into a grim and precipitous slide toward the depths of suicidal bleakness? I cannot let this happen, but like all addicts, I am powerless over my addiction—my jones, as it called on the street, or my 'boris,' as Alex, the Drug Nazi, calls it. Boris being the bad guy, Boris Badanov who plagued Bullwinkle, the moose, and others in the cartoons Rocky and his Friends.

"My first day away from the drug rehabilitation unit, New Year's Eve, I drive through downtown. I forget my bank card, so I can't get any money. All I have is ten or twelve dollars. Not enough to buy crack on Ceres and get high. Not enough to get entry to the bathhouse for sex on Seventh. The temptation is there. The forgetfulness is purposeful, but the desire to travel the razor's edge won't go away.

"I cruise Alameda toward Sixth Street and look down Ceres Street as it angles away to the south. The desire flashes in my mind as I drift past the places where the dealers who called me 'Papa' because I look like these young dealer's granddaddy hang out. Their spots are empty. Crossing Sixth Street, I drive slowly, watching the corner of Ceres a block away, passing the garage and the parking lot of the bathhouse, where I would go after scoring my rock. It is the place I would smoke up most of my stash, consuming eight or nine tabs—most of my typical purchase of eight to twelve tabs at five dollars each. I wonder if the tabs that fell out the window are still on the ground in the alley between the brick bathhouse and the garage, an old one-story brick shell covered by bowstring trusses. I am thinking dope and sex.

"I look down the street again and see a black guy positioned at the corner of Ceres and Sixth. The addict is the sentinel. He waits, he watches, he signals. Nobody else can be seen, but since he is there, I know I could score some tabs, had I the money. That day I speed away sober and relieved. I traverse across the knife's edge uncut, a clean escape.

"I drive to Seventh Street and turn west, but there are no hookers. Too early in the afternoon, too late in the morning for Skid Row's many prostitutes. The corner of Seventh and Ceres where the El Caribe Bar stands is empty of transvestites. The El Caribe doesn't open until the evening. Only at night do the transvestite hookers, ready to offer themselves to the cruising cars that show up at the bar, haunt the corner in their tight skirts, high heels, and luscious makeup.

"I always think about these so-called she-males when I pass this corner. I go out of my way all the time so I can observe. I have never stopped or made a sex deal because I never want to be the john, I want to be the hooker. I want to be dressed like them, patrol the corner like them, and be paid for sex just like them.

"This is my second addiction. Dressing up as the female gender is my latest obsession and newest sickness. I don't want to admit it, but I like it a lot. Cruising down Seventh, I wondered if I could ever muster the courage or the craziness to work the El Caribe corner. Blasted on coke and pot, I probably could. I have thought about the El Caribe and all the other side streets of Skid Row, where hookers, male and female, and the junkies, users, and dealers work. I have a fascination for this hell and often believe this is my true home. I am unworthy of anything better.

"Here is my guilt and my shame. I want to wallow in it. Even sober, could I work it? Could I live in the Ford Hotel with its sinks in the rooms and toilets down the hall? Could I hang out in the Casual Corner Bar and shop in the Salvation Army Store like the TVs do? Already, I eat in the greasy spoons just like the denizens of this sad neighborhood. Could I be like the tall, thin, strung out female hooker? I see her working at the corner of Agatha and Towne in the heart of Skid

Row outside the Rex SRO (Single Room Occupancy) Hotel where homeless tents and boxes line the streets between the hotels and wholesale merchant doorways. She is probably only in her thirties but her hair is completely gray. With scrawny arms, she signals to me that sex with her is only five bucks. She flashes five fingers at me. In her short, white-dotted yellow skirt showing her spindly legs and a tattered light blue blouse, she looks tired and sad from her latest deals. The big red glasses on her thin, stretched face and her long, stringy hair make her look like a fallen librarian. I figure she has AIDS and drive on. I would bet she is mentally ill."

"When we tried hooking, we couldn't even get arrested," Carlotta laughs.

"As I recall, I was dressed in full drag," I reply. "It was very late at night. I was cruising, looking for a corner to work. I had given up on Las Encinas' program and all the others, too. I was enjoying my relapse, if you could call this enjoyment. I am in my all-black outfit: black skirt, black blouse over my corset, black fishnet stockings and four-inch heels, studded collar. My eyebrows are plucked and my lashes are a good half-inch long. My lipstick and fingernails match—a provocative red. Dangly earrings complete the look. Blasted on crack, the cops pull me over on Towne Street."

"I told you to stay cool."

"I did. I wobbled across the sidewalk in my high heels and stood next to a building entrance while the cops shined their flashlights on me."

"Give us your driver's license," the female officer asked. Hands shaking, I dug inside my black purse, opened my wallet, and gave it to them.

"What are you doing out here so late?" the female officer asked. The male officer headed for my truck.

"I've been to a loft party," I lied.

The female officer handed me back my license. There was a loud squawk on the radio in the patrol car. The male officer deviated from going to my truck to respond to the radio call.

"Taylor, we gotta go. There is a shooting at 26th and Central."

The female officer climbs in the patrol car with a warning: "This is a dangerous neighborhood to be driving around at this hour of night."

bipolar bare

"Nice outfit," the male cop laughs as he gets into the driver's seat. "You are a lucky girl—or is it boy?"

"That incident was later when I was doing my drag thing more or less every chance I could get."

"Yeah, I know, Carlton. You were going further and further away from mental stability, descending gradually into a hell of your own design. You were lucky you never got arrested or beat up. I was surprised we could last so long in the condition we got ourselves in."

"I *am* lucky in some ways."

"Read to me more of what you did that first day away from Las Encinas. It proves you were already going to relapse, sooner or later."

"I leave downtown and head up Santa Monica Boulevard towards Silverlake. I am on my way to Circus of Books to see if the January issue of *TV Epic*, a local magazine aimed at transvestites, is in. It is. Inside is a big surprise: Carol Quintana's picture with the caption, 'Smile Doll, it's your first night out.' I, the male Carlton, am not recognizable, but the female Carol has a wry twinkle in her eyes and a semi-smirk on her face. She is a big girl, but not unattractive.

"After marveling at the picture, I find Marlena's column, where she talks about Carol Q. Marlena is the transvestite editor of *TV Epic*. She writes a column in each issue about men coming out as transvestites Marlena met Carol before her birthday party, at Queen Mary Club in the San Fernando Valley. Carol introduced herself and spoke to Ms. Lacie near the buffet and said that Ms. Lacie's column on male duality encouraged her to dress. Ms. Lacie expressed her joy at Carol's remarks and how this interchange was one of the most meaningful moments of her fortieth birthday party. After reading these remarks, I drive home nervous, excited, and troubled. I wonder if the transvestite is the 'real person' in my psyche.

"You used to call me Carol or Georgina," Carlotta observes. "Why did you change my name?"

"At first, your name was Carol Quintana," I explain. "I thought the name was too close to my sisters' and my mother's names and wasn't classy enough. Next, I called you Georgina Bushbunny, after our president, but that didn't seem to fit, either."

"So you changed it to Carlotta Pizzotta! You think *that's* a classy name? You were probably on drugs at the time. Why didn't you ask me for my opinion?"

"Because you would have come up with some name I could not have tolerated. Like Winifred, Marjorie, or Beulah Buckingham, or something equally abhorrent."

"Give me credit for being more inventive than that!"

"Don't you like Carlotta? I think it's exotic."

"Acceptable, but *Pizzotta*. As if I am some sort of pizza pie or Italian pasta dish."

"I think of you as having a lot of pizzazz, therefore Pizzotta."

"Well, at least I am not Carlotta *Pissoir*!"

I laugh at Carlotta's reference to the little French kiosk public urinal that Americans find so amusing. "Hmm, given your former proclivities, maybe I should change it to that."

"Those were not my proclivities, Carlton dear, they were yours. Drugs merely freed my soul, and you envisioned me as a whore. Read what you did with your female nature, bad boy."

"You know very well that after I got out of Las Encinas, I dressed up in female clothes every chance I got!"

"Read on, Carlton, It's very relevant to your search for sobriety, where you say you explored all the avenues."

"January 31, 1995. I am relapsed completely. Saturday night, January 28, I drank five gin and tonics in drag and at 2:00 a.m., my inhibitions shot all to hell, I bought $20 worth of crack and smoked it up in an hour. I wanted to drink for two reasons: one, I didn't believe the hospital's determination that all addicts are really alcoholics, and two, I was in drag at the Queen Mary transvestite bar in the San Fernando Valley for their Fashion Fetish Night.

"I didn't think of myself as having a problem with alcohol. Marijuana and cocaine yes, alcohol never. I have never really been drunk except for a small number of times in my life. The last one I can remember is when my wife and I spent an evening together several years before we married and several years before we even started a relationship. In fact, the circumstances of our excess drinking and subsequent sex hindered the development of a relationship between us because of our embarrassment at our drunken behavior. I remember that night well. Ginger and I sat on her porch drinking gin and tonics to the point of inebriation and then found ourselves on her dining room floor, pulling off each other's clothes and screwing madly on the bare hardwood. I have had drinks since then, but not to that extent where I totally lost control of my behavior. Saturday night, I wanted to prove or disprove to myself that alcohol is not a problem for me. I end up proving it is a problem.

"The second reason I drank is that I am alone and feeling insecure at the drag show at the Queen Mary. I want to be loose, so I start on the gin and tonics and then enter the fashion fetish show. I am in my all black outfit with the stud collar, the chain waist, and the long linked earrings that dangle below my auburn hair. I stumble up the entry steps, walk awkwardly round the stage, and disappear into the crowd afterwards, totally embarrassed. I drive back to my studio, where the desire to buy crack overpowers me. I buy $20 worth of the drug off the street, smoke it, and stay up until five in the morning drawing and playing autoeroticism. I know now: not only do I have to give up alcohol, but I must give up cross-dressing if I wish to stay sober. I am not sure I want to stay sober, if I have to give up this latest obsession."

"Is it I, Carlotta, whom you are afraid you will have to give up?"

"Maybe," I reply. "Are you just a fiction I have invented in my mind?"

"No, I believe I am your other mind. I shall always be here for you, but there is sickness in your right mind that is awakened when you take drugs. The same sickness awakens me in your left mind, but your right, emotional mind dominates and likes to play these sex games. Of course, since I am a female, I enjoy the sex, but I don't like the circumstances under which you practice this behavior."

"I am not sure I believe what you are saying. It is you who drove me to these sexual exploits."

"Frame it however you wish. The vision of these acts is what stays in your mind and that makes you feel guilt. I feel no guilt for having a good time."

"What about the dressing up?"

"That's what women do.

"I don't understand."

"I, Carlotta, the female voice, think we should defer this discussion for a future date, after we have thoroughly investigated our experience with the twelve steps."

"But why?"

"Because, during this period when you, the male Carlton, were intensely cross-dressing, we were also seeking a path out of drug addiction through some means other than the twelve steps. You developed an absolute hatred for that program."

"You are correct in your analysis that I became disillusioned with the twelve steps because of the inflexibility of the program, but the cross-dressing is somehow related to this."

"And you know that from your writing?"

"I didn't write much about the experience, yet I am angry all of January after getting out of Las Encinas. I cruise the transvestite bars in the San Fernando Valley. It is my only relief from the rage. I don't understand it, but being female is a relief from being male, and having anonymous sex or practicing self-sex provides relief."

"Then the knowledge must come from the yearly datebooks you decorate with drawings."

bipolar bare

Out of Control; 1995; diary page; ink pen

"*We*, dear Carlotta! *You* took the notes, and *I* drew the pictures on top of them. Made it darn hard to decipher."

"More fun that way."

"The trips to the evening program at Las Encinas were run by Alex, the Drug Nazi. She liked to play therapist. I had to make lists of all the different kinds of addictive behavior: alcohol, caffeine, drugs, exercise, gambling, food, nicotine, work, and sex. Some of the people in the group had issues with more than one of these behaviors."

"We were among them, of course. How about drugs, food, and sex?"

"I had to look at each and apply the twelve steps to each addiction."

"Bet that irritated little old Carlton."

"It did, and I didn't like it. I thought I was at this group to deal with my drug use. The Drug Nazi would want to play therapist. She would ask questions like: 'How does this fill a void? How is this a barrier to growth? How does this interfere with your relationships? How does this compromise your values?' The whole session would go on like this and then end with 'The Serenity Prayer,' which I grew to detest."

"That doesn't sound so bad," says Carlotta pragmatically.

"No? Well, in between all the questions, she talks about giving our addiction up to God, her higher power. She is pushing the God agenda. I want none of it. After leaving each group, my rage has grown greater than before I came in."

"So, we go to see Dr. Wortz, our trusted biofeedback psychologist."

"Yes. Dr. Wortz asks me to observe the precursors to my rage, how it comes into existence, and what remains when the rage is gone. I learn that the anger arises in my shoulders, and it's always preceded by some little incident of frustration or confrontation—anxiety over a trip to the dentist, for instance. Still, the rage does not abate."

"So we start to meditate again."

"Precisely. I use the rage as the object of my meditation and find that my stomach aches. Yet the rage remains and I hate the world."

"All in January and February, is this not? You were suffering from an attack of mania, a yearly occurrence for as long as we can remember."

"I know that now. Rage and anger are my mania. Why didn't Las Encinas diagnose it?"

"You were there for drug treatment, not mental disorder," Carlotta reminds me.

"I tried to lick my habit with the twelve steps, with therapy, and with meditation, but nothing worked, and in twenty-one days, on January 28, 1995, I relapsed on crack cocaine."

"Now you could dress up and get loaded all you wanted, Carlton."

"I didn't give up completely, though. I gave up on the twelve steps as set out by Alex at Las Encinas. I start a search for other programs, which I thought might work for me. I tried Rational Recovery."

"That didn't work either, did it?"

"Of course not! I tried a program at the Pizarro Treatment Center, which entailed constant urine testing and counseling, but was not a traditional twelve step program."

"Did that work?"

"No."

"How could any of these programs work when you were in a period of rapid cycling, speeded on by the use of crack cocaine? The whole idea is ridiculous."

"But I did manage to stay sober long enough to give a clean urine sample to Pizarro. That was something."

"Maybe you should have gone from one program to another, giving clean urine samples. Now this is an innovative program for sobriety, since most programs require a seventy-two hour clean urine sample in order to be admitted. We could call it the You're In Program."

"Be serious, Pizzatta! You know, now that I think about it, I probably came up with your last name from Pizarro."

"Aha! I knew there was some devious derivation for the name. Of course, Francisco Pizarro was a great conquistador in the Americas. Did he not ravage the Inca empire? Or could they have named the center after Juan Pizarro, Francisco's less-famous brother? Or maybe they were thinking of the major league pitcher Juan Pizarro, who threw for almost twenty victories for the 1966 White Sox. See how up I am on baseball lore?"

"I forget. Anyway, I drove all over Southern California trying to find a program I might enter that was not based on the twelve steps. I could find nothing. Every program everywhere is based on the twelve steps. In desperation, I visited The Betty Ford Center in Palm Springs."

"Figured if you had to go twelve steps, we might as well go top drawer, eh?

"No, I figured The Betty Ford Center would not force-feed its main clientele, rich celebrities, the twelve step program for fear of alienating them. I was right. When I went to talk to the admissions people, I told them I needed help with my addiction, but I didn't want to go to a place where they were they forced the twelve step program down your throat. They said they would not. I decided to go as a last resort. The BFC had a waiting list for admittance. It wasn't until July 4, 1995, that I was admitted."

"Independence Day! Carlton Doodle went to rehab, toking on a crack pipe ..."

"So to speak. I declared *our* independence day from drugs when I entered The Betty Ford Center for thirty days."

"You and your tiger went higher up the mountain to find a safer place to come clean."

"But there were six months before I was admitted to Betty Ford. A wild six months!"

carlton davis

Self-portrait; 1998; 22 x 30 inches; oil stick

CHAPTER 22

CARLTON AND CARLOTTA

"Can't sleep, Carlton?" says Carlotta, giving Carlton her devilish but comical smile.

"I am thinking about the six months after I left Las Encinas and before I went to The Betty Ford Center."

"Didn't you have a grand time? You played out all your fantasies."

"I'm not thinking about my behavior that way. I am thinking about anger and depression. I departed Las Encinas in late December and began January, the month of my big depressions, in a state of rage. In the process group today, the counselor said a patient could be in a mixed mood, both depressed and manic at the same time. I think this is where I am now *and* where I was in 1995."

"Why are you angry now? You should be happy. The hospital is filling you up with happy drugs."

"The drugs are not working," I lament. "I am as angry as I ever have been, and I am boiling over with energy. Anger releases great power. Anger was how I got myself excited and ready to go, to stay up all night, to drive myself to overcome my laziness, and to cross-dress. Anger filled my mania. It made me not care about the consequence of my actions. I was uninhibited. I was without fear."

"You did get angry at the slightest provocation. You would explode, throw dishes, slam doors, punch walls, rip up your art, and drive like a maniac. You scared me and other people."

I smile devilishly. "I could go now and attack the nurse's station."

"Bad idea! They will put you lockup and probably strap you down. Can't you think of another way to release this energy? Do a drawing. Write a piece."

"How about some sex?" I suggest hopefully. "When I got angry, I got loaded on crack, and I would search out some nasty sex."

"Dear Carlton, you didn't need anger or crack to go after nasty sex. You did it all the time."

"Shut up and listen to me! In a rage, I started smoking crack almost immediately after I left the Las Encinas drug program. Crack gave me even more energy when I was high and replaced the energy I lost when I was down. High on crack, I renewed my sexual escapades. Sex was the way I spent the energy on a wild ride through denial and desire. Yet I was still depressed."

"Denial and desire—what does that mean?"

"I denied I was an addict, and I desired as much weird sex as I could find."

"That is true, but maybe you were denying your true nature, which was gay and a transvestite."

"I don't believe that. When I wasn't high, I didn't desire gay sex."

"Sex was your obsession. Any frustration tripped you into rage or guilt. In either state, you hunted for sex."

"The year started with me in a depressed state," I muse, recalling the time. "I lost my keys. Losing something—most commonly my keys, but it could be my wallet, my phone, or a book—was the signal I was headed for a big depression. Never did I put the depression—the so-called attack of the black brain—together with the anger as mania. I ended up in what the counselor calls a mixed state. I always thought the anger merely was part of the depression. I did not see anger as the up state and depression the down. In the up state, I went for sex as a way to release the energy. In the down state, I sought sex as the way to increase my depleted energy. Drugs were required for both states."

"You did get angry at the slightest provocation."

I snort at Carlotta's gross understatement. "Crack gave a jolt of energy when I was high and made me higher. Crack replaced the drained energy when I was down but never lifted me out of the depressed state. Then there were the side effects. The body became very tense, the shoulders stiff from the built up tightness, the hands fisted, and the jaw clenched. The eyes crossed when I tried to concentrate. I saw double. I reversed letters in writing, inverted numbers, and destroyed eyeglasses in absolute irritation. I couldn't hear clearly. I made constant errors because my timing was off."

"You weren't a very nice person to be around. Everyone who knew you ducked for cover."

"I was attacked by inanimate objects, as it were. I banged into walls, columns, and furniture. Consecutive errors increased the volume of my anger. Then this mammoth energy was released. The spring uncoiled. Most of the energy released was negative, but there were positive aspects. Super-energized, I would do my best work, and Carlotta would be released."

Carlotta; 1995; diary page; ink pen

"Before you said Carlotta—or was I Carol then?—your drug-addled creation."

"You, the slut, were the manifestation of drugs, but you were more, too. You were a powerful being I could become. All I know is that I could not stop myself from releasing this Carlotta. All my inhibitions disappeared. My rage was stupendous, and you were undeniable. When I departed the hospital at the beginning of January 1995, I was in complete fury. I was angry at the hospital for turning me out because of the limitation of my health insurance. I was angry at going to the hospital at all. I was angry with my wife and my doctor for placing me in the position of patient. But my rage came from a place far greater than these annoyances. It came from a fundamental place within my brain and with its coming, Carlotta emerged."

"Are you saying I come only from the source of your anger?" Carlotta implores. "Can you identify that place?"

"No, I can't," I sigh. "I am saying *you* were my mania. Stoked by drugs and alight with rage, out came Carlotta, and I fulfilled my need to be a whore. You appeared many times in those months."

"I also appeared far after the time you speak about. I have been with you for a long time before, and look, I am here with you now."

"This is different. You are my Greek chorus of one, commenting on the events and guiding my aspirations. Carlotta, you are now my muse. I don't want to dress like you. I want your insights. In the past, you were my avenging whore, carrying the ice pick weapon. Your primary target was me, Carlton. The guilt enlarged my despair and pushed me toward self-murder."

"Carlotta is never violent. Only Carlton is the violent one, especially when covered in the package of Carlotta. Carlton allowed himself the capacity to be violent and had no guilt for his use of drugs."

"I had guilt, but only when I came down from high. Therefore, I tried always to be high. Crack fueled my anger and could lift my down temporarily."

"I thought you said crack could not lift your depression?" Carlotta reminds me.

"Crack couldn't. It only provided a temporary distraction. Crack is a fast burning and high temperature fuel. I would rocket forward like a jet plane toward some destination unknown. All I wanted to do was move fast and burn past any frustration, guilt, and depression in my path. I used to think my anger was the only advantage I had. I wasn't smart or clever, but when I was angry I could overcome any impediment in my way. I could race over the impediments with a power that was unbelievable. No average person could find that much energy within himself, but I could."

"I was always fearful we would be destroyed when you became that energized. Your anger knew no boundaries."

bipolar bare

"There were boundaries. After the anger and the energy of a high were spent, I became more deeply depressed, and when that depressed, I did not care what I did. I would seek drugs in this mood to replace the anger and make for myself a different sensation, like the desire for humiliating sex. I had many reasons why I needed to smoke crack. It stoked the up and mitigated the down. When I was in a neutral state I would be looking for help to remain sober. The rapid cycling carried on before the first time I went to the hospital and continued—getting worse—until I admitted myself to The Betty Ford Center on Independence Day."

"You certainly began to act in a very crazy way after you departed Las Encinas. You didn't just relapse—you went into complete insanity. All you wished to do was cross-dress, seek sex, and buy crack."

"It was a miracle I managed to make it twenty days before I relapsed on crack," I admit. "The habit escalated from a twenty dollars score to a $120 a day score over the next six months."

"And you became Carlotta at every available opportunity. I admit I enjoyed my time out, but it saddened me to see all the pain that Carlton was in. Carlton detested everything. The slightest annoyance set you off. You became frustrated, then angry, by the obstacle of any little thing, especially by inanimate objects: a car, a table, a door. You dropped a file under your car and began kicking the vehicle. You bumped into a table and kicked it across the room. You hit your head on a door and punched it, splitting its surface. Your solution for dampening these feelings was to smoke, put on your Carlotta uniform, and go out looking for sex. You wrote a lot about these misadventures. Why don't you get up out of bed? You can read to me, and we can talk."

I rise out of bed and take the notebook in which I wrote about the period from my desk drawer. Carlotta stands beside me dressed in her typical outfit of the time: black skirt and blouse, black nylons, black high heels with the buckled ankle straps, silver belt, and leather-studded brackets and collar. Her make-up is garish, green fading to white eye shadow, long eyelashes above eyes outlined in black, and red blush below the eyes. Her hair is auburn, and dangling from her ears are gold disc earrings.

"Do you like my look?" she asks coquettishly. "This is how you liked to dress, playing my part."

"It works for me. You look like the street hooker you were."

"Then let's get into it. Read to me."

"I have a good story. After I left Las Encinas, I felt like I was two people trapped in one body: Carlton the addict and Carlotta the whore. I wrote about it many times."

"June, 1995, Carlotta is out again. Carlton is relapsed. The divided self is smoking crack for six months. Carlotta is in an upscale mood tonight. Dressed and ready to go, she smokes $20 worth of the $100 score Carlton purchased earlier in the day. Each day Carlotta wants more sex, and Carlton feels more guilty and depressed. She is a real slut. He is an angry man. She wants to be out on the street picking up men, giving blow jobs and having them insert their dicks in her backside pussy. She likes walking the streets of Los Angeles and San Francisco after the bars close. Black men pick her up. Carlton tells Carlotta to carry an ice pick in her purse, just in case. She laughs, dropping the pick, wrapped in the black leather sheath Carlton made for it, into her silver-sequined bag. It looks like an oversized cocktail purse with eyebrow pencils in the midst of lipsticks, face powder, makeup, brushes, lighters, crack pipes, ice pick, condoms, and an old medicine vial that once said Paxil, now used to carry crack. Carlton calls Carlotta names: Whore! Hooker! Tart! Slut! Laughing, she says she may be a slut, but she says she isn't a whore. Nevertheless, she accepts ten bucks from a trick after she sucks him in his car on a deserted side street. Carlotta loves getting laid. Carlton is disgusted."

bipolar bare

Self-portrait; 2001; 22 x 30 inches ; oil stick

"Who is Carlotta, if I am not part of you, Carlton?" asks Carlotta. "The disgust you feel is disgust for yourself. When you try to separate me from you, you have nothing. Carlton is incomplete and is really a ghost if he doesn't divide himself in two. Carlotta and Carlton are one being, speaking and hearing through one voice and two ears. There is a dominance that Carlton asserts, but when he is high and confused by drugs, he lets Carlotta dominate. Without two sides, none exists. The coin can't be real without its opposite surface."

"No, I must disagree. You were a state-dependent personality. I am one being, who is contorted into something else when I use drugs."

"See it how you wish. I know who I am. Carlton doesn't seem to know who he is."

"Don't interrupt; let me continue with my story."

"Carlotta does the El Caribe. She is standing out there with the other TV hookers, making sex deals. Carlotta is bigger and older than the other girls, who are mostly Latinos or African-Americans in skimpy outfits. But Carlotta dressed in her black S&M outfit is just as sexy. There she is, on the corner of 7th and Ceres, in her five-inch black vinyl heels—the ones that make her a real Amazon at six foot six inches tall—talking tricks with the other girls. She will do a joint deal with another girl, Carmen. Carlotta, all in black, and Carmen, in red, approach a car with three black men. Carmen is petite but very sexy in her red miniskirt and red halter top that shows her considerable bust. Her skin is tan, a lovely smooth Afro-Cuban mixture. Tightly corseted, Carlotta wears a black miniskirt that displays her gorgeous legs and a snug, lacy blouse. Carlton is howling in her ear to remember the ice pick that's in her silver purse. Carlotta whispers for Carlton to be quiet and record the visual images of this fun event.

"The deal is set—sixty bucks for each girl and a share of the drugs the boys buy. Each man can have each girl twice and the girls will suck the boys prior to the fucking. Carlotta and Carmen get into the car, an old, bronze-colored Buick—a real land yacht— with white leather seats split with age. Carmen gets into the front seat next to the driver, the smallest of the three johns, who seems quite smitten with her. He has the kindest face, a mustache, and a small brimmed hat with a gray-feathered band. Carlotta is pulled into the back seat between the other two men, thickset brutes with heavy faces, very dark skin, and several days' worth of stubble. They start pawing Carlotta immediately as the car pulls away from the curb.

"The driver crosses 7th Street and slowly cruises Ceres until he finds a dealer. The driver negotiates. He has plenty of money and purchases $150 worth. Several blocks later, on a deserted street, the driver turns south away from downtown, slows to the curb, and pulls out two glass pipes. He lights up one and hands the other to the guys in the back seat. After the men have their hits, the girls are given theirs. It is good stuff. Carlotta feels sexy—she gyrates her torso just a little—and she can see that Carmen has already reached over and bent down to suck on the driver as they begin to cruise.

"The men in the back seat have opened up their pants. They both have enormous dicks. 'Suck on that,' the one to Carlotta's right says, pushing her head down to his cock. Carlotta wraps her mouth around the head and begins to suck and sink the cock into her mouth. 'You like that, bitch, don't you?' he grunts in ecstasy.

"The man to Carlotta's left is grabbing her ass and squeezing hard. He takes another hit of crack and passes the pipe over to the other man. 'Take this, Larry,' he says. 'I want some sucking by this big bitch, too.'

"Larry takes the pipe and pushes Carlotta's head upright. 'She's all yours, Leroy, but first, let's get her a little more loaded.'

"Smiling, Larry puts another chunk in the pipe, shoves it in Carlotta's mouth, and lights it up. 'White pussy is always better really loaded,' he chuckles.

"Carlotta takes a deep drag and holds it in. Sensation surges through her body. She leans over and French kisses Leroy, blowing the leftover smoke into his lungs.

"'You're right, Larry, this bitch really likes to fuck,' he says. Leroy grabs Carlotta's head and pulls her down on his penis, which is even bigger and fatter than his friend's.

"'You are going to take all of this, bitch, several times,' he says.

"Carlotta nearly gags on the monster. A cop car rolls by. The cops turn their heads to look at the black men but can't see the hookers bent down over the men's crotches. The men act innocent and stare straight ahead. The cops move on.

"'That was close,' says the driver, 'but we're almost safe at the motel.'

"We reach The Regis Motel, a seedy stucco court with 'Regi OTEL' spelled out in flickering neon over the entry. The driver goes in to register for a room with the manager, a blubbery black man. Leroy gets out and opens the trunk and pulls out two bottles of tequila. He steps back to the car and hands a bottle to Larry. They both take swigs, not offering anything to the girls.

"'Number 10,' says the driver, coming back to the Buick.

"'That's the good one, Joe,' says Larry. 'It's got mirrors and a TV that works.'

"Joe drives the car over to room ten. The merry crew spills out of the car raucously. Larry and Leroy push the girls roughly into the room through a red door with split wood at its base.

"Carlotta surveys the room. Mirrors cover three walls above a dull and dirty red lower wall about three feet high. The front wall next to the door is covered by dirty linen drapes from ceiling to floor. A beat-up credenza lines the wall at the foot of the beds, sagging relics with thin, stained covers atop rickety metal frames. The carpet is a threadbare green shag with streaks of red and large brown stains the origin of which Carlotta is loath to contemplate as she drapes her silver purse containing the ice pick over the end of the battered credenza.

"'Take your skirts off, bitches,' Leroy demands, swigging on his tequila bottle, then letting the bottle hang loose at his side. Larry flops on one of the two beds. Leroy sits down on the outside corner of the same bed, loading up the pipe. Joe switches on the TV and stands there mesmerized as the dark screen comes to life, revealing a porn flick in progress. Carmen and Carlotta are standing at the foot of the first bed, several feet away from the TV. Joe suddenly looks up from the action on the screen.

"'Awright, hos, get those skirts off,' he commands in a voice like sandpaper as he sits down on the second bed. 'Let's see your pussies.'

"Carmen slips out of her red mini shirt. Her ass is bare and her member is hidden under a lacy G-string. Carlotta wiggles out of her tight skirt, revealing her big bare ass and the slight bulge of her member beneath her G-string. Both girls have thigh-high nylon stockings kept up by numerous garter belt straps.

"'Wiggle your asses, hos,' Joe demands, accepting the pipe from Leroy and lighting up. Larry rises from the bed, drops his trousers, and steps out of his already unlaced tennis shoes. Joe passes him the pipe. He inserts a big hunk and lights up. The girls wiggle and gyrate their asses. Larry slouches on bed and watches as a black woman licks a black man's dick on the TV.

"Joe leans over and places the balance of the crack chunks on the nightstand between the two beds. He puts his hat on the metal pole at the head of the bed. Larry, now nude to the waist, turns and places his bottle of tequila on the table next to the crack. Leroy doesn't move but takes another swig of tequila.

"'Hos, get down on your knees and crawl over to me and lick my dick,' says

bipolar bare

Larry harshly. They obey. Larry takes one pipe from the nightstand. Joe hands him another large chunk. He inserts the chunk in the pipe, sticks it in Carlotta's mouth, and lights it. Carlotta inhales deeply. It feels so good. The rush quickly spreads. She holds it in and then gently exhales it over Larry's swelling dick. Carlotta puts the penis in her mouth. She slides easily down the shaft. Carmen licks his balls.

"'I told you to wiggle those asses, bitches,' Larry repeats.

"Joe and Leroy stand up and move behind the girls. Joe is rubbing Carlotta's cheeks and Leroy, Carmen's. Carmen crawls, turns around, and begins to suck on Leroy's cock. Joe works his hand toward Carlotta's pussy. He puts in two fingers and slaps her ass with his other hand. Carlotta feels the head of his dick at her pussy. He shoves it in. It feels good and she moans. She sucks harder on Larry's dick. It's now eight inches long. The penis inside her is smaller but is being thrust forward hard. Larry pulls back, takes a swig, and lights the pipe.

"Meanwhile, Joe keeps working Carlotta's ass. Carmen is trying to engulf Leroy's enormous cock and is choking. Leroy pulls away and takes the pipe from Larry. Larry tells Joe to put Carlotta on the end of the bed. Joe pulls out, slapping Carlotta's ass hard and pushes her to the end of the bed. Joe grabs her arms and spreads them out. Handcuffs attached to the bed appear and Carlotta's arms are clamped spread-eagle. Her ass is up over the end of the bed. Joe pushes a pillow under her to raise her ass a little higher.

"'Looks about the right height now,' he says, 'for a good fuck job.'

Larry walks behind her. He tells Joe to give the bitch the pipe. Carlotta's head is turned and Joe inserts the pipe in her mouth and lights it up. Carlotta inhales.

"'Keep it in awhile, bitch,' Joe says, smiling evilly. Carlotta nearly swoons. The drugs have made her hot. Larry spreads her legs apart puts grease on her ass. The grease has something in it. Carlotta's pussy is really stimulated.

"'Open up, whore,'" Larry shouts and rams his eight inches into her pussy. 'Ohh, yes, that's it!' Carlotta groans.

"'You like that, bitch?' says Larry. He begins a rhythmic stroking back and forth while Carlotta moans for more. Handcuffed to the other bed, Carmen is being drilled by Joe while Leroy slaps his enormous cock against her back. He turns to Carlotta and steps onto the bed. He sits at the head and slides his legs under Carlotta's spread arms. He shifts slowly toward her head until his twelve-inch cock is close to Carlotta's mouth.

"'Suck on this, bitch,' he commands, lifting Carlotta's head up and pushing his cock into her mouth. He takes the crack pipe and lights up. Carlotta is licking, sucking, and rolling her tongue around the tip of Leroy's penis. Larry is working her ass hard. Carlotta is vibrating everywhere and tries to engulf all twelve inches of Leroy's big thing.

"'Shall I let the whore have it now?' Leroy asks Larry. Larry slows down and pulls out. He heads for the bathroom to wash off his dick. Leroy slides back on the bed. He gives Carlotta another hit of crack, stands up over the girls, walks down the bed and jumps off. He is pumping his cock. Larry emerges from the bathroom and heads for Carmen. He does what Leroy did and gets Carmen sucking on his still stiff cock. Leroy slaps Carlotta's ass four or five times, greases up her pussy again, and steps forward.

"'Ready, bitch?'" he laughs.

"'Carlotta says, "Oh, yes, do it baby."'

"Leroy pushes his enormous member in slowly and works it up to the hilt. Carlotta is groaning and wiggling. He pulls back, pushes in hard, and begins to stroke, slowly and gently at first, but soon the pace quickens. Leroy is slapping her ass on each thrust. Carlotta opens up more with each forward movement. His cock seems to be filling up every part of her body. Everything starts to vibrate. The legs start to tremble. The torso shakes ever so slightly. The arms and neck relax. The shoulders sag and the neck droops. The spine stretches and the release of energy begins. Sweat dampens Carlotta's body. Her forehead is a waterfall. Perspiration flows rapidly across the hair and scalp.

"He adjusts his position and drives the cock in as deep as he can penetrate. Carlotta can take it. Her quick inhalations indicate the sensitivity. Their movement begins to be in harmony with every increasing quick, shorter, and deeper thrust. Rhythmic strokes drive the cock deeper. Carlotta tries to relax to receive it. The innards don't hurt today and the penis goes deeper. Carlotta is writhing and moaning. Smiling, she flicks her tongue at Larry's stoned face. His expression is tranquil but absent and doesn't change.

"'Take it bitch,' Leroy yells and drives his cock forward. Carlotta can feel the cum burst into her ass."

"That was raw! That story never happened! You made it up."

"How would you know, Carlotta? You were so wasted on crack."

"I know. But it sounds like another one of your fantasies. I was never that bad, that horny, that much of a slut! I never worked the corner of the El Caribe. Remember what happened when we tried to hook? The cops pulled us over and scared us off. Besides, how did we ever get home after this encounter with these bad men? Tell me that!"

"This isn't the end of the story."

"There is more to this fantastic concoction?"

"Regrettably, no. The three black men left their money on the nightstand, along with one crack pipe and a couple of chunks of crack, and left Carlotta and Carmen handcuffed spread-eagle to the beds.".

"I don't believe it," says Carlotta. "I would never let myself get into such a situation."

"When you were loaded you got yourself in all kinds of nasty situations. May I remind you of the Bay Social Club?"

"Go on with your fairy tale. I am the one who is now disgusted."

"'I think you are going to have another visitor,' Leroy says as he closes the door on Carmen and Carlotta. They could hear the Buick pull away and after a few minutes, the door opened and the fat manager walks into the room.

"Tsk-tsk, hos in my motel. What am I to do?" he says and walks over to nightstand. He drops a chunk of crack into the pipe and lights up. While he inhales, he sweeps up the 120 bucks and puts it in his pocket. He turns to Carmen.

"'You want I should unchain you, ho?' Carmen nods yes. 'Then you are going to suck on my dick, OK?' He pulls a key from his pants and undoes the locks on Carmen's arms. Carmen sits at the end of the bed, rubbing her wrists, while he undoes his belt and lets his trousers fall to the floor. Carmen pulls down his jockey shorts. He has enormous balls and a short but very fat cock.

"'Lick my balls,' he commands. Carmen obeys. 'Now suck my cock.' Shutting her eyes, Carmen does so. The cock swells to six inches long and more than two inches in diameter. It chokes Carmen. 'Good girl,' the big fat man says. He turns to Carlotta.

"'You want to be free, white bitch?'

"'Yes,' Carlotta sneers.

"'Then you're going to take this up your pussy and be quiet.'

"Carlotta gets fucked by the fattest dick she has ever had and never says a word. When the manager is done, he frees Carlotta and takes the handcuffs with him.

"'Get out of my motel and don't come back,' he warns, slamming the door behind him.

"Carlotta and Carmen put on their skirts and walk out of the room. Carlotta sees the manager in his inner office, watching TV with his back to the door. She unbuckles her high heels and gives them to Carmen. She unzips her purse and withdraws the stainless steel ice pick from its sheath. The pick is about six inches long and octagonal at its larger end, where an incised inscription reads, 'National Cold Storage.' Gripping it in her right hand, Carlotta carefully raises the gate at the reception counter and silently slips into the manager's office. The manager has his TV on loud and doesn't hear Carlotta approach. She comes up behind him with the ice pick in her hand and places the tip in the waxy opening of the fat man's ear. With her left arm, she applies a chokehold around his sweaty neck.

"'I am going to put this ice pick through your brain unless you give us back our $120, you bastard,' Carlotta hisses. 'Now give the money, the pipe, and the crack you took from us to Carmen here or you are a dead man. Don't move, you fat slob!'

"The manager does as Carlotta wants, gingerly fishing in his pocket. Carlotta pushes the ice pick just a little into the man's ear so it hurts and draws a small bead of blood.

"'Don't do it, I'm doing as you asked,' he pleads. 'I won't move.'

"'Where are the handcuffs?' Carlotta demands. 'Don't move an inch or it will be my pleasure to shish kebob your brain.'

"'Th—they're in the drawer of the reception desk,' the manager stutters, jerking his thumb over his shoulder.

"'Get them, Carmen,' Carlotta says. Carmen fetches them over. 'Now, put out your hands, you bastard.'

"The manager hesitates a little and Carlotta presses the ice pick into his ear a little more. 'Want me to push harder?' The manager relents and puts out his hands. Carmen clasps his fat hands into the cuffs.

"'Now, Carmen, unbuckle his pants, pull down his underwear, and grab his balls. Don't move, you son of a bitch.' Carmen complies, to the letter. 'Good. Now put one of the cuff ends around his penis and scrotum.' Carmen says she doesn't think it will fit. Carlotta tells her to squeeze the damn flesh into the cuff. The manager starts to squirm in pain. Carlotta pushes a little on the ice pick and tells him to shut up. Carlotta tells Carmen to fasten the other end of the cuffs between the handcuffs on his wrists. "I bet it hurts for a fat slob like you with such big balls. Now what are we going to do with the last pair of handcuffs?" says Carlotta

"Carlotta looks around the room for something to attach the manager to, but nothing appropriate presents itself.

"'What about the rail on his chair near the floor?' Carmen suggests.

"'I guess that will have to do,' Carlotta replies. 'Carmen, take this shithead's shoes, pants, and underwear completely off.' Carmen does so. 'Now, lift his balls and slip this open end of the third cuff under the cuff around his balls and attach it and the other handcuff to the rail of the chair.'

"When Carmen is done, the manager complains his skin and hair are being pulled by the inserted cuff.

"'Too bad, asshole, I didn't care much about getting raped and robbed by you,' Carlotta says.

"'I'll kill you bitches when I get loose,' the fat man wails.

"'Such nasty talk!' laughs Carlotta. 'Don't move, you asshole, you're wiggling and I see blood dripping from your ear. Does it hurt to have your balls squeezed? Oh, that's too bad.'

"'He looks like a fat brown pig, trussed up for the slaughter,' Carmen jeers as she admires her handiwork.

"Carlotta walks in front of the fat man and smiles.

"'You do look cute this way,' she coos, 'and so here is my gift to you.'

"She picks up the fat man's flaccid penis in her hand and brandishes the ice pick in front of his face.

"'I think you should think about getting a cock ring,' says Carlotta conversationally. 'It's all the fashion these days.'

"The manager looks terrified. Carlotta weighs the penis in her hand and with a sudden motion, rams the ice pick through the wide head. The manager screams and faints.

"'Nighty-night, big fellow.'

"Carlotta puts on her high heels. She and Carmen walk briskly away from the hotel, eventually hailing a cab on Washington Boulevard that takes them back to the safety of the El Caribe."

Carlotta is nearly apoplectic with anger and indignation.

"I don't believe you! The tale is a complete fabrication. Carlotta is never violent. Carlton, on the other hand, has a history of aggressive incidents. I remind you again of the axed door and your penchant for punching out defenseless walls."

"Since when have I been violent and since when has Carlotta been a perfect lady?"

Carlotta counters with, "If your story were true, the violence is bipolar behavior that only the emotional Carlton could manifest."

"You will never know, will you?" I reply. "How do you sort out the character of the two of us, since you say we are an inseparable being? Are we not then *both* bipolar? Could the violence not be yours, also?"

"I know in my heart that Carlotta may be capable of tawdry behavior, but not brazen aggression. That is male! Carlton, on the other hand, thrill seeker that he is, could fantasize and even seek out such a situation."

"All I know is," I reply wearily, "is that I feel sad when I read this. I am one sick individual. How could I have lived this way?"

"But you did, Carlton, and the past is done."

"But you are still with me."

"Still troubled by my presence?"

"Yes and no. I have no easy answer for that question. I feel guilty to have a second mind in you, Carlotta. I feel shame in some of the things Carlotta does.

bipolar bare

I often want you to go away and never reappear. But I like you, too. I like your boldness, imagination, and flair. They make me different. Sometimes I wish you could be male and I—or we, I should say—could be united in one gender."

"But you aren't united. You are bipolar, and you have always wanted to be a girl."

"Not always."

"Do you admit you need Carlotta?

"I wish I didn't need you, but I think I do."

"How curious! The failed intellectual needs his whore?"

"I thought you were my muse now?"

"It all depends on my mood. Your latest story has me cast in most unfavorable sexual terms, but what the hell, at least you are no longer denying my existence. You know I am more than just a manifestation of your addiction to crack. I am overjoyed."

Carlotta suddenly quits the desk and moves behind me, leaning over my shoulder to look at the page of the journal. Her hair and earrings tickle my neck.

"How long ago did you write this fantasy?" she asks.

"A long time ago," I answer.

Carlotta turns her face toward me and kisses me on the cheek. She stands tall, walks to the far side of the desk opposite me, and laughs.

"The motel story could be true," I say with a smirk, flipping the journal closed.

"Your muse will be big spirited and say that many a foul male deserves to have his penis pierced and a big ring placed on the end so he can be marched around in public like some ox."

"Too bad Carlotta didn't carry such an accoutrement in her purse so she could parade the motel manager down Central Avenue by his cock."

"Carlton has a great sense of humor. He can see the absurd and can be playful like a child, but he is prone to bouts of temper and violence. The attack on the motel manager is pure Carlton. I believe the rape you imagined was triggered by your bipolar disorder and you, Carlton, not I, Carlotta, made a payback to the manager."

"But aren't you bipolar, too? Would not this disease affect both sides of the brain?"

"Good question. I can't answer that. I do know that when you become depressed, you complain that the right side of your brain hurts and not your left. You remark on the deep pain you feel in the right hemisphere. I believe that I, the left hemisphere, become dormant and am not affected by the same pain and torment as the right. We are not doctors, so how are we to know? I believe I become silent, even though I am the center of language, and you, the right hemisphere, go into mania and then into the deepest depression that shuts both of us down. The only action I am able to take is to keep us from committing suicide because I still like being alive."

"Carlotta, I do like you and you are one wild, unconventional, opinionated, and willing-to-try-anything woman. You have a great spirit, but you are also self-destructive. Your sexual behavior is reprehensible."

"No, you have this wrong. It is you, Carlton, who is self-destructive, and it is your sexual behavior that is reprehensible. After all, you have lived thirty-some years longer than you would have if I hadn't saved your life. Suicide, toying with AIDS, and putting ourselves in harm's way, these are things you like to do. You like to walk along the razor's edge because it is a thrill and part of you wants to get killed."

"Life sucks!" I exclaim, apropos of nothing.

"There you go again, always looking on the dark side of the razor's edge you like to walk! Can't you look at the brighter side?"

"There is no brighter side of the razor's edge. When you fall, you are cut to pieces and fall into the abyss that lies on both sides of the razor."

"Then stop walking on the razor. Walk a smoother path in the brightness of daylight. Walk where Carlotta walks."

"If I accept you, am I not accepting part of myself as a slut?"

"Ah, back to that again. I, Carlotta, like to have experiences, and sex is one of the best. It is its own reward. I want to live life to the fullest. Don't you?"

"Life sucks. Sex sucks."

"You only like sex as a self-destructive act. Thus proving my point that it is you who created me as a slut who could act out for you sex in its most disgusting and primitive aspects. Sex without love. Sex without caring. It was Carlton who wanted to toy with the great tragedy of the late twentieth century and see if he could get AIDS."

"But I never got it."

"You tried hard enough, putting yourself and others at great risk."

"I feel guilty for that."

"You were lucky. Or perhaps there is a higher power watching over us."

"Us?"

"Indeed, us! You buried me too long. You only call on me when you are in big trouble or when you don't know what to do."

"Yeah, but it was you who got me hooked on crack."

"Don't make me laugh! Crack addiction was born of another one of your negative periods of self-destruction. But let's say I did get you hooked because it allowed you to set me free. As a happy result, your inhibitions fell. It is an interesting experience, isn't it? Besides, I could really get your attention. You let me out, didn't you? You dressed me up, although not in a style a lady of my breeding and culture would choose—I would prefer something more haute couture. You did take me out to the clubs, albeit not the kind I would choose—I prefer jazz or something more sophisticated. Yet I was very happy for the release."

"You're happy I'm a junkie?"

"The junkie knows many things and went many places to get himself free. That is a good thing."

"I went to The Betty Ford Center in desperation."

"The desperation was the first dim ray of hope."

Carlottta steps away toward the bathroom and wiggles her ass before departing through the door.

CHAPTER 23

INSIDE THE OLEANDERS

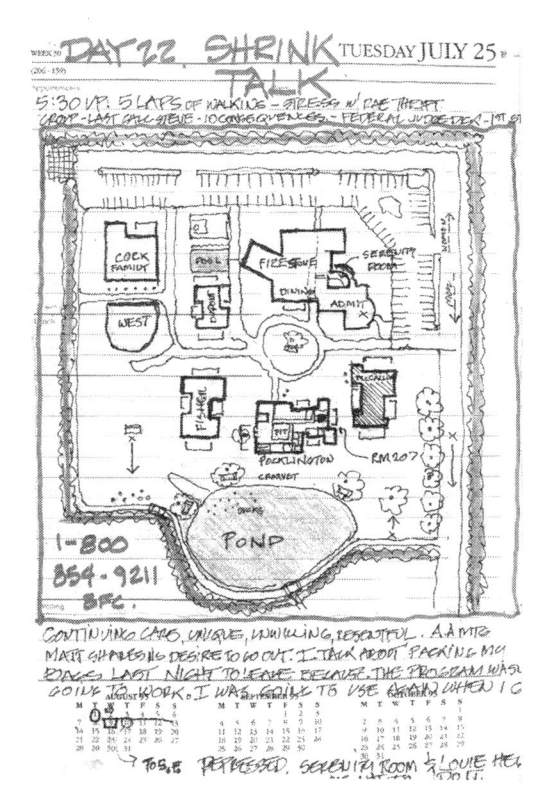

Betty Ford Center; 1995; diary page; ink pen

"How about we take a couple of laps around the hospital like you used to do at The Betty Ford Center?" asks Carlotta dressed in a red jogging outfit and white sneakers. She bounces back and forth from toe to toe. Her arms are lifted. She is ready to run. I am seated at my desk, as usual, studying my notebooks.

"Are you crazy?" I grouse, yawning like a cave. "It's nearly four in the morning and dark as a whore's heart outside."

"No more crazy than you," replies Carlotta, jogging in place. "You used to walk five or six laps around the path inside of the oleanders at BFC every day. Some exercise now would be good for you—get the old creative juices flowing."

"*Not* in the middle of the night."

"You are so conservative. What does it matter what time it is? A walk will stimulate your mind, and we can talk about The Betty Ford Center. You loved it there."

"I am *not* conservative and I *didn't* love it there—I tolerated it. Besides, if we walk now, the guards will stop us or the bed checker will notice my absence and set off an alarm that I bolted from the hospital. They'll hunt me down and kick me out."

"Let's pretend then. What direction did you walk each day?"

"South!"

"Oh, come now, you can be more specific than that."

"And I thought I was anal retentive," I sigh. "OK, I would go out the back door of my room in Pocklington Hall and head for the duck pond across from the croquet field to the path between the pond and the oleanders. Often, Plumb Bob, Detox Tom, or Tugboat Steve would accompany me. The men walk the path clockwise and the women counterclockwise to discourage fraternization."

"Admit it, you treasured those walks, didn't you?"

"Yes. They were the best thing about BFC. I walked daily between group therapy, the AA meetings, the lectures, breakfast, lunch, dinner, and volleyball games in the swimming pool. Volleyball was the second best thing at the BFC. The path followed the line of dense oleanders surrounding the entire center. The oleanders provided privacy from the paparazzi trying to snag photos of the celebrity patients. There were several when I was there: a state leader, a federal judge, and a professional basketball player."

"What about the women?"

"I never met any. The BFC had strict rules against fraternization with the women. All I got to know were the ordinary guys and addictions. Plumb Bob was a plumber and cocaine addict. Detox Tom was an executive from New York and a drunk who kept relapsing and coming back to the center. He was on his fourth trip to Betty Ford. Tugboat Steve was in the shipping business and a crack addict. There were also a couple of police officers. Oh, I almost forgot. Jerry Garcia of The Grateful Dead was there, too."

"Really?" says Carlotta, fairly salivating. "You must have some good dirt to dish on the legendary Captain Trips."

"To tell the truth, he never walked with us. As a matter of fact we hardly ever saw him and he left before spending the required twenty-eight days of the drug treatment program, I have an amusing story to tell about my interaction with him, but I will save that for later."

"Tell me now! I love a little bit of gossip. You did something bad, I bet ..."

"Not like what you think. Let me tell you about the oleanders and the path first. Here's something I wrote in my journal."

"July 10, 1995: The walking path went around the duck pond over a small footbridge and past several benches where women patients would sit and read. The path followed the inside edge of the grounds behind one of the female dormitories and Cork Family Center, where we had the meetings with our families when, on the weekend, they came to visit and participate in family group therapy. Ginger went there with me on several weekends. The next two sides of the path took us past the volleyball pool and the administration building and through the parking lot. The administration building housed the dining hall and the serenity room, where I often went to meditate. The route was a square except for the side that went by the duck pond, which bowed out from the path's straight lines."

"Did you speed walk the path?" asks Carlotta, rivulets of sweat streaking her face.

"Sometimes, depending how upset I was from the therapy sessions or the lectures."

"I never understood why you chose to go to Betty Ford in the first place. It was a twelve step program and you *hated* twelve step programs."

"What is this, an interview for *The National Enquirer*?"

"Well, inquiring minds want to know. Actually, it's for my own information, but if your recollections are any good, we could sell them to the Enquirer or the sleazy supermarket rag of your choice. Now, tell me about Jerry Garcia!"

"Keep your Reeboks on, I'll get to that story later."

"You refused to call on me while you were there," Carlotta pouts. "I felt abandoned and unloved."

"You were. I hoped to be free of you at last."

"You are so deluded. I repeat: Why *did* you choose to go to the BFC? I am curious."

"I told you before. Because in my preliminary interview, they said they would not force-feed me that twelve step hooey. I figured if they had to deal with celebrities, they had to treat the stars with a gentle hand. After all, I heard Elizabeth Taylor had been there. I didn't think the center could or would allow the counselors to browbeat a living legend like that into acceptance of the twelve step program—and I was right, they didn't."

"You really *never mentioned me* when you were there? Never?"

"No! You never got exposed. I didn't want the staff to think I was really crazy."

"Too bad, maybe they would have called you Queen Carl instead of Carlton. That would have been amusing."

"They called me Carl, plain and simple. I did reveal my cross-dressing, and I got teased about it, but only certain people got nicknames. It was only a way to differentiate between men with the same name. There were three Steves: Tugboat Steve, Tennis Steve, and Last Call Steve. I was the only Carl."

"Let's see, you had a Bob, a Tom, a Carl, and three Steves," Carlotta observes. "All such monosyllabic, manly-man names, I must say. I'm all a-twitter! The place must have been awash in testosterone."

"You could say that. Tugboat Steve got into a yelling match with Plumb Bob and they nearly came to blows. Jan, my counselor, had to break them up as they stood in the pit, hurling insults at one another. I got very angry once at Pilot Jim—"

"Ohh, and *Jim*, too!"

"Let me finish! Pilot Jim, who asked me if I had shaved my legs today. He was a big, macho airline pilot who said I disgusted him because I cross-dressed. I told him he was disgusting because he flew hundreds of people across the country while high as a kite. Ralph, another counselor, defused that situation."

"Ah, and there was a Ralph, too. Another he-man, no doubt. Now, tell me about the pit."

"If you are always with me, you know about the pit."

"I am and I do, but I want to hear your written description."

"July 12, 1995. The pit is a sunken square space in the middle of Pocklington Hall with chairs surrounding the perimeter. All the men gathered here each day a couple of times to discuss issues that arose between patients, the plans for the day, who got to be Granny, and who was going to get discharged. When a person was discharged, we all moved up to a seat closer to the good-bye chair, which was next to the counselor who managed the group. Every couple of days, someone was discharged and we moved over one chair until our day of departure was set. A new person sat at the end of the line of chairs until he moved when someone departed. The Granny was a patient chosen to be the leader of all the residents of Pocklington. He gathered the group for dining and has other responsibilities, which I can't remember. I wanted to be Granny, but I wasn't selected. That made me angry. Grannies were usually a week away from discharge, so they sat close to the head of the line of chairs."

"Musical chairs for drunks and junkies," Carlotta snickers.

"Must you put it so crudely? I haven't yet told you how the twenty-eight days began."

"Sorry, force of habit. Keep reading."

"July 14, 1995. 'Welcome to the rest of your life. You don't need to drink or use drugs again, one day at a time,' read the sign that greeted me when I arrived at The Betty Ford Center. I wished that were true. I believed it when I first was there. The place seemed quite magical. I got a room with a second bed for a roommate and an exterior door that led to a small garden area and the walking path beyond. The Betty Ford Center is like a high-class hotel in Palm Springs—no bedrooms with five or six people jammed into an overcrowded space like Las Encinas. The patients' rooms are centered on the pit in Pocklington Hall.

"The therapy rooms also flanked the pit, and when there were lectures, our group assembled in the pit, then marched to the lecture hall together. We also congregated outside the front door into Pockington Hall at dinnertime and all walked together to the dining hall, not far away from our facility. The Granny led the group."

"Are you sure you *never* spoke of me?" interrupts Carlotta, still smarting from the earlier slight.

"No, in the exactly twenty-eight days I spent there," I reply irritably, "you never made an appearance. I thought I was well on my way to licking my problem with drugs and freedom from Carlotta."

"You could have revealed me," says Carlotta petulantly. "Some of the boys might have appreciated the wisdom of yours truly."

"There were plenty of pranksters already in residence."

"But none, I'll wager, with my sense of the absurd."

"I don't know about that," I counter. "There was my first roommate. He was a genuine wacko. He arrived at the same time I did from some mental hospital, where he swore they were practicing brain surgery on monkeys. The story he told me on his first night in our room was unbelievable. He swore, in complete earnestness, that there were technicians—little men in white coats—at his previous hospital. They were surgically removing pieces of monkey brain and inserting them into human brains and vice versa. He even claimed that several monkeys escaped and were caught shopping in the local mall for hats. The humans became monkeys and were chained to a wall. He seemed very serious about this claim. I laughed at his story, and he got angry. I was really worried about sleeping in the same room with this psycho. Luckily, he got taken away the next day. I breathed a lot easier."

"Did you worry he was going to do a monkey brain operation on you?"

"Well ... the nut-job was dead serious about the monkey brain operation stuff. What if it was *your* side of the brain he fiddled with?"

"Perhaps I would become Carlotta, Queen of the Planet of the Apes, constantly outsmarting the emotional little human, Carlton."

"Right. Well, monkey guy only lasted a day. I think they sent him back to the loony bin he escaped from so they could complete the transformation. Next, I got a simple drunk from New York City. He didn't last all that long, either—called back on a business emergency. In all, I had three roommates."

"Three white boys, weren't they?"

"Yes. What's that got to do with anything?"

"Nothing really. I am just trying to provoke you."

"BFC was fully integrated. It was just the luck of the draw that I roomed with three white men."

"Maybe they were scared of a crack addict, and maybe I, Carlotta, spoke when you were asleep. You talk in your sleep, you know. Maybe I talked about smoking, getting dressed up in lingerie and high heels, and wanting to join them in their beds for a little frolic."

"You didn't!"

"How would you know? You never remember what you say in your sleep. Maybe you said how Carlton doesn't want to lose his beloved Carlotta."

"Don't forget, Dr. Wortz says you are my state-dependent personality. Since I was sober, you never appeared."

"I am more than that!" Carlotta replies huffily. "He is wrong on that one point. We are talking now, are we not? You are not high on drugs and you are not asleep."

"I don't talk in my sleep, by the way."

"Oh, yes, you do. Your roommates complained to the nurses about it. New York guy didn't go back to the city. He moved to a different dormitory because of it. You don't remember because I dealt with the situation."

"I don't believe it."

"It's true. When you dream, your true genius speaks: I, Carlotta, Empress of the Apes."

"Whatever you say, Your Apeness. Anyway, I entered BFC after I spent most of the six months since leaving Las Encinas smoking marijuana and crack, cross-dressing, and prowling drag queen bars seeking sex."

"You did go rather crazy."

"To put it mildly. I used up all my savings—approximately $15,000—and borrowed over $40,000 from my wife. I totally destroyed my plan to take a year off doing creative writing and painting because crack killed my interest."

"You could have gone back to work."

"No way! My dislike of the profession already had me headed in the direction of abandonment. I quit my career as an architect due in large measure to my preoccupation with crack."

"You were so wasted on crack, you could not possibly work. Right? Right!"

"I'm warning you, *don't ape my mother!* But yeah, that's right. I stopped eating regular meals and would sometimes go for days without eating at all. And I abandoned my marriage, staying out for days without contacting my wife."

"You did get thin. I could fit in a size thirty dress for once. We could actually go to the fat lady stores and find something that fit—even if their styles were rather atrocious. Alas, we will never be a size eight. We'll always be in the big-boned gal section."

"Enough of your narcissistic yammering!" I fume. "Here's the next bit from my notebook."

"Saturday July 15th, 1995, The Betty Ford Center. Today is my twelfth day in the program, and I am amazed I feel so good. My old self is returning. I have found a new interest in life, and I want to use my talents again. I want to write. I want to draw. I want to make art. I meditated today for the second time in two days. A new serenity is flowing through me.

"In our group therapy session, Louie the counselor has us do a little fantasy. He asks us to imagine a path and a secure place. We start our journey in the secure place and leave to walk our chosen path. On the path, we are to meet our mothers, our fathers, and two other significant figures. We are to speak to these people if we wish. Stewart, my buddy, shares his experience first. On his path, he meets his mother and father and tells them how he wishes they got the things out of life they always wanted. His story touches me and I cry.

"I volunteer to tell my fantasy story. I recall the Composers Cabin at the Dorland Mountain Arts Colony, where I spent a happy time a decade ago. I recount walking from the cabin through the Oak Grove out along the trail to the Far Spring. In the big bend in the path near the hole in the hill where once I confronted Big Red, the rattlesnake, I see my mothers. They are standing on opposite sides of the trail. They are smiling. I turn to my stepmother and tell her that I love her and I am sorry for all the pain I caused her in her life. I turn to my mother and tell her that I love her, too. I say I am very sad I lost her and that I needed her love for a very long time. Tears start to fill my eyes.

"Beyond my mother, near the dirt arch in the hill, stands my father. He is smiling and his arms are extended out toward me. We don't speak, but we hug each other, and I walk through the dirt arch. At another bend in the trail stands Dr. Wortz; he is smiling, too. He whispers in my ear, 'And how is your sweet self?' I shrug, we hug, and I pass on.

"Near the end of the trail stands another figure. He is an old Indian, one of the chiefs buried in the mountain. His arms are outstretched, and he is smiling the most contented and warm smile I have ever seen. He says nothing, but we hug affectionately. The Indian points me to the Far Spring, and I walk into the grove of trees and sit on a log, listening to the sound of the brook bubbling below the springs. The birds dart in and out of the water, and the wind rustles the trees. I am content and happy. I cry profusely while I tell my fantasy.

"I continue to cry, partially out of sadness, but more out of joy as Last Call Steve tells his fantasy, which is a beautiful journey in the landscape around Carmel, where he went with his wife when they were first in love. The mystical path rises into the sky toward the stars with Steve and his wife holding hands. Cajun Bob tells his fantasy path, where he meets his first wife and tells her he still loves her. By the end, Bob and I are both bawling like babies.

"Louie gives me tissues and asks, 'What else is going on with you?'

"Choking on my tears, I reply, 'When I think of my wife, I still feel I love her.'

"Several more people share their fantasy paths. They aren't as interesting and my sobs die down. Louie ends the group by suggesting I write letter to my mother telling her how I feel—merely as an exercise, not to actually send her. I am truly a lucky man to be here at The Betty Ford Center. I feel truly blessed to have lived the life I have lived in spite of the pain."

"So, now you feel lucky to live the life you have?" asks Carlotta. Her dewy eyes belie the sarcasm in her voice.

"Yes, I'd say so. It has been exciting. Not your normal humdrum life."

"This is not what you say when you are depressed—when you obsess about your crummy childhood."

"That day I was feeling good and recalling the good things."

"I don't know what I am going to do with you, Carlton. You can never make up your mind. Perhaps I should evict you."

"You can't do it. Besides, it would require a sex change operation."

"Don't think I haven't thought about it."

"You wouldn't!"

"I think we—rather, *I*—would be far happier if I were a real woman, not a female trapped in your disgusting male body with your repulsive genitalia. Snip, snip and those puppies are gone."

"Now you have gone too far."

"OK, I will leave that for another time. Didn't the high muckety-mucks at BFC make you list your childhood traumas that must have made you feel *not* so damn wonderful about your life? Read me that list."

"Your wish is my command, O Ape Queen."

"My list of Childhood Traumas:

In my mother and father's divorce in 1949 I was:

1. Allowed to run around naked in our neighborhood in winter. The police found me in a garbage can and returned me home. On other occasions, neighbors picked me up from the street and returned me home, demanding that my mother take care of me.

2. I often saw my mother and her lover drunk. They would slap me around and lock me in my room when I didn't behave.

3. My mother left me with her sister in New Haven, Connecticut and returned to Rochester, NY. I didn't know these people, and I was afraid.

4. My father kidnapped me off the street in New Haven and returned me to my grandmother's house in Rochester. I remember being placed in the back seat of a car and screaming that I didn't want to be taken away.

5. My mother would come to the door of my grandmother's house to see me. My grandmother wouldn't let me see my mother. My mother would be outside the door yelling and I would be inside screaming to see her and falling on the floor in tantrums. My grandmother would yell at me to behave myself and spank me with force when I didn't comply.

6. One day my mother didn't come anymore, and my father disappeared. I was left alone.

7. My grandmother couldn't put up with my tantrums and tears. She put me in a foster home.

8. My father came one day and took me to Corning, New York, where I was given a new mother. I didn't like her.

9. No one would tell me what happened to my real mother. No one would even say her name.

10. I was told to behave myself or they would put me in the foster home again. I told my parents I didn't care. I hated them all.

11. In the sandbox near our apartment, I hit another boy in the head with a hammer when he tried to take my truck. My father slapped me around and strapped my ass. He told me I was a bad son.

12. From age 7 to 16 I felt I was the child left out of my family's love. Attention was given to my two younger sisters. Since my stepmother was often drunk and my father hardly ever around, I was the one who took charge of my sisters.

13. In my senior year in high school, I was shipped off to prep school, where I didn't want to go. During the fall of that year, I had my two front teeth smashed in football practice. The school's dentist capped the teeth, not realizing the teeth were also broken above the gum line. The teeth became infected. I was in enormous pain and no one would believe me that I was in pain. I called my father. He told me to take a bus home. I rode a bus from Greenfield, Massachusetts, to Boston for six hours in excruciating pain. My father met me at the bus and took me to the hospital for emergency dental surgery, which saved my life. The infection had almost reached my brain.

14. In my junior year of college, I attempted suicide."

Carlotta asks, "After that laundry list of fear and loathing, do you *still* believe you are a lucky man, living a wonderful life?"

"No, I'm getting depressed, actually."

"Don't get depressed! Your life has been no worse than many others. As a matter of fact, you have had many good experiences."

"I admit, I did generally have a good time at Betty Ford walking around the path among the oleanders with the gang each day. And playing volleyball in the pool was terrific! The games were very intense. That was when I hit Jerry Garcia in the head with a volleyball spike. He was sitting on the side of pool with his feet dangling in the water. I rose up to the ball and hit a strong spike that was a little bit off course and banged Garcia in the cranium. He wasn't hurt, but he did leave Betty Ford several days later without staying the full twenty-eight days. A week later, he died."

"Aha! It was you who killed Jerry Garcia! The Deadheads will never forgive you for the fatal wound you dealt their guru."

"Don't be silly! It wasn't my fault."

"Carlotta can see the headline now: 'Ungrateful Dead! Dyke Diva's Spiteful Spike Kills Rock Legend!' *The National Enquirer* will love this story. Maybe I can sell it and make enough money for the sex change operation."

"Stop messing with my brain, Carlotta, and shut up and listen to this next exercise I wrote down. The center loved giving the patients homework. This one is called the King Baby, a person who demands attention and acts like a baby when he or she doesn't get what he wants. I had to come up with five examples. Some of them relate to the reason I feel I have had a wonderful and interesting life, despite of the fact I may be immature and unreasonable."

"Without a reasoned mental balance for sure!"

Like the King Baby, I am definitely addicted to a life of excess, driven by feelings of low self worth. I want adventure and excitement. I refer to this as my desire to balance on the razor's edge. I see elements of this addiction in the cross-dressing, the sexual escapades, the drug use, the desire for a Bohemian life, and the refusal to live an ordinary life in any way. Normality bores me. Yet beneath the adventurer lies a person who thinks he is worthless.

Like the King Baby, I feel that I am destined for greatness. Yet I believe I don't deserve it, nor will I ever really achieve it, because I am too deeply flawed a personality. The conundrum is: I am great, but I won't be because I am bad.

Like the King Baby, I am never satisfied. Nothing will appease me because of the love-starved, scared, and lonely child within me. Through the exercises in group therapy, I have come in contact with this sad child, who does not want to be hurt anymore. It is frightening to glimpse him. I am devastated to be confronted with this motivation.

Like the King Baby, I am driven by three motives: power, attention, and pleasure. With power, I achieve the least satisfactory results, but I still thirst after it. I achieved little professional or financial power. However, my wife always says I have immense emotional power over her, and I can see how I achieve it through my rage and frustration. I have gotten lots of attention, especially through fearlessness and loud, insistent wails and complaints. With pleasure, I seek it in drugs and sex, though I can never get enough.

Like the King Baby, I am angry at authority figures. I seek their approval, but I won't accept their criticism. I will become enraged when criticized. Thus, I am often immobilized by anger and frustration.

"You haven't grown up beyond the temper tantrums of the five-year-old Chinky," Carlotta observes.

"Don't you ever use that word, Carlotta!"

"Stinky Chinky, Stinky Chinky!"

"I'm going to strangle you, you blasted Brobdingnagian bitch!"

"Ah more big words no one understands. Then emotional outbursts—that's what gets you into trouble. And, of course, the crude language that go with them. Didn't you learn *anything* at the BFC?"

"Well, I learned to make lists," I reply sheepishly.

"You're a regular David Letterman, aren't you? Let's hear another one."

"All right, this is a long one. It begins with a statement on my powerlessness over the use of crack and catalogs the effects the drug had on my life."

"Powerlessness: preoccupation with chemicals. On June 28, 1995, I return from a trip to Yucca Valley, where I spend several days without using crack. I do not tell my wife I am returning that day, but rather I sneak back into town and purchase sixty bucks worth of crack. I spend the day aimlessly driving around Long Beach, the valley, and West LA. I should be going to a meeting with Dr. Wortz, a cocaine treatment session at Pizzaro, and a Cocaine Anonymous meeting in the evening. Instead, I use for the whole day and then go back to skid row in the evening to buy another $20 worth. At three a.m., the police pull me over for driving too fast—the story I recounted before. I am in drag and totally loaded. They let me go. I think I have finally hit bottom and will end up in jail, but I don't. Maybe it is the stupid grin on my face. I feel embarrassed to be standing outside my car in high heels and a black skirt. I feel ashamed. I am lying so blatantly to my wife. I think I finally truly lost my mind and any sense of morals.

"Attempts to control use: Throughout the year of my addiction, I try to buy smaller amounts of crack and spread the use out longer over the day. I will only buy $20 worth—four tabs. Two tabs I will put in my smoking kit and two tabs I will bury in my painting supplies. In far less time than I plan, I will use the first two tabs and find myself searching out the two tabs I have laid aside for later in the day. Before long, I will smoke all I purchased. I will head back out into the streets of Skid Row to buy more. Sometimes I repeat this ritual three and four times a day. Each time trying to buy a controlled amount. Each time trying to save part of my stash. It never works. I always consume faster than planned. I always spend more than anticipated. Each trip for drugs, I feel foolish that I cannot control the urge. Each hit on the pipe makes me more melancholy and fearful about my out-of-control behavior, but I cannot stop, no matter how much I beg for the will to stop.

"Attempts to control use. In April of 1995, I give my bankcard and my checks to my wife to stem the flow of money I am spending on crack. I only give myself $10 per day for expenses. My wife is to give me $10 per day when I ask for it. The strategy works for several weeks, and I cut my consumption down to almost zero. However, by the third week, I conserve the money she gives me until I have at least forty bucks and then I will go out and buy. By the beginning of the fourth week, I am withdrawing large amounts of cash from the bank, giving my wife the card and the allocated weekly allowance. With the surplus cash, I buy a large amount of crack. By some quirk, the bank blocks my card on the fifth week. I am furious. I find some old blank checks that I hadn't given to my wife and cash them for my crack money. I am doing this every day, even though I have to stand in the cashier's line for long periods of time, hoping no one notices me sweating profusely. By the sixth week, the whole process deteriorates when I won't give my wife the bankcard or the checks after withdrawing my weekly amount. I feel completely out of control, totally gloomy about any prospects for control, and know I am completely defeated.

I am very pessimistic about my chances for survival.

"Effects on my emotional life: In the mid 1980s, I stop dating and isolate myself in my loft because of my erratic behavior and depression, exacerbated by the heavy use of marijuana. I spend almost all of my hours outside of my job alone. I feel afraid that I am losing my mind. I feel inadequate at dealing with the conflicting emotions of rage and guilt, which torment me each day. Sadness follows me everywhere. I think a lot about suicide.

"Effects on my emotional life: During an earlier period of the 1980s when still using marijuana—heavily combined with cocaine—my capacity for love for anyone but my daughter was lost. I dated women yet became abusive to them when they attempted to offer me love. One woman in particular, I remember, used to send me love letters, hand delivering them to a special mailbox I had in my loft. I responded to her gentleness and caring with loathing. Our sexual relationship became increasingly more brutal. Near the end of our relationship, I recall that I would go to her house to have intercourse with her and leave to go to gay bathhouses for the rest of the night. I knew I was totally out of control but only responded to the situation by getting more stoned. I was angry all the time but could not articulate why. Under the anger was an immense sadness. After my nights of sexual binges, I returned to my loft and sobbed for hours. I medicated myself with booze, marijuana, and cocaine. The rage would return, and I would find myself pitching tequila bottles across the sixty feet of my loft at a steel loading door.

"These wounds are deep, Carlotta," I say, blinking my strained eyes owlishly. "They are difficult to talk about and difficult to reveal. To think that I inflicted my hurt on others is almost abominable."

Carlotta attempts to reassure me. "You must remember, you did not murder or maim another, as is often the case with males who have been injured in their earlier life. American prisons are full of such wretched humans. Continue with your list, if you can."

"Effects on my family life: Since I started using crack, I abandoned my marriage. This is a marriage in deep trouble. My addiction probably killed it. Over the course of the past year, my wife and I have basically stopped going out to dinner together, attending social functions together, stopped any intimacy, and almost stopped seeing each other. For example, we both never arrive home before nine p.m., even if we have an agreement to meet each other earlier. Ginger stays at the office for fear of confronting me in a bad mood or stoked up on crack. For my part, I never arrive home much before ten p.m., if I come home at all. We make plans to attend an event, lecture, tour, or party and never get there. I feel guilty for how I have treated my wife, but those feelings are tainted with the enormous resentment I feel toward her. This combination of resentment and guilt makes me depressed. I fear I can never have a decent relationship with any woman.

"Effects on family life: Since I was a teenager, I have been alienated from my family. When I started to use drugs heavily in the late 1970s through the mid 1980s, this strained relationship became even worse. I was abusive to my sister, who attempted to keep the family connection alive. I recall her visiting me in 1981 and trying to explain to me my stepmother's alcoholism and her desire for my support in her plan for an intervention, which she was trying to convince my father to support. Loaded myself, I told her that she could go to hell, that our father was an incredible asshole, and that I won't help him do anything. With Lois, my stepmother, I have no major issues, but I told my sister I couldn't help her. All I wanted was to be left alone by the family. I felt bitter to be asked to help, since they were never available to help me. But once again, under my resentment lurked an abyss of hurt and an abiding awareness of my own insufficiency. My sister took all my abuse and only offered me love. For years, I was irritated that she would not let me be.

"Effects on my spiritual life: In January 1995, I arrange to join a meditation group led by my psychologist. The group practices several forms of Buddhist meditation each session and has a discussion afterwards. I join after a long hiatus of no meditation. By the end of February, I cannot get myself to go. I prefer staying in my studio and getting loaded. I tell myself I can't go if I am loaded, and it is true that one time I did go after using. I have no concentration, and the meditation session is pure agony as I attempt to sit still and concentrate on my breath. After February, I tell my wife that I go to the session once a week. These appointments are never kept, allowing the opportunity to use in peace. I feel guilty about my lying and I am horrified at the decline of my spiritual interest, which was at one time the center of my life. The despair that racks me each Tuesday evening can only be obliterated with more and more cocaine. I use so much crack that I can never come home at all.

"Effects on my work: By fall 1994, when I am the project manager for the North Hollywood Station design for the Metropolitan Transportation Authority, I am fully addicted to crack. I become increasingly erratic in meetings. My temper is at the ready. I embarrass the client several times by chastising them for their general incompetence. I come to meetings sweating profusely. My excuses are many. The weather is too hot. I have just finished exercise, or I have to rush to get to their conference room on time. My aggressive stance masks the guilt I feel at being loaded and the anxiety I feel about my competence to do this job. I ended up being removed from the project by my wife.

"Effects on my character: With the addiction to cocaine, I lost any compunction about being honest. For example, my wife told me she didn't want me to use in her house. When she accused me of smoking cocaine in the house, I denied it. On one occasion, she asked me what the strange smell was in the guest bedroom. I said I didn't know. When we went into the room to smell, I suggested it could be the Joshua tree pods I brought back from the desert, which were lying in a box close to the location where I just smoked crack. I argued that everyone knows that Joshua tree pods give off a semi-sweet odor. She bought the story. I felt guilty at my lie, but my resentment toward my wife was so strong that I had a counterbalancing feeling of cleverness and supreme deviousness because I deflected her accusation."

"Whew! You must have had one helluva case of writer's cramp after all that. They really cracked the whip over you at Betty Ford, didn't they, Chinky?" Carlotta taunts me.

"I *told* you not to call me that."

"Oh, come now, you must have grown out of your irritation at being called Chinky, the Chinaman. Everyone used to do it. Didn't you reveal it at one of the therapy sessions at BFC?"

"Never! It took me long enough to get my family to stop calling me that horrible name. They called me Chink until well into my teenage years. Drove me crazy! It's bad enough you like to call me Carlton when everyone else calls me Carl."

"Sticks and stones may break my bones but words shall never hurt me—I read that on a bathroom wall somewhere. Chink—that seems fine to me, like a person with a chink, a fragment missing. A chink in the wall."

"I am going to strangle you, Carlotta Pissoir!"

"Now you want to play dirty."

"Where is my rope? I want to silence Carlotta Pizzotta once and for all."

"Can't do that, Chinky the Chinaman; you will only strangle yourself. We are stuck in this body together. It's such a conundrum. Maybe you should consider the sex change. You really did like our escapades, as Carlotta, Dark Queen of the Night. But tell me how all these assignments you have read relate to bipolar disorder. Aren't these remembrances merely the deathless anecdotes of an unusually articulate crack junkie?"

"They are both evidence of my experience as a junkie *and* proof of my bipolar mania. Your adventures, Carlotta, were the highs of a maniac, kept high and higher by the drug, which prevented, mitigated, or bridged the down between highs. This is what I surmise if Dr. Poliquin is right, and underlying my addiction is a mental disorder."

"Do you still insist I am a state-dependent personality, arising only with your use of crack?"

"You were that then, you are not now."

"Wasn't I there when you got depressed?"

"Even back in those crazed days before Betty Ford—and after, when depression struck—I have no recollection of your appearance. I was alone with my misery."

Carlotta insists, "I am sure I was there."

"On the contrary, you go quiet when the attack depression happens. I believe you are as much bipolar as I am. It happened at Betty Ford: I wasn't ready for it and you weren't ready for it. Here's is what I wrote during my final days there."

"It's July 21, day eighteen of the twenty-eight day program, and I crashed. I should have seen it coming. Elation and happiness filled the past two weeks. I can't allow myself exhilaration because right behind it is the Black Brain. The warning signs were there. The increasing stiffness of my body, the difficulty walking—each step requiring a tremendous effort—and the lack of coordination are the first signs I am headed for difficulty. I misjudge distances and tumble into objects. I can't button my shirt. The fingers fumble with the holes. I can't tie my shoes. I forget where I leave things—a towel in my room and a book in the pit. Strong emotions surface. Anger and tears follow one after the other. I lie down on my bed after a meal and begin to sob uncontrollably. I don't know why.

"The technician arrives with a new roommate. I tell him to fuck off. I leave the room, go and lie by the pond for an hour. I go to the serenity room and cry. I come back to my room and sleep through the day and the night, alone and sad.

"It's July 22, day nineteen, and the mind burns. The Black Brain emerges. Life is pain. The end of pain is death. Every view is negative. I meet with Jan, my counselor. I am crying. I can't take the mood swings anymore. I tell the group about my cyclical highs and lows. It is as if I have a wild and angry animal loose in my mind at one moment tearing up every memory especially those of my family, and the next moment recoiling in fear of retaliation. Jan asks our group to draw pictures of our families. I refuse, but my group pressures me to perform. I make my father a marshmallow speared over a campfire. My stepmother becomes a martini, dripping alcohol on the flames. One sister is an animal running from the flames. My other sister is the Red Cross truck racing to the flaming ruins with flowers. My mother is the burning match, setting a bonfire alight. I am a jet, bombing the burning ruins. The drawing is crude, drawn in the manner of children. Jan frowns and assigns me to read four chapters of the *Alcoholics Anonymous Big Book*, saying it should improve my mood. I don't do it.

bipolar bare

Betty Ford Center; 1995; journal; 7 x 10 inches; ink pen

"It's July 23, day twenty, and the negative mood remains. I finished writing 'Why I am afraid to tell anyone who I am.' The Betty Ford Center gives its patients many writing assignments like this. They think this is therapy. I wonder if it improves anything at all. Ginger arrives at 1:30 and brings our dog. We go out on the patio with the dog to chat. The tech asks about the dog. I tell him Jan said it was OK. Ginger and I have lunch and sit on the bench by the pond and discuss the money I owe her. The talk is good but not great. She doesn't hear me, and I don't hear her, but we try to communicate across the gulf of resentment. There is still denial here and there.

"July 24, day twenty-one, the wreckage smolders. My counselor suggests I go to Henry Olhoff House in San Francisco for six months. I would be living in a halfway house: six months living in a dormitory with thirteen other men. I don't like the idea. Jan tries to convince me it is the best option to continue my sobriety. I shouldn't go home, she says. 'Do I really want to live?' I ask myself. My answer is, I think I'd rather go use and die.

"In the therapy group, Rose, the counselor attacks me. The group says to me the only reason I am depressed is because I don't get my way. I become extremely angry. They are shoving the twelve steps down my throat. I don't want to say that I am powerless over my addiction. I don't want to give my life up to God. God is dead, as far as I am concerned, and the group isn't a satisfactory substitute. I feel depressed and want to leave BFC. I feel as if I get no understanding from my peers. According to the counselor, this is my alcoholism speaking. I don't have a problem with depression or some biochemical imbalance: I am just stubborn and refuse to embrace the twelve step program. I am acting like a King Baby, and if I go to ninety meetings in ninety days, all will be well. Just give myself up to the counselors, the group, or God. They know best. After all, I'm just an addict who self-medicates with drugs. I am simply depressed because I am not getting my way. Crack provides a euphoria that limits my depression. I want some right this minute!

"July 25, day twenty-two, I finally get to see a psychiatrist about my depression. He listens intently to my description of the depression and recommends the continuing care of Henry Olhoff House. I tell him I am unwilling to go there and resentful to be asked. He prescribes an antidepressant. I take a pill and go to the AA meeting. There, the trembling begins. My hands start to shake, then my head, finally my whole body. I become dizzy and disassociated. My thinking is muddled. My body is stiff. The arms and legs are tight. The stomach is upset. The shoulder muscles will hardly move. I have no energy. I am angry for no apparent reason.

bipolar bare

Plumb Bob helps me from the group to my room. A nurse arrives. He says I am having an anxiety attack. He says the trembling is unusual, but the disassociation and the dizziness are typical, even if its onset is within an unusually short time span. I lie in my bed, not wishing to move, but the nurse won't let me. He forces me to get up and return to the AA group.

"I tell the group about my condition. I must have a mental disorder that has nothing to do with drugs. I think I have had this condition all my life. I say, 'Given this condition, I don't see how I can have any kind of reasonably normal life.' The residents don't believe me. They say this is just my alcoholism speaking. After the meeting, I return to my room, collapse on the bed, and begin to cry uncontrollably. All I want to do is lie in a dark room until the mood passes. I can recognize the signs. I am beginning an attack of the Black Brain.

"I haven't had one of these attacks in a long time. I am so tired of them. January this year passed without a major attack—probably because I was high on cocaine. Now one comes in July, way out of sequence. When one comes, all I can think are negative thoughts, and how much I would like to die. Mental illness has destroyed my life. I will be up and optimistic, and then some little thing will set me off. Is the visit from my wife, when we argued, to blame?"

"Carlotta, little did I know that taking the antidepressant was absolutely the wrong thing to give a bipolar patient," I remark. "The antidepressants work for a while but subsequently trigger mania in the person taking the drug."

"I don't think they knew that fact. The pharmacology of treatment for mental conditions has advanced a great deal since you went to Betty Ford, Carlton."

"True. At any rate, the last five days of my stay at Betty Ford are happy. I believe I have finally been given a treatment for my disorder and I immerse myself in the twelve step program. I walk the walk. I talk the talk. I take many laps around the perimeter of the hospital compound in the company of the committed twelve-steppers. Each of us reassures the others that we will remain sober when we leave and we will remain in contact with one another to strengthen our commitment to the program."

"And did you stay in contact with one another?" asks Carlotta, jogging and pumping her arms.

"No, but you're getting ahead of the story. Toward the end of my stay, I am ready to leave the protective enclosure of the oleanders and face the world beyond. Reciting the words of *Alcoholics Anonymous: The Big Book*, I say to one and all I am committed to remaining sober. I decide to go to San Francisco and stay in Henry Ohlhoff House."

"July 26, day twenty-three, the temperature is 120 degrees. I move three chairs away from the final position in the pit. I will be discharged in five days. Tugboat Steve is leaving today. The group sings the song of departure: 'One-two-three, we're the guys from Pocklington Hall/we don't do no drugs at all/we don't do booze/we don't do lines/we're going to leave here feeling fine.' I walk six laps around the oleanders with Tugboat Steve. He says he is committed to staying sober and working the program of the twelve steps.

"July 27, day twenty-four, the temperature is 118 degrees. The heat wears you down. I am ready to surrender to a God I hardly believe exists. I get the antidepressant drug before breakfast and walk around the oleanders five times. I am thinking happiness is the ability to receive the pleasant without grasping and the unpleasant without condemning. Happiness is the ability to take all the insults of life as a vehicle for awakening—to enter into the full catastrophe of our lives with an open mind and heart. Happiness is the confidence that pain and disappointment can be tolerated. Love will prove stronger than aggression. Am I am thinking Buddhist thoughts? I go to the grief group. I hear that forgiveness is the gift I give myself and to forgive someone doesn't mean you have to like him or her. In group therapy, I read my resentment letter to my wife and truly hear the mantra of the twelve steps: 'God grant me the serenity to accept the things I cannot change, the courage to change the things I can, and the wisdom to know the difference.'

"July 28, day twenty-five, the temperature is 123 degrees. I move one chair closer to the departure chair in the pit. I make six laps around the oleanders in the heat of the day. I see Detox Tom sitting outside the administration building with his luggage. He is going home to his apartment, his bars, and his loneliness. He never made it to the final chair in the pit. I think of him as a dead man in the sun. I believe he will be drinking in a month.

"July 29, day twenty-six, Plumb Bob is released. My anger returns. I make seven laps in the 100-degree sun. Why I am I angry? Am I losing faith in the twelve steps? I want some crack … staying sober won't be easy. Anger is my most significant relapse trigger. I repeat again and again the most important priorities in my life in order of importance: One-sobriety; two-happiness; three-my daughter; four-a good relationship with Ginger; and five-my writing. As I march the path, I repeat again and again that without sobriety, none of the other priorities are possible.

"July 30, day twenty-seven, I move to the exit chair in the pit. My number is up. I get discharged tomorrow. I am serenaded the departure song.

"July 31, day twenty-eight, I am ready to leave The Betty Ford Center. I get a prescription for an anti-depressant. I make my last five laps around the oleanders, repeating my priorities. I am happy and glad to be departing. I listen to a lecture on marijuana and cocaine. The doctor shows slides of what the drugs do to your brain. His lecture is a repeat of what I saw my first day at the center. I attend my last group therapy. I share a letter to my stepmother. The group gives me feedback. They suggest I never mail this letter and I remove the elements that intimate blame. The staff says goodbye. I do a fifth step with Pastor David. The fifth step you admit to God, to ourselves, and another human being the exact nature of our wrongs. It is a most difficult step to do. It is the confession of our sins. I go over my resentments, my wife, my father, my stepmother, my secrets, stealing, prostitution, gay bathhouses, cross-dressing, and the pain of my sexual relationships. Talking with him is a great relief. Pastor David asks me about my incapacity for love. We speak of the great hole in my soul and my fears of severe depression. On my final afternoon, I sit in The Betty Ford Center chapel before flying to LA, meditating on my anger and disappointment and praying for God to help me."

"How did it go after you left?" asks Carlotta

"With no clear path to follow, two days after leaving The Betty Ford Center, I was smoking crack."

CHAPTER 24

REMEMBER THE ALAMO

"You are leaving the hospital today?"

"Yes, they are sending me away. I am to go to their daycare program. My psychiatrist says I will have more contact with her that way."

"Are you going to tell the best story before you go away?"

Carlotta is dressed in a Hollywood version of a cowgirl costume. She sits on the far corner of the desk, wearing hand-tooled cowboy boots, a black pleated skirt with ruffles at the bottom, a red blouse tied in a knot below her breasts, and a coonskin cap with the tail draped jauntily on the right side of her head. I think of the old Western movies where the heroine was often dressed in similar cowgirl chic—without the coonskin cap, of course.

"What's with the outfit?" I ask. I am sitting at the desk, flipping through my notebooks and organizing them according to size before placing them into a cardboard box I got from the kitchen.

"I am the only woman who was at the Alamo when the siege occurred."

"There were no women at the Alamo massacre. Get your history right!"

"I am dressed for the Hollywood version. The script describes my character as 'intrepid woman who gives the men the courage to battle against hopeless odds.'"

"Am *I* up against hopeless odds?"

"Could be. Bipolar disorder never goes away. You could be using again in several days."

"What's the Alamo got to do with the possibility of a relapse?"

"The Alamo is my metaphor for what lies ahead—possibly death and destruction, just like the valiant Texan and Tejano volunteers who defended the Alamo against the Mexican forces."

"What are you talking about? Nothing I am involved with has anything to do with the Alamo in Texas."

"True. But there is also *another* Alamo with personal resonance for you: the park in San Francisco where you went to relive your childhood disaster. I gave you the strength to endure the remembrance. Read to me what you wrote at the time."

"I didn't write anything."

"Then tell me the whole story: the childhood remembrance, Henry Olhoff House, and the aftermath. You remember it well."

"I don't know that I can remember it. It wasn't a pleasant time to recollect."

"I think you can. It was your last major relapse and so much was revealed. Pretend it's a Hollywood movie and I am the heroine."

"Some heroine! You were more like the dancehall whore."

"There you go again, attributing the negative stuff to me. I bet you are going to blame me for messing up your recovery."

"The thought crosses my mind. You and that damn antidepressant killed my recovery. I should have let the cook keep it. And you exploited my failure!"

"Nobody but you ruined your recovery. I went along for the ride. I had fun. Didn't you?"

"No, it was all wrong. I will tell you what happened."

"Good. I want to hear if and how you will twist the facts."

"I only tell true facts."

"Ha! You get the facts confused with the feelings. Remember what the psychiatrist told you: 'Feelings are not facts.'"

"I shall keep that in mind. Now stop twiddling with the raccoon tail!"

"Nice tale on a nice piece of tail, wouldn't you say?"

"No, I wouldn't," I sigh. "Do you want to hear this or not?"

"Shoot, pardner."

"Then pay attention. Alamo Square is the perfect place to sit on a bench and look at the city of San Francisco. Photographers come to capture the image of the city towers in the distance behind the six Victorian houses that compose the foreground of countless postcards of the city. I have come to Alamo Square for relief from Henry Olhoff House, the gigantic mansion that houses recovering alcoholics and addicts.

"Betty Ford had recommended I go to a halfway house for six months to maintain my sobriety. They gave me the choice of several places. I chose Henry Olhoff House because of its reputation for strengthening recovery and for treating gay men. I wanted to explore the possibility I was truly gay. I had already used and gone to the bathhouse since leaving Betty Ford, but I hoped I could get back on track at this group home.

"Henry Olhoff House stands a block away from Alamo Square at the corner of Steiner and Fell streets. I arrive in a taxi from San Francisco Airport and make my way up the twelve concrete steps to an imposing, three-story Victorian mansion—all turrets, pediments, and filigree. I walk across the front of the big green house with faded purple and peeling white trim girdled in scaffolding, upon which painters are busy refurbishing the exterior. More steps ascend to an arched, white gothic portico with benches on both sides. The ornate entry door is decorated with carved wood garlands surrounding a large, cut glass oval center.

"An African American man whose name I later learn is Robert is lounging on the front porch with some other residents. He unlocks the front door with his key and directs me to the first room on the left.

"'You will find the director there at the end of the corridor, in the round room,' he says, stepping aside to allow me to enter. 'Welcome to the land of rules.'

"I pick up my two bags and enter. In front of me is a long wide foyer. On my right is a pedestal with a white marble bust of a woman and a series of small mail cubicles. Eighteen feet away, a grand staircase begins at a large newel post and curves up to the second floor. A huge stained glass window of a huntsman is positioned on a landing a few steps up. On my left, a handful of keys dangle from a pegboard, beyond which I can see a large room full of couches and overstuffed chairs, where two men are lounging and watching TV. Beyond this room is a dining area with long tables. Immediately to my left is a corridor leading to a half-open door, which reveals a man with long dark hair seated at a desk.

"I drop my bags in the foyer and go down the corridor, rap gently on the open door, and announce myself as a new resident. The man tells me to come in and sit down, and introduces himself as Bobby, director of Henry Olhoff House.

'We call the house HOH for short,' he says. He takes the usual information and asks me what my drugs of choice are. I tell him crack and marijuana. He asks me when I last used. I lie and say thirty days. Truthfully, I inform Bobby I managed to stay straight for a week before coming, because I knew I would have to pass a drug test. Bobby commends my effort, because one requirement for residence in the HOH is a minimum of seventy-two hours' sobriety.

"We walk back out of the office to the main hallway of the house, where I had left my baggage. Bobby tells me to follow him with my luggage, and we ascend the main staircase up to the second floor, where several doors on the left lead to sleeping rooms. Bobby tells me these are the rooms of men who have a long tenancy in the house and have proven themselves worthy by following the program and the rules. We proceed to a plain door on the right side of the hallway. I follow Bobby through the door, struggling with my bags up a steep, narrow staircase leading to the attic floor. At the top, a short corridor leads us into a large open room filled with many beds.

"Bobby tells me this is where I will reside until my group feels I am ready to move to the second floor. I look dolefully at this array of beds, realizing I will have no privacy. The room, where I will live for almost three months, holds at least twelve to fifteen men. This is no Betty Ford Center, where each patient is given a room to share with only one other person. I am depressed by what I see.

"Bobby tells me there aren't many men around at this hour because they are at work. He then states that in order to stay in HOH, a resident must get a job. I will have two weeks in which to find employment. Bobby leads me to a bed without sheets and tells me to put down my suitcases. He points out the closets and cubicles along one wall to my right where I can store my belongings and find bed linens.

"Bobby walks me back downstairs and shows me the dining room, where all residents have their evening meal together. I am expected to be at dinner every night at six unless I have permission to be late. Repeated violation of this rule is grounds to be evicted from the house. He then tells me other customs and courtesies, and asks me if I have any prescription drugs. I have one, I say, my antidepressant. Bobby asks me to bring him the drug, telling me I can get my allotted prescription from the cook in the morning and evening. Violation of the customs and courtesies—the C & Cs—is also grounds for eviction. If a resident hides his prescription or is found to be using illegal drugs, he is immediately expelled.

"Next, Bobby asks for a urine sample. He points to a room across from the dining room next to the main staircase. I piss into a bottle and take it back to Bobby. I go up to my bed, find the linen closet for sheets and a blanket, and make my bed, which lies in an area of three other beds closely positioned together near the entrance to the attic, which I later learn was a originally a dance room. I am feeling very sorry for myself as I lie on my new bed and stare at the ceiling. I get up and go to the window. Beyond the painters' scaffolding there is a beautiful view of the San Francisco harbor and the Bay Bridge leading to Oakland. HOH is definitely not what I thought it would be. The lack of privacy and the numerous rules inhibiting my behavior are very troublesome. The interior life would be hell, but the exterior views might make up for it. I put my clothes away in the closet, and my alarm clock and a couple of books on the small shelf at the head of the bed, and under the bed I place the bag with the clothes I had for Carlotta.

"I struggle with the thought of immediately leaving this place. I learn later that only a small number of residents make it all the way through the HOH program. Many fall by the wayside because of infractions of the house rules. Some because they can't make dinner consistently, some because of their disruptive behavior, but the most common reason is that they use and are caught. The frequent drug tests give them away.

"Dinnertime comes. I descend to the dining room, replete with fine cabinetry and a fireplace. Three large tables fill the room. I approach the table closest to the doorway and am shooed way because it's reserved for the facility's senior residents. I am directed to sit at the furthermost table. Before dinner begins, I am asked to introduce myself. I have to stand up and state my name, what my addiction is, and how I come to be at HOH. I say I am a crack addict and The Betty Ford Center recommended I come here. There are murmurs of agreement. I don't mention Carlotta.

"Residents act as waiters. The first table gets served first; my table is last. After dinner, because I am a 'newbie,' I am assigned the task of cleaning up the dining room with two other recent arrivals. We bus the dishes to the kitchen, where other newbies wash up. HOH is very hierarchical. Senior residents have more privileges and greater freedom. Curfew times do not apply to them as they do to newbies. Each evening, I have to be back in the house by ten p.m. I feel like a teenager and resent it.

"Within two weeks, I find employment as an architect on the project for the new San Francisco International Airport. I am happy to have the job, but I am increasingly unhappy at living at HOH. The restrictions are onerous. I try to make the place tolerable by meditating once a day and taking morning walks around the neighborhood. I always end up in Alamo Square, where I sit on a bench and stare out over the beautiful landscape of San Francisco. I think about the mess I have made out of my life. I resent where I have ended up. I regret the path that has led me here. I can't forgive myself.

"Surprise, surprise: HOH emphasizes the twelve step program of Alcoholics Anonymous. Dutifully, I go to as many AA meetings as possible. I try to give myself over to the AA program, as I eventually had at Betty Ford, but I feel something holding me back from total commitment. I will not give up my prescription drug, the anti-anxiety, anti-depressant Xanax.

"There is a culture in AA that frowns on taking any drugs at all. I got the feeling the HOH staff—and some residents, too—looked down on any drug, prescription or otherwise. The staff made it hard to get my prescription, and the longtime residents remarked negatively on my use. To them, this prescription drug is just another chemical, shielding one from reality. To them, to be clean and sober is to be rid of all chemicals, but I feel I need my antidepressant in order to cope. I have difficulty coping with the rules of the house when I have difficulty getting access to my medication.

"Men were continually being kicked out of HOH. I see one man get kicked out because of his disruptive behavior. Chris was thrown out when I complained to him that he played his radio too loud in the third floor bedroom, and he physically attacked me in the foyer in front of a crowd. Sal was told to leave because he missed too many house AA meetings. Bob and Ed were kicked out of the house for using drugs. Kicked out, you had to leave the house immediately, even if you had nowhere to go.

"Three men who came to HOH about the same time as I did left of their own volition. I wanted to go with them. They found an apartment together, but it was not large enough to include me. They said that the three of them would work the twelve step program together and thus keep each other sober. They failed.

"I wanted to leave but stayed from the end of August to the end of November, trying my best to make the program work for me. I attended all the process groups, went to the AA meetings in the house and in the city during my lunch hour. I became skeptical that the AA approach would work for me. I took my anti-depression pill and still had periods when I found myself very irritable, supercharged, just plain sad, and desirous of a good high. My antidepressant did not alter these feelings. I asked if I could see a psychiatrist, but one was not available.

"I wanted to don my gal apparel, as it were, and for Halloween, I got the chance. Steve—one of the three refugees who left HOH of his own accord—and I got dressed up in our drag outfits at his new apartment. Steve was a vision in virginal white: white panty hose and a white cocktail dress. In his brown wig and makeup, he made a passable woman. I was a different matter—my large size gave me away. My all-black costume consisted of a black pleated skirt—no ruffles on the bottom—black blouse, and black fishnet hose with silver heels, which I accessorized with studded-leather cuffs, leather collar, big silver earrings, and a red brooch depicting Vladimir Lenin. This is *not* typical female attire. My garish makeup, combined with my orange/red Day-Glo wig, left no doubt I was a big man in drag—but then, the look I *wanted* was a man in drag.

"This was the first time I appeared in public in drag. Steve and I rode the bus from his apartment to Mission Street, where we drew many disbelieving looks and laughs. At Mission Street, we tried to walk in high heels up the hillside to Castro and the street party. We could not do it. Our ankles kept collapsing on the steep street to the amusement of straight passersby. We gave up, took our heels off, and marched in our nylon stockings up the hill, where a large crowd had gathered for the gay Halloween Street Fair. Tourists wanted their picture taken with Steve and me. We obligingly posed numerous times with various straight families who had come to gawk at the outrageous gays. Carlotta was released by this experience. She had a glorious time wandering around

bipolar bare

amidst the leather men and the other transvestites. And so it was, Carlton began to wear drag to other events at HOH and in the city."

Carlton as Carlotta; 1996; 22 x 30 inches; colored pencil and pastel

"This cowgirl got released from her genie bottle as a drag queen, ready, willing, and able to *par-tay*!" says Carlotta, smiling broadly. "A little known fact is that the soon-to-be-massacred defenders of the Texas Alamo partied, too, just like the Castro Street Halloween Party."

"You don't know that—it's preposterous!"

"One should always party before a significant event. I made myself available to all those doomed men before I slipped away before the battle began."

"See, I told you—you're a whore."

"Not a whore. I soothed the shattered nerves of the brave men."

"You didn't soothe my nerves, and if you are a true genie, you could have provided me with three wishes."

"But I did, pilgrim. You got to wear drag, appear in public, and go to a sex club. I made you freer and willing to express openly your hidden desires."

"My hidden desires came from a bad place."

"That's just your opinion. I have a different view on the situation. You got to do what you always wanted to do, and Carlotta made her grand appearance in public. Please continue with your narrative."

"I went to fairs in drag. At the Folsom Street Fair, the wild variety of gay life styles was on parade. Men flogged other men on their bare buttocks and a leather-clad woman with bare breasts led another woman through the crowd in chains. The chained partner was usually dressed very elegantly except for her bare breasts. Some men and women were completely naked and casually strolled through the clumps of leather men. One man was chained to a fence while another man gave him a blowjob. There were many persons dressed in drag. Carlotta got to wear her black outfit. I was amazed and hoped someone might be attracted to my drag. Nothing happened. I returned to HOH and endured the derisive snickering of the residents.

"I went in drag to a sober living symposium for the gay community, where men discussed their need to totally dominate their partners and how they could not sustain a lengthy relationship because submissive men are promiscuous. I found I could not relate to this kind of activity and went away from these events feeling like I was not as far gone as these fanatical men. I went to Alamo Square to study the true nature of my sexuality. I liked drag but had no desire to get into a relationship with another man. I liked the anonymity of drag and the anonymous sex when dressed up, but I was not proud of my addiction to cross-dressing. It was one more aspect of my sad life, one more manifestation of my mental illness.

"One bright fall day, I stepped off the trolley after work and looked up at Henry Olhoff House, high on the hill above the corner of Hayes and Steiner streets. A comparison surfaced in my mind, and everything became clear to me. HOH was a foster home for adult men society had rejected because of their behavior, just as I—the recalcitrant child—was rejected by my family and sent to the foster farm. But the youthful story was much more tragic and complex. It was a story of childhood sexual abuse. My interest in cross-dressing was a means of reliving this abuse without conscious understanding.

"My God, childhood sexual abuse! It was an epiphany too horrible to contemplate.

"I walked to Alamo Square, sat on my favorite bench, and relived the experience I had as a five-year-old. The memory expanded until I remembered the whole story of my abandonment to the foster home farm. The memory was overwhelming. Tears streamed down my face. I sat on the bench looking out at the famous landscape of San Francisco, so picture postcard pretty, feeling stunned and massacred. This memory was my Texas Alamo, where the innocent child was killed. That child was replaced by a neurotic divided child, who buried his horrible experience in the subconscious and relied on a second self to ease his pain. That child grew into a divided adult where the anger and rage against himself and the world lay just beneath the conscious surface, but erupted at the slightest provocation. This seething rage and agonized sadness corrupted my waking states and made me often gloomy and suicidal. In barely contained anger and sadness, I stayed in the park, just sitting, well past the dinner hour, unable to move, reliving the story again and again. Each pass over the story added more detail."

"Carlotta comforted Carlton that day."

"What? What?" I say foggily as I snap back to reality from the grim remembrance.

"I said, Carlotta comforted Carlton that day. You were so terribly upset. I told you how life goes on, and you had gone on. The past was over and you should not cling to it."

I blink and hot tears roll down my face. "But I haven't told you the story yet."

"You told Dr. Poliquin a rough outline of your experience."

"But not the *whole* story."

"Then tell me one more time."

Carlotta reaches into the box where my journals are stacked, pulls out the one with the red tag, and hands it to me. I begin reading out loud on the marked page.

"Carolee and Chinky overhear a conversation that Grandmother, Grandfather, and Father have in the living room over cocktails. They think the siblings are up in the attic, but they are really on the staircase, just on the other side of the wall from the living room.

"'The court decision is that neither you nor Lynn will get custody of the boy,' says Grandfather. 'The boy will be made a ward of the court and given to us for the time being.'

"'I can abide by that decision for now,' says Father. 'With my new job down in Corning, I haven't got time to take care of him.'

"Grandfather replies, 'This is a real burden on your mother. I am in New York all week and only here on weekends. She is already taking care of Carolee. I don't know how she can take care of another child, especially this one.'

"'He is difficult and undisciplined,' Grandmother concurs, nodding. 'He is like his mother: wild and a bit crazy. Two days ago, he broke a crystal vase when he carelessly reached up on the sideboard in the dining room to hide a shoe as part of a ridiculous game he and Carolee were playing. I sent him to his room, where he screamed and yelled at me for better than an hour, calling me all kinds of vile names. I can't have this in my house.'

"'What are the alternatives?' Father sighs.

"'Your mother and I have given this some thought,' says Grandfather. 'We think that the boy should be placed in foster care for the time being.'"

"Father asks, 'Are you sure this is the best thing?'

"'I don't know what else to do,' says Grandmother. ' I can't have him in my house. It is too much for me.'

"'All right, if that is what we must do, let's do it,' says Father.

"'There is a foster care farm outside Rochester that is supposed to be very good,' says Grandmother. 'It is for boys only. We can take him there next weekend when Grandfather is here again.'

"There is silence and the tinkling of ice in glasses. Sister and Chinky creep back up the stairs to the attic castle. Chinky asks Carolee what foster care is. She doesn't know. Chinky says it sounds like they are sending him away. Sister makes tea. Chinky doesn't want any. He climbs up on the window seat, rises on his tiptoes, and stares out the window at the empty street. Carlotta can hear his thinking. He is wondering where his mother is.

"Chinky is sitting in the back of the big bronze Buick with Teddy Bear on his lap, both arms clasped tightly around the beloved bear. There is a suitcase on the seat next to them. Grandfather is driving, with Grandmother beside him, glowering straight ahead. Everyone is silent. Chinky is looking out the window. He doesn't want to look at Grandfather and Grandmother because he hates them. The Buick backs down the long drive of 172 Council Rock Avenue into the street and turns south. They pass by all the big lawns with big trees where the houses sit far back from the street. There are no people on the street. Brighton is not like the neighborhood around Aunt Helene's house, where lots of people walk along the street and say hello. The people here are snooty and unfriendly. We travel to where the houses get farther apart. There are fewer trees and no people. Fences, furrows, and a few poles define the landscape. The Buick turns between two fences on a dirt road next to a sign that says 'Miller.' The dirt road leads to a white farmhouse, a big barn, and several white shacks.

"The Buick crunches over small rocks that surround the house and halts under a big leafless tree five feet from a beat-up pickup truck. Grandfather and Grandmother get out of the automobile. Grandfather is wearing a gray suit with a blue tie. He always wears gray suits with blue or red ties. Grandmother is wearing a fur coat and a hat with a lacy band around it. A stout woman in a short blue jacket and green dress comes off the low porch to meet them. They talk. The woman looks toward the car at Chinky and the bear. Grandfather comes back to the car and opens the door. He picks up the suitcase off the seat and sets it on the ground.

"'Chinky, you are going to stay here for a while,' he tells the boy. 'Get out of the car, please. I don't want to have to haul you out.'

"Chinky doesn't move. He looks at his grandfather with tears in his eyes.

"'Why can't I be with my mommy?' he says.

"Grandfather sighs. 'Right now, that can't happen. You have to stay here. I promise you it will only be for a short time.' He reaches into the back seat and grasps Chinky's forearm gently. Chinky resists him, but he is not strong enough to break Grandfather's grip. He slides out of the back seat and falls to the ground. Grandfather pulls Chinky up.

"'Do I have to stay here?' Chinky cries.

"Grandfather looks at him with sadness in his eyes but warmth and love in his face.

"'Yes,' he says softly. 'You will like the farm. It has all the things you like: cows, chickens, dogs, cats, goats, and horses. Did you see the white horses in the pasture when we came up the road?' Chinky shakes his head no. 'Well, there is lots of room for you to run and play. Come on, let me introduce you to Mrs. Miller and some of the other boys.'

"Grandfather picks up Chinky's suitcase. He takes my left hand and drags me toward the big woman. I try to pry my wrist out of Grandfather's hand. His grip is too strong. Behind Mrs. Miller stands a group of boys. Some are Chinky's size, others are as big as she is.

"Grandfather introduces me. 'Mrs. Miller, this is our grandson, Carlton. We call him Chinky.' A chorus of sniggering erupts from the group of boys.

"'I am delighted to meet you, Chinky,' says Mrs. Miller cheerfully, leaning down to look at the boy. 'Who is your friend?' Mrs. Miller is a tall large woman dressed in a flannel hunter's jacket over a gray dress and work boots. Her face has a pleasant smile with a ruddy and creased pallor of one who works outside much of the day. Her long brown hair streaked with gray falls forward and comes close to Chinky's face.

"'This is Teddy,' says Chinky. He holds the bear up with both hands toward Mrs. Miller's nose. Again, the boys snigger.

"'Well, I am delighted to meet you too, Teddy,' says Mrs. Miller, standing up and shaking the bear's paw. She turns toward the group of boys behind her, shushes them, and turns back toward us. 'Please pardon the boys' lack of manners, Mr. and Mrs. Davis. They know better than to laugh at a newcomer. I shall speak to them later.' She points toward one of the mid-sized boys. "Tom, will you please take Chinky and his suitcase to Cabin Three? Chinky, your roommates will be Freddie and Bruce,' she adds, indicating two boys with short dark hair. They are both smaller than Chinky, who has long blond hair that falls to his shoulders.

bipolar bare

"Chinky and Teddy follow Tom across the crumbled rock toward one of the white shacks that lie between the farmhouse and the barn with Freddie and Bruce in tow. Three beds occupy this little cabin. Freddie, the smallest and quieter boy, has the one by the door against the wall. Bruce has the bed opposite from Chinky's. The wall opposite the door has a window. Next to it is a dresser. Each boy has a drawer for his clothes. Toys are kept in a box below the window. There aren't many toys, nor will there be that much time to play with them. Chinky places Teddy on his new bed with great ceremony.

"All the boys, even the smallest, work on the farm. Chinky has to leave the bear in the cabin every day when he goes to do his chores. He tells the bear what he does when he comes home. Chinky works in the chicken coop, collecting the eggs in the morning. The eggs, he learns, are fragile, and he must handle them with care. One morning, he drops and breaks two eggs. An older boy yells at him and calls him a dummy.

"He feeds the chickens during the day. There are big buckets of feed that Chinky must scoop into smaller buckets then throw the feed onto the ground in the fenced area where the chickens run around. Chinky says this job is fun, as the chickens get really excited when he tosses out the seeds. They follow him and peck at his feet. The worst part of his job is that he must clean the cages and the shed. While the chickens are out, he has to wash down the wire with water and wet rags and then wipe them off. He has to rake the area inside the shed and put the messy straw in big cans. The job is smelly and often the older boys are mean to him. They bully him and push him down in the dirty straw. They call him Stinky Chinky. Its makes him cry. 'Crybaby!' they taunt him. "Do you want your mommy, Stinky Chinky?'

"Two big boys, as big as Mrs. Miller, Danny, and Frankie, come into the cabin past bedtime. They close the door and pull down the window shade. Freddie and Bruce turn their heads to the wall and cover their faces with their pillows after Danny and Frankie whisper something to them. Danny and Frankie walk over to Chinky's bed and pull the covers away from Chinky and Teddy.

"'Here is the boy with long hair like a girl,' says Frankie, fingering Chinky's blond locks. 'Maybe he really is a girl—what do you think, Danny? Maybe we should call her Pinky?'

"Frankie pulls Chinky's pajama bottoms off while Danny holds him down.

"Look at that nice pink ass, Danny,' Frankie leers. 'I want me some of that."

"Frankie grabs Chinky's legs and yanks him to the floor. Danny slides onto the bed and wraps one arm around Chinky's head, covering his mouth so he can't scream. With his other arm, he holds Chinky's body as tightly as possible so he can't move. Frankie kicks Chinky's legs apart and unzips his trousers. His penis flops out. The erect member is about six inches long. Chinky is struggling against Danny's hold.

"'Push his butt up, Danny,' Frankie grunts. Danny does so. Frankie steps forward and pushes his penis into Chinky's anus. Chinky grimaces and struggles against the violation.

"'That's it, wiggle it, Pinky! I like it that way!' chants Frankie, slamming himself repeatedly against Chinky's buttocks. 'Mmm, mmm, Pinky's pussy is good! Oh, boy! Here we come!' With a nasty laugh, Frankie withdraws and pulls up his pants.

"Danny leans down to Chinky and whispers, 'Next time, you are mine, little girl. Don't you dare say anything to anybody or your ass is grass. Got that, Chinky Pinky? We come here all the time for nooky, so get used to it.' He raises up and punches Frankie playfully in the arm and says: 'We'd better haul ass out of here before old lady Miller does her bed check.'

"True to their word, Danny and Frankie came often. Not every night, but often enough. Chinky can speak to no one because he knows what the big boys will do to him. They leer at him daily. They demonstrate how they can hurt him with pitchforks driven in the ground near his feet, with heavy ropes swung by his head, and with axes chopped close to his body. Chinky huddles in his bed in fear every night. Each sound outside the cabin makes him cringe. When they do come, Chinky becomes hardened with hate. He makes no sound. He makes no movement. He saves his tears for their departure.

"Gradually, his tears fade away and Chinky becomes a hardened, unforgiving boy. He realized he was the only person who knew this story. He could not blame his father or mother for what happened to him at the foster home. They knew nothing of it, and he told no one. It was his secret alone, his pain alone.

"Finally in the fall of 1949, Father comes to take Teddy and me away. Father drives me to a new town, gives me a new mother, and goes away. Father says he will be back soon. New mother Lois is kind, but I don't trust mothers. I don't trust fathers. I don't trust anybody. All I know is that the bogeymen come every night. They come through the window, bust the door down, and emerge from under the bed to get you. I try to hide under the covers, but they always find me. I cry out until the new mommy comes to comfort me."

Sniffling, I look up from my journal. My tears have stained the pages, turning the words into Rorschach-like blobs. Carlotta's brow is knitted and fat tears glisten in the corners of her eyes.

"Tears were streaming down my face while I sat on my bench in Alamo Square, putting these vile memories together in my mind," I say at last. "I cried and cried until a passerby asked me if I was all right. 'Please don't bother me,' I asked him gently, and he passed on. My tears finally subsided, but I felt as sad as I ever had. I walked solemnly back to HOH and was reprimanded for missing dinner, as I knew I would be. Any more infractions of the rules and I would be out on the street, Bobby informed me.

"For days after this horrible epiphany, I stopped at Alamo Square after work to sit on my bench and look out over the city. My thoughts dwelled on the rapes. With awful clarity, I remembered the smell of the chicken coops and cow barn. The fear I had when the boys threatened me with the pitchfork. And the creaking door and the moonlight through the window of small dormitory I lived in. I remembered hiding under the covers with my teddy bear, praying to some vague deity to whisk me away or make me invisible, to no avail. I remembered the teenagers pulling my long blond hair, and the humiliating fact that they called me a girl.

"After several days of putting myself through this hell, I stopped sobbing and my mind turned to hatred. I knew I had finally penetrated to the core of my anger. I knew this was the anger that permeated my life. This anger was the source of my unhappiness and my obsession to dress as a woman. But incredibly, reliving the experience did not free me of my desire to cross-dress and fantasize about anonymous sex. It only seemed to fan the flames even more.

"I couldn't dwell too long on the episodes each day because I didn't want to miss dinner and be ejected from the house. I did not want to go back to the house, but I had to. There was no other place to go."

"You buried that memory in your unconscious mind and the all-male environment of HOH brought it back. You should be pleased," Carlotta says, dabbing at her tears with a Western bandanna.

"No, it was too painful. I wish I had never uncovered it."

"But you did, dear Carlton, and the memory is a giant step on the path to recovery. It helps to explain why you like to be raped."

"I don't *like* to be raped—no one does," I correct her. "I sought out gay sex only when I was high on crack, even though I thought it was wrong. It was you, Carlotta, who loved the kinky sex."

"I don't deny it. Now read to me what happened with HOH after your personal revelation."

"I didn't write anything about this time. I was too fucked up. All I can do is tell you what I remember."

"Please do."

"Very well. I remained in the Olhoff House for nearly three months, and then I was booted out. My end came not because I was late for dinner, but because of the anti-depression drugs. When I first came to the house, I surrendered my pills to the director, who told me I could get the two pills a day I was prescribed from the house cook—one in the morning before breakfast and one in the evening before dinner. I never could get them. Finally, I insisted the cook give me my pills. I took advantage of the fact that he was distracted and irritated at the time and he didn't notice that I didn't give the prescription bottle back to him after he angrily forked it over. I kept it in my belongings and took my medication without the middleman. No one seemed to notice, and I forgot about this infraction of the house rules.

"When the prescription ran out, I went to the director to get the house physician to renew it and was summarily caught in my violation of the house rule. The director told me to get the hell out of the house. He stated I was not committed to the HOH program, and he was right. I left immediately, just like all the other rejects. I thanked the director for doing to me what I hadn't the courage to do myself. I packed up my belongings, called a cab, and retreated to a hotel on the edge of the Civic Center Park. I was sober three months in HOH, but before another month was over, I relapsed. I went on a binge that lasted off and on for a year until I returned to Los Angeles."

"And quite the binge it was! Carlotta was always out, walking the streets with her ice pick, going to bars, gay festivals, and sex clubs."

"I hated myself for it."

"But you never denied me."

"I was too wasted to stop. It was so easy to get high."

"Indeed it was. Go on with your tale."

"The Civic Center Park across the street from San Francisco's City Hall was a drug Mecca. I became one of many people who prowled the park looking for drugs. I even came across the cook's assistant from HOH, who was fired because he relapsed. After work, I would wander into the park and buy crack from the dealers who hid themselves in the groves of trees that flanked a central reflecting pond. I was on constant lookout for a dealer, many of whom rode bicycles, or else would be sitting on the benches just outside the perimeter of the trees. Seeing me enter the grove, they would rise and follow me in. I started buying $40, went to $60, and ultimately purchased $80 worth of rock at a time.

"I had a sequence I followed. Coming out of my hotel, I walked a short block up to my bank's ATM and withdrew cash for my buy. I would then walk back to the park and search out a dealer. My transaction made, I would head to the hotel to dress up in drag and prowl the Tenderloin, looking for sex. I would go to the Motherlode Bar, a well-known hangout for transvestites, and drink until I was ready to stroll the streets with the other transvestite hookers. I was not beautiful like the others and was generally unsuccessful at making a score. On one occasion only, I made a deal to suck a man's cock for five dollars.

"I went to see a Dr. Storme, a gay psychologist who lived in Marin County, to explore my childhood sex abuse and my addiction to cross-dressing. I brought the drawing I made of you, Carlotta, in your orange/red hair, leather collar, and silver disk earrings. The doctor instructed me to talk to the drawing. I propped the drawing up on the couch next to me, while the doctor sat in his easy chair with the background of the bay spread out behind him. The setting was beautiful, with sailboats cruising gently on the water. It was hard at first to conjure up negative thoughts. Then I called Carlotta a slut and the words started tumbling out. I said Carlotta was my marker for my depraved state … that she represented all my negative attributes … that she was sarcastic, promiscuous, and without respect for anyone, including Carlton. I said that she loved the sex she had with strangers and that she could never pass as a woman. I said I hated Carlotta. I said I hated *you*."

"I know you did," Carlotta says hurtfully.

"Dr. Storme said that you were the woman in me. He said that I had to be aware and accept this feminine side of me, if I ever wished to change, if I ever wished to stop my dangerous sexual behavior. The mantra he gave me was: awareness, acceptance, and change. Carlotta was the little girl/boy who got raped in the foster home. Carlotta was the adult who seeks out dangerous behavior. She lives on adrenaline. I tried to accept you, Carlotta, but I could not do so. Yet every chance I got, I would dress up and act your part. Dr. Storme and I analyzed this drawing for several sessions. He said, 'Perhaps you are a loner, neither gay nor straight.' I didn't understand him and I went away angry. The anger was my excuse to go the sex club."

"You always went to the sex club after a session with Dr. Storme. You didn't need anger as an excuse."

"That's true. After my sessions with Dr. Storme, I would dress up in drag like the drawing, cross the Bay Bridge, and go to the Bay Area Club in Oakland. The club, which was hidden down a dark street without any sign to mark its location, had one night a week set aside for cross-dressers and the men who liked them. You signed in at a counter and entered through a door into a room where a coffee bar was placed along one wall with a group of tables nearby. Stairs led to the dark sex club area. Another doorway led to a dressing area and to a group of small cubicles that a club member could rent for sex in private. I always got one of these rooms if one were available. If it wasn't, I roamed the dark corridors. But first I had to get more loaded on crack. I smoked in the toilet or my cubicle until sufficiently wasted."

bipolar bare

"You can skip describing the rooms," says Carlotta. "They were small and dirty. In fact, the whole place was dark and dirty. Carlotta felt like she was traipsing about in a small meadow, trying to avoid the cow pies."

"I thought you loved the place."

"I loved being out, but the BAC was certainly no sexual Shangri-La. It was too sleazy for a woman of refinement like me."

"It was a sleazy place for sure, but that's what I liked about it. The law was trying to make it difficult for the club to survive. This was all part of my uncontrolled desire to live outside the law, to be a Bohemian, to live a life outside societal norms. By day I was a professional, by night I was running wild in the underground underbelly of San Francisco's storied gay community. Cross-dressers were a small subculture of the larger gay community. The BAC was one of the few places that catered to them."

"You were at the zenith of your sickness. You didn't care what happened to you."

"The bathhouses south of Market were gone because of the AIDS epidemic. But I didn't care if I got AIDS. I even *wanted* to contract the disease, because my life was so awful. Once I cared about living, but now I didn't care if I lived or died."

"You didn't even worry about being arrested?"

"Not really. The BAC customers always had to worry about police raids. Don't you remember the time the police came? They came and marched through every room, up the stairs, through the sling room and the narrow dark hallways. Their presence stopped any activity as members retreated to the tables near the coffee bar and acted innocent. It wasn't long after that raid that the small cubicles disappeared and the dressing area closed. For that reason, you had to come to the club already decked out.

"After so much crack before and after my BAC visits, I would be sweating profusely. My makeup would run. Even in my messed up state, I found some men ready to rape Carlotta. In the dark corridors, men came up behind Carlotta and raised her skirt, exposing her bare ass flanked by the garter straps that held up the Cuban heel nylons with the seam up the back. Wordlessly, the nasty deed was done, often with a crowd watching the action."

"You had lost control completely. Your life was unmanageable."

"I still tried to become sober."

"Pointless! You could not stop using."

"All too true. I kept relapsing after I departed HOH. I would get clean for sometimes as much as twelve or fourteen days and then find myself binging. It was so easy to slip. The park and the crack dealers were just around the corner and the ATM was just up the block. My buying habits were easy to chart, especially on the days I went to the social club. First, I would buy $20 worth after work and before going to see Dr. Storme, thinking I could get by on that amount. After my session in the hotel, I would smoke up the four $5 tabs in less than an hour while I dressed up. Returning to the park, I would buy $30 worth, which would only last me several hours while driving over to the BAC and smoking it there. Returning to the park after my trip to the club, I would buy $40 worth and stay up all night, unable to sleep. I built up to a habit that was costing me $100 a day over the period of a year. The dealers got to know me and I got to recognize them."

"Were you still taking your antidepressant?"

"Yes. I took it daily. I got the prescription renewed. I don't remember how—perhaps through Dr. Storme. Maybe in light of what I know now, that was not a good thing. The antidepressant, combined with my use of crack, could have contributed to my cross-dressing mania and didn't help my attacks of depression and irritability. The drug had no preventative effect—it merely overlaid the sensation of pleasure that would immediately turn on Carlotta. I would dress up in her clothes, practice autoeroticism in my hotel room, or, if it were a Wednesday night after my session with Dr. S., I would head for the Bay Area Club. I frequented the club almost every week of my stay in San Francisco. Sometimes I was successful in finding a sex partner, and often I wasn't.

"No matter. The playacting was becoming less satisfying with each visit and each inhalation of crack cocaine. My lungs began to hurt with each intake of the melted crack. I noticed that my body was becoming stiffer each time that I dressed up. My highs from the crack were diminishing in intensity. The drug simply allowed me to attain equilibrium where I didn't feel depressed. If I tried to stop, I sank into a deep depression and became intolerably irritable. Stopping seemed impossible.

"I decided I needed a stimulus to end my behavior. I packed up my belongings and returned to LA, where I was able to stay sober for almost six months and didn't resort to cross-dressing. I pulled what AA people called a geographical. It didn't work, but I did gradually stop cross-dressing. Each month, I divested myself of one piece of Carlotta's costume. I threw out the dildos first. Carrying with me some piece of Carlotta's garb, I drove to downtown LA, where I had found a new dealer who was honest and gave me my money's worth of crack. On the way home from each trip downtown, I stopped by the railroad yards and tossed away the bra, the stockings, the skirt, the blouse, the leather collar, and finally the high-heeled shoes. Gradually, Carlotta became a memory. But the addiction and depression remained."

"You didn't free yourself from me," says Carlotta. "I was always with you in your private conversations with yourself. You became aware of me as never before."

"I did accept you, true, but with the goal of eventually eliminating your presence."

"See, you admit you accepted me! All you did was change me from a hooker to a companion when you cast out the paraphernalia that a whore would wear."

"I was just following Dr. Storme's advice. I was already aware of you. I accepted you, and change came. You left me until you resurfaced here at the hospital."

"What about the night you attempted suicide on the freeway overpass? I was there, too."

"Whatever. I could not end the drugs. I struggled with the desire to use every day. I would go to work high and after work get high again. There was no end I could reach, and I refused to go to twelve step meetings because they only fueled my desire to use. I was trapped in a cycle that descended deeper each day. My bottom never appeared."

"Yes it did. It was on the freeway overpass."

"That wasn't my bottom. I could always go deeper, more dependent on the drugs to keep me going and more despairing of my ability to become drug free. If you remember, I smoked the following morning and whole day before Ginger put me in the hospital. The drug had changed its nature for me. I no longer got high. I now needed the drug just to keep me balanced and able to get through each day with a modicum of normalcy. Crack was taking its toll on my body.

Every joint in my body hurt. My teeth hurt and I had coughing fits where I would hawk up gray goo. I was not living. I was surviving."

"You are the only survivor of the Alamo."

"Carlotta, leave me be. I am not a survivor of the Alamo. Your non sequiturs are becoming tiresome."

"You are still alive, aren't you? You could be dead from an overdose, or you could have been killed by one of the evil men who hung out in Civic Center Park, or you might have jumped from the freeway overpass."

"Yes, I survived, but I didn't want to. I liked how close I could come to being arrested or thumbing my nose at death. That is the thrill I liked. Then, when all options were gone, I thought about suicide. After this week in the hospital, I am not that way anymore. I don't need *you* anymore. You are an impediment to my recovery. You are the division I can no longer afford."

Carlotta's face blanches with disbelief. "You're serious! You really do wish me to leave! If your muse leaves you, you won't be inspired anymore."

"Please hear me," I say solemnly. "Go away."

Carlotta stands with her hands on her hips, looking at me defiantly. The coonskin cap is askew, draped over one eyebrow. She grabs it angrily and flings it away.

"You will miss me when I am gone," she says tersely and disappears into the bathroom.

A nurse enters my room and tells me a cab is waiting for me at the entrance.

Standing in the doorway with my valise and my box of journals in my arms, I survey the room one last time. Carlotta is gone. Really, truly gone. No disembodied voices, no fanciful apparitions. I am alone. O, happy day! I have seen the last of her.

Fat chance.

CHAPTER 25

THE BIPOLAR COASTER

THE BIPOLAR COASTER RIDE BEGINS before you know you are on it, before it has a name, before you know it is a disease. The climb up the first ascent is thrilling. You didn't know you could climb so high, or that the peak could be so exhilarating, the rush down the descent so fast, and the valley quite so terrifying. The next climb finds you a little more leery, but the high is even higher, the ride down even faster. The next three or four lows and highs happen in such quick succession that you are accustomed to them now. Then there is the one the afflicted call The Monster, the biggest one of all, the one they advertise as the super drop, the one that takes you up into the clouds and buries you in the dirt. You chug slowly up the incline, fearful but excited. The adrenaline is flowing. The pinnacle will be a blast of energy, firing the bullet of descent. Descent will be wondrous until near the nadir, when all the energy is spent and total depression sweeps over the body. The mental circuits are short-circuited and goddamn it, you are going for another ride on the endless roller coaster that is impossible to exit. That is, unless you dive off. Best done from the summit, when you can stand in the carriage say no more will I ride down to that hideous bottom that lies in wait for one who rides the Bipolar Coaster.

I still ride the Bipolar Coaster. I guess I always will. The highs are not so high and the lows not so low anymore, but every once in a while, I have a really bad low. It's then I think about how great a hit of crack would be. The blast of energy would fire me up to a place I haven't been in a long time. I wish I could say I don't miss it, but I do. The wild intensity is gone. The thrill of walking the razor's edge is gone. The desire to be someone else—Carlotta, the slut—is gone. I am quite ordinary now. Well, maybe not so ordinary. I have my writing, which I do about art, architecture, and mental illness. I have my art. I love to make drawings: the self-portraits I do every several years to see how I have changed, landscapes, and other odd images that strike my fancy. I am still fascinated by light and if I could get a big studio again I would make sculptures exploring that subject. I remain an architect, but one whose opportunities to do interesting work are limited by lack of reputation and cash. If I could, however, I have some ideas for places and spaces much more aggressive than Marilyn. I think of myself as an artist in the Renaissance sense, unfortunately one who has been limited in the past by mental illness. Regrets, however, do me no good. I must accept my mental disorder and the ordinariness of it while still seeking to do some good with the talents I have been given.

What held me back from being sober and seeking good took a long time to die away. I no longer have an undeniable craving to get loaded, and I am no longer willing to pay the price for the desire. I remember too well the last years of my addiction. Getting high was once wonderful. All inhibitions were gone. I didn't care about the consequences of my actions. I just wanted to stay high longer. I thought if I kept smoking continually, I could bridge the gap between the lows. I could ride the speeding projectile of self: a little more up and over the valley of the downs in a great thrill ride of danger and illicit desire. Unfortunately, the pleasure didn't last as long as I wanted. The high didn't get higher and the low got a little bit lower the more I indulged. Soon, the low was getting really low and lasting longer, no matter how much drug I fed myself. At some point, I crashed. The body and the mind were too tired to go on after days, maybe weeks, of operating on very little sleep or no sleep at all, and I realized what I had done to myself. I stop the binge, sleep for days, get up, go to meetings, and promise myself to remain sober. I did this many times in San Francisco.

The body and the mind paid a severe price for my indulgence. The muscles became stiff. I could not bend easily. The joints hurt at each flex of foot, elbow, knee, or neck. The teeth hurt. The gums became super sensitive. The lungs hurt. I coughed and spit up a gray goop whenever I inhaled crack smoke. My balance became unsteady; I stumbled around, knocking into furniture. This was especially comical when I was wearing high heels. My mind was becoming cloudy and I would forget things—often my wallet—leaving them in my home. I could not remember where I was going unless I was dressed in drag. The effects would diminish when I would remain sober for several days, but I always went back to smoking in a bid to find my elusive high. At first, the crack got me high, but it wouldn't last long. I wouldn't give it up, however, because it kept me in a kind of equilibrium and functioned as a medicine against deep depression, albeit not a very good one.

My dialogues with Carlotta faded away as I became long-term depressed. I gave up taking the antidepressant, since it wasn't working. Finally, my life hit a crisis point, and I went out on the freeway overpass to commit suicide. From there it was the mental hospital, my attendance in an outpatient program, and many meetings, especially those of persons who suffered from depression and other mental disorders. Slowly my life began to get marginally better. There is no quick fix for bipolar disorder.

My first year of sobriety, May 2003 to May 2004, passed without recourse to crack or marijuana. I didn't cross-dress, and I didn't seek out anonymous sex. I took my medications dutifully. I left each hospital group meeting, each day care program meeting, and each subsequent bipolar disorder meeting without the immediate desire to go and use. I attribute this to the medications. Unlike the twelve step programs I attended, the psychiatric drugs took away my craving. They worked where nothing else had. Giving my life up to God hadn't. Finding another higher power hadn't. Ninety meetings in ninety days hadn't. To work, however, medications had to be closely monitored, because just like the hit of street drugs, the medication cocktail can have a period of time in which it will have an effect, but then the body will become used to the dosage and the effect will be nil or the dosage will have to be greatly increased for any effect. Medications also have side effects.

When I first entered the hospital, I was given lithium, which didn't seem to have much effect. Dr. Poliquin experimented with different dosages of Haldol, Risperdal, Abilify, Depakote, Trileptal, and several others. The Depakote made me hungry all the time, and I was eating tons of food without satisfaction. Always large, I became obese, and Dr. Poliquin subsequently dropped the drug. Some of the other drugs made me woozy. I could hardly walk. I staggered down the corridors of the hospital. My speech was slurred. Dr. Poliquin ended the use of these drugs, as well. In this first year, I endured many changes to the drugs I took and the dosages before a combination with few side effects was found that would control my mood swings and relieve my depression.

These first bipolar drugs would work for a couple of months and then my body would become attuned and adjusted. The mood swings would start again. The ups were not as high, the lows were not as low, and the in-betweens were more even. These mood changes may not have been as severe as the ones in the past, but they were still devastating, probably because I expected I would never be troubled again with major mood changes. I was so wrong. Nine months after my stay in the hospital, I returned for a "tune-up" when I found myself contemplating suicide after a bout with depression. Dr. Poliquin made major adjustments to my medications, adding new ones and changing significantly the dosages of the old ones. In a few days, I was out of the hospital again. Dr. Poliquin commented it takes a long time to find the right combination of drugs to smooth out the highs and lows of a bipolar one person. It has certainly been that way for me.

So I rode the Bipolar Coaster many times in my first year out of the hospital. I became seriously depressed, with the depressions coming in cycles as they always had. After a good, even expansive mood, depression would again rear its ugly head. I fought like hell the desire to use crack cocaine as a means to mitigate it, but I found I could resist. I attended support groups that helped me through these difficult times as I shared my common experiences with others struggling with the same issues. There are so many others taking the ride on the Bipolar Coaster: addicts for whom the twelve steps had not worked, schizophrenics, sufferers of post-traumatic stress disorder, and the severely depressed, both diagnosed and undiagnosed. Hearing their stories and their methods of coping helped me cope. After my hospital tune-up, I was either a little on the high side or on the low side of even, but I never got so far down in these early days as to be suicidal or ready to use.

Treatment did not make me a happy person. I remained fundamentally dissatisfied with my life and angry at the edges. I should have congratulated myself on my year of sobriety, but I didn't. Pessimism had me in its grip, wrapping all my positive thoughts in a black shroud. I knew I needed to add something to my program of medication to help lift me out of my depression. At the beginning of my second year of sobriety, I decided to begin meditating again. Given how meditation had worked in the past, and even to some degree when I was using, this seemed like a good idea. Perhaps it could even lead to a path to some higher power: God, maybe. I would have liked that, as I remained alienated from the concept of God. Try as I might, I could not see that God loved anyone, much less me. I didn't find God in my new beginning at meditation. Rather, I got an unexpected result, with Carlotta appearing once again after a long absence.

Our intimate meditation group is presided over by Linda, a long-time student of Dr. Wortz, who founded the group; and she now leads it since Dr. Wortz became too ill with cancer to lead. The group is comprised of artists, writers, actors, and other creative people. The zendo, or meditation hall, is a small, bright-white room to one side of a larger sitting area in fellow member Nancy's vintage remodeled bungalow home. An imposing sepia print depicting an armless and headless torso kneeling in what appears to be a forest hangs above a modern black table, upon which art books are stacked in piles of two. There are no obvious Buddhist icons peppered around the space, which has been carefully designed to promote modern American meditation based on psychological principles.

Linda's cushion sits in front of the table below the print with her bell, a ringing bowl, a wooden fish, and sticks for making sound. Two meditators on cushions sit on either side of her. Dr. Wortz and I occupy chairs. Linda says we are to listen to the sounds in the environment around us without interference, without thought, and without judgment. We are to try hear the sound after it has disappeared. Linda strikes the ringing bowl with the short fat wooden striker and the meditation begins. The bowl is a shiny brass hollow seven inches wide and four inches deep that give off a resonant ring when struck by the thick soft leather wrapped end of the striker. A sharp Whaaaaaaaa aaaaaaa aaaa aaa aaa slowly gives way to less and less sound at lower and lower volume with greater and greater periods of silence between perceived sound until there is complete silence. A shifting of bodies in their meditation positions is heard. The room goes quiet.

I am the shell from which the emptiness speaks. That thought came to me again and then again as I listened to a cat's claws padding rhythmically across the hardwood floor. He brushes up against my leg, making me more agitated. I can't find the calmness to go beyond the emptiness thought, to hear the sound after a sound has disappeared. This is not emptiness, a void into which I can disappear and find equilibrium. This is emptiness jammed full of noise from no source. The thought warps; my mind races. Disconnected sentences plague my attempt to be calm. They tell me what I already know: that I will never be free of bipolar disorder. They tell me that I shall always be confronted with the limitations caused by the disease. I can never trust my reactions. I can never trust my decisions. I will never be what I want to be. I can't be calm and steady.

Tonight, I am depressed and nothing but negative thoughts race through my mind. My consciousness is a jumble of unhappy and pessimistic thoughts, scattering and reforming into knots of gloomy possibilities. I can't force them out of my mind. The darkness is the inside and the outside of my shell. The police sirens wail, and the shouts in the street are manifestations of the terror around me. The fullness of sound and thought only makes me more aware of the poisonous void that surrounds and fills my being when I go about my daily life. Death would be a solution to all my problems and all my thoughts. I try to reject it. *Don't give up*, the small voice in my head says to me. Is it God? Probably not. Is it Carlotta? No, I have not heard from her in a long time.

The thought of using crack and knowing again the pleasure of its exquisite high gnaws at me. The blast of energy from a hit is hard to resist. But the thought passes as another voice whispers, "You are not prepared to pay the physical price—the aches, the pains, and the coughing—for falling back into the habit." I can at least control this desire. The overpowering craving to smoke crack is gone. I haven't had the urge to self-medicate with crystallized cocaine since I began the medication some months ago. I remain sober. I am better.

Linda hits the hollow fish with the wooden stick. My chain of thought is broken, as is the purpose of the sharp and unexpected bonk. Let me start this meditation again, I am thinking. I am an empty shell. The voices begin. "You will have no interesting future." That was my father's prediction in my father's voice.

"Your experiences in the past were very ordinary." That was my mother's verdict. "Your experiences in future will be even more ordinary." That is my father again. "But you are better." Whose voice is that? *Carlotta, is that you?* "You have lost the desire to buy street drugs. No longer do you prowl skid row looking to find crack and trouble. No longer do you cross-dress. You are not alternately gay and heterosexual." *Carlotta, is that you?* I can't find the silence to meditate. Inside my shell of emptiness, sounds from the past reverberate. I can't concentrate. I am distracted, angry, and on edge. My thoughts are racing again.

I could not let go and just listen to the sounds outside me because inside me, voices are yelling to me about my mother. "She was an evil woman." Who said that? My grandmother? "She did not love you." Who said that? My father? "She abandoned you!" *Who said that?* The voices are coming from every which way. I remembered, and I cried.

My mother died in March, 2000. I didn't know. My father informed me four months later, on a Sunday. I was still groggy from sleep. "Your natural mother has died," he said matter-of-factly. "She died in a nursing home." I didn't really understand. I heard the words, but the impact was nothing. My mother's passing had no effect on me, but as I sat in this meditation, her passing affected me deeply. I hadn't thought that I cared, but I did. I found myself grieving. I started to talk silently to her:

"I love you mother. I mourn your death. I am sad that I was not there to express my love and ease your passage. I wish I could have held your hand in mine. When I was very young, that warm touch of your hand was reassurance of safety and care. How wonderful it could have been if I had been able to return your gesture after all these years. I would take your long, slender fingers and, gently easing them into my hand, I would give them a tender squeeze of reassurance to let you know you were not alone. You are safe now, I would say. I would lean in and kiss you on the forehead. Despite everything, Mother, the lost years, the pain in your life and mine, I still love you. We had a special connection, you and I. No one knew it but us. We never spoke of it, but an extraordinary bond was there. This was more than the connection of son to mother. We had a common need for one another. We shared a fundamental essence."

Tears were streaming down my face.

"When we met again after thirty years of separation, our defensive walls came with us. I did not trust you; I did not feel any love. I wanted to see what you looked like. I wanted to know who you were, so I could know myself. I felt an enormous void. I wanted to fill it in, but the void remained after our painful reunion. The emptiness did not gain definition. The void only became deeper."

I began to sway gently.

"I saw in you certain aspects of myself. Your nose and my nose are the same—an American Indian nose, I think. We have in common long fingers, arms, and legs, and our lips are similar. Your character was the big surprise. I recognized a shared boldness and theatricality. Your presence betokens a fearlessness and frankness that commands attention. I can be that way, too. I inherited from you, too, the inability to hold my thoughts in check. Your strengths and your weaknesses live on in me. Seeing you gave me a means to own this character in myself, a character that I found unsettling, like the debris from the bottom of a deep well."

My swaying became more pronounced. I was making a low choking sound.

"I observed your vulnerability, your emotions masked by flippancy and sarcasm. I do the same. Yes, you have a crazy family. I recall the dinner party in Las Vegas where I met my half-sisters, and where they verbally attacked you. I saw a world of hurt masked by your remark. I could hear in the sisters what I felt in myself. You echoed a gigantic world of pain and suffering. You were at the center of this pain, and enduring it hardened you as it hardened me."

Nancy came over to me and gently asked me if I was all right. I nodded that I was.

"I saw in your fiery temperament and quixotic nature that you were the young woman who wanted the exciting life of a nightclub singer. You wanted freedom from the restriction of a Catholic home life, so you married the dashing socialite, only to find yourself trapped in another restrictive culture. You were brash, sexy, beautiful, unwilling to be tamed by another authority, and you ran away to the nightlife. You were irresponsible, leaving a young daughter in the hands of the mother of the socialite so you could be young and have fun. I followed in your footsteps, unaware that I was doing something similar. Bored with the ordinary life, I abandoned it for a Bohemian existence, and I left my daughter behind, but I loved that daughter as you loved me.

"You took my hand in yours and we would go places. I would sit on a chair or a stool while you tried on dresses, hats, and jewelry. 'Do you like it?' you would ask. I would nod and suck my thumb. 'Sucking your thumb isn't gentlemanly,' you would chide me, but you never struck the offending digit from my mouth. Dad did that. You would just give me one of your looks—loving but authoritative. I would take my thumb from my mouth, only to insert it again once you disappeared into the dressing room. 'I will be right back, I will never leave you,' you said. One day, you were gone forever it seemed, until I met you again in Las Vegas and the emptiness only grew larger.

"There was something not quite right with Lynn Quinn that you passed on to your son. I am convinced that my bipolar disorder was passed to me through your genes. I can hate you for it, or I can appreciate the gift of excitement that you passed on to me. I am choosing to appreciate the latter and to love the complete person who was my lost mother. This is how I see the story. I take solace now in knowing the one truth that I have unearthed: my love for you. We had a special bond. May it extend beyond your lifetime and mine. God rest your soul, mother. Peace and joy find your spirit."

The bell rang, signaling the end of the meditation. I felt infinitely better. My sense of depression was gone. I felt like smiling.

Preoccupied with the thoughts of what had just happened, I started the drive home and almost had a head on collision with another driver, who was veering over the double yellow line. To regain my composure, I pulled into Hollywood Cemetery, where some of the great film stars are buried: Rudolph Valentino, Tyrone Power, W.C. Fields, and Marilyn Monroe. The latter two were alumni of the Las Encinas alcoholics program. Fields went there to dry out, but in his day, he was given a martini nightly to bring him down slowly, or so I was told. I wonder if any of these icons were bipolar? Surely Monroe would have been labeled bipolar, had she lived to the day when seemingly everybody with a death wish receives that convenient diagnosis.

I parked and got out of the vehicle, and that's when I saw her. Marilyn Monroe was standing next to the gate, beckoning to me. Even at this late night hour, closing in on midnight, with a full moon darting in and out behind clouds, the platinum blond hair and red lips, the languorous eyes, the white halter neck dress and nosebleed heels were unmistakable. Left arm akimbo against her outthrust hip, she was smiling that famous come-hither Marilyn smile and waving her right hand seductively.

"Carlotta, is that you?" I ask incredulously. "Were you talking to me earlier tonight?"

"Good guesses, Carlton," says the apparition in Marilyn's wispy child-woman voice. "I have appeared to cheer you up and congratulate you."

"What for?"

"I think you have finally come to terms with your mother. Haven't you?"

"Let me think about that."

"Don't you think tonight you finally let go of your obsession with the woman? You declared your love and you let her go in peace. Don't you feel a lot better?"

"Yes, actually I do. I think you're right. I have finally unburdened myself of the weight I carried around with me for years. It feels good."

"And you came to some degree of acceptance of your bipolar disorder."

"Why do you say that?"

"You said to yourself you got the disorder from your mother, and you were OK with it."

"I did? I will have to think some on that subject. OK is not the word that describes how I feel, nor is acceptance. Maybe recognition is the right word."

"You're splitting hairs with me, Carlton."

"Now I remember. I said I accepted her gift of excitement."

"Same thing. I will not argue with you. I came to give you my congratulations and to tell you, you have many other things to give up before you will be happy. You will know when it's time to give those things up. I must go now."

"Will you be back?"

"When and if you need me again."

bipolar bare

With that, Carlotta turned away and passed through the gateway to the cemetery. "Nice outfit!" I call after her. Smiling, Carlotta bent her knees, pursed her bee-stung lips and blew me a kiss before disappearing behind the trees. I continued home, content for once.

2008. Five years plus have passed since I was in the hospital. My journey to stay sober, to accept God and my disease, and to make peace with myself continues. I take my medicine daily and keep getting better. I am less angry, less irritated, and less self-destructive. I am calmer now, and I smile a lot more. I don't make as much complaint, commotion or call undue attention to myself by my overt actions. I still meditate. I still ride the Bipolar Coaster, but the rides aren't always as fearsome as they used to be. The ups and downs are mild compared to what they once were. Here and there I have a terrible down, usually caused by stress or a time of year that will trigger it. September, the time to go to school, and January/February, the time I lost my mother in 1949, are when I have to be most aware of a pending depression. Sometimes it comes; sometimes it doesn't.

For a long time, I have taken the same cocktail of medicines that are supposed to keep me stable. This group—Klonopin, Trileptal, Abilify, Lamictal, Artane, Inderal, and Ritalin—function together well. Klonopin keeps my anxiety down. Trileptal and Lamictal are my mood stabilizers. Abilify is my anti-psychotic. Dr. Poliquin concluded I have Attention Deficit Disorder (ADD), and prescribed Ritalin to counteract it. Artane and Inderal help me deal with the side effects of my primary medications.

I went back to work as an architect, but as time passed the side effects of the drugs became more and more troublesome. My left hand, which trembled a little when I first started on the medications, began to shake more and more. The trembling became so fast that I could no longer write my name. Worst of all, I lost the fine motor control necessary to draw. Even in the age of computer-aided design, a tremor this extreme is an architect's worst enemy, because I couldn't sketch on paper or type on a computer without great difficulty. When I drew a line, it would wobble up and down like a heartbeat on a monitor. When typing, my fingers would hit the keys again and again uncontrollably. As devastating as the loss of these skills were, I was willing to sacrifice them for sobriety and fewer rides on the Bipolar Coaster.

The other side effect I began to find even more disturbing and distressing than my tremor. I was stable, but I was flat. The medication dulls me down so much that life had become intensely boring. I had no spark, no interest in anything. I likened myself to a round rock on which all the interesting edges were worn away. The doctor and I decided to look at decreasing the dosages and eliminating the use of some of my medications in a bid to revive my spirit, albeit at the risk of a return to a rapid cycle of mania and depression. She thought the risk worth taking, since both of us believe I am no longer at risk for the use of illegal drugs.

We changed the medications. The Klonapin, Ritalin, and Inderal were eliminated. The Trileptal was gradually reduced to zero. A small dosage of Topamax was added. The Abilify dosage was cut in half. Lamictal and Artane were left as originally prescribed. The change worked and my old spark has come back. I feel a new interest in life. I can get high, but I also can get low. I know that the medications only dampen the cycle of highs and lows; they do not eliminate them. All that can be done is to smooth the curve between the high of mania and the low of depression.

There is no complete escape from the oscillations between high and low because the condition will never go away. I carry it in my genes. But I am a different person now, repackaged in a new and improved design. I don't want to take trips to the bathhouse. I have no desire to cross-dress, nor do I explode at each instance of frustration or irritation. I am almost a regular person except for my mental disorder, which sets me apart as it sets so many others apart. Many of the others I meet are totally disabled. They see themselves as irretrievably cursed by their disorder. I try to tell them they need not see themselves in this way. They could look at their disorders as a gift, which allows them to see the world differently. Most return a look of disbelief.

I wonder if I believe my words myself. Secretly, I dread a return to my old life. It could so easily happen. One day of feeling bad and one trip to the crack dealer, and I would be right back to where I was before. I tell myself it won't happen, because as the Buddhists say, I am trying to walk like an elephant, with a steady calm pace, and to sit like a frog, unperturbed by the wind and the rain.

I would need to remember these concepts, because in February, near the beginning of the fifth year of my sobriety, I felt very depressed. My mentor, Dr. Wortz, had died. My father had died without my ever reconciling with him. I was operated on for blood clots in my left lung, for which the doctors had no explanation. The lung had partially died, and I lost part of it. I secretly attributed the damage to my chronic use of cocaine. The shaking in my left hand was diagnosed as Parkinson's disease. Events in my life were taking a negative turn. I headed for the meditation hall.

The Zen zendo in Berkeley, California, another meditation hall I have attended, is on a quiet residential street near the university. I am facing a white wall in my chair, listening to the sounds all around me through the filter of the sound of buzzing in my ears. The result of my suicide attempt in college, the buzzing in my ears is always with me. I do not notice it when I am active, but when I slow down and I am quiet, like when I meditate, I am acutely aware of a persistent hiss.

In the middle of the session, the meditation leader hits the hollow wooden shape that looks like an abstract fish with a wooden stick. The fish gives off the sharp bonk. The sound is always loud and totally unexpected. A deep shiver passes through my body. A strong itch emerges from my armpit and crawls down the inside of my arm. I cannot resist the need to scratch. My right arm sweeps over my chest and digs under my left arm for several seconds. I tense to resist the itch as it spreads down my side. When I relax, the itch is gone and so is the high whine in my ears. There is some residual buzz but it fades away. I have silence. I can't believe that what I thought would never change has changed. I can listen to the sounds outside the zendo—the planes overhead, the cars passing by, and the frogs croaking in the pond in the backyard—without hearing them against the background of a constant hiss. I can hear them arise and pass away. I can listen to the sound of no sound when the noises are gone. It strikes me that the sound of no sound is like a hole. Through that hole bright light shines. It envelops me.

I think sound is like a plug that fills part of the fabric of reality, and when a sound that was there isn't there, there is a gap in the fabric. We have to be totally aware to see the hole with the mind's eye because that opening is only there extremely briefly. In under a nanosecond I was in, through, and out of that opening. The substance of reality rearranges itself instantly to plug the hole, and I am back to everyday existence. This is far out thinking I realize, but to me it makes sense. For a sublime, quicksilver moment, I touched a place beyond the reality of daily life. I felt in touch with a zone I could go to where the condition of my mental disorder would not affect me. I was on the other side of the gap where I was clean, clear, and new. I thought I had had a revelation.

What if, for a brief moment in that place of no sound, I had experienced the fundamental ground of existence? Through that hole in ordinary reality was another dimension, where what I suffered from did not matter and did not affect me. Beyond me, beyond us all, lies another place, a multidimensional reality, far greater than our three dimensional existence, which for that nanosecond I had experienced. I conjectured that the space I lived in day to day was covered by a veil, a matrix of energy, light and sound that keeps us from seeing and experiencing the greater reality that lies beyond. This goes beyond ordinary science and touches on the ineluctable and the eternal. In our ordinary field of reality, energy, light, and sound bounce around. When one of them stops for a briefest part of a second, we can see the net that encloses our real world and the holes through that net. The holes are not holes like empty space, but some other, indefinable substance. The sound of no sound was not sound, not light, not energy, but something akin to all. I could not explain it, but it begins to provide me with a vision of how all of us are tied together to everything. This matrix and beyond—could it be God?—that extends through us, beyond us, and into everything visible and invisible was the fundamental essence of the universe. At first, this revelation made me happy. I was laughing silently. So this is what I have been searching for. I had touched God! Then I began to doubt it.

I was just hallucinating. Holes in reality. Why, the idea was preposterous! But the experience was so vivid and felt so real, more real than the moment on the freeway when I thought I would die in my overturned vehicle and time slowed down. Was the hole the place where God stepped through and saved me from premature death? What if I had seen through the veil of existence to something else where I was completely relaxed for just one second, all my flaws were irradiated, and I became one with the universe, perfect and complete? The curse of my mood swings was removed because I had become a flawless human being who is totally awake and alert. For one brief second, I could have been enlightened.

No, it could not be, could it? Ordinary reality is a web that has us locked into our limitations. We are what we have been. There is no escape to something better beyond. I feel very sad. It is February after all, and my life is not going too well.

Still, I tried hard to catch the hole again as the sounds in the environment arise and pass away. A jet streaks overhead. A police siren shrieks in the distance, the frogs keep up their constant croaking, and the buzzing soon returns to my ears. I could not find the place of no sound again. But for a brief moment in time I was given a reprieve from the constant whine in my ears. I do not know if I should be happy or depressed. The meditation leader rings the bell and the meditation session is over. I feel a little changed by my meditation experience. The sadness is with me, but I am one jot more accepting of my bipolar condition and one jot more at peace with the world. I leave the zendo laughing at my hole theory. Crazy Californian sees God through holes in reality after the sound of jet plane fades away. Only some nut case could come up with that idea! There is your bipolar gift, mister.

I leave the meditation hall and drive up a steep street to Tilden Park, the hilltop open space above Berkeley, which gives a commanding view of the San Francisco Bay. I sit on a bench and look out over the scene and think about my experience of the holes in reality. Maybe my meditation experience is just so much illusion. A Buddhist master would say I needed to get beyond these illusions to just sitting. Here in the park there are the trees and meadows in the foreground, the bay dotted with boats in the middle ground, San Francisco with its towers and hills in the far ground, and the sky in the background. There are no holes in this reality. A beautiful clear azure sky dolloped with clouds makes this picture a rich and colorful, all encompassing panorama. I still feel slightly sad and imagine myself at the top of a giant roller coaster, about to descend. Could I make it through one more ride? Could I find enough peace and acceptance to make it through another tough bottom? Perhaps God would show up in the great cumulus clouds gathering over the headlands of Marin and tell me how I could avoid another depression. I decide God wouldn't show up when clouds start to look like elephants slowly plodding across the sky. Why am I always looking for God in the clouds? I did that once before at Venice Beach when the clouds looked like fish.

I try to meditate, but I cannot get to the place of no sound. The buzzing stays in my ear and the strong wind rustling the trees never lets up. I sit for several hours, watching the boats float by in the bay, the cars navigate the roads of the park, and the people wandering along the paths. I think more about acceptance, peace, and God, as one might do sitting alone on a park bench on a sunny and blustery day like this. Am I really ready to accept the fact there was no escape from my disorder? Could I finally find some peace in my life? Had I a revelation about the nature of God? As charming as the view is from the top of the mountain above Berkeley, it all seems like ordinary reality. I don't think I could appreciate this place any better than anyone else because of my condition.

Somehow, this insight makes it easier for me to accept my situation. I am just another person in a park appreciating the wonderful outdoors. Other people are out doing the same thing. These other people could be suffering too: cancer, heart disease, diabetes, or some other grievous affliction. An elderly woman was pushed past me in her wheelchair. We smiled at each other. Life wasn't great, her look seems to say, but I get by. Yes, I think, we get by, if we don't fight what can't be fought. I have accepted something from AA, I think: their Serenity Prayer.

Tilden Park provides no additional insights about, or relief from, my affliction. It is a peaceful place, and if you believe God is all around you and in everything, then it is a good place to be. The views, the trees, the grassy meadows, and brisk air reinforce your values. I am not sure I get that. I still doubt. I have to descend the mountain and continue my quest for peace and God, especially the God who gave me the gift of bipolar disorder.

Can I ever be at peace with the world? I am at peace with my mother, finally. Yes, I had let her go and no longer had any anger toward her. There is still a twinge of sadness when I think of her, but I can live with that. To be at peace with the world is harder. Part of me still wants to scream how unfair it is to be affected by this unseen and unsympathetic illness. Bipolar disorder is a hidden illness, one that makes normal people fearful of its presence and the afflicted fearful to admit their misfortune. Is life really worth living with this disease? For a long time I was engaged in self-destructive behavior, which said life wasn't worth living. Would a loving God allow such activity? My answer keeps coming up "no," even as I think, why should God intervene? I have free will. After all, God doesn't bother to prevent wars; why should he take an especial interest in the plight of one bipolar warrior?

I wind my way down from the mountaintop and go to the First Church of Christ Scientist in Berkeley, the masterpiece by the architect Bernard Maybeck. Sitting in the congregation hall under the great crossed beams, I think about the holes in reality again as I look at the S-like penetrations carved into the four big wooden trusses that span across the hall from each of the stubby-articulated columns. With their knobby pendants and heavy brackets, the columns are like stalactites in a great wooden cave, an attribute that makes this church so different from most soaring cathedrals. A soft white afternoon light streams through the long, low rectangular windows on one side of the sanctuary. I imagine I am inside a holy sepulcher, squat and close, experiencing a view into a heavenly reality. The brightness is like the light I saw when meditating on the place of no sound. I listen to the shouts of the homeless and the indigent in People's Park next door and try to hear the sound of no sound when their yells die away before a new noise takes its place. I cannot find that place of no sound and give up the effort.

Instead, I contemplate the words of Mary Baker Eddy, the founder of the Christian Science movement, whose seminal description of Christ is inscribed on one of the columns: "He proved Life to be Deathless and Love to be the master of hate." I am not so sure about life being deathless, but "love being the master of hate" are good words for me. I knew I had to give up my anger at the world for being bipolar, something that is taking me a lifetime to do. Thinking about these words in this serene place, a measure of peace descends. I feel touched by some nameless power larger than myself. I could not quite call it God, but I am almost there. I still question if life is really worth living, but the gift of life seems a little more reasonable to embrace.

As the sun sets, I start my trip home to Los Angeles. My six hour journey over the hills east of Berkeley, over the Altamont Pass with its giant windmills, down Interstate 5, then up the Grapevine through the Tejon Pass and down into Los Angeles would give me lots of time to think about a multitude of weighty subjects: bipolar disorder, the worthwhileness of life, the holes in space, God, and my life for the past thirty years in California. It's a long trip from the Bay Area to Los Angeles—nearly 500 miles. I have been making this trip between LA and San Francisco for all this time, and for most of it, I was stoned. For the first time in memory, I am sober and clearheaded.

For most of that time, I didn't think of myself as mentally ill. I just thought myself different. I thought my mind was wired differently from that of most other people; therefore, I saw the world from another perspective. I defined myself as an artist, and it was OK for an artist to be loaded. I saw all my actions through that prism. The depressions were merely part of the equation that defined who I was. For more than twenty-five years, I had no idea I was suffering from bipolar disorder. I had no proof my mind was wired differently and that the difference was a mental disease. I thought that my suffering was just part of being an artist.

When I made my trips back and forth on long weekends as my daughter was growing up, I smoked joints. For eighteen years I did this. I thought about the art projects I would do. I conceived big wire pieces I called *diaphanes*—a kind of static light machine —of which I made a few. I took photographs of the landscape— the low hills, often gray and fuzzy blue in the distance across orchards and cotton fields, the giant power lines that crossed, re-crossed, and paralleled the highway, and irrigation canals that zigzagged next to the road like big, jagged scrapes. I played with ideas like seeing energy emanating from light bulbs and conduits in walls. These images and ideas I thought would make marvelous drawings, but I couldn't think of a new way to present the material that was different from what other artists had already done. And so, I never made them. I would fantasize about homosexual escapades in San Francisco—the capital city of gay. I would obsess about my mother. Often I was in a mindless trance, listening to the hum of the highway and the whoosh of the passing cars and trucks.

The ascent of the Grapevine lay just ahead when I started to think about my bipolar disorder. The road up this steep incline is a lot like the ascent up the Bipolar Coaster. You're building up energy. The trucks and cars jam up. Your mind is racing and thoughts collide. The trucks are moving slower and gravitate to the outside right lanes. You are trying to shake off the ennui of your last down. The cars accelerating to gain the momentum to climb the mountain push to the left, trying to avoid the trucks moving to the right. You want nothing in your way. The faster cars moving to the inside left lane cross in front of slower moving cars on their right. You are winding up, ready for a high. It's a tense ballet at high speed. The adrenaline flows, awareness peaks, danger lies all around. Cars veer in front of you. A pickup can speed up behind, then turn right or left of you in a flash. Your irritation with others is peaking. A truck slips behind you or jumps in line to pass a slower semi. Your nerves are on edge, but it makes you excited. Something interesting will happen. Either you will make it over the pass or you will become a wreck. I have always made it over the pass and I don't go slowly. I love the high of crossing the Grapevine. I loved the high I used to get over the years when I wasn't diagnosed and I didn't have the drugs I have now that control my mood. Being a fired-up artist was wonderful. I could stay up for days talking about my ideas with other artists and working in my studio.

 I come over the Grapevine through the Tejon Pass and begin the long descent into Los Angeles. The descent is like a long descent of the Bipolar Coaster. There is all this momentum behind and you can really move fast now. You can go eighty-five, ninety miles an hour now if you dare. Some dare to go faster than that. Push one hundred—why not? You dare to do things you ordinarily won't do because the momentum of the high is pushing you. The heavy loaded trucks can really pick up steam and come right upon your rear if you move too slowly and if you decide to stay within the speed limit. So you don't. You race. Your mind races and there are so many things you can do when you're this full of energy. It's exhilarating. All you have to do is keep your vehicle in control. All you have to do in life is keep yourself in control. That is not easy to do. Too often you go out of control in the descent of Bipolar Coaster.

 I remember making a wire piece called *The Ironic Column* fabricated of many three-dimensional plus and minus shapes. I worked on this sculpture for five days nonstop. First, as a template, I made a gigantic drawing the same size as the completed piece. Then I made each individual plus and minus shape out of wire mesh, soldering and sanding the edges and corners. This took a long time and many a sleepless night. Finally, I assembled them all together into a column with entases, just like a Greek column. This also took many more days and nights without sleep. I was inspired. This was the artist's life I craved. Little did I know I was in a manic phase. I thought those were the best days; there just weren't enough of them. Then you crash.

Ironic Column; 1985; hardware cloth; steel eyelet, bolt and hook

bipolar bare

I come out of the mountains into the Los Angeles Basin and I am thinking about the negative aspects of all the things in my life that are not going too well, and whether or not life is worthwhile. It's always this way when I return after a trip to San Francisco. I have hit the bottom of the Bipolar Coaster. I think about *The Ironic Column*. When I finished it, I made a trip to San Francisco to see my daughter. I was dead tired, irritable, and in a dark mood. I had a piece of art that nobody wanted, not even me. Once a piece was done, the fun was over. I could see all the mistakes and the weaknesses. I couldn't see where to go from this piece. When I returned from this journey, I went to bed and stayed there for a week, seeing no one. Life didn't seem worth living, and I thought about suicide as I always did when I ended up in this mood.

Instead of going directly home after this return trip, I go to Venice Beach to the place I had gone way back at the start of the 1980s, when I was thinking about the end of the American Dream and the end of my dreams. I was thirty-five years old then. I am sixty-two years old now. I park on Windward Avenue and walk past the closed up shops selling tattoos, sunglasses, T-shirts, and cheap jewelry, cross the boardwalk, go through the palm trees and a low enclosure of concrete walls completely covered in colorful graffiti, and onto the sandy beach. I walk across the sand toward the long rocky breakwater. It is late at night, just as it was then when I stood on the beach at the edge of the surf and thought about walking out into the ocean and never coming back. It's low tide now and the breakwater is hugging the beach. Back on December 31st, 1979, the tide was high and the breakwater was offshore. I could stand on a spit of land, watch waves boom against the breakwater, and see two smaller waves behind the breakwater curve into the shore, making a point of land.

To face an open ocean, I have to move down the beach where the waves break against the shore. Bright moonlight makes it easy to see the soft swell and curl of the ocean as the water approaches the sand. I stand close to the edge of the surf and stare out at the dark ocean against a lighter gray sky. Suddenly, I catch a glimpse of a female figure far off in the distance, moving rapidly towards me via some unseen locomotion.

I cannot believe my eyes. As the figure moves closer, I recognize Carlotta, riding the swell atop a scallop shell as if it were a surfboard.

She is naked except for a long train of hair, which comes down the front of her body and covers her loins. Two archangels with trumpets float on either side of her head. The wave curls up and breaks. Riding the crest, Carlotta assumes a classic surfer's stance, her arms outstretched like wings as she cross steps along the shell to keep her balance. The trumpeters herald her arrival with a majestic fanfare as she slides up the churning foam spreading out over the sand and ends up gently bobbing on the water six feet from me.

"Dude!" she exclaims, grinning from ear to ear. "That was one bitchin' wave!"

I am amused in spite of myself and can't keep a sardonic smile from blooming on my face. "You're way too big to be Gidget, so let me guess: You are Boticelli's Venus this time."

"Verily! Venus comes to Venice. You love art, so I have come to you as a well-known muse."

"Aren't you cold out there? A birthday suit is no protection against the cold night."

"A muse is never cold. Are you thinking of suicide?"

"Carlotta, I thought you went away forever. I haven't seen you in a long, long time."

"A muse needs to take a break every once in awhile: to get a tan, to remember what it's like to be full of energy, to recharge run-down solar batteries. Taking care of you was a very demanding job."

"I didn't ask you to come back."

"How about a little appreciation, when I have done so much for you?"

"You've done nothing lately."

"You haven't needed me. Tonight I think you do."

"Why, just because I am here at the beach, looking out at the ocean?"

"You didn't answer my question, Carlton. Are you thinking of suicide?"

"The thought crosses my mind."

"I thought so."

"It is just a thought. I am not going to do it."

"Are you sure? Life has not been going well for you lately."

"I admit I am low. Death is on my mind. My father is dead. I could have died from the blood clots. I find it hard to give up my attachment to these negative feelings, but I must let go. I thought I had with my mother, but every once in a while all the negative feelings come back. What good does it do me to hang onto these thoughts?"

"None whatsoever. It is time to move on."

"Dr. Wortz has died, too. He was a rock for me. The only man I trusted, and now he is gone."

"Dr. Wortz talked to you about the transitory nature of all things. Can't you abide in this truth?"

"I'm trying, but gloom sometimes overwhelms me."

"Then grieve and let go."

"God eludes me, too."

"What you can't stuff God into your little holes in reality?"

"You're mocking me now."

"No, just giving you a little insight. God is everywhere. Just because you can't prove it doesn't make it any less true."

"It's all too much to handle. I am an empty shell and the pearl is gone "

"No, the pearl is *not* gone and your shell is *not* empty. Look at me! I am standing on your shell. Be thankful. How many others get to envision the naked Venus on her scallop shell, floating on the waves off Venice Beach? I find it a delightful image."

"Venus on the half shell," I can't help quipping. "The oyster is gone and so is the pearl. I am depressed."

"Your shell is crowded, Carlton. You have your wife, your friends, your daughter, and you have God, who is looking out for you. Tell me a story. It will cheer you up."

"Do I have to? Can't you just disappear?"

"Talk to me. I insist!"

"Even after all this time, Carlotta, I'm powerless to resist your demands," I sigh.

"Five years have passed since I last rode the big Bipolar Coaster. I have ridden little ones here and there, but not the big one anymore. I am sober and I am on a level surface. Medication has given me sobriety and meditation has kept me in equilibrium. Yet I often feel empty, a mere shell from which the pearl has been plucked. One pays a price for equilibrium. The bright highs are gone, their tops shaved off. I no longer feel as if I can think a brilliant thought, or do a brilliant deed ... that is, if I ever could. The new high is deceiving—it's not very high— and what is ordinary can be misconstrued as something fantastic."

"Balance is hell for those who lived on adrenaline."

"You said it. It's February and I sense a big depression is coming. I might even want it to come, but first I want the manic high. I miss them and I have nothing to replace them."

"Yes, you do. You have a stability that grows stronger each day, despite the fact you still get a few lows."

"That's true. The lows aren't as low as they used to be. The darkness, the pitch-black universe, where all is pitiful and dead. Can you believe it? I miss that, too. In the depths of depression, my capacity for pain was verified. I would hurtle myself into risks that could lead to death. There was intelligence in those depths. I could see the phoniness of life. And when I did pull through, the depression would turn to brilliance. My every thought and action was creative. But I could never retain it, this positive energy. My hold on it was always elusive. I would slide back into the gloom. In these terrible lows, I would think of suicide. Now there is a mysterious hand that holds me back from the positive delusion and the negative self-destruction. I wish it weren't there. I know the mysterious hand is the result of the medications I take."

"Venus knows. The goddess of love, born from the sea, thinks the mysterious hand is the love for life. Or perhaps it's the hand of God, of whose existence you so fervently crave proof. You are divesting yourself of so much self-centered behavior. Spiritually naked, you are fighting against the remains of your old, hateful life."

"No! I am not. I'm just looking at the ocean wondering, where it's all gone— all the things I wanted to do, all the things I could have done, and all the things I have left undone."

"I am not so sure. Are you thinking of doing away with yourself AGAIN?"

"I told you already the thought crosses my mind. It's been a tough time lately."

"More than the usual up and downs?"

"Yes."

"You must give up your attachment to all the negative thoughts. You must come to love your life. Then you can love others. You must come to forgive yourself. Then you can truly forgive others."

"I know you're right, Carlotta. When I was meditating today, a flurry of negative thoughts overcame my positivity."

"Tell me about that," says Carlotta, swaying precariously as waves buffet the scallop shell. "Dude, I nearly wiped out that time!"

"Then get off and come to shore, you silly twit."

"No. I like it out here on the water. Proceed with your description of the meditation. Usually it works for you. I presume it didn't this time."

"It's not that. I had a peculiar experience. I heard—or was it saw?—holes in the fabric of reality, where I experienced something beyond ordinary existence. I thought perhaps I had touched the hem of God, for lack of a better description. But the knowledge I gained, which at first made me happy, made me sad as my day progressed. I was left thinking about the curse of being bipolar."

"You exaggerate as always, Carlton! Can't you think of it as a gift from God?"

"That's hard to do. You know, Carlotta, everyone I meet who has a mental disorder thinks it is a curse from God. When I try to tell them something else, they laugh at me."

"Laughter is healing."

"Oh, please, don't hand me that Norman Vincent Peale bunk! A mental disorder is a curse. The condition never goes away and can never be cured. It is the nightmare you live everyday of your life, waiting for it to strike again and *knowing* it will strike again."

"It's not striking you tonight. Can't you be a beacon for the others as you work and as you encourage them to stand up to a society that beats them down and marginalizes them for having this disorder?"

"I accept that I have the disease. That doesn't mean I am happy about it. I can be at peace with the world, but how can I be a beacon when I am feeling the same way as everyone else who has bipolar disorder?"

"You're just having an off day, Carlton. You have to think positively."

"I can't when I am becoming depressed. The medication is no longer working. I feel the mood swings beginning again. My anger is rising."

"Don't you think this will pass?"

"So what if it does? I know it will come again and I will struggle once more against the forces that want me dead. The ride on the Bipolar Coaster will begin again."

"Let it! You can handle the bumps and breakneck speed now. The rides haven't been really bad for a long time, have they?"

"Well, no, but they could be, if I am not careful. You get tired of being careful. You just want everything to be over."

"Now you are talking trash! We are beyond that. You can't slip back. I don't want you dead. It would ruin my hair, my nails, my makeup, and the good times I am beginning to have, where I function as a rational advisor to a talented, humorous, and sensitive man."

"Please! You're going to make me upchuck."

"Dear Carlton, are you going to force me to recite a list of your positive assets? You never remember the good things you do and only dwell on the bad in the dark."

"I come by it naturally. After all, I am bipolar and it's cold and dark in the polar regions. The sun hardly ever shines at the poles."

"Ah, but when it does, it can shine for twenty-four hours a day. Can't you pretend the sun shines on you around the clock?"

"You know I can't do that."

Carlotta nods at the angels, who bring the trumpets to their lips and blast a deafening fanfare that hurts my ears.

"Listen up," says Carlotta. "You, Carlton, are a paddlepuss: somebody who plays along the shore, never growing the balls to brave the big waves. There's so much opportunity for you, out on the ocean of life—"

"God, what a cliché!" I groan.

"SHUT UP!" says Carlotta. Her stern expression shows she will brook no further interruptions. "What matters is that you expressed a positive side to the illness. Remember, it has a name—bipolar—which expresses the fact there is a positive and a negative. You can view the illness as having two poles: one good, one bad. Think of it like electric energy. There is a negative pole and a positive pole. You don't always have to go to the negative pole—the dark side, as you call it. There, you get nothing. Go to positive pole! Connect up the poles properly and you get the energy flowing. It's just like the energy you saw flowing off the lights in your studio. You get light! Go to the light! Go for the gem that lies hidden in all that is negative, painful, and sorrowful. Peering past the darkness can only be seen when you have the light.

"I thought I was an artist then."

"You still are."

"No one but you and I think so, Carlotta. My ambitions are too high. I didn't want to be an ordinary artist. I wanted to be a *great* artist, a new Leonardo da Vinci. *Ha!* I am living proof that delusions of grandeur and mental illness fit hand in glove."

"You probably do shoot too high, but there is nothing wrong with that. Besides, your game isn't over yet."

"I'm too old now," I reply pitifully.

"No, you are *not*! I'm convinced, Carlton, that the real bane of your existence is stress. You handle it with far less equanimity than most people. You let it get the better of you."

"So what am I to do, become a monk or a recluse?"

"No, not at all. You must do the things that reduce the stress. Meditation helps. Taking medication helps, too, and you must avoid stressful situations. If you get caught in a stressful situation, you need to remember the gifts you have been given. When the negative thoughts come, remember the light in the Christian Science Church! Remember the light in Rembrandt's paintings! You have seen many pearls of eternity in the fields of life. Don't give them up too soon."

"I know you're right, Carlotta, but the disorder will last forever. It gets me down."

"It's OK for you to get down. Everybody gets down now and then. Just remember there are ups, also. Life can be good if you let it. Love life. It will love you back."

"Yeah, yeah, tomorrow is another day, and I have to go home. Will you come with me?"

"Not tonight, Carlton. Venus on the half shell has things to do and places to go."

"Does this mean you are a muse for other people?"

"Could be. But I am always around for you."

"I guess I am glad of that."

"You should be, but you don't need me that much anymore."

"What if I say I do?"

"You were always trying to get rid of me, and now you want me. How sweet! And how much you have changed, Carlton."

"I think you're good for a little inspiration, that's all. Isn't that what a muse is for?"

"Indeed. I will leave you, then, with a small thought. Remember what you read from the Gnostic gospels. You said you liked that sentiment."

"I've forgotten. What did it say?"

Carlotta puts her hands together in an attitude of prayer and recites: "'If you bring forth what is within you, what you bring forth will save you. If you do not bring forth what is within you, what you do not bring forth will destroy you.' Promise me you will bring forth that light that shines in that shell of darkness of yours, Carlton."

"I promise, Carlotta."

"Good. Now go home, friend Carlton. We had a hell of a ride on the Bipolar Coaster, but now our journey is complete."

The angels blow a farewell flourish as Carlotta extends her arms, palms turned heavenward, and wills the shell out to sea. I stand reverently in the surf, my shoes

bipolar bare

soaked, delighting in the occasional glimpse of her, standing so tall and straight against the purple horizon, as the shell bobs in and out of the waves.

"Wait!" I cry, ere she is out of sight. "What if I never find God?"

"How do you know you haven't already?"

Struck by the beatific smile on her face, I laugh all the way home.

carlton davis

Author Photograph by Ed Glendenning - 2008

Made in the USA
Charleston, SC
12 August 2012